FREEDOM IN THE
WESTERN WORLD

*From the Dark Ages
to the Rise of Democracy*

Books by Herbert J. Muller

FREEDOM IN THE WESTERN WORLD
FREEDOM IN THE ANCIENT WORLD
ISSUES OF FREEDOM
THE LOOM OF HISTORY
THE SPIRIT OF TRAGEDY
THE USES OF THE PAST
THOMAS WOLFE
SCIENCE AND CRITICISM
MODERN FICTION

FREEDOM IN THE WESTERN WORLD

From the Dark Ages to the Rise of Democracy

HERBERT J. MULLER

HARPER COLOPHON BOOKS
HARPER & ROW, PUBLISHERS
NEW YORK, EVANSTON, AND LONDON

First HARPER COLOPHON edition published 1964 by Harper & Row Publishers, Incorporated, New York, Evanston, and London

LIBRARY OF CONGRESS CATALOG CARD NUMBER: 63-8427

To Albert K. Babcock

ACKNOWLEDGMENTS

Since it is often said that our democratic society does not properly esteem its scholars, writers, and thinkers, I wish in particular to express my gratitude to the Foundations that help to support them better, perhaps, than almost any past society did: specifically to the Rockefeller Foundation, for a grant that enabled me to devote a full year to this volume; to the Center for Advanced Study in the Behavioral Sciences, where I spent a most pleasant and profitable semester; and to the Fund for the Republic, now the Center for the Study of Democratic Institutions, for a grant that allowed me to spend a summer working at Cambridge University and in Florence.

I am also grateful to my friends and colleagues Professors Roy Battenhouse, Morris Bishop, John Fisher, and Rudolf Gottfried for critical readings of several chapters. And again I am more deeply indebted than I can ever properly acknowledge to the many historians whose specialized researches I have drawn on, or whose brains I have picked.

CONTENTS

ILLUSTRATIONS

PREFACE

This book is a sequel to my *Freedom in the Ancient World,* the second of a projected three-volume History of Freedom, carrying this history to about the year 1800. Although it is designed as a complete work in itself, not assuming a knowledge of the previous work, it is based on the same premises, which I should therefore restate. I am adhering to the broad but relatively neutral definition of freedom as "the condition of being able to choose and carry out purposes." This includes the most common meaning of the absence of external constraints, or freedom *from* coercion; the idea of actual ability with available means, or effective freedom *to* do what one wishes; and the assumption of a power of deliberate choice between known alternatives, involving freedom *of* mind and spirit, which is hardest to specify but still distinguishes human freedom from the ability of other animals to carry out their instinctive purposes. In the words of Christian Bay, "A person is free to the extent that he has the capacity, the opportunity, and the incentive to give expression to what is in him and to develop his potentialities."

So defined, I repeat, freedom means concretely freedoms of various kinds, which may be at least roughly specified. Among the most fundamental is political freedom, involving some means of control of rulers by the ruled, some protection of the individual against government by legal rights or civil liberties. (I continue to make no distinction between "freedom" and "liberty," which in common usage are practically synonymous.) But government remains only an essential condition, and it has plainly been affected by other basic interests—commerce, technology, religion, morals, etc.—that oblige a historian to consider the society or culture as a whole. And so considered, I have grown more unhappily aware, the history of freedom may amount to a history of civilization. Since almost everything of any consequence that men have done has had some conceivable bearing on my subject, I am wide open to sins both of commission and of omission, and at least one reviewer has commented that my theme is "probably impossible." Certainly I have here again included much material of indirect or tangential bearing, which may give the reader a fuller consciousness at once of the complexity and the richness of the subject, or perhaps more than he bargained for, but which may also obscure my theme, make the reader wonder where he is going and why. On the other hand, I have almost as certainly slighted works and events of more consequence than some I have chosen to dwell on. I should never attempt to disarm criticism (a strictly impossible effort anyway); but I owe some statement of the principles that have guided my selection and emphasis.

In general, I have concentrated on the major developments that have affected Western civilization as a whole, entered the main stream of its common culture or living tradition, and so are known to educated men in all its nations. (Let me postpone the large question of what constitutes this civilization.) In so doing I have looked to both the economic or material and the cultural or spiritual conditions of freedom. Among these are the gains in collective wealth and power, through commerce and technology, that have effectively enlarged the capacities of men and widened the range of choice. A related concern is creativity in art and thought, to me the clearest proof of the reality and the value of human freedom, and in any case a vital factor in its history. This in turn involves the history of ideas, especially ideas that promoted—or discouraged—freedom of mind, a confidence in man's powers or potentialities, a belief in his dignity or his fitness for freedom. As for the most obvious topic, the social and political structure that mainly determines who shall enjoy such freedoms and to what degree, I have naturally dwelt on the extension of rights, opportunities, and incentives to larger numbers of men. It is always possible to argue that the primary social concern should be provision for the elite, the few who are capable of creativity; but since all societies offer privilege and power to some few, I assume that a society becomes objectively freer as it gives more of its members more chance for self-expression or self-realization, and some say in their rule.

Regarding the vast deal that I have perforce excluded, I make no apologies at all for ignoring most of the political and military history that filled the conventional histories of the past: the many dynasties whose rise or fall made no appreciable difference in social or political structure, the many wars out of which little or nothing came except suffering for the victims and some transient fame for the victors. My concern remains the broader political developments, such as the rise and the decline of absolute monarchy, and the broader social consequences of war in general, including a few particular wars (like the American Revolution) that dramatized issues of freedom. I do make some apology for scanting when not ignoring the history of many peoples, from Hungarians, Finns, and Czechs to Canadians, Latin Americans, and New Zealanders; but at least I thereby imply no disrespect. While taking for granted that their history is worth knowing, possibly more honorable than much that was made on the main stage, I have freely disreregarded all achievement that did not enter the common Western heritage or significantly influence the main march of events. I feel unhappiest about the many creative artists, writers, and thinkers whose works I have slighted out of the necessity of selection, especially because I cannot be certain that my selection has always been judicious. All I can say is that I have singled out works that seemed most significant for my present purposes, either as positive influences or as expressions of major developments, and that my choices have not been dictated merely by personal prejudices. I much prefer St. Francis to St. Thomas Aquinas, John Huss to John Calvin, but I judge that St. Thomas and Calvin are clearly more important in a history of freedom; I am unable to believe that the greatest poets and the profoundest thinkers are necessarily the most influential, and suspect that no artist has affected life so much as the inventor of double-entry bookkeeping; and if, as I like to think, there may be some truth in the saying "Let me write the songs of a people and I care not who writes its laws," I still cannot find in this a good excuse for dwelling here on the music of Bach and Mozart.

In as sober a piety (I hope) I have insistently complicated the issues of a history that, broadly considered, has been a clear growth and spread of freedom as I define it. Western civilization has notoriously achieved unprecedented gains in power, or effective freedom to carry out human purposes, which promoted its extraordinary faith in progress; it has been the most boldly adventurous and continuously creative of the great societies over a thousand years, in part because the most committed to a spirit of individualism; it has struggled to establish the fundamental freedoms of thought, speech, and press; as consciously it has declared ideals of political freedom, culminating in the rise of democracy; with this it has extended opportunity to an unparalleled extent by free public education; and lately it has even conferred equal rights on women, who all along have made up half the human race. Today, however, I hardly need add that the growth of freedom has by

no means been steady, uniform, or a simple progress. Every major
advance has created further problems, accentuated both old and new
threats to freedom, beginning with the notorious abuses of wealth and
power and leading to the price men have to pay for all cultural or
spiritual goods. I have continued to emphasize the invariable costs of
freedom as not only a historic fact but a methodological principle,
essential to an understanding of the human condition in general and
the state of the modern world in particular. And if this principle may
now seem a commonplace, it involves me in more difficult issues.

Philosophers have typically been devoted to various concepts of
"true freedom," the idea that a person is "really" free only when he is
being his "true self," acting in perfect accordance with reason, doing
his duty to God or state, or in general doing what is right and good.
The trouble remains that such true freedom turns out to mean very
different things, inasmuch as philosophers have never been able to
agree on how to tell one's true self, or on the dictates of reason, conscience, or God in social behavior; so in these terms I still mean by
freedom "a state in which a person may decide for himself what is right
and good, what to do with his freedom, what kind of self to become."
We may hope to discuss more profitably the problem of freedom *for*
what if we define it neutrally, distinguish the question of its conditions
from the question of its proper uses or ends. Yet I should now emphasize
that we cannot evade this further problem, simply as we try to understand the history of Western freedom. We all know that freedom can be
abused (at least by the other fellow), and the very growth that has
enabled more men to think and live more nearly as they pleased forces
more consideration of what they have chosen to believe and how they
have been pleased to live. The rise of democracy in particular has forced
the question of the uses or ends of freedom, for from the outset its
advocates have explicitly declared such moral ends as justice, equality,
the natural rights of man, and they soon began worrying over the quality
of democratic culture. And though we may try to be neutral or wholly
objective as we survey these issues, none of us is or can be in fact
neutral—we are all committed to certain values, or notions about what is
right and good. Then the trouble is that we are making value judgments, which many historians say are none of their business and most
social scientists insist we have no right to make.

Now, the effort to avoid such judgments is quite honorable. The
primary aim of a historian ought surely to be to understand what has
happened and therefore what has come to be, like it or not. He should

know that value judgments always betray some preconception or bias, personal, national, or cultural, and that they can never be scientifically verified; history itself is the plainest demonstration of the actual relativity of values, the impossibility of complete agreement upon them. That I have "naturally" sought to record the history of freedom objectively, impartially, is a tribute to the modern temper, for this effort was hardly natural before the rise of the scientific spirit. Nevertheless, the very effort calls for an awareness of the essential, inescapable limits to objectivity, beyond one's personal limitations. It is itself a commitment to the values of a disinterested pursuit of truth, of the intellectual honesty and freedom required by this pursuit, of the sympathetic understanding it makes possible—values not universally recognized by the wise and holy men of the past. It implies further social and cultural values from the outset of research, for these determine a historian's selection of what is "important"—a judgment that he has to make, and that grows harder with the immense wealth of factual knowledge accumulated by researchers who like as not thought they were merely sticking to the facts. Judgments about what is natural, right, and good for man are only most conspicuous in a historian's conclusions, whatever understanding of history he professes. All history comes down to a history of culture, and the ultimate value of a study of it is the light it gives on the means and ends of a conscious animal who lives by values of his own creation—values that alone make it worth being a human being, and alone can justify the as strictly undemonstrable belief that it is better to be a civilized being.

By the same token, however, a historian is not left at the mercy of personal or cultural prejudice. While subject to the discipline of the scientific spirit, the publicity of the scientific method, he is also supported by a basic consensus that has widened with the growth of civilization. Thus there is a pretty general agreement on not only the "importance" or value of creativity but on what have been the great creative achievements in art and thought. The very awareness of cultural pluralism has made possible at once a more objective and a more sympathetic understanding of diverse cultures, and has thereby in effect widened the consensus still more; for men who dispute the relative merits of Buddhist and Christian scriptures, Greek and Gothic architecture, Chinese and Renaissance painting, Hindu and Western philosophy, may still do honor to them all, agree that all are far superior to the trash that may edify, delight, or bemuse addicts of our mass media. And so with the touchier issue of moral judgments.

Histories have always been strewn with such judgments, of course, if only because of the common agreement that such practices as murder, cruelty, treachery, and dishonesty are bad. Of more concern in a history of freedom are practices like slavery, judicial torture, and burning for religious belief that were once generally accepted. I assume that we should try to understand such apparent barbarities, avoid simple condemnation of the societies that approved them, and always guard against the inveterate tendency to self-righteousness, especially in view of the notorious barbarities of our own time; but by the same token I assume that we might as well call them by their bad name, not pretend to be neutral about them, especially because they are now almost universally condemned in principle. They point to the as universal acceptance in theory of the once revolutionary "rights of man," the "human rights" approved by the United Nations—a political development so extraordinary that we may forget that these rights were always implicit in the ethical codes taught by all the world's higher religions.

Accordingly, I add with some pride as well as humility that there is little if anything really new in this history, except perhaps its focus. I have been content to follow through the conventional "ages" or "movements" accepted by most historians, with the qualifications emphasized by recent research: the ages of course have no clear beginning or end, the movements never proceed in separate channels or on straight lines. The familiar periodization corresponds closely enough to the major developments in the history of freedom as I read it, if only because the issues of freedom have long been a primary concern of most historians, tacitly when not explicitly. Similarly, I have not committed myself to any novel theory of history or to the drastic reinterpretations of major happenings that periodically cause some stir, for if these are usually stimulating and illuminating, they are always partial and one-sided. Whenever a scholar asserts that the basic cause or the essential truth about something or other is "*not* this, *but* that" I find it a pretty safe rule to substitute "both this and that," and probably then some. An obvious example is the economic interpretation of history. This has afforded new insights that have become part of our intellectual stock in trade, indispensable to understanding, but it may also be too easy a way of creating an illusion of depth or finality; its practitioners have commonly tended to reduce and impoverish history by minimizing other cultural factors, in particular the independent power of conscious ideas and ideals that I believe has been most conspicuous in Western history, and of late most amply demonstrated by Marxism

itself. Briefly, I take my cue from a study of the presidential addresses
of the American Historical Association, from 1884 to 1945, which
revealed that the presidents disagreed over all their basic concepts and
objectives, agreed only on the idea that their subject was broad and
rich. I find the disagreement wholesome, since I assume that history
never can be an exact science; and I want first of all to keep it broad and
rich, as befits a study of human freedom.

A word, lastly, on the great Eastern civilizations, especially China
and India. I have given them but passing mention in this volume, partly
because they had little direct influence on European culture during
the period covered, chiefly because they experienced little independent
growth in freedom. In my first volume I pointed out some basic reasons
why these societies have contributed far less than the Western world
to the theory and conscious practice of freedom. I would therefore
repeat that they cultivated values that may be considered higher or
holier. These included a tranquillity or peace of mind that is often
called "spiritual freedom," and that further complicates my subject;
with it went a religious tolerance that Europe would achieve only after
centuries of strife. Still, such "spiritual freedom" also helps to explain
why they remained relatively unconcerned about political freedom,
failed to develop any tradition of freedom under law or of government
of and by the people, and made no sustained effort to extend rights,
opportunities, and incentives for other modes of self-realization. That
many free Americans now appear to hanker most of all for peace of
mind merely emphasizes another corollary of my neutral definition,
that freedom no more assures contentment than it does wisdom, virtue,
or holiness. At any rate, I propose to dwell on the Eastern societies, or
in general what is now politely called the "non-Western world," in
my concluding volume. Only by understanding their quite different
cultural traditions can one appreciate the literally extraordinary drama
now going on, as men all over the world are taking to Western ideas and
ideals whose growth is surveyed in this volume.

Herbert J. Muller

THE RISE AND FALL
OF ISLAM

It might well seem Western conceit that reduces the history of Islam to a mere prologue to the history of Europe. Certainly there is nothing more extraordinary in religious history than the triumphant beginning of Islam, as within a generation after the death of Mohammed (A.D. 632) his upstart followers surged all over the Middle East, permanently establishing his faith in regions that Christianity had taken three centuries to win, and now lost for good. They proceeded to develop a new civilization far in advance of contemporary Europe, in brilliant centers from Baghdad to Córdoba; its superiority was nowhere more conspicuous than on European soil, in Spain. For centuries Islam stayed in advance, contributing much to the intellectual development of the West. When it began to fall behind in creativity it was still vital enough to inspire the Ottoman Turks, who finished off the Byzantine Empire, the last remnant of Christendom in Asia, and built an empire of their own that long menaced Europe. When it fell behind in military power too, Mohammedanism remained one of the world's major religions, which today numbers some 300,000,000 followers. The Moslem world, now astir, is again a force that the West must reckon with.

Yet this stir has been due to Western impact, after centuries of torpor; and the torpor indicates the reasons why Islam may properly be subordinated in a history of freedom. While it had some potentialities for a free society, it failed to realize them. It never established popular or constitutional government, introduced any notable measure of political freedom, and at length it lost the intellectual and imaginative freedom it had known in its brilliant period. It grew rigid in orthodoxy, capable of little but military and commercial adventure, at a time when Europe was entering its Renaissance. Under the Ottoman Empire it remained an essentially closed society, autocratically ruled, intellectually stagnant. The history of Islam remains a major episode in world history, important in its own right; but its primary interest in this work is as an object lesson, illuminating by contrast the conditions of Western freedom.

The immediate key to its history is the Prophet Mohammed. The dramatic entrance of the Arabs on the world stage—out of their deserts, out of nowhere—was indeed not quite so sudden and startling as may at first appear. They were hardy warriors who for centuries had given some trouble to their neighbors by raiding expeditions; they were aided by the weakness of the contemporary Byzantine and Sassanian empires, which were exhausted by wars on each other; and they were not simple barbarians, some of them having grown accustomed to city life in such prosperous caravan centers as Mecca. Nevertheless, the Arabs hitherto had been a relatively primitive, obscure, insignificant people, in keeping with their desert habitat, their endless blood feuds, and their worship of the Black Stone. They had never been a nation until Mohammed gave them a new faith. It was the Prophet who united and inspired them, and then himself inaugurated the holy wars by a raid on the Byzantine province of Syria. Upon his death the wars went on under the leadership of caliphs (meaning "successors") who were wholly devoted to him. The armies that overran Persia, Mesopotamia, Syria, Egypt, north Africa, and Spain may well have been fired more by lust for plunder than by religious fervor, but they were Moslem, always fighting under the banner of Mohammed. As they conquered they spread his faith, which remained the national faith of the whole Middle East. No other religious leader has ever had so plain, direct, immediate an effect on the course of history. Christopher Dawson, a devout Christian historian, has said that his Koran is the most influential book in world history.

Such assertions can be made more confidently about Mohammed than about Moses, Buddha, or Christ because much more is certainly known about his life, his teaching, and the early growth and spread of his faith.[1] We must qualify, to be sure, the conventional saying that

---

[1] I am referring to historical knowledge by objective, public standards on which men of different faiths or no religious faith can agree. They cannot agree, of course, on much that believers hold as sacred truth—for example, the virgin birth and the resurrection of Christ. Since my concern here, as later with Christianity, is the historical consequences of Mohammedanism, not the metaphysical questions of its truth, I should emphasize that these consequences are roughly ascertainable, but also that they are too mixed and often contradictory to permit agreement in judgment. I am substantially repeating the judgment of Mohammed and his work stated in Chapter 8 of *The Loom of History*, noting perhaps too briefly the ideal possibilities stressed by liberal Moslems today, but dwelling on the actual historic record of Islam that they perhaps discount too much.

Islam grew up in the full light of history. Inevitably it grew up as well in a jungle of fabulous legend; triumphant piety bred not only the familiar miracles but literally hundreds of thousands of contradictory *hadith*, traditional sayings and doings of the Prophet, setting later theologians the hopeless task of deciding which were authentic. (The conscientious al-Bukhari accepted only seven thousand of them.) If the legends help to fill what H. A. R. Gibb has called "the gap between the bare facts and the tremendous results," they are hardly a satisfactory explanation. But they do testify to the tremendous power of a real personality. There is little or no question about the main facts of Mohammed's career and its immediate results.

He was an unlettered Arab, in his own words "the Prophet who can neither read nor write," and never pretended to be divine or to have superhuman powers. At about the age of forty, after he had acquired some position by marrying a rich widow in his native Mecca, he felt a calling like that of the prophets of Israel: he asserted that the Angel Gabriel had commanded him to preach the one true God, do away with the many false gods worshiped by the Arabs. His preaching converted some poor people but naturally antagonized the respectable, pious Meccans, especially when it threatened the town's profits as a sanctuary and hostelry for pilgrims. Hostility grew so violent that the Prophet fled to Medina one night in A.D. 622—the hegira that marks the beginning of the Mohammedan era, with a historic certainty and exactitude that cannot be claimed for the birth of Christ. At Medina he became a man of the sword, the political and military as well as spiritual leader of a community, who warred on the Meccans, and also on some neighboring Jewish communities. After eight years Mecca gave up. Mohammed returned in triumph with his army, to be accepted as the Prophet of Allah, and to consolidate and extend his community in the year or so remaining to him. He was the only great religious leader whose life ended in worldly success.

Meanwhile his followers had been taking down the Koran, which he said the Angel Gabriel had dictated to him in installments. As an impassioned, illiterate prophet, Mohammed was incoherent and inconsistent enough to keep theologians busy in interpretation and disagreement, and his followers split into sects; but there is again little question about his basic teachings. Unlike Christian Scripture, much of the Koran was written down during his lifetime, and the rest from memory within a few years later. However obscure, ambiguous, and uncertain in the order of its composition, the great bulk of it almost certainly

represents the word of Mohammed himself. It contains no conflicting
testimony by different apostles, no reinterpretations such as those of St.
John and St. Paul. His gospel is plainer and more nearly uniform than
the gospel expounded by the various authors of the New Testament.

The God of Mohammed came out of Judaism and Christianity. Although the Prophet had only a superficial acquaintance with the Bible
(regarding the Crucifixion, for instance, as a Jewish falsehood) , he recognized true prophets before him, from Abraham and Moses to Jesus,
and therefore respected Jews and Christians as "people of the Book."
He claimed only that he was the last of the prophets, completing their
work in a final revelation, and above all purifying it of later corruptions. Basically Mohammed preached an utterly pure monotheism. Over
and over again he insisted that there was no god but God—Allah; at
least half of the Koran is taken up with denunciation of every form or
suspicion of polytheism and idolatry. Allah had no Son, no Mother, no
Holy Ghost, and he was never to be represented in human form, by
graven images, or in the trappings of sacraments. If Mohammed somewhat obscured his absolute transcendence and oneness by admitting the
traditional angels and evil spirits, the latter led by "the Satan," he did
away with all human intermediaries between man and Allah, condemning the priests and monks whom men "have taken as lords beside Allah."
Denying the divinity of Christ, he as resolutely insisted that he himself
was "only a man, warning you."

The warning was necessary because of another uniform, emphatic
teaching—the Christian doctrine of Heaven and Hell, together with a
Last Judgment and Day of Resurrection. Heaven was a literal Garden,
which as in Christianity was open only to true believers; Hell was a
literal Fire, the destination of all unbelievers and sinners. Mohammed
spelled out some ritual requirements, such as daily prayers and fasting
during the holy month of Ramadan in which the Koran had been revealed, but like all the great religious teachers he insisted on the primacy of righteousness. True believers had to earn the delights of the
Garden by good works, which he also specified in detail. The gist of his
teaching is in this verse: "It is not righteousness that ye turn your faces
to the East and the West; but righteous is he who believeth in Allah
and the Last Day and the angels and the Scripture and the Prophets;
and giveth his wealth, for love of Him, to kinsfolk and to orphans and
the needy and the wayfarer and to those who ask, and to set slaves free;
and observeth proper worship and payeth the poor-due."

Now, as might be expected, Islam did not remain pure, but went the way of popular religion everywhere. The "lords beside Allah"—mufti, dervishes, fakirs, wonder-working saints, etc.—all came back, with the usual accessories of salvation cults, while Mohammed himself was endowed with the usual miraculous attributes of divinity.[2] The Prophet had left some openings for the return of pagan idolatry by concessions to Arabian tradition, notably the retention of the sacred Black Stone in Mecca. In the main, however, Moslems have been more faithful to his teachings than Christians have been to those of Jesus, and their whole culture bears much more plainly and deeply his imprint. This gives more point to our immediate concern here—the bearings of his gospel on the issues of freedom. As might also be expected, the bearings are ambiguous; like the prophets of all gods, Mohammed (or the Angel Gabriel) had far more to say about the duties than the rights of men. But first we must note that, like the founders of all the higher religions, he asserted principles that could support men's claims to dignity and worth, and therefore to rights.

Liberal Moslems now stress a basic democratic principle shared immediately with Judaism and Christianity—the principle of spiritual equality and brotherhood. It is perhaps more emphatic in the gospel according to Mohammed, if only because all men alike were dwarfed by the transcendent mightiness of Allah; Maude Royden went so far as to say that Islam "proclaimed the first real democracy ever conceived in the mind of man." In keeping with this principle, which entered Moslem law as a theory of political and civil equality, Mohammed shared the concern of Jesus and the prophets of Israel over the habitual oppression of the poor; he attacked the extreme economic inequalities that limited the real freedom of the many. More explicitly, according to tradition, he insisted on racial equality: "The white man is not above the black nor the black above the yellow; all men are equal before the Maker." His religion would accordingly have an advantage over Christianity in the conversion of Africans and Asiatics. He was also most explicit in his concern to free simple worshipers from the priesthood, with its stock in ritual or sacrament, that everywhere stood between them and God, and that might live off them when not exploit

---

[2] One miracle of some historical consequence, still celebrated annually in the Moslem world, was the transportation of the Prophet one night into the seven heavens, where he met Jesus and others, and was further gratified by a view of the sinners roasting in hell. He took off from Jerusalem, specifically from the blessed rock now enclosed by the great mosque called the Dome of the Rock, to which the Angel Gabriel had whisked him from Mecca. Accordingly a holy city for Moslems, as well as Jews and Christians, Jerusalem became the bone of a good deal of holy warfare, as it still is.

them. A Moslem needed no priest, not even a church, in performing his daily worship; or in a mosque he might still pray alone, in true spiritual equality with all other Moslems bowed down before Allah. The caliph of Islam was never a pope, nor did its clerics have the possibly awful power of sacraments essential to salvation.

More broadly, the gospel of Mohammed was like that of Jesus a means to regeneration. It was no less a new religious start because in the name of an old God, for it not only purified worship but raised the spiritual sights of men. It was an especially invigorating gospel, calling for daily active service of an always purposeful God. Unlike Hinduism and Buddhism, or the Platonic versions of Christianity, it did not disparage the natural, temporal world. For the purposes of earthly life, even the apparent limitations of Mohammed might be more to the good than saintliness. While always preaching with an eye to the Garden, he was a worldly man, shrewd in business and politics, who frankly enjoyed the pleasures of food, jokes, and the company of concubines and eleven wives, and who set up his kingdom squarely in this world; but he thereby underwrote the value of the only world in which men may surely exercise and enjoy freedom.

As a crusading faith in the One True God, Mohammed's gospel naturally inspired considerable fanaticism—another legacy from Judaism and Christianity, distinguishing this family of religions from the major religions of the Far East. It was more liberal in this respect, however, than medieval Christianity or early Protestantism. Although Mohammed turned on "the people of the Book" when they refused to recognize him as the true Prophet, he had acknowledged some spiritual kinship with them. His triumphant followers did not systematically persecute Christians and Jews, or try to suppress or destroy their faith; they were content with subjecting and taxing them, allowing them freedom of worship. When they took Jerusalem they did not massacre its Christian inhabitants, as the later Crusaders exultantly massacred both Moslems and Jews, but guaranteed their security. Most of the Christians in Syria, Palestine, and Egypt voluntarily became converts to Islam, the more readily because many were Monophysite or Nestorian "heretics," liable to have nose and ears cut off by decree of Byzantine emperors. That in time Moslems grew more fanatical was due primarily to the Christian Crusaders. Even so, the later Ottoman Turks granted full religious freedom to their Greek subjects, members of the Holy Orthodox Church—a freedom they would scarcely have enjoyed under the dominion of contemporary Rome.

More ambiguous was the effect of Mohammed's teaching about predestination. As a fervent missionary, he was bound to imply now and then that men were free, responsible agents, able to save their own souls. More often and more plainly he preached that Allah was responsible for literally everything in his creation, including disobedience and unbelief, as an Almighty must be. ("Whom Allah will He sendeth astray, and whom He will He placeth on a straight path.") Predestination remains the orthodox doctrine of Islam. Logically, this belief should induce a fatalistic resignation, since a man cannot by any effort of his own alter his predestined fate. Psychologically, it is likely to have the very opposite effect. True believers naturally tend to assume that they have been elected for salvation, and to be braced, heartened, even fired by the conviction that the Almighty is behind them. They may redouble their efforts, just as did the Puritans, or more lately the Communist believers in historical predestination. The early followers of Mohammed demonstrated conclusively enough that his gospel had filled men with new confidence, liberated immense energy.

Still, the doctrine of predestination comes down to a denial of actual human freedom. In the bad times that lay ahead for Islam it could and did support a good deal of fatalistic resignation, instead of active effort to improve society or reform the state. It recalls us to an evident absurdity in the description of Islam as the "first real democracy." For Islam never produced an actual democracy, never stimulated any concerted efforts whatever toward one until recent times. Although it kept clear of the vulgarity of racial prejudice, it never realized in political practice the theory of equality stated in its law, nor the as nominal principle that "the fundamental rule of law is liberty." Economic inequality grew ever more glaring, in states now notorious for the rotten wealth of the very few and the wretched poverty of the masses. These shortcomings may be attributed to a corruption of the teachings of the Prophet, as they are by virtually all Moslem reformers today. Outsiders may agree that Mohammed was sincerely concerned with social justice, and may add that he could hardly be expected to anticipate the problems that would arise as his little community grew into a great empire. Yet to a Western eye the shortcomings of Islam seem due at least in part to his gospel, which tended most obviously to discourage the growth of freedom—political, intellectual, or religious.

To begin with, no deity of the higher religions is so despotic as the Allah of Mohammed. While he remained as exclusive and jealous as the Christian God, granting salvation only to true believers, he was more arbitrary, having cursed the vast majority of men with unbelief, and refusing any rational explanation of his exorbitant scheme. To Moslems he was "Compassionate and Merciful," the Prophet often said, but as often "severe in judgment"; the accent was on the need of fear. Nor was Allah disposed to permit any question of his variable moods, any assertion of human standards of justice. As a later theologian explained, "The Lord of the Worlds is not under a Law." Above all, Allah insisted on the absolute dependence of man, the complete submission of his own purposes. *Islam* itself means "surrender to the will of God." The proudest title man can aspire to, says the Koran, is "slave of Allah." Prostration in prayer, the Moslem mode of daily worship, can be beautiful in its simple humility; but it may remind us that in all the great states of the ancient East men typically prostrated themselves before the Great Kings, despotic Lords of this world who also were under no law.

In his own humility, Mohammed claimed no credit for his inspired missionary work—it was all Allah's doing; yet he was naturally as dictatorial in spirit. He was a prophet, not a philosopher or a seeker of the truth. In laying down the law for man, he demanded unquestioning obedience and permitted no freedom of conscience, no idea that men have a right to seek and worship God in their own ways. Outsiders must wonder why God chose to present his final, complete revelation to mankind through an illiterate member of an obscure tribe; but taking Mohammed at his own word, as a mouthpiece of the Angel Gabriel, we can only repeat that he dictated and denounced in a manner that allowed no dissent. At most he offered a text that seems to provide for inconsistencies: "If we abrogate or cause any verse to be forgotten, we will replace it by a better one or one similar." Theologians could therefore keep happy, or forever perplexed, in a hunt for abrogated texts. But there was no getting away from the absolute truth of the Koran, the literal word of the Angel Gabriel.

To outsiders, again, this appears to be a distinctly fallible word. If it was perhaps deliberately adapted to the understanding of its rude Arab audience, it in any case reflected their limited knowledge, civility, and spiritual reach. Mohammed was indeed much superior to his society and distinctly elevated its moral code, even by some of his dubious precepts. Thus in legalizing slavery he called for a more humane treatment of slaves and encouraged his followers to free them; in legalizing polygamy he was regulating a practice that had been unrestricted, permitting men to have only four wives; and in general he was more specific than the recorded Jesus in condemning current evils because much more practical, explicit, and thorough in his teaching. By the same token, however, he tied his law more closely to the customs and the needs of his undisciplined people. His elaborate regulations include much indiscriminate legalism of no particular ethical or spiritual tendency. In one verse he could preach brotherliness and charity, in the next verse directly confirm the old eye-for-an-eye principle of justice. He as positively legalized some barbarous customs, such as slavery, that Jesus tacitly accepted but did not approve in so many words. And the apparent fallibility of a gospel that Moslems were required to accept as sacred truth was magnified because the Angel Gabriel also adapted his dictation to the varying fortunes of Mohammed, and spoke most emphatically after the military triumphs, when the Prophet was practicing something rather different from a gospel of universal brotherhood.

Hence the fateful doctrine of *jihad*—the sacred duty of war on idolaters. In his early days at Mecca, when the Prophet had only a small following and no worldly power, he urged the faithful to reason with unbelievers: "Let there be no compulsion in religion," reads the Koran. As a war leader at Medina, he announced that "God is free from any obligations to idolaters, and his Apostle likewise," and he commanded his followers to "slay the idolaters wherever ye find them"—thus abrogating, it is said, 124 other verses recommending tolerance. Since he had himself put to death all the men in a Jewish community he had conquered, selling the women and children into slavery, he explained: "It is not for a Prophet to hold captives till he hath dealt slaughter through the earth." Aside from this occasional ruthlessness, it may be said in extenuation of Mohammed that only by war could he have succeeded in primitive Arabia, and that at least he was free from the hypocrisy of Christians who profess a belief in the Sermon on the Mount. Nevertheless, it is indisputable that the triumphant Prophet preached the method of violence, not of reasonable persuasion. He not only split mankind into "righteous Believers and sinners" but in effect denied human rights to unbelievers. As a prophet he might have foretold that the holy wars would lead to spiritual disaster in Islam too; for success in these wars fatally corrupted its rulers, while also facilitating the subjection of the masses of Moslems to their autocratic rule.

There remains the most notorious violation of the theoretical principles of equality and liberty in Islam—the treatment of women. This was not wholly the fault of Mohammed. One reason why he had more to say about the status of women than about any other social question was a clear desire to improve their status: he not only limited polygamy but commanded husbands to treat their wives humanely and as impartially as possible, just as he treated his own, while he did not specifically enjoin his own practice of segregating his wives and concubines. Yet he did specifically deny women equality, declaring that Allah had created them inferior, authorized their subjection to men, made them "the least in Paradise" too. Among the God-given rights of men was that of divorcing a wife at will, whereas women could not sue for divorce on any grounds. Warning husbands that "thy worst enemies are the wife at thy side and thy concubine," he told them to "use the whip" on disobedient women. Sometimes he forgot his own pleasures (or perhaps remembered them too vividly), sounding like an early Christian saint: "Women are the faggots of hell." Taking him at his literal word, at any rate, the faithful proceeded to degrade women to an extent unparalleled in any other higher religion. There is only to add that the degradation was a curse upon the men as well, especially the young, for it denied them the natural freedoms of social life enjoyed by almost all other peoples.

All this may fall short of the essential truth about the religion of Mohammed, in particular the possibilities of "spiritual freedom" in the service of Allah. But it points to an essential aspect of the truth that must be remarked in a history of freedom, particularly because as the latest of the world's major religions Mohammedanism might appear to have a legitimate claim to be the loftiest, or the best suited to a "free man's worship." The Prophet did not merely "purify" the religion that came down to him from Judaism and Christianity. In some basic respects he crudely simplified it, if only to adapt it to the needs of his relatively primitive, warlike people. He simplified most obviously by his crass literalness, as in his sensuous pictures of the Garden—a masculine paradise on a cool mountaintop, streaming with honey, furnished with couches, silver goblets, silk garments, perfumes, "boys of everlasting youth," etc. (Among the special rewards for the faithful killed in holy wars was marriage to "seventy dark-eyed virgins.") His elaborately detailed law, with its innumerable prohibitions, was likewise a complete discipline that left nothing to chance or choice, telling simple worshipers and warriors just what to do on all occasions. Even the seemingly transcendent, ineffable Allah was an anthropomorphic deity easy enough for his people to understand. Mohammed could tell them a great deal about Allah, after all, including how he looked and acted when seated on his throne; and his inscrutable arbitrary ways were no puzzle to men in the ancient East, where despotic gods and god-kings had always been the rule.

Such basic simplicities, together with its insistent ethic, made the gospel of Mohammed an admirable one for rude peoples like his own. It could at once inspire, uplift, and discipline them, on the record more readily than other religions; thus it made a world power of the nomadic Turks. But there remains considerable question of its suitability for purposes of further growth, intellectual or spiritual, or more specifically for independence of mind and spirit beyond manliness on the battlefield. Such doubts are borne out by the history of Islam.

Its political history was plainly disastrous, by its own standards. Orthodox Moslems place their Golden Age in the reign of Abu-Bakr and Omar, the caliphs who succeeded Mohammed, and who remained true to his spirit as they conquered much of the Middle East; but this glorious age lasted little more than a decade. The third caliph was assassinated, by a party led by a son of the first one. The murder of the next caliph, Ali (the Prophet's son-in-law), led to not only civil war but a permanent schism over the rightful succession, splitting Islam into the major sects of Sunnites and Shiites. It also led to the establishment of the Umayyad dynasty (661–750), which moved the capital from holy Medina to Damascus; although these caliphs were a worldly success, expanding the dominion of Islam from India to Spain, they won among the faithful a reputation as tyrants and unbelievers. The Abbasids who overthrew them, after another civil war, generally maintained a show of orthodoxy but as generally were worldly, licentious, and impious. Under their rule, from a brilliant new capital at Baghdad, the empire won by the holy wars soon began breaking up, showing nothing like the staying power of the Roman and Byzantine empires. The seeds of its sorry destiny were already sprouting in the reign of Harun al-Rashid (786–809), the famous symbol of the power and splendor of Islam— a reign that began in harem intrigue and murder, and ended in civil war between his sons. By the next century assassination had become the common fate of the caliphs of Baghdad. They lost almost all authority, political and spiritual, serving chiefly as window dressing for their army of Turkish "slaves," the real rulers of what was left of their domains. Early in the eleventh century the slaves put an end to the sordid pretense of their rule. Caliphates that sprang up in independent provinces, such as Egypt, rehearsed the same story of splendor, corruption, and decay.

In building its empire Islam had reverted to the ancient tradition of the Oriental sacred monarchy.[3] The first caliphs ruled like tribal chieftains, consulting other Companions of the Prophet and dividing up the spoils of war among the faithful. The Umayyad caliphs ruled as monarchs set apart from the people, soon denying the right of criticism as well as access; they adopted the appurtenances of an Oriental royal court, including harems with eunuchs. The Abbasids in Baghdad grew more autocratic as they consciously took to the style of the Persian-Sassanian emperors before them. They had themselves crowned with the diadem, proclaimed their divine right to rule as "Deputy of God," solemnized their majesty by holding audience from behind a curtain, and proved it by squandering ever more wealth in luxury. While making free use of an executioner whom they added to their retinue at court, they further emphasized the fact that Moslems were subjects, not citizens, by making the army their own property, recruiting it from foreign slaves. That eventually they became puppets of these slaves, and all along were liable to routine assassination, only accentuates the failure of Islam to develop republican or constitutional government: any political means of keeping rulers responsible to the ruled, any institutional safeguards against either tyranny or utter incompetence, any effective tradition of liberty under law. Periodic rebellions, usually in a religious guise, effected no lasting change in the structure of either society or the state.

Now, this failure is surely understandable. It is almost inconceivable that the inexperienced Arabs could have administered democratically the empire they so quickly won. Having no concept even of political sovereignty beyond simple rule by chieftains, they naturally looked to the political forms of the Byzantine and Sassanian empires before them, while sensibly employing many of their officials. Their only other guide was the little theocratic state set up by Mohammed, a potential sacred monarchy in that it made no distinction between church and state, and was ruled by one man. The dilemma of his successors, for whom he had made no provision, was summed up in an exclamation attributed to Omar: "By God! I know not whether I am a Caliph or a King. And if I am a king, it is a fearful thing." Still, the fact remains that the caliphs

---

[3] On this tradition see Chapter 2 of *Freedom in the Ancient World*. The gist of it was rule by absolute monarchs who either were themselves divine (like Pharaoh in Egypt) or were divinely appointed, and upon whose sanctified authority there were no definite checks beyond custom or prudence. It was the invariable form of government in all the empires of the East—Egyptian, Babylonian, Hittine, Assyrian, Persian, Byzantine, Sassanian.

very soon decided that they were kings, and ceased to think it at all fearful; they rewarded themselves with increasingly generous shares of the booty and set about keeping power in the family. ("Give the kinsman his due" reads a convenient command in the Koran.) One might have expected something better of a state based on a higher religion, avowing a principle of equality. And though the man Mohammed could not have been expected to draw up a constitution for a nonexistent empire, the trouble was in part his authoritarian spirit. In ruling his own community he had laid down principles of social justice, but he had hardly proposed submitting his law to discussion or allowing his people to amend it.

It did not help, either, that Mohammed's law remained in theory the basis of all law in Islam—unlike Christendom, which operated chiefly on common or Roman law and admitted the legislative power of the state. A God-given law cannot be openly discarded or freely amended. Moslem jurists perforce did alter the Sacred Law, as they had to accommodate it to the needs of large and diverse nations; yet they did not regard it as man-made, or subject to ratification by the people, and the alterations in turn were likely to seem inalterable. As for government, the jurists chiefly rationalized the fact of absolute monarchy. "Were there more than one God," they read in the Koran, "the universe would go to ruin"; so they argued that princes on earth could not share their authority either. When kingship brought on the chaos it was supposed to prevent, they proposed no alternative. In effect they agreed with the authority who remarked that thinking people capable of choosing their rulers was as obviously absurd as thinking them capable of choosing their prophets. Once more religion gave its blessing to autocracy as it had since the dawn of history.

That Islam had nothing really new to offer political theory, and in practice nothing so rational as the Greeks and Romans had achieved, was dramatized by its most successful political creation, the Ottoman Empire. A small tribe of nomads about the year 1300, the Ottoman Turks rose under an exceptionally long series of vigorous, able sultans, who gave Islam the strongest empire it had yet known. To administer their empire, the sultans developed a remarkable institution: a huge royal "slave" family of soldiers and officials, numbering up to 80,000, whose members were carefully selected from their Christian subjects (chiefly peasants), as carefully trained, promoted on a strict merit basis, and thereby enabled to rise to the highest offices in the state, including grand vizier. This system, strikingly similar to that devised by Plato for his imaginary Republic, reached its zenith under Suleiman the Magnificent early in the sixteenth century.[4] But under Suleiman corruption set in, thereafter the system grew rotten with nepotism and graft, and with its failure the Ottomans proved helpless. At its best, its main object had been conquest and the collection of taxes, in the service of the sultan, not the people. It deprived the Turks themselves of both political power and political experience, making them utterly dependent on the capability of their rulers. The sultan himself was not carefully selected and bred, nor was his character notably improved by the early revival of a practice going back to the Persian Empire centuries before Christ: upon ascending the throne, he had his brothers executed. (Selim the Grim, father of Suleiman, made a clean sweep of his nephews as well.) The long, inglorious decline of the Ottoman Empire was accentuated by a royal bombast so preposterous that it might pass as a burlesque of the traditional style of the Oriental King of Kings. ("The command, under the Sublime and lofty Signet, which imparts sublimity to every place, and under the imperial and noble Cypher, whose glory is renowned throughout all the world, by the Emperor and Conqueror of the Earth, achieved with the assistance of the Omnipotent, and by the especial grace of God, is this"—in this case a concession to foreigners.) There were the familiar accompaniments of barbaric splendor, harem intrigue, corruption, and assassination in the Sublime Porte, while peasants toiled faithfully in poverty and ignorant piety, until this century remaining obedient, resigned, inert.

In their rise the Ottoman Turks had most plainly demonstrated the values of Mohammedanism as an inspiration and a discipline. Even before their decline they illustrated as plainly its possible drawbacks for purposes of independent, critical, creative thought. They adorned their empire, especially their capital of Constantinople, with a notable architecture; but otherwise they contributed scarcely anything of note to literature, philosophy, science, the humanities—not a name worthy of rank with the great names in Islam before them, or with the many more great names in contemporary Europe. Their formal literature was

---

[4] It is discussed at greater length in *The Loom of History*, pp. 305-310. This curiosity of political history was no contribution to the growth of free institutions, of course, as the Christian recruits were given no choice, torn from their families, and forced to become Moslems, while at all times the sultan had absolute power over their property and their life; but it should be added that they were generally loyal, even proud, since no stigma attached to their rank as "slaves." Busbecq, a European envoy at Suleiman's court, remarked that the Turks selected and bred men with a care that Europeans reserved for dogs, hawks, and horses, and that the system compared favorably with the aristocratic system of Christendom, in which rank depended solely on birth, not merit.

characteristic, consisting chiefly of an artificial, imitative poetry rigidly bound by rule. That down to 1850 Turkish poets employed only the Ptolemaic cosmography was in keeping with the whole Ottoman curriculum, which remained faithful to tradition and grew ever more hopelessly inadequate as the West kept making revolutionary advances in science and technology. Education was controlled by the *ulema*—the men holding religious office. There was no printing press in Constantinople until the eighteenth century, no Moslem press in the Arab world until the nineteenth.

We are accordingly brought to the cultural history of Islam. This was far more complex, varied, and fruitful than its political history; it ranks Islam among the world's great civilizations. Yet it too contrasts sharply with the history made in the West, in ways suggestive for a student of freedom.

Art was mostly true to the spirit of Mohammed, in particular his ban on the representation of the human form. Although in some regions, especially Persia, the ban was ignored, painting and sculpture were generally restricted by it and never flourished as they did in the Italian Renaissance. Today some students of art might say that Mohammed rescued artists from possible bondage to realism, gave them the greater freedom of abstract or nonrepresentational design. All may agree that Islam developed a distinctive style of great beauty in architecture and ornamental art, suited to its chaste mode of worship; it made fine builders of most of its converts, who worked with most loving care on their mosques. By the same token, however, Islamic art lacked autonomy and became a conservative force. It is a reminder that outside the Western world art has rarely been independent or rebellious, much more often serving primarily the vested interests of gods, god-kings, and ruling classes.

Imaginative literature owed much less to the Prophet. His spirit possibly had something to do with the failure to cultivate such major forms as drama and epic (or any major forms in music), but otherwise writers exhibited considerable freedom. Poetry was typically romantic, sensuous, and erotic, wedded to the theme of love, in the old pagan tradition of Arabia; the world-famous *Arabian Nights* came out of the same tradition. A rich vein of mystical poetry might be attributed to Mohammed's inspiration except that the God known immediately by mystics is a God more of freedom than necessity, never a severe judge who has predestined most of mankind to unbelief and damnation; the mystics of Islam were always liable to charges of heresy. More plainly heretical were many sophisticated, skeptical, irreverent writings in the brilliant cultural period of Baghdad, down to the eleventh century. Their spirit is best known to Westerners in the later *Rubáiyát* of Omar Khayyam. This critical spirit owed mainly to the discovery of the thought and learning of ancient Greece, through Byzantine scholars in Syria. Thereupon the conquerors from the Arabian deserts acquired a remarkable passion for knowledge—a passion that their unlettered Prophet might have approved, but scarcely inspired or guided. Although the early caliphs frowned on the books of the idolaters they ran across, at Damascus the worldly Umayyads began showing some interest in them, patronizing translators who were popularly known as "sorcerers," and under the Abbasids in Baghdad such studies grew much more extensive, systematic, and respectable. A son of Harun al-Raschid set up a "House of Wisdom" for translators and students. Islam was soon turning out scholarly editors, then philosophers and scientists. It became the main center of intellectual development, livelier and more enterprising than contemporary Byzantium, far ahead of contemporary Europe.

In the course of this renaissance the thinkers of Islam showed high promise in their own right. If as philosophers they chiefly worked out variants of Platonism and Aristotelianism, they were independent enough to risk heresy—an essential condition of freedom of thought. Ibn-Rushd, who became famous or infamous in Europe as Averroës, anticipated the daring effort of St. Thomas Aquinas to reconcile Aristotle with the truth of revelation. Behind him was the school of Mutazilites, freethinkers who tried to make the faith of Islam entirely rational. Something of a scientist too, he carried on as well the tradition of the great al-Kindi, "Philosopher of the Arabs," master of both Aristotle and natural science, to whom were attributed some 265 works. In science the followers of the Prophet did their most original and important work. The advances they made—especially in mathematics, chemistry, physics, astronomy, and geography—are too technical to be detailed here; but suffice it that they helped substantially to prepare the way for the great age of exploration and discovery in Europe, and for the rise of modern science.

Long before this the scholars of Islam had put the Western world incalculably in their debt. It was immediately through them that Europe—just emerging from the Dark Ages—began to recover its classics, as Arabic editions were translated back into Latin. Toledo in Spain (recaptured from the Moors in 1085) became the main channel for this one-way traffic, in which Europeans acquired the all-important

Aristotle while having little or nothing to offer in return. Likewise Islam transmitted Greek mathematics and science, together with its own major works, such as the immensely influential compendium of medicine by ibn-Sina (Avicenna) —a means to an ordinary kind of freedom that histories can never do justice to. It passed along other contributions from the farther East, most notably the "Arabic" numerals, including the zero invented in India; a vast improvement over the clumsy Roman numerary, these greatly facilitated the further development of science and technology. Europe might well have got along without all this help; but as is was, the most lasting good that came out of its Crusades on Islam was all that it learned from acquaintance with a civilization much superior to its own. The first book printed in England, appropriately, was *The Dictes and Sayings of the Philosophers*: a translation from a French version of a Latin recast of an Arabic work.

At that, Europe was not yet acquainted with the most astounding genius produced by Islam—the historian ibn-Khaldun (1332–1406). Having had no important followers in Islam, and remaining entirely unknown to Europe until the nineteenth century, he had no influence whatever on the history of freedom, or on any history; but even so we must pause over his work. Ibn-Khaldun now stands out as the first scientific philosopher of universal history, the first thinker anywhere to offer a closely reasoned, empirical theory of the nature and the course of civilization. As history was in his view a science embracing all social phenomena—not only political but geographical, economic, cultural, religious—he may be called the first sociologist as well. Like many other works that have had no perceptible influence on the main march of events—the plays of Shakespeare, the paintings of Rembrandt, the symphonies of Beethoven—ibn-Khaldun's *Muqaddimah* (or Prolegomena to the study of history) must be considered important simply because it was a great creative work, another token of the values that give man a distinctive history and make it worth telling; but it is also significant here for the light it throws on the history of Islam.

The major conclusion of the *Muqaddimah* was a law of growth and decay: an invariable law that recalls the ancient Greek theory of cycles, but differs in that it was derived from an empirical study, supported by an analysis of natural causes, and illustrated by many penetrating insights into social processes. This theory was not calculated to inspire or invigorate men, or to influence the course of history. So far from holding any promise of salvation for Islam, it was made possible only by the political failure of Islam—the growth and decay of the early caliphate, a story since repeated in all the provinces, and become at once so monotonous and so hectic that ibn-Khaldun judged the "normal" life span of a dynasty to be only three generations. In analyzing this failure he rejected the popular notion that men had once been uniformly happier and more virtuous, instead dwelling on the ambivalent causes of degeneration, the natural tendencies to softness and corruption as civilization reached its goal of "sedentary culture and luxury." In particular he emphasized the common failings of the dynasts in Islam, such as the dependence on mercenaries, the favors lavished on an inner circle at court, the exploitation and waste that discouraged both cultural and economic enterprise, the enforced subservience of the many that weakened "group feeling" or loyalty. Ibn-Khaldun had the advantage of firsthand knowledge. No mere academic, he had devoted most of his life to public affairs, often holding high office.

It is depressing that so extraordinary a work as the *Muqaddimah* should have been so soon forgotten and long neglected. It is not at all surprising, however. Ibn-Khaldun was a native of north Africa, whose family had lived for generations in Spain. For some time creativity had been largely confined to the outlying regions of Islam, which were exposed to fresh influences; a blight had long since settled on its heartland in the Near East, beginning well before this was devastated by the Mongols of Jenghiz Khan, and Arabia itself had returned to its primitive state. Now the provinces were by no means all aglow either. Ibn-Khaldun remarked that the sciences had disappeared from Spain, where there was no longer a shadow of the intellectual disciplines; north Africa was busy chiefly in political intrigue and civil war fought over no principle higher than personal ambition, so he quit it for Egypt; and though he was pleased to find much more intellectual activity here, his account of it indicates nothing really independent or original. His own work was in fact to be the swansong of Moslem philosophy and science: Islam would produce no more thinkers of consequence.

One might say that it was simply exhausted, or experiencing the common fate of creativity—great movements in thought always peter out sooner or later. Yet Islam was now becoming a military power under the Ottoman Turks, it would go on building and adorning great mosques, it was still busy in commerce, and it might have been stimulated by the revolutionary goings on in Europe. One may suspect some deeper reasons for the long centuries of intellectual torpor, which ibn-Khaldun did not foresee. And there are plain enough clues in the limitations of his own thought.

As a public man he was not far above the sordid political life of Islam, fawning, intriguing, and shifting allegiance with little scruple. More important, he was fundamentally not superior to it as a political philosopher. While coolly analyzing the inveterate failings of the dynasties, he continued to take for granted the necessity of autocratic rule, identifying the state with the dynasty. That the rulers claimed all glory for themselves, permitting the people none, he thought unfortunate but unavoidable. He repeated the stock argument that only rule by one man could prevent anarchy, without suggesting any institutional means of preventing the abuses that were producing anarchy in his own time. In arguing that injustice was poor policy, he dwelt chiefly on injustice to property owners; he showed no concern for the many poor, or the theoretical principle of equality. Nevertheless, he insisted that the Islamic state was based on religious law. He mentioned an alternative that he called "rational politics," which is concerned with the public interest in this world, but he quickly dropped it: "God made this type of politics superfluous for us in Islam at the time of the caliphate." Habitually he ended his empirical analysis by affixing a religious tag: "This is how God proceeds with His servants."

Such fatalism was in keeping with the dogma of predestination, which ibn-Khaldun explicitly affirmed; but it points to a profound inconsistency in his thought. While he naturally professed a respect for intellect and the "intellectual sciences," and deplored their disappearance in Spain, he also deplored the fact that they had "seduced" many Moslems; intellect must always bow to tradition and be on guard against "innovations." He gave considerable attention to the "sciences" of speculative theology, dream interpretation, and angels, but dismissed physics in a page: good Moslems should leave it alone because it was of no use in their religious affairs. He warned against the study of philosophy (a science he lumped with alchemy and astrology) as especially dangerous to religion because of its faith in reason, and declared that logic itself was safe only if the student were first "saturated with the religious law." In particular Moslems should give up all speculation about causes. "And you were given but little knowledge," Mohammed had said in the Koran; so "we have been commanded completely to abandon and suppress any speculation about them, and to direct ourselves to the Causer of all causes." The orthodox piety of ibn-Khaldun seems so much at variance with the rational, empirical spirit of his work that one may suspect him of being a politician in these matters too, afraid of expressing his real convictions; at least he had good reasons for such fear, since a friend had been lynched as a heretic. In any case, he reveals the most apparent reason for the intellectual stagnation that lay ahead. This was the triumph of orthodoxy, the return to the infallible Koran.

The triumph had been signaled by the fate of the Mutazilites, the rationalists, whose doctrines ibn-Khaldun described as "pernicious." While they accepted the Koran as a divine revelation, they held that by reason alone man could recognize the Creator, distinguish right and wrong, and that reason was necessary to interpret the Koran, as the Prophet had often spoken figuratively. Thus Allah did not really have a face and hands, really sit on a throne. They also held Allah up to rational standards of justice: as a good God he would never deliberately create evil, predestine his creatures to eternal damnation. They insisted that men were free agents, themselves responsible for the good and evil they did. Similarly they ridiculed the traditional way of dealing with all the contradictory *hadith*, the supposed authenticity of which was decided by an oral chain going back to some companion of the Prophet, not by the sense they made. These freethinkers accordingly contributed to the sophistication, and no doubt to the skepticism and irreverence, of Baghdad in its heyday; but the lasting consequence of their rationalism was the conservative reaction they inspired. Led by al-Ashari in the tenth century, this culminated in the triumph of al-Ghazzali ("Algazel," d. A.D. 1111), who gave orthodox theology essentially its final form.

Although himself a philosopher, al-Ghazzali concentrated on the dangers of inquiry, the inevitable contradictions of rational theology. In his immensely popular work *The Incoherence of the Philosophers*, which attacked the deplorable influence of the Greeks, he expounded a simple, basically uncritical faith resting on tradition and the Koran. When Averroës then exposed the as plain contradictions of this faith in *The Incoherence of the Incoherence*, the followers of the Prophet decided that he was only proving the vanity of reason. The Mutazilites lost out on every major issue. Their defeat had been anticipated by the loose-living Abbasid caliphs, who maintained their show of piety chiefly by persecuting them, executing many, once going so far as to decree a ban on all research and philosophical discussion (this by a caliph celebrated for a different kind of research, having slept with every one of his four thousand concubines). These caliphs had little spiritual authority, however, and by the time of al-Ghazzali had disappeared from the scene; so the significant thing is that he triumphed rather by voluntary consensus of the faithful. Or more precisely of the *ulema*, the large body of men holding religious office and constituting a clerical aristocracy. (Ibn-Khaldun was among them.) Apologists for Islam make much of the idea that technically it has no papacy or church; but the *ulema* became about as powerful as any priesthood, not only interpreting and administering the Sacred Law but controlling education.

The orthodoxy that prevailed was a somewhat debased form of the creed of al-Ghazzali, in keeping with his repudiation of the claims of reason. Truth is all just as it is written in the Koran. If the Koran is sometimes ambiguous, as Mohammed himself admitted, he had added that "only God knows how to interpret it," and true believers would simply believe. Allah has a real face and real hands, and sits on a real throne (in some unimaginable anatomical manner) ; he will raise the dead in the flesh, and send them to a real Garden, a real Fire; and as the only Creator, he has it all worked out beforehand—he *did* will all folly, unbelief, evil. If this predetermined hell on earth and in the hereafter seems unreasonable or unfair, the faithful will not inquire "in what sense" or "why," because "such inquiry is Innovation in Islam." One conservative summed up the victorious creed to which ibn-Khaldun formally subscribed: "Belief is a duty. Inquiry is heresy." As a result, the caliph who had his way with four thousand concubines finally had it with intellectuals too: for all fundamental purposes the research and philosophical discussion did stop. As philosophers were denied the right to make Allah rational, scientists too were denied freedom of research; their inquiries might lead to Innovation. Most of the works of the great al-Kindi disappeared, the more readily because thinkers—including ibn-Khaldun—had never really come to grips with the basic principle of science. The medical compendium of ibn-Sina survived, as it represented no serious threat to the true faith, but its survival was another testimony to the halt in inquiry. It was still being used in this century, even though it was as far behind the times as was the primitive lunar calendar that Islam likewise clung to.

There remained one source of spiritual stir and lift—the mystical movement known as Sufism, to which al-Ghazzali had lent some authority. It was bolder, more varied, and much more popular than mysticism in Christendom. In the name of a God of love, it produced the saintliest men and most eloquent religious writings of Islam.[5] It also produced

[5] Jesus might have uttered the prayer of Hallaj, who had said "I am the truth," and who in 922 was crucified for blasphemy:

"And these thy servants who are gathered to slay me in zeal for Thy religion and in desire to win Thy favor, forgive them, O Lord, and have mercy upon them; for verily if Thou hadst revealed to them that which Thou has revealed to me, they would not have done what they have done; and if Thou hadst hidden from them that which Thou hast hidden from them, I should not have suffered this tribulation. Glory unto Thee in whatsoever Thou doest, and glory unto Thee in whatsoever Thou willest."

much poetry of a humanistic cast, as the Sufis disguised their heretical intimacies with Allah by metaphors of love and wine. But although Sufism remained too popular for the orthodox to suppress, it failed either to reform or to reinvigorate Islam. Beginning as a revulsion against the worldliness of the Abbasid caliphs, it tended to an unworldliness that flourished on the social and political failures of Islam; most of its holy men were given to quietism. Among its intellectual attractions was the Neo-Platonism on which it had drawn, an assertion of the unimportance or even the unreality of the temporal world. (This borrowed theme was a favorite in Ottoman poetry, which thereby depreciated the world in which the early Ottomans had distinguished themselves.) On popular levels it strengthened the tendencies to fatalism, the habit of complete submission to Allah and to caliph or sultan, more especially because here it was debased by many idle dervishes and fakirs who expoited the generosity and the superstition of the poor.

Like all other Moslems, the Sufis expressed nothing but reverence for the Prophet; and this brings us back to his crucial role. The unfailing reverence was a tribute to the power of a great personality—so great, and so human, that Mohammed survived the popular effort to make him over into a conventional miracle man or a mere god. It also generated, however, an inveterate, invincible traditionalism harking back to the simple mentality of his early followers. The multiplication of *hadith* began as they sought authoritative answers for all questions not settled by the Koran. The *hadith* ran into hundreds of thousands because the faithful put the seal of the Prophet on every idea they cherished, and at the same time were loath to risk any possible contempt of tradition; the popular way of dealing with an embarrassing *hadith* was not to suppress it but to invent a contrary one. So the industry flourished even though one traditional saying plainly condemned it: "A book other than the book of God! Do you not know that nothing but the writing of books beside the book of God led astray the peoples that were before you?" In discussing the "science" of *hadith*, ibn-Khaldun admitted its difficulty, and could not forbear expressing some respect for one authority who had accepted only seventeen or so as authentic; yet he did not question the appeal to tradition as the final arbiter of truth. Neither did he ever question the infallibility of the Prophet. And though he stated that "infallibility is a primary necessity of prophets," he never considered the independent claims of other prophets. "The religious law," he explained, "has forbidden the study of all revealed scriptures except the Koran."

Today liberal or sophisticated Moslems can still find many texts in the Koran to suit their varied purposes. Some even declare that Islam has a peculiar genius for science as well as democracy because of its emphasis on the unity of God, the reverence for the empirical fact made possible by its removal of the distinction between the phenomenal and the transcendent. To outsiders the conservative reaction that smothered science and natural philosophy seems truer to the literal, authoritarian spirit of the Prophet. Certainly Mohammed himself displayed no scientific spirit or reverence for empirical fact as he dictated the Koran. He left no room for doubt or dissent, but sealed his teaching with the finality of revelation, and sealed it so irrevocably that even today very few Moslems dare to say openly that the Prophet was a fallible man of his age and the Koran a human document, not the word of God himself. At any rate, the historic record is clear. The orthodoxy that triumphed was a complete repudiation of the Greek spirit—the spirit of free inquiry and criticism, by rational standards. Islam succumbed to its heritage from the ancient East.

As it succumbed, the Greek spirit was growing more active in Europe, then entering the Renaissance, embarking on the career that would make Western civilization the most boldly, richly, continuously creative civilization in all history. Though ibn-Khaldun was provincial enough to consider the works of unbelievers unworthy of serious attention, he mentioned having heard that the "philosophical sciences" were greatly cultivated in the country of the European Christians. "Existing systematic expositions of them are said to be comprehensive, the people who know them numerous, and the students of them very many. God knows better what exists there. 'He creates whatever He wishes, and His is the choice.' " One who is as ignorant of Allah's choice in this matter may remark that the country of the European Christians had the advantage of remoteness from the ancient East, but also of a more direct heritage from Greece and Rome, more deeply engrained in its tradition.

In our longer, wider perspective—which intellectual brilliance could not make available to ibn-Khaldun—we may reflect on further possibilities. We may roughly distinguish Europe from almost all the great Asiatic societies in that their whole culture remained more clearly based on religion and more thoroughly permeated by it, beginning with their characteristic institution of the sacred monarchy. Islam may in this respect be considered the furthest development of Asiatic tradition, as it grew up on a higher religion that governed its whole way of life, even to details of dress and food; the many actual separations and conflicts of interest within it led to no concerted, lasting efforts to achieve open independence from religious authority. By ordinary standards Islam remained a religious success, losing very few of its adherents to Christianity, continuing to make converts in the face of Christian competition. It more nearly achieved the uniformity and fixity of belief that some contemporary Christian thinkers maintain are essential to both social and religious health; it was much truer to its scripture, and to absolute standards of truth; it firmly denied the autonomy of science or any other mode of truth, just as its basic law governing all major activities remained a Sacred Law. The history of Islam intimates that such conditions are not necessarily conducive to a lofty spirituality. Much more plainly it suggests that they are not conducive to the growth of freedom.

PART I
THE ORIGINS OF
WESTERN CIVILIZATION

Chapter One	*T H E B A C K G R O U N D*

1. The Prehistoric Prelude

As our theme is the growth of freedom in the Western world, to an extent never approached in the East, we may be pleased to think that the prehistoric cave drawings in Europe represented the greatest known cultural achievement of man up to that time, and apparently the most brilliant culture that food hunters have ever developed anywhere; but if so we should be sobered by the fate of this culture. Among other things it illustrated a moral that Westerners have grown most keenly aware of: nothing fails like success. These skilled hunters and painters of the mammoth and the reindeer were evidently incapable of adjusting themselves to new conditions of life as the glaciers retreated and forests began spreading over Europe. Excavations throughout northern Europe tell the story of a slow but steady retreat. Descendants of the cave men, or inheritors of their culture, fell back to the north with the mammoth and the reindeer, until the encroaching forests had them backed against the Baltic Sea or the Arctic Ocean.

Here they proved resourceful enough to adapt themselves to coastal life, learning to build seagoing boats out of skins, to harpoon seals, to catch fish in wicker traps and nets, and to make other equipment still in use by fishermen today. Some even managed to maintain themselves in arctic regions, most likely siring the modern Eskimos. Under these rigorous conditions, however, the northern peoples could barely maintain themselves; none went on to develop a rich culture. Neither did other hunters and food gatherers who learned to live in the forests. Europe would achieve nothing of note until much later, after food growers and metalworkers began coming in from Asia. It was in the Near East that man discovered agriculture, learned how to work metals, and then rose to civilization. Europe remained far behind in culture until the Minoans built up a civilization on the island of Crete—and

27

then western Europe stayed barbarian for another thousand years or
so. There was manifestly no magic in European air or blood.

Certainly there was no common consciousness among the many diverse peoples and cultures of prehistoric Europe. The Greeks would
begin to talk about Europe and its conflict with "Asia," but still with
scanty knowledge of either the history or the geography of these artifi-
cially separated continents; otherwise we can hardly speak of a European tradition at this stage. Nevertheless, the assorted barbarians did
develop some distinctive ways in their remote land. Knowing that their
descendants or inheritors would eventually overtake their Oriental
teachers, start creating the most dynamic of civilizations, we might
make out some possible seeds or portents of this eventuality.

One portent was a contrast between the Danubians, the best known
of the early incomers, and the later Battle-ax folk. The Danubians were
a simple, peaceful, agricultural people who entered through the Balkans,
spread over central Europe, and reached as far as the Baltic, moving
along steadily because they quickly exhausted the soil in the small plots
they cleared. In spite of their wastefulness, they might be regarded as
progenitors of the peasant tradition. The Battle-ax folk, so called because of the stone axes found in their graves, were herdsmen who came
in from the east about 2000 B.C. and spread over northern and central
Europe. They were almost certainly Indo-Europeans, the first to arrive
of these peoples who were to dominate European history.[1] As warriors
who ruled or dominated the peasants in the regions they invaded, they
might be called heralds of the aristocratic tradition, the nobility to
come. More plainly they heralded another tradition: Europeans would
remain more warlike than the Egyptians, Chinese, Indians, or most
other civilized peoples. They would stamp even their Christian religion
with military metaphors, such as "soldier of the Cross." The military
virtues, always popular in spite—or because—of the wars they breed,
do not guarantee independence of mind and spirit (as Islam shows);
yet they may contribute to such independence. The fact remains that
Europeans—barbarous or civilized, in Greece, Rome, or Western Christendom—have typically distinguished themselves in the arts of war as
well as the arts of peace.

---

[1] The early history of the Indo-European peoples is sketched in my first volume, pp.
31-34. It should be noted that they were no "race," but mixed peoples who spoke related
languages, and that those who called themselves "Aryans" settled in India and Persia
("Airyana" or Iran), not in Germany.

Another potentiality was indicated by the many megalithic tombs along the Mediterranean, Atlantic, and North Sea coasts. Although the huge stones used in their construction have led some scholars to believe that they were built by "Children of the Sun" from the Near East, those in northern Europe were evidently the work of native peoples, since their furnishings include very few imported objects. (Stonehenge in England, a temple to the sun, is a comparable work.) In any case, the remarkable technical skill that made them possible was due to the spread of Oriental culture by this maritime route. Western Europe was profiting by a growing trade in metals, as it was rich in copper and tin, and it also faced both the Mediterranean and the Atlantic. Peoples living along its extended coasts, with their many good ports, could prosper as the Greeks did when they realized the possibilities of sea trade. Eventually they would make the Atlantic a pathway to the Americas.

Meanwhile there appeared other pioneers known as the Beaker folk, because of a distinctive kind of drinking cup invariably found in their graves. They were bronze-smiths and traders who roved all over central and western Europe in armed bands, possibly selling beer, but dealing especially in metals and finding customers among the Battle-ax herds-men. They introduced the Bronze Age into most of northwestern Europe, including England (where for a time they took over Stonehenge). In their wake, along the trade routes they established, spread the art of metalworking. It was a very gradual spread, over some centuries in the second millennium B.C., but during its course the relatively poor, backward European peoples realized some of the possible advantages of a fresh start in remote lands.

Well before the end of the second millennium they were doing fine work in metal, in styles of their own, and were also mining and trading on a large scale. By this time there were some fairly wealthy chieftains among them, as well as warrior aristocracies like the older Battle-ax and Beaker folk, but there were still no great kings or kingdoms, no power-ful priesthoods. Artisans and merchants were free men, not hirelings. Although we have little direct knowledge of their doings except for their finished products, one reason we know little is that there were no palace or temple shops, no towns large enough to support them indefi-nitely. For the most part they must have been itinerants. They were evidently stimulated by their varied markets, far-flung operations, and adventurous, perhaps dangerous life, for they proved more inventive than their contemporaries in the ancient East, began developing new types of artifacts much more rapidly.[2]

In thus anticipating the European genius for technology, these craftsmen also foreshadowed another major theme—the importance of the creative individual. In prehistory such individuals are perforce anonymous, at best being commemorated in some later myth like that of the master craftsman Daedalus, and their inventiveness is obscured by the slow pace of change, the gradual diffusion of new skills, and the conspicuous uniformity in artifacts. Today their importance is commonly minimized because of our awareness of their dependence on culture, and of the deep, unconscious, involuntary processes of historic change. Yet nothing would seem plainer than that every new invention must have been the work of some individual—not the automatic outcome of an impersonal process, nor the product of a committee of embryonic organization men. Even the very gradual improvements in skills or changes in styles were due to minor innovations that could only have been the work of individuals. The diffusion of new arts and skills itself required some exceptional men bold enough to break the cake of tribal custom, perhaps defy the patriarchs or the head magician. Hence the faster pace of innovation in prehistoric Europe meant among other things that there was now an increasing number of enterprising, imaginative, more or less unconventional men. We may doubt that their works were always welcomed or that their tribal societies were eager for change; but at least these societies were growing more disposed to accept change, encourage the innovator, and thereby were anticipating a civilization that would provide more opportunity and incentive for the creative individual than had any of the great Eastern societies.[3]

---

[2] Gordon Childe tells this story in the last chapters of *The Prehistory of European Society* (1958) , completed shortly before his death. He perhaps tells it too proudly, exaggerating the freedom and the originality of European craftsmen; but their work in bronze unquestionably became independent and progressive, no longer a crude imitation of Oriental work.

[3] In *Change and History* Margaret Hodgen has made a pioneering study in this field: a detailed history of technological innovation in England, shire by shire, parish by parish, over its entire history. Three major periods of innovation—the twelfth and thirteenth centuries, the sixteenth and seventeenth, and the Industrial Revolution beginning in the late eighteenth—reflect the larger "movements" made familiar by historians, and illustrate the deep, impersonal processes of historic change that the innovators may be quite unconscious of. But a close study of these periods, as of the whole span, gives much more prominence to the work of individuals other than the few famous inventors. Thus it was not strictly "England" that produced or underwent these innovations: they occurred primarily in certain regions, more specifically in certain towns or parishes, and always were the work of particular men, who in the sixteenth century begin to be identified by name in the local records. Of the more than 12,000 parishes in England, down to 1900, fewer

By about 1000 B.C. iron too was being worked in central Europe, and again its use spread rapidly—much more so than in the settled land of Egypt. The Greeks in particular exploited the revolutionary social and economic potentialities of iron as a source of cheap tools and weapons, enabling the little man to come up in the world as an independent farmer, artisan, or merchant. Outside of Greece and Italy, no people were stimulated to raise their culture to a level worthy of the name of civilization, but at least Europeans were now catching on more quickly. Some developed a culture considerably more advanced than that of the later Germanic tribes pictured by Roman historians; excavations of the great cemetery at Hallstatt in Switzerland, and of the snug, well-built town at Biskupin in Poland, have revealed peoples who were by no means half-naked savages. They bring us to another pre-Germanic, Indo-European people who made something of a name for themselves as they entered recorded history—the Celts.

For several centuries toward the end of the first millennium B.C. these Celts dominated most of central and western Europe. They had an art of their own fine enough to make later Roman influence seem decadent. Julius Caesar praised their smiths, who made iron tires for their war chariots and were reputed to have invented chain mail. Although their mysterious priests, the Druids, also acquired some reputation as philosophers, Caesar's account of them belies the intimation that the Celts had been much affected by the spiritual ferment of the first millennium that produced the higher religions; the Druids believed in the transmigration of souls, an idea that presumably came from India, but they still believed in primitive gods and carried out human sacrifices. Like other Indo-European peoples, the Celts made their name chiefly as warriors: they were the dreaded "Gauls" who once sacked Rome itself and later swept into Asia Minor, to harry the Greeks for years and to give their name to the province of Galatia. It took a Caesar to conquer them in Gaul. Others who were forced out of mainland Europe, as Germanic peoples pressed down on them from the north, retained their vitality; in Ireland they would distinguish themselves in the Dark Ages that lay ahead. They point to the diversity of race and culture that has so greatly enriched Western civilization, as now one people, now another took the lead in a fresh development.

---

than 20 per cent ever took up a new craft or industry, and most of these ventured upon an innovation but once. Most of England, in other words, remained a traditional agricultural society, at most adopting improved tools made by more enterprising men elsewhere.

2. The Dark Ages

In the textbooks of the past, the fall of Rome to barbarians in A.D. 476 was a major turning point in history, dramatically signaling the collapse of the Roman Empire and inaugurating the Dark Ages. To recent historians this famous year seems no more important than it did to contemporary Romans, who mostly failed to notice that the Empire was no more. The barbarians had been infiltrating it for more than a century, forming the bulk of its army, gradually dominating its administration; now they assumed more formal control of the western half of the Empire, replacing a Roman with a German dynasty. They had no idea of destroying the Empire or building a new German one. They took over all the basic institutions or forms of the Roman state; they retained Latin as its official language; they sought to acquire Roman culture, which they recognized as superior to their own; they too were Christians, or soon became converts. Romans of the old school might be unhappy over their German masters, but if so they resigned themselves to a status quo little different from what it long had been. The Roman emperors at Constantinople in the East acquiesced in the new regime.

Similarly the Dark Ages no longer look so dark. This was surely no period of mere stagnation, being as turbulent as any, nor did it descend to pure savagery. It produced some great men, from St. Benedict and Pope Gregory the Great to Charlemagne and King Alfred. Scholars continued to study the ancient learning; writers turned out some new books. Lights glowed in such hitherto dark regions as Ireland, which gave birth to the genius of John Scotus Erigena. Rostovtzeff, a leading authority on the social and economic history of the classical world, even questioned the concept of a decline or decay of civilization in the end of Rome. There was a decline of classical civilization, he granted, but with it came a shift to Christian values; what seemed all-important to men brought up on Greco-Roman culture no longer seemed vital to most men—it seemed futile when not false. In *The Making of Europe* Christopher Dawson went still further, asserting that the so-called Dark Age was actually a dawn: it saw the conversion of the West, the foundation of Christian civilization—the real "making of Europe."

Yet such assertions come down to the swing of the pendulum, the familiar story of overcompensation for previous slight or neglect. Granted that there was no sudden collapse or complete disappearance of civilization, the period from A.D. 400 to 1000 was unmistakably a dark age in Europe, predominantly barbarous. The Germanic peoples proved wholly incapable of matching the feats of the Arabs, who in overrunning a world with a much higher culture than their own not only preserved this culture but began building on it a civilization of their own. They could neither maintain the Roman Empire nor create anything to take its place; the kingdoms of Goths, Visigoths, and Vandals were alike transient. The Merovingian Kingdom of the Franks that succeeded to the rule of Gaul under Clovis, at the end of the fifth century, fell as far short of civilization by any accepted standards; King Clovis was a pure barbarian, uncontaminated by any Roman ideas of the state or of citizenship, who treated his kingdom as a personal possession. From the sixth century on, all western Europe—excepting Arabic Spain—had no strong states, no great cities, no civil service, no banking system, no good roads, no formal schools, in general no communal means of maintaining a high culture. The nobility consisted chiefly of illiterate warriors whose main pleasure was killing game, or one another. The learning of the clergy was shot through with crass superstition and ignorance, typified by Bishop Gregory of Tours: he branded as sinful the use of medicine instead of religion in curing disease. To appreciate the actual decline one has only to look to the eastern half of the Roman Empire, which had not fallen when Rome did; for whatever one thinks of the Byzantine Empire, no historian would deny it the name of civilization. We may disagree on how tragic the decay of classical civilization was, or whether in the long run it was a setback for the cause of freedom; but it is only because Western civilization finally emerged out of the Dark Ages that historians can regard this period as anything but a decline or decay.

One reason for emphasizing the actual darkness is the popular notion lingering on from romantic theory that the Germanic peoples were unspoiled noblemen of nature, and Western freedom was born in the forests of Germany. As barbarians these peoples did have some tribal military virtues, but they remained rude barbarians, "democratic" only in the bonds of kinship that unite all primitive peoples, hardly up to any idea of legal rights or citizenship in a state. Neither was their behavior notably improved by conversion to Christianity, since the warriors were baptized en masse at the orders of their chieftains. Rather, they helped to barbarize the Church, as King Clovis of the Franks most conspicuously did. A darling of the Papacy because he was converted to the orthodox faith, instead of the Arianism of the earlier Germans, he was an especially brutal, bloody autocrat who became more ferocious as a Christian; then his many crimes were no longer considered crimes. Gregory of Tours, his biographer, recorded them with only the pious comment "Thus day by day God cast down his enemies before him, because he did what was right in His eyes." The Dark Ages established the tradition of routine violence and bloodshed that has come down through Western history.

Christopher Dawson himself points to another reason for dwelling on their darkness. "The foundations of Europe," he wrote, "were laid in fear and weakness and suffering—in such suffering as we can hardly conceive today," even after the disasters of world war. Crisis was the normal state of the period, which in this respect was a fitting prelude to a civilization whose history was to be a series of revolutions. Only against this fearful background can we understand and appreciate the works of the great men of the Dark Ages, above all of Pope Gregory the Great—the man who is generally credited with laying the foundations of Western Christendom.

He lived at a time of appalling pessimism (*c.*540–604), when Rome still had memories of its imperial greatness but no material means of sustaining it. New barbarians, the Lombards, had overrun northern Italy; the city was now a beleaguered island in a barbarian sea, with no allies to aid it; and its impotence was crowned by famine and plague. "Today there is on every side death, on every side grief, on every side desolation," wrote Gregory; "on every side we are being smitten, on every side our cup is being filled with draughts of bitterness." With no worldly hopes whatever, except for the speedy end of the world and of his own sickly life, he nevertheless worked with tremendous energy and determination in the Papacy to which he had been summoned against his will. Lacking any military force, he administered and defended Rome by spiritual authority, preserving its independence by negotiating a treaty with the Lombards. He carried through extensive reforms in church and monastery, spelling out a strict discipline in letters of advice to bishops and abbots over western Europe, while also dispatching missionaries to convert the barbarians, notably St. Augustine to England. He maintained the primacy of the Roman See against the much greater temporal power of Constantinople; all Christendom in the West looked to him. Since he had no idea at all of building a new order, we must later reconsider the foundations he laid, with some doubts of their adequacy for a going society; for his was a religion of terror, reflecting the barbaric superstition of his age. In any case, he thoroughly earned his common designation as "the father of medieval Christianity."

Within a generation after his death Christendom had to face a new threat, as the Arabs began pouring out of their desert under the banner of Mohammed. After conquering the old Roman province of north Africa, they crossed over into Spain and threatened further advances until they were turned back in France by Charles Martel, in 732. They continually menaced Europe by their command of the Mediterranean, disrupting the trade that had gone on since the fall of Rome. According to Henri Pirenne, it was the Arab invasions, not the Germanic, that ended the ancient world by transforming the Mediterranean from a Roman to a Moslem sea, effectually ending all sea trade with the East, and moving the center of European gravity to the north. ("Charlemagne, without Mohammed, would be inconceivable.") Although scholars are still debating and discounting his thesis, there is little question that the Arabs did bottle up Europe and bring about a further deterioration. Among their later conquests was Sicily, from which they harried Italy as far as Rome.

The first clear sign of a European recovery was the empire founded by Charlemagne at the end of the eighth century. Short-lived though it was, the Carolingian Empire had a lasting symbolical significance that will concern us shortly. In our present context it is significant as an abortive effort, and a prelude to the worst crisis of all: upon its collapse Europe reeled into chaotic darkness. In the tenth century it sank to its nadir as Christendom was threatened on every side by more barbarians and infidels.

From the Mediterranean Saracen pirates kept raiding the coasts, while other bands of Moslems camped in the Alpine passes, blocking trade and preying on travelers. From the east came terrible raids by the Hungarian Maygars, devastating large areas in Italy and France. From the north came as devastating raids by the Vikings, or Norsemen, who wiped out the promising monastic culture of England and Ireland and with the Hungarians kept France under a reign of terror. "Everywhere there is nothing but dead bodies," wrote the chronicler of St. Vedast "—clergy and laymen, nobles and common people, women and children." For the rest, little is directly known about this blackest of centuries, but the evidence indicates an almost universal deterioration in all spheres of life. Towns shrank into mere fortresses; commerce dwindled into an occasional trickle, through a primitive rural economy. Most rulers could have little if any political or economic policy beyond the exigencies of military defense. The Church too reached its moral and spiritual nadir, which in Rome was marked by the rule of Marozia the Senatrix—in Dawson's words, "mistress, mother, and murderess of Popes." (The affairs of these popes were so scandalous that even Gibbon dared report them only in Latin footnotes.) Altogether, there was good reason for the legend that men were terrified as the year 1000 approached, expecting it to be the end of the world.

One might wonder, though, why Christians should dread the end of such a world as this. Apparently they still had some spirit, even some hope for this world. And the year 1000 in fact opened a century that was a real dawn. The catastrophic tenth century that laid waste the surface of Europe plainly had not destroyed its vitality, but somehow had roused it, stirred new creative forces. Among these, it turned out, were the very Norsemen who had stricken it with terror; as "Normans," converted to Christianity, they would be among the leaders in its resurgence. Another portent was a rising consciousness of "Europe," as a cultural rather than a mere geographical term. The first known use of the term in this sense, since the fall of Rome, was by the ninth-century historian Nithard, who wrote that Charlemagne "had left all Europe in the greatest happiness." Europe had become something like "the West" that we speak of. So we must now pause, to consider what had come through the Dark Ages, what composed and distinguished this society, what gave rise to the new civilization.

3. The Nature of "Europe" in the Year 1000

A more precise name for our society at this stage is Western Christendom. Eastern Europe—Russia and the Balkans—was largely occupied by other Indo-European peoples, the Slavs, but these were converted by the Holy Orthodox Church and owed their high culture directly to Byzantium; they did not participate significantly in the history that now concerns us, were little affected by the major developments in the Middle Ages or later the Renaissance and the Reformation. Still other Slavs who became Catholics—the Poles, the Czechs, and the Croats— point to what most obviously held western Europe together during the Dark Ages: the Roman Church. At the dawn of the new civilization this was the main source of power, order, and unity, all that came to distinguish it alike from Islam and Byzantium. As its people grew more self-conscious they called their society "Christendom"—the standard name until the fourteenth century, when "Europe" began growing more common.[4]

From the onset of the Dark Ages the Church had gained in prestige, most notably by such heroic efforts as Gregory the Great's, but also simply by political default of a crumbling empire and the political incompetence of its barbarian converts. If it was unable to control these converts, no kingdom within its realm was strong or independent enough openly to defy its authority or to proclaim the supremacy of the state, establish the "Caesaropapism" of the Byzantine Empire. It became the largest landowner in western Europe, the greatest financial power. It was the one civilizing agency, virtually monopolizing literacy and learning; without its aid no ruler could hope to administer a kingdom of any size. During the catastrophes of the tenth century it practically took over what remained of government in large regions, as towns looked to their bishops for not only spiritual but political leadership. During this crisis, too, the Church proved its spiritual vitality. We know of its dark state chiefly through the writings of St. Odo, Abbot of Cluny, who led a movement of monastic reform that by the next century had affected the entire Church.

St. Odo represented one of the most characteristic and important institutions of Western Christendom—monasticism. Early in the sixth century St. Benedict had published his celebrated Rule for monastic life, exemplifying a Roman as well as a Christian spirit. Whereas holy men in the East had been prone to an extreme asceticism, when not to the life of the hermit, the Benedictine Rule was essentially social, calling for co-operative labor, regulating the government, the economy, and the common life of the monastery. It found immediate favor as a practical means to both material and spiritual self-sufficiency, enabling the monastery to carry on through the most troubled or chaotic periods. In time it was followed by almost all the many thousands of monasteries in western Europe.

---

[4] The Poles, like the Catholic Magyars of Hungary, may remind us that under any name the new civilization of course had no precise boundaries. They were on its fringes culturally as well as geographically, contributing relatively little to its major developments, remaining less progressive by the standards of peoples to the west of them. For this reason some historians now prefer the name "Atlantic civilization." I am adhering to the conventional "Western" because the non-Atlantic peoples of central Europe, above all Italy, obviously played an important part in its history.

The long-range consequences of this Benedictine Rule are incalculable. It most strongly affirmed the Christian principle of the dignity of
manual labor, which classical tradition had disparaged, and so fostered
the practical spirit that would revolutionize Western civilization. Werner Sombart argued that it laid the foundations of capitalism by instituting the regular, punctual life—the bourgeois ideal of being "as
regular as clockwork"—which no previous society had considered necessary or natural. Immediately, at any rate, monasticism did more than
any other institution to preserve the rudiments of civilization during
the Dark Ages. The monasteries not only set an example of moral order
and discipline but were the libraries and the schools of Europe. To
learn their Bible, their liturgy, and their monastic duties, monks had
to learn reading and writing, and something of the available arts and
skills. They took the lead in almost all the more promising cultural
developments, as in Ireland and England, and later were the architects
of the early cathedrals. For if they suffered as much as any other group
from the barbarian invasions, the institution of monasticism was almost
impregnable. "Ninety-nine out of a hundred monasteries could be
burnt and the monks killed or driven out," Christopher Dawson ob-
serves, "and yet the whole tradition could be reconstituted from the one
survivor, and the desolate sites could be repeopled by fresh supplies of
monks who would take up again the broken tradition, following the
same rule, singing the same liturgy, reading the same books and thinking the same thoughts as their predecessors."

Eastern Christendom, whose Holy Orthodox Church had not yet
broken with Rome, also did much to keep civilization alive in the West,
apart from the major contribution of Byzantium to all Christendom in
halting the main Arab drive at Constantinople. There was always some
trade with the Byzantine Empire, and some diplomatic intercourse between Rome and Constantinople. Because of these relations Italy never
sank into such barbarism as did lands farther west, while Venice became
the one European city to flourish during the Dark Ages. With the beginnings of political revival, under Charlemagne and the later German
emperors, Byzantine influence grew more pronounced; Charlemagne's
church at Aachen was an early example of the tutelage that gave Venice
its St. Mark's and remained apparent in Romanesque art. Even distant
England owed to Byzantium a great archbishop of Canterbury, Theo-
dore of Tarsus, who late in the seventh century organized its church
and brought in a store of precious books.

Much more important, however, was the direct influence of classical culture. Not long after the fall of Rome Boethius wrote in prison his noble *Consolation of Philosophy*, steeped in Greek philosophy, which for many centuries was one of the favorite books of the Western world; though a Christian facing death, he consoled himself with no hopes of heaven, instead expressing the old pagan ideal of freedom of mind in defiance of tyranny, time, and death.[5] But other writers of the Dark Ages who are now read only by scholars, and make hard going even for them, have no less claim on our gratitude. Thus one can hardly exaggerate the importance of Cassiodorus, a contemporary of Boethius. An insufferable pedant (who as a chronicler, incidentally, failed to notice anything exceptional about the famous year 476) , he was nevertheless a genuine lover of literature, learning, and the liberal arts, and an indefatigable collector of the great works of pagan antiquity available in his time—works still suspect to the pious, as they later were to Pope Gregory the Great; except for his zeal many of them might well have been lost to Europe. In the next century Gregory of Tours, now a prey to barbaric superstition, lamented the decay of learning and the want of an audience; yet he carried on, writing in poor Latin his *History of the Franks* for the edification of posterity, including copyists unable to spell. Bishop Isidore of Seville then displayed as monumental industry as ineptitude in a chronicle of the "whole world," an encyclopedic hodge-podge of dull and dubious lore; remaining for many centuries a revered authority, he at least served as a bulwark against the ignorance that had engulfed most of Europe. While thereafter a few writers, like Bede in England and Erigena in Ireland, stand out from the prevailing mediocrity and monotony of the literature of the Dark Ages, even the dreariest copyists and imitators helped to preserve the all-important classical tradition of high culture.

Utterly anonymous men likewise preserved the basic arts and skills of the ancients. They did some beautiful work in jewelry, ivories, and ornamental art, but chiefly they illustrate how simple craftsmen in the "minor" arts can preserve a tradition, the foundation for major work, when there are no great original artists or possibilities of major creative work. Though the Dark Ages were too poor and chaotic for men to engage in monumental public works, few technical skills were lost. In technology, in fact, this was by no means a benighted era, as historians have recently begun to discover. Even in conventional "drum and

---

[5] Once quoted by almost all the greater writers, his work is no longer widely read; so one may be surprised to learn that its translators included such a diverse lot as King Alfred, Jean de Meun, Chaucer, and Queen Elizabeth.

trumpet" histories we may run across some surprising details, such as
the powerful artillery employed by the Vikings in their siege of Paris
(886) and the catapults employed by its defenders. More surprising
were some significant advances in agriculture and industry, which will
concern us shortly. In passing we may note two examples bearing on the
major interests of both the Dark and the Middle Ages—war and religion. During the seventh century armorers in France developed a
pattern-welded steel that was greatly admired in Islam, and in the next
century the first church bells were cast in bronze, eventually to ring all
over western Europe, in order to tell time and to scare off the demons
inherited from antiquity.

The most conspicuous classical legacy, and one that brings us closer
to the Middle Ages, was the political tradition of the Roman Empire.
While men in the Dark Ages were indeed quite unable to organize and
administer a real empire, ancient Rome had none the less given the
Church its organization, its law, and its tradition of statesmanship, best
exemplified by Gregory the Great; and the Church operated over wide
areas. Memories of municipal government lingered on in Italian towns,
and remains of public works stood up in France too. (Nîmes and Arles
even survived as settlements within a Roman amphitheater, which
served as a fortress.) The grandeur that had been Rome was never forgotten. The Frankish empire founded by Charlemagne was called Roman and believed to be merely a revival of the ancient one; in the year
800 he was crowned in Rome, the "Eternal City." So was the German
King Otto, who in 962 again restored the undying Roman Empire.

We are brought to the celebrated fictions on which the living faith
of the Middle Ages was founded. The empire of Charlemagne was
Roman only in name, or by grace of the Roman Church. It had no legal
system, no civil service, no senate, no Roman institutions of any kind
except the imperial Church. It was a pretty poor empire by any standards, based on a simple rural economy, lacking cities, foreign markets,
good roads, a treasury for public works—lacking almost everything
beyond an army, a court, and a harem. Its artificiality was symbolized
by its official language, Latin: a learned language that its emperor could
not read or write and its common people did not speak. By the time a
later German emperor formally added "holy" to its name, the empire
nominally embraced lands that were thriving on commerce and industry, at last worthy of being called civilized; but Voltaire still spoke truly
when he gibed that it was neither holy nor Roman nor an empire.

Now, we must keep wary when dealing with such fictions. It has become too easy to see that the luckless men of the past lived by mistaken, even absurd beliefs; so we may fail in a decent respect for them, and forget that the historians of the future will point out that we too lived by myths. In particular we need to guard against the elementary but insidious fallacies flowing from this kind of awareness—the conclusions that the "real" causes were what we see, that the absurd beliefs had no real effect, or that they could have only a harmful effect. The conception of a civilization—the gleam in some eyes—may be as important as its birth. Medieval men were unquestionably inspired as well as confused by their fiction of a Roman Empire. While it helped to make Charlemagne a legendary cultural hero, the illiterate emperor had himself been inspired to make his kingdom worthy of it, bringing poets and scholars to court and exhorting churchmen to establish schools. "If your intentions are carried out," the educator Alcuin wrote him, "it may be that a new Athens will arise in France, and an Athens fairer than of old, for our Athens, ennobled by the teaching of Christ, will surpass the wisdom of the Academy." Later on Christian culture did in fact flower in France. With the fiction of the Roman Empire, moreover, came such potent ideas as constitutional government and natural law. If they too may be called fictions, they were certainly of major consequence in the history of Western freedom.

Yet we must also keep aware that fictions are fictions, even apart from the absurdities and in time the deliberate frauds they may inspire. They commonly blind men to their own original achievements, and to the new problems arising from them. Charlemagne earned his legendary fame by his own magnificent energy as well. His empire was a bold creative effort, the more daring because it was so deficient in both material and intellectual resources. While strengthening both king and church, it stirred some vigorous controversy at court over the proper relations between them—a portent of the violent conflict to come, but also of active, independent thought. More important, his empire foreshadowed a distinctively new civilization because it was the creation of new peoples, remote from the old centers. Although blessed by Rome, it further differed from the Roman Empire in that it was a northern, inland empire, no longer centered on the Mediterranean. Out of these lands, in the midst of the catastrophes of the tenth century, came the vigorous German kings who restored the Empire, and also strengthened Christendom by deposing a couple of the most infamous popes in Rome. Italy, where Roman tradition remained strongest, had produced Gregory the Great and St. Benedict, but after Cassiodorus it produced no

thinker or scholar of note until St. Thomas Aquinas—and he went off
to Paris. The domain of Charlemagne gave birth to Gothic art, and was
the center of the brilliant renaissance of the twelfth century.

Einhard, the contemporary biographer of Charlemagne, reports that
the most Christian Roman emperor authorized the preservation of old
Germanic vernacular literature, which was essentially pagan. His age
would be immortalized, suitably, in the French *Song of Roland*: an epic
nominally Christian, fired by devotion to God, king, and country, but
celebrating primarily the heroic ideal, and at that not very classical in
spirit either, rather different from both Homer and Virgil. (Apollo,
incidentally, here joins Mohammed and Termagant in an "unholy trinity" supposedly worshiped by the Saracens.) So we are led back to
"Europe." The Roman Church and the heritage of classical culture provided the foundations for a civilization; they gave the new civilization
its essential unity and much of its strength. Yet they were only potentialities: having them, Europe had remained in darkness for centuries.
Evidently new forces were at work, other potentialities were being realized. And among these, again, was the diversity of its peoples—a diversity that would always menace its unity, but also fertilize and enrich
its culture, help to generate new growths.

The earliest of the northern peoples to show promise were the remote
Celts in Ireland, at the time of Gregory the Great. Not knowing that
Gregory had censured a Gallic bishop for the study of Latin grammar
and poetry, they took enthusiastically to this study. Their renaissance
culminated in John Scotus Erigena, by all odds the most original
thinker of the Dark Ages. So bold as to assert the primacy of reason over
authority, he was later adjudged a heretic; but such rationalism would
dominate Western thought. Meanwhile Irish monks had carried the
torch to the Anglo-Saxons in England, the next people to take the lead
in Christian culture. They in turn sent out St. Boniface, who enlarged
Western Christendom by converting the north Germans and organizing
their church, and Alcuin of York, the most prominent figure in the renaissance at the court of Charlemagne. At home King Alfred the Great
set about translating the Christian classics into Anglo-Saxon, so that "all
the youth now in England of free men who have the wealth to be able
to apply themselves to it be set to learning . . . until the time when they
can read English writing well."

The youth of England soon had to stop learning and to fight for their
lives against the Vikings, whose devastation for a time put out the lights
in Ireland and England; but these Norsemen were to create much more

than they destroyed. While they were far from being such "noble" savages as Tacitus pictured the early Germans, they had more energy, courage, initiative, and independence of spirit than these Germans; and they were as far from being mere savages. They were well ahead of other peoples in western Europe as metalworkers, notable especially for their iron axes. Above all, they were the most adventurous seamen in all history to their time, surpassing Phoenicians and Greeks alike as they sailed the rough Atlantic in their open long-ships, even reaching the coast of North America some five hundred years before Columbus. Their feats were not only extraordinary but historically significant, for they realized as the Anglo-Saxons had not the possibilities of commerce along the Atlantic and North Sea coasts, on which western Europe would prosper. They themselves largely gave up raiding for commerce and consolidated conquest. Trade with the East led them far down into Russia, where they built up the brilliant kingdom of Kiev; here they looked to Constantinople, adopted its religion, and so passed out of Western history. In Sicily, which they reconquered from the Arabs, they set up another notable kingdom, where under Arab and Byzantine tutelage they realized their genius as builders. (The Cathedral of Monreale is a superb example of both their aptitude as pupils and their independent imaginativeness.) Likewise they built the first strong states in western Europe, especially Normandy. When from here they again attacked the Anglo-Saxons they created the historic England.

Before their conversion to Christianity, all these northern peoples had produced poetry that throws some light on their achievements, and remained of some consequence in European literary tradition. It too was diverse, ranging from magical Celtic romance to grim Germanic epic and saga, but generally it expressed heroic ideals comparable to those of Homer at the dawn of Greece, asserting the hero's superiority over his commonly tragic fate. Germanic religion in particular wrested its values from an unflinching tragic view of life. It taught men to fear neither death nor the gods, with whom they were fellows in both victory and defeat. The gods too were subject to an inexorable fate, a doom that was to end their world; and if this idea of the twilight of the gods reflected the coming of Christianity, it was no less significant that they went down valiantly as the heroes did, in a consciously hopeless fight. Upholding "trust in one's own might and main," the epics and sagas were another assertion of man's freedom in the face of necessity. In the words of W. P. Ker, they declared "absolute resistance, perfect because without hope."

This spirit could help to carry men through the common terrors of life in the Dark Ages. If it would not necessarily stimulate energy and creativity, it would work against passive submission or resignation.[6] The epics reflect as well a basic realism of peoples still incapable of a lofty spirituality, but also unable to afford the fancy courtly ideals played up in the later romances of chivalry. Although their society was aristocratic, there was no great gulf between chieftains and followers if only because no great surplus of wealth. The chieftains were not Sir Lancelots but leaders in common enterprises; both they and their men apparently enjoyed their heroic poetry. It brings up the possible uses of adversity that the Dark Ages eventually took advantage of.

As the Roman Empire crumbled, provinces could no longer depend on the central administration but had to shift for themselves. In the loosely organized, disorderly kingdoms that followed, smaller communities still had to provide for their own defense; the feudal system that grew up was among other things a system of local self-reliance. It involved serfdom for the many, but no longer outright slavery; with the wealth, power, and order of the Roman Empire, chattel slavery also largely disappeared from western Europe. Through the recurrent raids and upheavals peasants too had often to rely on their own arms and efforts. In general, the violent transitions of the Dark Ages broke up ancient customs and forced men to think and act for themselves. They might not do so intelligently enough—otherwise men would always surmount crises. But in western Europe many did develop a practical spirit, and habits of enterprise and resourcefulness, that made possible the rise of civilization.

Great effects, one may like to think, must have great causes. The leadership of a revitalized Church might then seem the most appropriate explanation for the rise of Western Christendom. It was clearly an important factor, as the reforms initiated by St. Odo spread through the Church; one sign was the emergence of such vigorous clerics as Burchard, who in the symbolic year 1000 became bishop of Worms, took over the rule of the town, presently began building its monumental

---

[6] Any ideal of passivity was unlikely, indeed, to flourish in the climate of western and especially northern Europe. Ellsworth Huntington's studies in the influence of climate on civilization led him to conclude that Europe enjoys about the optimum climate for purposes of stimulation. This is not a mild, equable but a variable kind, short of the extremes of cold and heat, with frequent storms; there is considerable evidence that people do not work so well when the temperature remains uniform, and more obvious evidence that they are likely to be torpid in tropical climates. Europe again demonstrates, however, that climate is only a condition of high culture, not a basic determinant, for in its optimum climate Indo-European peoples managed to remain barbarians for several thousand years.

cathedral. Still, it was only one of the factors, and not clearly more important than less exalted ones. Another early sign of recovery was a revival of commerce. A major stimulus was Venice, which from the eighth century had been flourishing on its commerce with Byzantium and Islam—repeatedly ignoring papal threats of excommunication. It spurred the growth of other cities in north Italy, notably Pisa and Genoa, which for the sake of God and trade then co-operated in successful warring expeditions against Saracen outposts in the Mediterranean. The religion of Venice remained business, under a thin Christian veneer; it carried on an especially profitable traffic in Christian slaves (Slavs), whom it sold to Moslems for their harems. And if in defying orders from Rome it perhaps trusted to its relics of St. Mark (which it had stolen from Alexandria), its disrespect for the popes was typical of the period. Rome itself was by no means venerated throughout Western Christendom. In 1084 it was sacked by the Normans, more ferociously than it had ever been by barbarians in the past.

A related stimulus, of a still more typically European kind, was the technological enterprise of the Dark Ages. Historians have only begun to realize how much the barbarians from the great plains of Eurasia contributed to the Western world that they began by breaking up.[7] Their inventions included trousers and felt hats, barrels and tubs, the stirrup and the heavy plow, the cultivation of rye and oats, and the use of soap. In western Europe their descendants made increasing use of the water-driven mill, which appeared late in the Roman Empire but was little used by the Romans, and they developed the crank, a device unknown to the ancients, essential for connecting reciprocal and rotary motion. In agriculture they invented a three-field system of rotating crops and fallow that greatly increased the productivity of land from the time of Charlemagne on. (The Greeks and Romans never learned to make hay either.) In the ninth or tenth century they developed almost simultaneously three apparently slight but revolutionary inventions—the horse-collar, the tandem harness, and the horseshoe. The ancients had harnessed the horse with an ox-yoke, which choked the beast if it pulled hard; the horse-collar enabled it to pull fifteen instead of three or four times its weight, and with the tandem harness provided Europe with much more power at no more expense of human labor. Conceivably it alone might explain the sudden rise of energy and prosperity after all the disasters of the tenth century.

---

[7] "Technology and Invention in the Middle Ages" by Lynn White, Jr. (*Speculum*, April, 1940) is a good compact summary of the findings in this long-neglected field.

The upshot is the usual mixture of spiritual and material factors, perhaps unseemly, but not simply incongruous. The Church could not have carried out its civilizing mission without the material wealth and power provided by commerce and technology, to which its monks contributed. Needless to add, however, neither has the genius for business and technology proved simply a boon to Christendom. It points toward more pronounced incongruities bequeathed by the Dark Ages, seeds of deeper disharmonies that were already sprouting at the court of Charlemagne, an ambitious warrior with many wives and concubines. The radical dualisms at the heart of Christianity itself—of body and soul, the temporal and the spiritual, the City of Earth and the City of God— were intensified as it was revitalized and transformed by the energy, passion, willfulness, and imaginativeness of its barbarian converts. The resultant tensions help to explain why Western Christendom became the most dynamic, the most continuously creative, and the freest of civilizations, and also perhaps the most troubled, for historians the most troublesome.

| *T H E   M E D I E V A L   S O U R C E S   O F   F R E E D O M*

1. The Basic Incongruities

In a history of freedom, the first and last thing to be said about medieval society is that it was not basically a free society. One may argue that it was devoted to higher purposes than are the modern democracies, that it did fuller justice to man's spiritual being, that by hierarchical order it gave men more psychological security, possibly made them *feel* freer; but by any objective standards the great majority of men were not in fact so free as they are in the democracies. Our theme remains an unmistakable growth in freedom. Then we may add that this growth did not begin with a simple break from the Middle Ages, any sudden renaissance, reformation, or revolution. All the major forces that made for Western freedom were at work from the outset. All involved conflicting tendencies too, inaugurating a history that has never been a simple progress; they help to explain why many men now look back nostalgically to the "Age of Faith," and why many others who are affluent and politically free may not look or act like free men. So it is well to begin this ambiguous history by dwelling on the violent contradictions of the Middle Ages.

In general, they were the invariable contradictions between the ideal and the actuality. Only a cynic or an utter materialist can deny the reality and the power of the faith that inspired the Crusades, built all the Gothic cathedrals, produced a St. Bernard, a St. Francis, and a St. Thomas Aquinas, governed most of the great art and serious thought of the period, and led a relatively poor society to devote so much more wealth and energy to the service of its God than modern society does. Only a bigot or an utter sentimentalist can overlook the pride, greed, lust, hate, and cruelty that ran through the whole society, corrupting above all the Church itself, and leading Dante, the sublime poet of the age, to picture it as degenerate if not morally and spiritually bankrupt. One who views the Middle Ages as a golden age, unified and secured by its lofty faith, cannot even appreciate its grand achievements, in particular the arduous effort to run reason, law, and order through a welter of barbarism, ignorance, and anarchy. Medieval men always lived, as they built, most dangerously, in a political and economic insecurity aggravated by a violence they took for granted.

More specifically, the contradictions stemmed from the dual traditions of Christianity and heroic barbarism, symbolized by the two main forms of medieval architecture—the cathedral and the castle. Although the Church tried to regulate war by the "Truce of God," which called for peace on holy days and over weekends, the feudal aristocracy owed its privileges to the sword and considered war quite legitimate. No civilized society in the East more openly honored a reckless, often brutal violence. For out of the dual traditions had come two equally popular ideal types—the saint and the knight. The knight was by definition valiant, loyal, and chivalrous, but his profession was fighting, his primary allegiance was to a warrior overlord, and his chivalry extended only to fellow knights, not to such fellow Christians as peasants. Like the old heroes, he often fought for no cause higher than love of fighting and fame; the continual wars of the period sprang from personal ambitions and animosities. And though medieval men had more than the usual aptitude for keeping incongruous aspirations in separate compartments, the incongruities were deepened by the mingling of the dual traditions. The saint and the knight came together in the soldier of the Cross, the Crusader; and then atrocity was blessed. Hence the First Crusade—in its fervor the first major demonstration of European unity and sense of high mission—began the active persecution of Jews in Europe, went plundering and slaughtering its way from the Rhine to the Jordan, and sealed its triumph by a wholesale massacre of Moslems in the Holy City. The cleric Raimundus de Agiles recorded its ecstasy: "In the temple and porch of Solomon one rode in blood up to the knees and even to the horses' bridles, by the just and marvelous Judgment of God!"

A related source of contradiction was the youthfulness of an age that was not actually a "middle" age, but a beginning of something new, quite different from classical antiquity. One sign was its boundless energy and passion, the insatiable "Faustian" spirit that dared all, expressed itself most gloriously in the Gothic cathedrals—restless, asymmetrical, incomplete, always suggesting an aspiration to speak the last word that can never be spoken. Medieval men were as thoroughly unclassical in their conduct, tending to carry everything to excess; they set up no Apollonian ideal of balance, moderation, or restraint, knew no clear mean between their extremes of love and hate, hope and fear, ecstasy and despair. Above all, they were willful. They were the more willful because of the very obsession with the deadly sin of pride, to which Christians were especially liable in their self-righteousness. Or even their humility: Gregory the Great was himself aware of the pride of self-conscious humility, as in the man who "walks with himself along the broad spaces of his thought and silently utters his own praises." Subtler thinkers than he kept noting these dangers, yet continued to feed the peculiar pride of Christendom. "God humbled himself in order to be exalted," St. Augustine had said; St. Thomas Aquinas drew the lesson for those created in the image of God, remarking that "the Son of God became man in order that men should be like gods"; and the exalted Dante gave free rein to the fiercest pride in the world's great literature. Saints and sinners alike could be extravagant in humility or abnegation, but rarely were meek, mild, or poor in spirit. On the lower plane of everyday life, medieval extravagance translated such ambiguities into bizarre contradictions. As youngsters love to make up rules, so they bound themselves by elaborate forms and codes, commandments backed by the most awful religious sanctions; and they compensated by a fantastic license and irreverence. In their glorious Gothic cathedrals the young met to make love, whores prowled for customers, students in holy orders might play dice on the altars.

Such naïveté was most apparent in the celebrated fictions of the Middle Ages, beginning with the Holy Roman Empire. In their imaginative ignorance of the past they revered, the youngsters were passionately devoted to their ideal theories, and as loftily unconcerned about the vulgar actualities. "At no time in the world's history," commented Lord Bryce, "has theory, professing all the while to control practice, been so utterly divorced from it." The divorce was easier because they could revere the sacred institution or office no less if the men who ran it notoriously, habitually profaned it. They all revered Rome and the Vicar of Peter, and they mostly despised the Romans, hated the popes. They entrusted their eternal salvation to their spiritual shepherds, and believed that bishops had an especially poor chance of getting into heaven.

As medieval men grew more sophisticated they grew more aware of these glaring contradictions: yet maturity also tended to deepen the contradictions. In the twelfth century—the great century of the Gothic cathedrals, the Crusades, and a brilliant intellectual renaissance—men

seemed most energetic, confident, exuberant; while at the same time
the felt need of moral and spiritual reform generated a growing sense
of crisis, even of impending doom, as religious spirits proclaimed that
men "had almost forgotten God." The thirteenth century, crowned by
the works of St. Francis, St. Thomas, and Dante, seemed still darker to
many contemporaries, especially Dante. For the example of the medieval saints and the growth of medieval theology widened the gap between
ideal and popular Christianity. Popular religion was increasingly degraded by such gross superstition as the cult of holy relics, a craze fed
by the saints themselves. (When St. Thomas died in a foreign monastery, the inmates promptly decapitated and boiled him in order to preserve his precious remains.) Similarly the growing prosperity through
commerce widened the gap between medieval economic theory and
practice; churchmen denounced more vehemently the evil of buying
cheap and selling dear, and especially of charging interest on loans,
while the Church itself got ever more deeply involved in business and
finance, made increasing use of moneylenders. The growing sophistication affected even the rude knight, in a strange but typically medieval
fashion. He became addicted to the ideal of courtly love, the compound
of the ascetic and the erotic symbolized by Sir Tristram and Sir Lance-
lot; and as the object of this love was neither marriage nor the frank
fulfillment of physical desire, as poets celebrated passion for its own
sake—a passion impossible to satisfy, for which men would sacrifice all
—it became essentially as aberrant as Greek homosexuality.

Now, corrupt as all such worldliness often was, it was not simply the
seamy side of medieval life. It involved attractive qualities of humor,
candor, exuberance, adventurousness, and gusto that helped these sinners to dare and achieve much more than any society of saints ever
could. It recalls the simple humanity obscured by both the saint and
the knight, as in the earthy, satirical *fabliaux* and the many lyrics with
refrains like "Let's away with study," "The pretty fruits of love," "This
song wants drink." It produced such charming works as *Aucassin and
Nicolette*, which also reminds us that there was more popular skepticism
than appears in most accounts of the "Age of Faith." (The hero remarks
that he would rather go to Hell than to Paradise, which is full of dull
pious folk.) It gave us Chaucer. Indeed, it may be considered largely
responsible for the glories of medieval art, even to the great cathedrals
—works often denounced by churchmen, especially St. Bernard, as
signs of worldly pride and ostentation; for if Christianity provided the
occasion for most art, saints rarely created it or expressed an enthusiasm

for it, and the wealth of elaborate, sometimes grotesque ornament suggests that its inspiration was not purely religious.[1] Medieval worldliness led to a growing naturalism, humanism, and individualism that anticipated the Italian Renaissance, the characteristic passion of Western man to savor, know, feel, and express all the manifold possibilities of life in the natural world. In short, it promoted a spirit of freedom.

With all its anomalies, at any rate, such worldliness must be kept in mind as we consider the elements of actual and potential freedom in the Middle Ages. These may be traced to four major sources: the Christian religion, the classical tradition, the feudal system, and the urban bourgeoisie. For purposes of analysis we may consider them separately, noting that the first two were heritages of the ancient world, the last two were indigenous growths. We must keep an eye, however, on a process of continuous interaction, through which all had ambiguous and unforeseen effects, in a hierarchical society that was not consciously devoted to ideals of freedom. Medieval bishops, scholars, barons, and merchants would alike have been startled, and mostly dismayed, by the long-range consequences of their efforts.

2. *Christianity*

Given the current fashion of regarding Christianity as the fountainhead of Western freedom, it seems necessary to rehearse the tiresome, obvious charges. Throughout Western history until this century, the major established churches did not lead the struggle for freedom, but on most fronts offered the most stubborn opposition to it. They authorized the persecution of Jews, infidels, heretics, dissenters, freethinkers. On principle they denied freedom of conscience, freedom of speech and press, so long as they had the power to do so. They fought the unorthodox theories of science, the main agent of emancipation of thought. Like established churches in all civilizations, moreover, they were typically allied with the ruling class. When the movement toward popular government got under way, they still supported monarchy or aristoc-

---

[1] "I say naught," St. Bernard wrote to an abbot, "of the vast height of your churches, their immoderate length, their superfluous breadth, the costly polishings, the curious carvings and paintings that attract the worshiper's gaze and hinder his attention"; but he went on to say plenty. The gist of his complaint was that men were "more tempted to read in the marble than in our books, and to spend the whole day in wondering at these things rather than in meditating the law of God."

racy; and as late as the nineteenth century religious orthodoxy remained generally illiberal, more often opposing than leading the movement toward social reform, or the emancipation of the working class. In every chapter we have to return to this unhappy theme. As for the Middle Ages, at best freedom was simply not a vital concern of even the most high-minded churchmen, any more than it had been with the great prophets of Israel. The immediate concern of Christian thinkers was order, their ultimate concern was salvation in a life to come; so the saintliest of them could accept, or like Thomas Aquinas explicitly defend, the institution of serfdom if only because a serf had an equal chance for salvation.

Yet another reason for recalling this theme at the outset is to clear the way for an appreciation of the very important contributions that Christianity nevertheless did make to Western freedom. Because it began by embracing so many diverse, contradictory tendencies, from Jewish, Greek, and Roman sources, Christian tradition itself has provided ideals to belie every charge in the foregoing indictment, lined men up on both sides of every major issue of freedom. We must accordingly take some pains to distinguish between Christianity and the Church, or any of its established churches. The medieval Roman Church embraced virtually all of Western Christendom, its spiritual authority was hardly questioned, and its practical authority was very great; but even so many laymen and many members of its own organization were always critical of its official policies and often bitterly opposed to its leaders, in the name of Christian ideals. Such incessant, unseemly conflict was another distinction of the most dynamic of the higher religions, which has thereby influenced a great deal of secular thought and effort, including the thought of men who have rejected its dogmas.

To begin with, the Church itself remained on the forefront of the rising civilization in the early Middle Ages, as the major civilizing agency. By both precept and example it taught political rulers most of whatever they knew beyond the arts of war, especially ideals of law. It provided for formal education, then higher education in the universities; all the learned men were in holy orders. Similarly it provided the means for most of the creativity in art and thought. In spite of its repressive tendencies, it permitted considerable freedom in thought, at least as much as most thinkers needed, and certainly enough to make room for a great deal of eager inquiry. It contributed much to technology too, directly through the works of its monks, indirectly through the works it commissioned; for men had to learn much in order to build and adorn the superb, enduring cathedrals.

For ordinary men the visible churches housed the common faith that most clearly unified the society of western Europe, led it to call itself Christendom. Everywhere men attended the same Mass, celebrated with the same ritual, symbolizing the same beliefs about the Redeemer and their hopes of salvation. Both physically and spiritually the Church indeed dominated the medieval town. Typically its towers or spires stood out above all others, drawing men's eyes skyward; it was the principal civic center, the scene of the great annual festivals and communal processions; it was the scene as well of the major occasions of family life, the christenings, weddings, funerals; and its square was commonly a gathering place, a social center for daily life. While it was itself always a haven for those in distress, with it were connected the charitable institutions by which churchmen carried on the tradition of caring for the needy, to an extent the Greeks and Romans never had. In such respects no other historic church had provided more amply for the needs of simple worshipers.

The great cathedrals were not indeed creations of the "folk spirit," any more than of pure Christian idealism: the churchmen who built them often extorted the labor and the pennies of the folk. Nevertheless, the cathedrals demonstrated that Europe had now evolved a genuinely, distinctively Christian art, beyond the classical forms of its early basilicas. In their soar they testified to religious exaltation as well as worldly pride, and to the capacity for sacrifice and devotion to an ideal—qualities that no free society can afford to disdain. (Even godless Americans might be humbled by the thought that the small town of Chartres built a cathedral that New York cannot match, and that in France alone some eighty cathedrals were built in one century, all by towns much less wealthy than small American cities.) At the same time, the admixture of worldly pride—to most of us more pardonable than it seemed to St. Bernard—involved other reasons why the inspiration of Christianity was a liberating influence.

One was again a view of earthly history that made much more difference than we may realize until we consider other great societies. Hindus and Buddhists agreed on an ideal of nonattachment to the natural, temporal world, which they regarded as either evil or unimportant when not illusory, while Hindus also agreed with most of the later classical thinkers in conceiving earthly history as only an endless, pointless series of cycles. Although Christianity was always given to strong otherworldly tendencies, it was bound to cling to the idea inherited from Judaism that life on earth was very real and properly very earnest, befitting a purposeful, personal Creator. Despite all its holy men who fled the world, it could never formally renounce the temporal world as illusory or valueless, or conceive history as a mere cycle, because God himself had appeared on this earth, in the flesh, in historical time. And as the unique appearance of Christ was for his followers the turning point in human history, so it held an undying hope of a new start, a regeneration. This historic drama of redemption, visibly represented in Christian liturgy, helps to explain why there was very little quietism or fatalistic resignation throughout the Dark Ages. Now, in a society on the rise, the hope became a more positive inspiration. Long before the Italian Renaissance medieval men were using its vocabulary—*renasci, reformatio, regeneratio, renovatio;* the *Vita nuova* of Dante is only the best-known example. Western Christendom was realizing its distinctive religious spirit—in the words of de Rougemont, the spirit of ardent Quest, contrasted with the serene Way of the Far Eastern religions. The Way might be wiser; but it was less likely to promote the cause of freedom.

On lower levels, or among ordinary men incapable of high Quest, a more direct contribution to this cause was the potentially democratic gospel of Jesus, in particular the idea of equality in the brotherhood of man. For medieval churchmen this meant only spiritual equality—an equality in death, not a social or political equality in life; they took for granted a hierarchical social order, corresponding to the order of the Church, which logically implied a principle of natural inequality, and which effectively kept most men in their place at the bottom of the hierarchy. Nevertheless, there was more democratic feeling in the Middle Ages, and a deeper, liver sense of community, than there had been in the Greco-Roman world, with all its alien peasants and its millions of slaves. Men felt equally at home in the church, which was daily open to all. The ecclesiastical hierarchy was at least no hereditary aristocracy or caste system; poor boys might become bishops, even popes. Lowliness was no disgrace for a religion that from the beginning had sought out the poor, been aimed primarily at the lowly. If the conventional sanctification of poverty and its blessings enabled wealthy churchmen to enjoy their wealth with better conscience, the openly declared respect for the poor, and for the manual labor by which they lived, was still a revolutionary reversal of the social values of antiquity.

More to the point, the biblical tradition of indignation at social injustice was still alive. St. Odo, the monastic reformer, had denounced the oppression of the poor in a style reminiscent of the prophets of Israel. Few medieval saints and fewer popes expressed a comparable indignation, but some lesser churchmen did, and more "heretics." The popular heresies that began flourishing early in the Middle Ages, such as that of Peter Waldo's Poor Men, typically returned to the spirit of Jesus and his early followers, emphasizing the gospel of equality. The sophisticated Jean de Meun anticipated Rousseau by describing an egalitarian "state of nature" in his immensely popular *Roman de la Rose*. Above all, some of the lowly began taking seriously a more democratic idea of equality, and acting upon it.

> When Adam delved and Eve span,
> Who was then the gentleman?

—this medieval verse came down through the generations, and with it John Ball's dream of "equal liberty, equal greatness, equal power." The power of the Christian gospel was demonstrated by a wave of great peasant uprisings in the later Middle Ages, unparalleled in almost any of the Eastern societies except Islam, where nothing came of them. In Europe the uprisings were promptly and brutally put down, but they inaugurated a tradition of revolt that remained very much alive. They set the immediate terms of the long political struggle for freedom, which was generally a struggle for more equality, against the excesses of privilege.

A related Christian principle that has counted for more than all the cant it has inspired is the dignity of the person, even the sanctity of personality: every person must be respected because he was created in the image of God, endowed with a personal soul. Needless to add, he never has been or will be fully respected, and certainly he suffered plenty of indignity in the Middle Ages; high churchmen degraded him on principle, stressing his natural depravity, racking and burning his body in order to save some other souls. Still, the idea of the sanctity of the person survived all such barbarities, to mark another significant difference from the Greco-Roman world. It was included in the all-embracing gospel of love preached and lived by St. Francis: the person was the neighbor whom one should love as oneself. From Waldo to Wyclif, heretics anticipated Protestantism by insisting on the personal responsibility of every man to God, his right to worship God directly without need of priestly intercession or sacraments. When Westerners later began to assert "the rights of man" they could more readily believe that these were "natural rights," even though the overwhelming majority of men throughout history had never enjoyed them, because most believed that they were God-given. The barbarities of our own time seem worse because of the still-live Christian sentiment that you simply can't do certain things to people.

The struggle for the effective rights of the person was aided by another distinctively Christian principle—the separation of church and state. Never clearly separated in the civilizations of the East, in the Greco-Roman world, or in Moslem theory, they were potentially sundered by a single statement of Jesus: "Render unto Caesar the things that are Caesar's, and unto God the things that are God's." It was a profoundly ambiguous, fateful statement. It could be used, as through most of Christian history it was, to justify Caesarism or absolute monarchy; it saddled Christians with a dual allegiance, and an endless, hopeless confusion over just what things were Caesar's and what were God's; and it led to endless conflict, in Europe beginning with the struggle between the popes and the emperors. Whatever Christ's intention was, it bore out most clearly his statement that he came to bring not peace but a sword. Yet the outcome was a clear gain in both political and religious freedom.

The separation of powers implied a higher law above the state, which all medieval monarchs dutifully recognized in their coronation oaths. In *Policraticus*, the earliest medieval political treatise (1159), John of Salisbury maintained that kings were bound to obey this law, else their subjects were not bound to obey them; he leaned heavily on the Old Testament, citing the prophets who opposed the kings of Israel. Hence the basis of royal claims to rule by divine right was also a basis of opposition to tyrannical kings, or to any who outraged Christian conscience, intruded upon the service of God. Likewise it served as a basis for opposing the despotic pretensions of the medieval Papacy, or any church that claimed sovereignty over political life; it implied a limit on spiritual as well as political power. Men could accordingly maintain on principle their own ways against both church and state. Today many Americans like to think vaguely that their nation is somehow "under God," and all must hope that their government is conducted in something like a Christian spirit; but few who cherish freedom and know its history would wish to end the fundamental separation of church and state.

The medieval theologians who kept wrestling with the problem of the relations of Caesar and God represented still another element of freedom in Christianity—a tradition of rationalism that led men to inquire into the sacred truths, to seek understanding instead of blind faith, in effect to maintain the grounds of a free man's worship. This rationalism, which owed directly to the classical heritage, will be considered more fully in the following section. Here we should note that although it bred many a heresy it got substantial support from the medieval Church, which often took the liberal side in controversy, even supporting such radicals as Thomas Aquinas. On the question of free will, for example, it agreed with St. Thomas that man does have such freedom.

But this characteristic controversy brings us back to the more troublesome reasons for the dynamism of medieval Christianity. Classical philosophers had not worried over free will, or even recognized the problem; it became a problem for medieval men if only because of their boundless aspiration and willfulness, but more directly because of the tradition reaching back through St. Augustine to St. Paul that held for the doctrine of predestination. This followed logically from the assumption of an omnipotent, omniscient God, as it is never clear how man can do anything not willed and foreknown by the Almighty, much less defy his will; though St. Thomas demonstrated conclusively enough that man must be free in order to be a responsible moral agent, he did not show *how* man can be free. In time his Church acknowledged that man's freedom is a mystery, beyond reason. Meanwhile reason was getting into further trouble, and preparing to give still more. Faith remained primary, since the truth of Christianity finally rests on divine revelation; the Church perforce condemned as heretical the early assertion of Bérenger of Tours that truth could be attained only by reason, not by revelation. While it came to accept the belief of St. Thomas that most of the essential truths of Christianity can be demonstrated by reason, other theologians argued that they could not be and had to be taken on faith; and these others were plainly right—else all intelligent men exposed to the truths would long since have agreed upon them. Moreover, there remained the venerable antirational tradition of Christianity. Pope Gregory the Great, "the father of medieval Christianity," denounced curiosity and the appeal to reason as the root of heresy, declaring that only unquestioning faith was acceptable to God. If a doctrine was incomprehensible, so much the better: "Nor is faith meritorious to which the human reason furnishes proof."

In short, the Church continued to embrace the basically inconsistent attitudes engrained in its tradition. So too with the paradoxes stemming from the radical dualism of Christianity. It taught that man had been created in the image of God, made fit to share an eternity of bliss with

his Creator, and that he was a fallen creature, a sink of natural depravity; that the world had been created primarily for his sake, out of over-
flowing goodness, and that God's creation was a vale of tears or a devil's
snare, to be despised and fled; that human history on earth was intensely
important, and that all that mattered was the life to come; that life
was sacred, and that it was wretched and vile. As for ethics, it taught
that man should love all his fellows as himself and hate all infidels and
heretics, that he should resist not evil and crusade against it, that he
should respect himself and loathe himself, and always that he should
choose to do good, in the knowledge that he was utterly dependent on
the grace of God. Always he must at once love and fear God, who was
himself merciful, jealous, loving, and wrathful.

Given such apparent contradictions, Christianity could inspire many
different ways of life, including the life of freedom in reason. No less
fruitful were the contradictions themselves. For want of a Way, duty in
Western Christendom was never uniform or clear; men had to think and
to choose. Out of the conflicts, especially between reason and faith,
church and state, the sacred person and sacred authority, grew the ideals
of freedom of thought and conscience. In this view Christianity promoted freedom because it never achieved the unity, certainty, and fixity
that it always aspired to, and was much more catholic than its greatest
Church.

3. The Classical Tradition

"We are like dwarfs seated on the shoulders of giants," said Bernard
of Chartres in the twelfth century. "We see more things than the
ancients and things more distant, but this is due neither to the sharp-
ness of our own sight nor the greatness of our own stature, but to that
giant mass on which we are raised and borne aloft." By now we can see
that these pious dwarfs saw considerably fewer things than the ancients,
had a pretty dim view of things distant, and could not see at all the
foundations of the giant mass. The classical heritage that the Dark
Ages had preserved was a miscellany of fragments salvaged from the
rhetorical tradition of the late Roman Empire. The recovery of more
works of antiquity in the century of Bernard, which stirred a wild,
unclassical enthusiasm, was a haphazard affair due chiefly to the Arabs,
much like shopping in a thieves' market, as works preserved by these

infidels were imported or smuggled in from Moorish Spain. The precious heritage still amounted to odds and ends; Europeans were unable to read the Greek originals, knew most of the greater writers and works only by name, knew very little of the history of Greece and early Rome, remained almost as ignorant of antiquity as they were reverential. The heritage was always colored and confused by Christian thought, and especially by the originality of medieval men. A few contemporaries of Bernard of Chartres, such as Walter Map, were already complaining that the illustrious feats of "moderns" were being slighted because of this craze. In general, men gave the classical heritage at once more and less credit than its due. Scholars are still busy tracing, discovering, or discounting its influence.

Yet there is little question that the influence was immense. Much of it was direct, notably the thought of Aristotle; much more that was indirect, pervasive, and therefore somewhat uncertain was more profound. The immediate example was the renaissance of the twelfth century, the "golden middle age": a renaissance that as clearly marked a turning point in Western history as did the capitalized one several centuries later. The energy that was producing such original medieval creations as the Gothic cathedral was now fired by a passion for learning. The whole movement was indeed no mere "rebirth" of antiquity, as the very excitement suggested; medieval men were finding themselves, growing up on their own, and in the process were evolving another highly original institution, the university.[2] Nevertheless, the ancients were the source of the learning they so eagerly sought, the model they set themselves to emulate. The ferment of the century rose directly out of a self-conscious effort to recover their classical heritage, and it got headier as they succeeded. "There is no more worth-while occupation in this world than philosophy," Siger of Brabant would exclaim. "The only wise men are philosophers." Certainly the Christian Bible itself was no more likely to stir a passion for learning or philosophical inquiry than was the Koran. The most Christlike of the saints, Francis of Assisi, was hostile to this rage, while the Church soon condemned Siger's ideas about philosophy.

The implicit radicalism of the movement was plain enough in Peter

---

[2] Appropriately, the enthusiasm of scholars was parodied by such popular stories as "The Lay of Aristotle," telling how "the master of those who know" was saddled by an Indian maiden and ridden on all fours around a garden. This story, which was carved in some Gothic churches (showing Aristotle properly crowned with his doctoral bonnet), is perhaps as good a key as any to the medieval mentality.

Abelard, the most prominent of its pioneers. He was sufficiently critical of the Church Fathers to list in his famous *Sic and Non* some hundred and fifty contradictions in their teaching. Here Abelard exemplified the youthful daring of the age, which made of theological disputation an exciting game, a kind of scholarly tournament; but behind his lust for victory (not to mention his more famous illegitimate love affair with Héloïse) lay serious convictions that made him the first "modern" thinker in Europe. He insisted that in order to believe one must first understand, and that it was absurd to preach what one did not understand. As he was confident that the Christian faith was perfectly reasonable, he maintained that all knowledge was positively good, even doubt was good. He paraphrased the biblical saying "Seek and ye shall find" by a saying of Aristotle: "For by doubt we come to investigate and by investigation we ascertain the truth." In effect he became an apostle of freedom of thought, known in his own day as "the Socrates of Gaul." His faith in reason was such that he believed even heretics should be reasoned with rather than tortured.

The extraordinary fame won by Abelard was not due merely to his boldness and brilliance. Teachers have never since had such authority as they did in his eager day, when books were still rare and men who had mastered them were rarer. The main issue, at any rate, was his faith in reason; and this was soon brought to a head by St. Bernard. An austere adherent of the tradition of Gregory the Great, Bernard was horrified not so much by the particular heresies of Abelard as by his basic assumption that sacred truth was subject to inquiry and ought to be comprehensible. "He sees nothing through a glass darkly," cried the saint, "but stares at everything face to face"; and he succeeded in getting the unabashed starer condemned and disgraced. Even so, he won only a partial, temporary victory. While the Church would never give reason complete freedom, neither would it openly endorse the pious obscurantism of Bernard.

Immediately Abelard had a good deal to do with the advancement of the university, a spontaneous outgrowth of the revival of learning that soon became the chief means of its spread. Students by the thousands streamed to Paris from all over Europe to listen to him; from now on the burgeoning University of Paris was the most influential school in Europe. While it continued to attract almost all the greatest thinkers of the Middle Ages, universities everywhere served as centers of the new enlightenment. In time, as we might anticipate, they underwent the natural fate of educational institutions, becoming strongholds of conservatism; but first they quickened as well as trained the mind of Europe. Although under the wing of the Church, they largely governed themselves, determined their own curriculum, and in practice acquired considerable academic freedom; they were more independent of political authority or pressure than modern universities have generally been, while individual teachers were freer from bureaucratic controls by administrators and educationalists. Likewise the Scholasticism they nurtured was in this age of ferment by no means the uniform, pedantic, dreary affair it seems to most moderns. It was a bold philosophical venture that raised basic issues, stirred lively controversy among dozens of schools of thought, bred some skepticism and more heresy.[3] At that, it did not uniformly dominate thought; there were also influential schools of law and medicine, the latter becoming a scandal as centers of skepticism. And the influence of the universities was the more liberalizing because their students came largely from the middle ranks of society, young men ambitious to rise in the world. Knights and barons were not given to a passion for higher learning, nor had four years at a university yet become part of the social routine for young gentlemen.

Soon after Abelard's day his pupils found a new excitement in the discovery of Aristotle. The study of this pagan philosopher was the more daring because he was best known through the commentaries of Averroës, who stressed implications of his philosophy that were heretical by both Moslem and Christian standards; in 1209 at least ten men were burned in Paris because of intimacy with Arab and Jewish disciples of Aristotle. Yet the eager students persisted in risking the wrath of high churchmen, risking their very souls. Abelard scored a posthumous triumph over Bernard in the thirteenth century when Thomas Aquinas came to the University of Paris. The new master vindicated his faith in reason, and in the reasonableness of Christianity, by a radical synthesis of Christian doctrine and Aristotelian philosophy that was condemned as heretical by the conservatives of his time, but eventually became the orthodox theology of the Roman Catholic Church.

If the synthesis of St. Thomas no longer satisfies many men outside his Church, and for that matter is unintelligible to ordinary Catholics today, it was none the less a magnificent effort, unsurpassed in the entire

---

[3] Even the favorite example of the futility of Scholasticism, the question how many angels can stand on the point of a needle, grew logically enough out of concern over the nature of spiritual substance—a vital concern if one takes seriously the idea of an immortal soul. The question hardly makes for profitable debate; but it might seem less silly if moderns began to think a little about the soul they vaguely believe is "going" to heaven.

history of thought for its combination of imaginative breadth and patience, thoroughness, and rigor.[4] Extraordinary though it was, it was an absolutely essential effort if Christianity was to meet the challenge of Greek rationalism. "The truth of our faith," he wrote, "becomes a matter of ridicule among the infidels if any Catholic, not gifted with the necessary scientific learning, presents as a dogma what scientific scrutiny shows to be false"; and at the time Aristotle represented the best available knowledge of the natural world, the apparent sum of Greek science. The empirical premises of St. Thomas could and did survive all criticism of his theological superstructure, as well as the later efforts of his Church to stand on dogmas that scientific scrutiny showed to be false.

It is now as hard to appreciate as to exaggerate the importance of the medieval acceptance of Aristotle, especially for the history of freedom. In the first place, he provided a rational antidote for the Platonic idealism and intuitionism that through St. Augustine had largely dominated Christian thought, shielding it from natural knowledge or empirical criticism. "The origin of our knowledge is in sense," St. Thomas declared, following Aristotle and anticipating John Locke, "even of those things that are above sense." While taking for granted the revealed truths of Christianity, he made the dangerous admission that these truths, to the very existence of God, were not self-evident but seemed so only because of custom; his appeal to experience, as to reason, left an opening for revolt against the authority he accepted. Similarly he followed Aristotle in trying to bring matter and mind, body and soul, into organic unity, and thereby gave more dignity to the natural world and the natural man that Platonism had depreciated. If both might be trusted to take care of themselves, they took on worth from the authority of Aristotle, now regarded as the master of masters. Westerners could henceforth be optimistic about their lofty position in the natural world, more frankly devoted to their characteristic ideal of self-realization in it.

Most important for the long run was the simple but novel belief that reason was the key to natural knowledge. While men in the Dark Ages might have discovered as much by their practical interests, they had not gone on from practice to conscious theory; only now did Europe

---

[4] In his *Summa Theologiae,* for example, he tried to meet all possible objections to Christian doctrine, and thought up no fewer than ten thousand of them, all stated and answered with scrupulous care. Skeptics today may be more impressed by many of the objections than by his answers to them, but they should be no less awed by his work—and by the thought that it was designed for beginners in theology.

begin to realize its distinctive confidence in the power of reason. Eventually science would give it more confidence than the Greeks themselves ever had for their practical purposes, but they prepared the way for this too. With Aristotle came an ordered body of knowledge, classified under the various sciences, which incorporated the Greek idea of a lawful universe that the Middle Ages transmitted to the great pioneers of science in the seventeenth century—a metaphysical assumption that by then was taken for self-evident truth. It inspired a few remarkable medieval pioneers, thinkers who had little immediate influence but kept alive the scientific spirit. Thus Adelard of Bath, a proud contemporary of Abelard, recorded his enthusiasm over the possibilities of the science he had discovered through the Arabs, adding that he preferred Arabian to Christian science because it followed reason instead of authority. Such men as Albertus Magnus, Robert Grosseteste, and above all Roger Bacon began concretely to realize and define these possibilities. Bacon's passion for mathematics and natural science led him to speak not only reverently of the "heathen" savants of Greece and Islam but contemptuously of the churchmen and scholars of his own day. He most explicitly attacked the principle of authority as the major obstacle to the pursuit of truth. On the uses of physical science he was amazingly prophetic, foreseeing such possibilities as airplanes and automobiles.

Bacon also anticipated the rise of science by attacking Aristotle, foreseeing why he would become something of an intellectual nuisance. In making Aristotle the supreme authority, medieval thinkers enthroned not the scientist in him but the logician and metaphysician, and his logic permitted only deduction, not discovery. Still, the classical heritage contained much more than Aristotle, who had been no such authority to the ancients—as with further knowledge of them men began to realize. The most fertile element in this heritage remained the free, critical, inquiring spirit of the Greeks: the spirit exemplified by Peter Abelard, which had induced his followers to welcome the heterodox philosophy of Aristotle, "the revenge of paganism" on Christianity; and this spirit was still active in the late Middle Ages, when Scholastic philosophy was running out in the sands of endless verbal dispute, and the Arabs had returned to their Koran.

Meanwhile the ancients had made their all-important contribution to Western freedom—the broad tradition of liberty under law. Christianity in itself provided no political theory, simply because its founders were not in the least interested in the subject: Jesus offered only his statement about Caesar and God, St. Paul added only an emphatic injunction on the necessity of obeying Caesar or the powers that be. Hence Christians got their main political ideas from the ancients, immediately from the Roman Empire in which their religion grew up. In Italy the dim, confused memories of municipal self-government which led towns to give magistrates the title "consul" (a title they had not actually had outside the city of Rome) were live enough to foster the rise of an independent citizenry. A twelfth-century writer noted that the Lombards "are so attached to their liberty that, to avoid the insolence of rulers, they prefer to be reigned over by consuls than by princes." In the same century the people of Rome itself set up a senate, then under Arnold of Brescia maintained a republican commune that for ten years rejected the temporal power of both the pope and the emperor. And though Arnold was excommunicated and hanged, the republican principle remained alive in the kingdoms too.

It stemmed from the Roman idea that the state was a *"res publica,"* or public thing: the people were the source of law and authority, the emperor was properly their servant. As early as Charlemagne this idea gave some validity to the fiction of his Roman Empire, for he used the following formula: "Charles the Emperor . . . together with the bishops, abbots, counts, dukes, and all the faithful subjects of the Christian Church, and with their consent and counsel, has decreed the following . . . in order that each loyal subject, who has himself confirmed these decrees with his own hand, may do justice, and in order that all his loyal subjects may desire to uphold the law." While medieval thinkers all assumed that kingship was the most natural and proper form of government, they mostly agreed in denying the king absolute authority, putting him beneath the law, which they declared was the property of the people and could be modified only with their consent. John of Salisbury not only asserted that "good laws were introduced for the sake of liberty" but took pains to distinguish the true king from the tyrant, one who ruled by force and therefore was a public enemy; he went so far as to justify tyrannicide—the first known Christian writer to have this possibly doubtful honor. Short of killing, St. Thomas Aquinas also declared the right of resistance to tyrants, and though he was vague about just when and how men should go about it, he at least agreed with Aristotle that tyranny was the worst form of government. Dante, an ardent champion of the Emperor against the Papacy, summed up the ideal theory of government in emphatic Roman terms: "The aim of such rightful Commonwealths is liberty, to wit that men may live for their own sake. For citizens are not for the sake of the Consuls, nor a nation for the King; but contrariwise the Consuls are for the sake of the citizens, the King for the sake of the nation."

Long before Dante such ideas had been buttressed by the intensive study of Roman law, a code far more rational and equitable than any of the God-given codes to date. Due primarily to the recovery of Justinian's Code—another major contribution of Byzantium to Western Christendom—this secular study was centered in the University of Bologna. As its influence radiated over all Europe, another ancient idea that had lived on became clearer and more conscious. The "higher law" above the state to which Christians appealed was recognized as the "natural law" announced in Stoic philosophy centuries before Christ, and rationalized by the Roman jurists. This was supposedly a universal, immutable law, binding on both rulers and ruled, the criterion of the justice of all actual laws; the idea also came through that an unjust law was not really a law at all. Since in theory it applied to all men alike by virtue of their common possession of reason, it specifically embodied a principle of equality. In the Age of Enlightenment thinkers would derive from natural law the doctrine of natural rights.

Medieval theory remained consistently vague about all these ideal principles, especially about means of instituting them, and medieval practice fell far short of them. In the next chapter we must emphasize that outside of England states failed to develop legal, constitutional means of enforcing the principle of limited power, or of resisting tyrannical kings; open resistance amounted to disloyalty or treason. Later medieval jurists, moreover, played up a different idea that had come down from Roman imperial tradition, with the sanction of some Roman jurists: the emperor was above the law and had absolute authority to make it. In this spirit Christian thinkers could and did maintain that kings were responsible only to God—an idea naturally congenial to kings, since God was not invariably prompt in punishing despotic abuses of their power. Yet the ideal theory of constitutional government counted for more in the long run. It too was stated more emphatically in the late Middle Ages, especially as men resisted the papal claims to supreme authority. In the fourteenth century Marsilio of Padua even drew out the democratic implications of the idea that law and authority derive from the will of the community: "Those matters, therefore, which can affect the benefit and harm of all ought to be known and heard by all, who thus may attain the beneficial and repel the opposite"; and to the traditional objection that most men are too stupid or vicious to judge soundly, he answered that if few were wise enough to make laws, every citizen could be a proper judge of them, just as he could be of a house or a ship he could not make. In the next century Nicholas of Cusa summed up the whole classical doctrine in a statement that might be mistaken for a revolutionary manifesto:

> Every constitution is founded on natural law, and if it contradicts this it cannot be valid. . . . Since by nature all men are free, all government . . . arises solely from agreement and consent of the subjects. For if men are by nature powerful and equally free, a valid and ordained authority of any one person, whose power by nature is like that of the rest, cannot be created save by election and consent of the others, just as law is established by consent.

Later on we must consider, too, the obvious objections to this cloudy idea of natural law. Many thinkers have remarked that there is not in fact any such universal, everlasting law; some have pointed out that the derivative idea of natural rights has often been used to resist the spread of legal rights, since the customary always looks natural, and custom has long sanctified the subordination of the many. At this stage we need only to note that Western peoples have clung stubbornly to the classical doctrine, and that on the whole it unmistakably made for the growth of freedom. Thomas Hobbes was a radical, not a conservative, when he argued for the absolute sovereignty of the monarch. John Locke, and after him the signers of the American Declaration of Independence, were revolutionary in that they carried through the implications of the theory of natural law, and acted upon them; but they were still in the line of the oldest political tradition in the Western world.

4. The Feudal System

Technically defined as "vassalage with fief-holding," the feudal system has also been described as no system at all, only "licensed anarchy" or "a chaotic fact." Certainly it was based on no conscious theory— there was not even a word for it until the eighteenth century. It involved no such ideas as "commonwealth," "state," "citizenry," or "the people." It was basically uncivilized as a local, rural arrangement, substituting private for public law, designed primarily for military purposes, and sustained by force. As unchristian in principle as unclassical in political form, it contributed mightily to the confusions and contradictions of the Middle Ages. With increasing prosperity and the rise of

greater lords, or kings, it grew at once vaguer, untidier, and more complicated; a landholder might owe allegiance to several different lords,
who in turn were allied or embroiled with kings or high churchmen.
While their knightly ideals governed medieval thought to the end, the
lords themselves lost much of their political power and more of their
political function, serving chiefly to consume when not to destroy.

As there has long been some tendency to idealize feudal society, in
terms of knighthood and *noblesse oblige,* we should again note at once
that this was not at all a free society. It was the quintessence of hereditary aristocracy, privilege by birth instead of proved merit. A virtually
impassable gulf separated the ruling class of lords and their fief-holders
from the masses of peasants. Whatever their virtues or their vices, the
rulers monopolized wealth, power, and prestige. However loyal, content, or secure at best, the peasants were mostly serfs, bound to the soil,
forced to work for the lord; as the Abbot of Burton boasted, they possessed in law "nothing but their own bellies." There was constant talk
of "liberties" and "rights," but these were only the privileges of the
few; feudal privileges were a primary grievance in the struggle for freedom down through the French Revolution, into the last century. Peasants suffered as well from the military tradition engrained by feudalism,
the more because of the social stigma preserved in the connotations of
the common name for them—"villeins." Feudal lords had a natural
scorn for the manual labor dignified in Christian theory, and in war
those belonging to the enemy were fair game for pillage and slaughter,
without compunction or courtesy. Chivalry was at most only for other
chevaliers.

Nevertheless, there were elements of potential freedom in feudalism
too. However chaotic, it was not lawless or simply barbarous; it began
by forcing responsibility on the privileged. However primitive, it was
no mere tribal system either, but a highly distinctive kind of social
arrangement, reflecting the energy, resourcefulness, and self-reliance
that enabled Western Christendom to survive the Dark Ages. The common use of the term "feudal" as a loose synonym for "aristocratic" has
obscured the fact that, excepting Japan, no other society developed a
strictly comparable system.[5] And it was not simply ironical that out of

---

[5] See *Feudalism in History,* edited by Rushton Coulborn—a book rather oddly dedicated
to the study of uniformities in history. Although specialists in various societies, such as
India, China, and Russia, conscientiously looked for a feudal period, they uniformly
found only some kind of tribal or aristocratic organization, involving lords but not the
characteristic relations of lords and vassals found in medieval Europe.

feudalism came Magna Carta, which Anglo-Americans would revere as the historic charter of their liberties.

Although serfdom may be traced to the *coloni* of the late Roman Empire, the distinctive medieval institution of vassalage first appeared about the time of Charlemagne. Its essence was simple and practical: in return for military service, a lord awarded his vassal a fief, or land, with peasants and privileges, and the vassal might in turn award smaller estates to subvassals or knights on similar terms. Society was thus separated into warriors and peasants, with churchmen on the side to administer to both (though some churchmen were also lords or vassals). By this division of labor peasants might be exploited but were also protected; they were relieved of fighting and sustained on manors that were largely self-sufficient. Only by some such simple, local organization as this could a nontribal society survive at a time when there were no strong states, and men lacked the knowledge, experience, and material means to administer a large state.

On the whole, then, Western Christendom repeated the story of the rise of civilization. Again wealth and power went to the few, at considerable expense of freedom and justice to the many. Only so, it would again appear, can a society rise above barbarism. A ruling class that may squander the increasing wealth in war and luxury, perhaps brutally exploit those who do the hard dirty work, nevertheless provides order, fosters commerce, industry, learning, the arts—leads the way to civilization, which may then eventually provide more freedom and justice for the many. During this process in Europe the warriors were partially Christianized and civilized; some became noblemen or gentlemen in fact as well as name, giving more substance to their chivalric ideals. Yet medieval feudalism also had some unintended by-products that made Western Christendom fundamentally different from the early civilizations. It maintained many centers of local independence by a kind of military stalemate, as mounted knights were usually no more able to take a castle than castles were to conquer them. It delayed the rise of bureaucracy, which might have discouraged enterprise or stifled independence, while it permitted the growth of free towns. Above all, it helped to prevent the early development of anything comparable to the Oriental sacred monarchy, to which Islam had promptly reverted.

In some basic respects the feudal system was the antithesis of Oriental despotism. The essential principle of rule was contract, not God-given right or dominion; it was an embryonic form of the "social contract" on which later political theory would be based. "Vassal" was an entirely

honorable term with none of its modern connotations of bondage or servility; the vassal freely made a contract with his lord that imposed obligations on them both. The powers of the lord were clearly limited and
defined: he had no right to assess arbitrary taxes, demand any services
beyond those specified, make his own laws, or interpret the contract to
suit himself. In case of dispute, the vassal's case was settled by a court
of his peers. In all this there was no abstract idea of political liberty or
human rights, any more than of civic duty or the common weal. There
were only concrete liberties that came down to customary privileges,
private rather than public rights. Still, they constituted a safeguard
against arbitrary rule, which by custom was extended to serfs too and
gave them some rights in return for their services. (The celebrated
droit de seigneur, incidentally, was not accepted custom.) In view of
the many overlapping authorities on the medieval scene—lord, king,
town, and church—there could be no absolutism unless one succeeded
in dominating all the others. Feudalism helped to frustrate both papal
and royal efforts at domination.

Another simple, practical, but quite original institution that grew
out of it was parliament. This too was unplanned, in no sense a creation
of embattled men resisting tyranny. Lords were accustomed to calling
in their vassals for counsel or consent, especially when they wanted military or financial aid beyond that required by contract; "suit to court"
was no honor but one of the vassal's obligations, to be discharged at
his own expense. Kings found it as convenient to summon councils of
nobles for similar purposes. Given the classical tradition of government
by consent, these councils came to be regarded as in some sense representative of the community, even though they in fact represented a
very small minority, and they grew more representative as kings found
it profitable to include some townsmen, chiefly for purposes of raising
money; so the outcome was a kind of political assembly that had no
counterpart in classical antiquity. Given feudal tradition, these assemblies were wont to claim that the king must ask them for any money to
be raised by taxation. The American revolutionary slogan "No taxation
without representation!" may be traced back to the Middle Ages.

The kings accordingly began to find the parliaments inconvenient.
As the monarch grew more powerful he ceased to summon them; during the ascendancy of absolute monarchy the parliaments disappeared
almost everywhere except in England. Memories of them lived on, however, and were revived with opposition to the kings, especially at the
beginning of the French Revolution. In England Parliament had a con-

tinuous history, supremely important in the history of freedom, which calls for a separate chapter later on. But as early as 1215 England had produced its Magna Carta, the cornerstone of its liberties.

This was a typically medieval cornerstone, resting squarely on a myth. The actual agreement between King John and his barons was a severely limited one, arising out of a practical conflict over money. John was selfish, unscrupulous, despotic, and cruel, yet he had a legitimate complaint: the king was not getting his share of the national income under a rising money economy. The barons were ultraconservatives, literally reactionaries, trying to retain feudal privileges made obsolete by this economy; most of the provisions they forced John to agree to were unintelligible to the later generations that worshiped Magna Carta. The barons made no appeal whatever to the welfare of the people or the nation, not to mention any rights of man; their only concern was their own welfare. This was plain enough in the most celebrated 39th clause of the charter: "No free man shall be taken, or imprisoned, or disseised, or outlawed, or exiled, or in any way destroyed, nor will we go against him or send against him, except by lawful judgment of his peers or by the laws of the land." Here "free man" meant only the barons and their sort; they would have been aghast at any suggestion of ordinary men's claiming such privileges. Magna Carta was then left unsigned because King John and most of the barons were illiterate. Innocent III, the greatest of medieval popes, added a fitting epilogue. John had fought him bitterly too until the pope decreed that he be deposed, whereupon he had given in and sworn eternal loyalty to his liege lord; so now, at John's request, Innocent graciously declared Magna Carta null and void.

Nevertheless, he was even more shortsighted than the barons—Englishmen paid no attention to his decree. In the next two hundred years the kings of England were obliged to reissue such charters some thirty times. Magna Carta at least affirmed the basic feudal principle of contract and limited power: the king had to obey the law of the land, could not make it to suit himself. Likewise it asserted the principle that the king could not levy taxes as he pleased, but must get the consent of some council. For two centuries Englishmen then forgot about the charter of their liberties, until Sir Edward Coke resurrected and misinterpreted it as a means of resisting King James I, who fancied himself as an absolute monarch. The privileges claimed by the barons had gradually been extended to more and more of the people, and by this time almost all Englishmen were "free men"—even the "villeins" whom the barons despised; the 39th clause was made out to be a declaration of their basic rights. Thus the anachronistic charter served as the platform of Parliament in the struggle with the kings through the seventeenth century, and with the winning of this struggle it became the most revered national document, venerated by conservatives too.

The history of Magna Carta accordingly gives Anglo-Americans food for second thoughts. It is a matter for irony—but a more complex irony than sophisticates are usually given to. It has its counterpart in the American Constitution: another document drawn up by conservatives, now fearful of the common people, which was attacked by most democrats of the time, and is today revered by almost all Americans, who assume that it was a great popular document. Again we are led to the real power of "fictions," which realists are likely either to discount or simply to deplore. Those who deplore might reconsider the power of the ideals behind the fictions, and the real need of symbols, if not of myths. The fact remains that in this manner—at first unconscious, thereafter generally confused and often misguided, yet also deliberate, resolute, often high-minded and heroic—Englishmen and Americans won their liberties.

Conservatives might learn a further lesson from the history of Magna Carta. As usually happens, the feudal barons helped to destroy the system they were trying to preserve unchanged; in Western history privileged defenders of the status quo have a remarkably consistent record of shortsightedness. But there remains a more complicated lesson for liberals too. Despite the defeat of King John, the future belonged to the kings; eventually they put down the barons and ruled as absolute monarchs. And despite their frequent abuses of their power, the rise of monarchy was as natural a development as the rise of the feudal system, and to some extent clearly salutary. A strong central power was essential to put an end to feudal disorder, and to provide a broad, firm economic and political basis for a growing civilization.

The confused moral is underlined by the singular history of Iceland. Early in the feudal era, when kings were beginning to emerge, some sturdy, independent Norsemen refused to submit to their power. They defied the wave of the future by sailing off to Iceland, where they maintained their independence, wrote their great sagas, and established the oldest parliament in the Western world. Only they too were literal reactionaries. They entered a backwater, cut themselves off from the developing civilization on the continent, and played no further part in the history of Western freedom. In view of their admirable spirit, we may wonder what they might have done had they sailed farther and settled on the American continent. As it was, they settled on a poor, barren island where they remained sturdy, but could hardly develop a rich culture or make much creative use of their freedom.

5. *The Urban Bourgeoisie*

Medieval writers were wont to say that society consisted of those who worked, those who guarded, and those who prayed. As those who worked were peasants, there was no approved place in feudal society for merchants. While lords looked down on them, the Church more positively disapproved of their activities. "The merchant can please God only with difficulty," St. Jerome was reputed to have said, and St. Augustine was plainer and harsher: "Business is in itself an evil, for it turns men from seeking true rest, which is God." There was good reason, indeed, for the persistent hostility to this restless, anonymous "middle" class. The plainest motive of the merchants was sordid—only to buy cheap and sell dear; and often they sold dear enough to hurt. But there was much better reason for hostility than the nobles and churchmen could realize. These merchants were revolutionaries, destined to wrest the power from those who guarded and prayed, to destroy feudal society, to subvert and split Christendom, and to spearhead the intellectual, political, and industrial revolutions that would prevent Westerners from ever finding "true rest."

To be sure, they were quite unconscious revolutionaries. In the early centuries they were by no means engaged in a conscious class struggle with either the nobility or the clergy, their best customers. Neither did they preach the great social virtue of free private enterprise. As they simply went about their business they were hardly any more aware that they were laying the material foundations of Western civilization, providing an economic surplus that would enable more men of leisure or learning to deplore their sordid activity. At that, their motives were not purely commercial. Like Datini, a fourteenth-century merchant of Prato, they were likely to inscribe their ledgers "In the name of God and of profit"; and if there was always some question whether God really came first, they were mostly devout Christians. Many were dedicated men, in a way ascetic, almost mystical in their dual devotion. For such reasons too they had an enormous influence on the formation of

Western civilization, even though they were a small minority, and for a long time neither had nor sought political power outside the towns in which they lived. Their influence was as mixed as their motives, and it became more dubious as business became a religion, God ran a poor second to profits; when their business class rose to be the ruling class, many men would consider them the major enemies of freedom. Yet for centuries these still-unconscious revolutionaries were indisputably major agents in the growth of freedom, to which they made a plainer, more direct contribution than did the Church.

As we have seen, among the earliest signs of dawn in the West was a revival of commerce. The activity spreading from Venice led to successful sea expeditions against the Saracens; the launching of the First Crusade (1096) signaled European domination of the Mediterranean. Another, largely independent center was Flanders. Here a growing wool industry soon stimulated England, France, and the Hanse towns on the Baltic. The power of England in particular was built up on wool— the "noble dame" to which the poet Gower penned an early apostrophe; though with the note that "where thou dwellest is never free of fraud and trickery."

The merchants of Venice had a long professional tradition, learned through Constantinople. In western Europe, however, the antecedents of the merchants are obscure, as professionals had virtually disappeared from here. Apparently they came out of the peasantry—adventurous sons who were inspired or forced by unsettled times to take to peddling or sailing. When they appear, at any rate, it is always as free men, owing allegiance to no lord, traveling from land to land to buy cheap in one and sell dear in another. How they rose in the world is indicated in the biography of St. Godric, a poor peasant boy born toward the end of the eleventh century, who started as a peddler, joined a band of merchants, got into foreign commerce, "chaffered most freely and assiduously," made "great profit in all his bargains," and built up a great fortune, which by the grace of God he then renounced to become a saintly hermit. Before then St. Godric showed all the instincts of a capitalist, not only by his shrewd eye for bargains but by his habit of at once putting his profits to work in more business instead of hoarding them. In the twelfth century such men expanded business so vigorously that this "golden middle age" has also been compared to a modern industrial boom age. And they did so entirely on their own, without government aid, even the elementary aids of a settled society, such as good roads, regular communications, standard coinage, police protection, or any assurance for the security of their fortunes or the safety of their lives. The letters of Datini of Prato give a vivid idea of what they still had to contend with as late as the fourteenth century: the constant dread of shipwreck, piracy, banditry, insurrection, war, famine, and pestilence.[6]

Under such circumstances the merchants had to be experimental, resourceful, and adventurous. One might expect them to be more intelligent and enterprising than the landed nobility, which is never a naturally progressive class. But the question remains why they proved so much more energetic and inventive than Roman businessmen ever were, and socially more enterprising than businessmen in almost any civilization except early Greece. Moslem merchants, for example, had early learned to take to the sea and become adventurous sailors, they carried on a vast, far-flung trade from Scandinavia to China and the East Indies, and at home they built up flourishing industries, notably in metalworking, pottery, textiles, and carpets; yet their business enterprise led to no significant changes in the Islamic state or church, in particular to no growth of political or personal freedom. Here, I think, one can only say that the merchants of Europe fully exploited their opportunities and their possible advantages, including the advantage of adversity. They had behind them the practical, experimental tradition of the Dark Ages, and around them a society at least free from the economic evil of slavery. The difficulties and dangers besetting them forced them to co-operate; they early banded together for self-protection and soon formed trading companies, got into the habit of corporate organization. In particular they took full advantage of the personal liberty they enjoyed, in a feudal society that gave them no honorable status but did grant them freedom, as the nobles wanted their goods. Their private enterprise was perhaps freer and bolder because their society did not yet highly esteem the type of the sound, solid businessman, who for social purposes may be sound asleep or solid from ear to ear.

The merchants also stimulated and financed the remarkable advance in medieval technology, anticipating the revolution to come. Like the early Greeks, they were apt at learning from the older peoples they traded with; it was a twelfth-century merchant, Leonardo of Pisa, who acquainted Europeans with Arabic numerals and their immense superiority over the clumsy Roman numerals. But from the tenth century on a tide of invention at home brought many new devices, ranging from the button and the clock to means of producing cast iron. Apparently

---

[6] See *The Merchant of Prato*, by Iris Origo (New York, 1957).

they included such major inventions as gunpowder, the compass, and the spinning wheel, once thought to be importations from the East. They spurred the growth of industries—textile, chemical, metallurgical —for which medieval technicians made increasingly efficient use of mechanical sources of power, like water mills and windmills, devising much machinery unknown to the ancients.

The ugly word "power" recalls the vulgar materialistic aspect of all this activity, which might seem unbecoming the rise of Western Christendom. Still, power remains essential to effective freedom, and the advance of technology served intellectual or spiritual purposes too. It contributed a great deal to the development of not only science but art; an early wave of experimental chemistry, for instance, made possible the arts of stained-glass windows, frescoes, and oil painting. It led to such revolutionary inventions as the printing press, which made literature—including the Bible—available to ordinary men. By that time the learned had probably forgotten a medieval inventor who is still almost unheard of and unthought of. Everybody knows of the Crusades; but possibly a more important historical event, and certainly a more beneficial one to mankind, was the invention of spectacles by an obscure Italian in the thirteenth century—an invention that has enabled millions of men to make more use of their eyes and their head. In this view even the hammerforges and the bellows invented for the water mills have an ideal aspect. The chief glory of the Middle Ages, Lynn White ventures, was "the building for the first time in history of a complex civilization which rested not on the backs of sweating slaves or coolies but primarily on non-human power."

A particular glory of the medieval bourgeois, no less materialistic in its origins, was the free town. Its growth was primarily due to the merchants, who again had to start almost from scratch. With a few such exceptions as Venice and Rome, the surviving towns in the tenth century were little but fortresses, known as "burgs" (or bourgs, or boroughs). Bands of merchants began settling outside their walls for trading purposes, or between foreign expeditions, hence becoming known as burghers or bourgeois; gradually they built up their suburbs, which in time completely surrounded and dominated the original burg. By this time, too, hundreds of new towns were being founded. Very little is known of the growth of these towns until the twelfth century, inasmuch as the few records of the time were kept by clerics, men scarcely aware of their historic importance and unlikely to have much sympathy for them anyway; but the basic conditions seem clear enough. As trade and industry expanded, especially the manufacture of cloth, the merchants necessarily had to employ workers. Because their main source of supply was escaped serfs, the growing towns often had trouble with feudal lords in the vicinity; a typical conservative of the twelfth century spoke of these "detestable communes." The communes nevertheless managed to remain independent, by fighting or bargaining, often with the help of greater lords who had the wit to see their usefulness or simply wanted their goods. They acquired charters granting them various rights, such as bearing arms, coining money, and setting up their own courts. As the charters amounted to another "social contract," so the burghers acquired status as members of the Third Estate—hardly an exalted rank, but at least an assured place in the medieval order.

In this process the burghers displayed as much genius for self-government as for commerce. They originated their own law, a rational law of contract suited to needs for which feudal law was wholly inadequate. Since their first need was always city walls for self-defense, they devised a system of public taxation that had no feudal equivalent, and that anticipated the graduated income tax. By an administration at first made up of more or less democratically elected officials, they provided for the erection of public buildings, the maintenance of markets and quays, the regulation of trade and industry, the prevention of fraud, the assurance of ample supplies of cheap food for artisans. They elaborated, indeed, the most complete social legislation in all history to their time; it included protection for workers and bans on woman and child labor. To their modern descendants all this may have an alarming "socialistic" aspect, the more so because feudal government never got into business (though they should remember that the lords likewise gave no such aid to business as they now take for granted government should give). By contrast with feudal society, at any rate, the towns were models of peace, law, order, and civility. They early became the main centers of progress in the Middle Ages.

The medieval free town accordingly resembled the Greek *polis* in being autonomous and walled, while incidentally preserving the agora or the Roman forum in its piazza, plaza, or platz; yet it was another quite original creation, essentially different from both the ancient and the modern city. Wholly urban, it maintained its autonomy within a larger province or state. Except in Italy, it housed few if any lords or estate owners; the feudal nobility kept to their manors or castles in the country. It was wholly bourgeois too in that the burghers had developed it all by themselves, in Italy with some memories of Roman municipalities, but nowhere with any real model. And it was more thoroughly permeated by the spirit of community than were the later cities, even apart from its relative smallness. Among its most characteristic institutions was the merchant or craft guild, primarily economic in function, but also something of a brotherhood with social and religious interests. Among its historic innovations was the provision of hospitals, almshouses, and homes for the aged. Altogether, the early town was a more genuinely Christian community than the feudal manor was, than any large state could ever be, or than the papal city of Rome ever was after Gregory the Great. It most completely embodied the medieval social ideal, expressed by St. Thomas among others, of a unity of economic function, corporate organization, and civic freedom.[7]

Again, these burghers had not consciously set themselves any such lofty ideal. Although generally peace-loving men, they were not pacifists on principle; war was simply bad for business. Similarly they had no passion for freedom in the abstract. In this respect they were no more idealistic than the barons of King John, had no more idea of the rights of man and no more concern for the welfare of the country at large; they simply wanted freedom for themselves—the freedom they needed to go about their business. Nevertheless, the important point at this stage remains that they were free, and had flourished in freedom. Since the merchants needed some assurance as well for the escaped serfs who worked for them, it presently became established that a man who had lived in the town for a year and a day was legally free; so a burgher was by definition a free man. In spite of the class divisions between merchants and workers, and the increasing differences in wealth and power, there was a degree of equality in citizenship, a relatively free association. The official emblems of the town were typically emblems of fraternity; burghers were sworn to aid their fellows in defense of the town. They were united in the civic pride that early started erecting cathedrals, to the greater glory of God and the towns-people.

---

[7] In *The City in History*, Lewis Mumford adds that the medieval town was by no means so filthy as is commonly supposed. Although scarcely sanitary, it was less dark, dirty, crowded, and slummish than cities later became, with the aid of freer private enterprise by landlords, and never so foul as the industrial cities of modern times. Among its forgotten provisions were public bathhouses, while in Germany the better homes even had bathrooms—supposedly a nineteenth-century innovation. More important, medieval townsmen lived with an eye to color and beauty, in street and market as well as church. The common acceptance of drabness and ugliness as normal is another reason why Americans often do not look or act like free men.

Although the towns were destined to lose their independence as the nation-states began to form, first they enabled the bourgeois not only to rise in the world but to transform this world. Most decisive was the impact of the "detestable communes" on feudal society. As they offered an escape to freedom for many serfs, serfdom broke up earliest and fastest in their vicinity. Indirectly it was weakened no less by the growing population and wealth resulting from the growth of trade and industry. Many monasteries and feudal lords had large reserves of uncultivated land, which it was now possible and profitable to clear and till, but to attract the needed men they had to offer special inducements and could no longer bind these men to the soil; hence there grew up villages or "new towns" occupied by tenants instead of serfs—free peasants who were often called "burgenses," after their unconscious liberators. As unwittingly the burghers weakened the barons by developing a money economy. This made it possible for kings to hire troops and officials, instead of depending upon vassals, and increasingly they chose officials from the bourgeois, men of proved administrative competence. Kings favored them the more because they needed the support of the towns in their struggles with the barons; the bourgeois returned the favor by usually supporting them.[8] The feudal nobility preserved its social superiority for many centuries, but by the end of the Middle Ages it had lost much of its military and political power, and tacitly acknowledged its losses by starting to build town houses.

Other indirect influences of the urban bourgeois, generally as unpremeditated, were perhaps more significant in the long run. As liquid capital eroded the power of landed capital, so the mobility of the merchants and the steady drift to the towns weakened the principle of fixed hierarchy, while the habit of rational calculation further weakened the power of custom and tradition. Among the salutary consequences was the rationalization of medieval law: a society grown more businesslike dropped the crude methods of proof, the trial by duel and by ordeal, that had satisfied the knights' rude sense of justice or rude faith in God. At the same time the international operations of the merchants opened up Europe to foreign influences. The spirit of trade, which in these days was a spirit of adventure, prompted feats more daring and potentially world-shaking than any performed by knights and Crusaders, most notably the journey of the Polos across Asia to the

---

[8] One exception was England, where the towns supported the barons against domineering kings. But this is another reason why the history of England calls for a separate chapter.

Great Khan of China—a journey that took them through some lands
that no Westerner would see again until the nineteenth century. Marco
Polo came back talking of "millions" of everything; his popular narrative of his travels told of cities far greater and richer than any in Europe,
in a civilization much older and more sophisticated. Growing knowledge of this kind shook the cozy, parochial, bandbox world of medieval
Christian theory. Some men started worrying over questions it raised—
how all the new species of animals discovered could have got on Noah's
Ark, and whether each continent had had its own Adam and Eve.[9]
Others began looking beyond the horizon, until eventually Columbus
was led to discover America—looking for a new trade route to the fabulous riches of the East.

As for the Church, the still-pious bourgeois started repaying its distrust of them long before they earned it by claiming complete autonomy
for business and a profit system. In the eleventh century a number of
towns rebelled against their bishops, depriving them of the political
authority formerly exercised over the burgs. Their spirit of liberty kept
them suspicious of ecclesiastical authority; more conflicts broke out
over the control of the municipal schools. Hostility was deepened by
the very piety of the burghers, who were indignant over the corruptions
of the Church. But in the long run their deepest influence on Christendom was the most obvious one, due to their naturally worldly spirit.
Their towns were the first to adopt the vernacular instead of Church
Latin for official usage. As their guilds took over from the monks the
building of cathedrals, so they broke the ecclesiastical monopoly on
learning and art, produced a new class of laymen who had more freedom in teaching, writing, and creating. With their worldly success they
grew more interested in secular as well as religious art and thought;
they began building themselves palaces, accumulating libraries, commissioning artists. Merchant princes would be among the chief patrons
of the increasingly worldly art of the Renaissance.

By this time Europe was much richer and stronger. It was not, however, basking in the prosperity or the freedoms achieved by the bourgeois. Most men were still poor, and many of them were more hostile
to the wealthy burghers than the feudal lords and churchmen had been.
One reason was another of their major innovations—capitalism. Medi-

---

[9] Such heretical curiosity had cropped up earlier in the Emperor Frederick II. Wondering
whether children untaught from birth would speak Hebrew, the "oldest" language, or
Greek, Latin, Arabic, or what not, he had a number brought up with never a word spoken
to them. Unfortunately, the children all died.

eval capitalism was primarily commercial or financial rather than industrial, but by the twelfth century it was developing on a greater scale than it ever had in antiquity. Large trading companies became closed corporations, taking pains to exclude both retailers and workers. Moneylenders became great bankers; in the thirteenth century Italian banking houses were operating all over Europe, dominating finance. Men in other countries soon followed their example in the profitable management of capital. Double-entry bookkeeping—another medieval invention that has had much more lasting influence than the celebrated Crusades—facilitated the growth of powerful commercial firms.

St. Godric should remind us that these capitalists were by no means simple villains in the medieval drama. They brought down interest rates, stimulated productive enterprise, helped to keep the European economy more expansive and vigorous than that of the Roman Empire had ever been. For the most part they dealt more generously with their employees than feudal lords did with the peasantry. Outside of Italy they seldom sought or directly wielded political power, and certainly they were engaged in no conspiracy to rule Europe; they had no Karl Marx to make them conscious of their historic role. Still, other men needed no Marx to learn distrust or resentment of their operations. Large merchants early began trying to corner grain in times of famine, and large companies continued to seek monopoly. Much of their enterprise was speculative, not directly productive; fortunes might be made chiefly by luck or unearned increment, with little if any gain to the community. Rash speculation led now and then to the bankruptcy of great banking houses, causing commercial crises from which the poor were likely to suffer most. The manipulation of large capital developed habits of abstraction and impersonality that already were widening the gulf between capital and labor, embittering their conflict. Whether or not the greater capitalists abused their power, they were too powerful for towns or small principalities to regulate. At best they wanted freedom only for their own operations—as the medieval burghers had from the outset. No more than the saints or the barons can the bourgeois be regarded as the heroic protagonists in the history of Western freedom.

| # THE BREAKDOWN OF THE MEDIEVAL ORDER

1. The Major Causes

In *The Waning of the Middle Ages* Johan Huizinga remarked the strange obsession with death reflected in late medieval art, as in the skull and bones that adorned even drinking pots and the rings of whores. It expressed a horror more earthy than religious—a horror of physical death and putrefaction, more intense and macabre than has been evinced by any other society, past or present. It seems stranger in a Christian society, in which death presumably meant a blessed reunion with one's Creator, an escape from a world commonly described as a vale of tears; for if death might also mean everlasting torture, it was apparently not so much the fear of hell as the decay of the despised flesh that obsessed medieval men. Still, their horror was not really so strange. Excepting some saints, these men had always loved the pleasures of the flesh, been lustier than men in most other societies. They had always known, too, a sense of crisis or impending doom; in every generation men proclaimed the spiritual bankruptcy of their society, the desperate need of reform—and the reforms never lasted, if they took at all. Their life had always been full of terrors: fantastic terrors of demons inherited from Pope Gregory the Great, and more of their own making; terrors that should logically have made them welcome the release of death, but understandably made them cling to life the more dearly. The greatest of their popes, Innocent III, had preached a sermon on the misery of the human condition that could make Schopenhauer seem almost radiant; and ordinary men who might share the earthly pessimism of Innocent could not enjoy his earthly pomp and power, or his assurance of supernal bliss.

At any rate, the prophets of doom were right. *Their* world was in fact coming to an end.

Now, it is important to remember that the Middle Ages never actually realized its ideal of a united Christendom, under the spiritual authority of a Catholic Church. From the outset its Holy Roman Empire had bred conflict between pope and emperor. Feudal princes continually warred on one another, and as they grew into kings got embroiled with the Papacy too. One reason for the passion for unity was the growing disunity, often verging on anarchy. And if medieval men regarded violence and physical insecurity as normal, there is reason to doubt that they enjoyed as much psychological security as Erich Fromm and others make out. Churchmen were obviously prey to spreading fears. They grew harsher and more systematic in the persecution of heretics or scapegoats, setting up their Inquisition, and they appealed to terror in their preaching as well; after 1200 Christ was represented more often as Judge than as Savior. The anxieties of ordinary men appeared in not only the peasant rebellions but signs of hysteria, such as the dancing and flagellation manias that swept through the countryside. Perhaps most pathetic, and most ominous, were the periodic millenarian movements, in which apocalyptic tradition was revived with a dreadfully literal seriousness. Prophets or messiahs held up the vision of some kind of egalitarian heaven on earth, in which the poor and oppressed would come into their own, but the way to it usually led through massacre and terror, or holy bloodthirstiness; for the "signs" of the Millennium always included a preliminary reign of sin or preternatural evil, first the hordes of Antichrist had to be eliminated—usually beginning with the Jews in the vicinity.[1]

Yet it is no less important to recognize the reality and power of the medieval ideal. Although this was not strictly universal, embracing only those of the proper faith, it was more catholic than the national ideal that superseded it; and it was no mere fiction. In the early Middle Ages men were likely to think of themselves first as Christians, not as Germans or Frenchmen; as such they united in the Crusade to recover the Holy Land, which deepened and vivified their common consciousness of Western Christendom. They were agreed on the essential truths about the meaning of the human drama, from the Creation through the Redemption to the Last Judgment. The learned all communicated in the universal language of Latin, the unlearned communed in the same rituals; together they glorified the same God in similar forms of art.

---

[1] Norman Cohn offers a thoroughly documented history of these movements in *The Pursuit of the Millennium*. He perhaps exaggerates their importance and their addiction to terrorism, especially because he sees in them a source of modern totalitarian movements; but there is no mistaking the anxieties on which they fed.

Alike they traveled freely over Europe, a land not yet fenced by fixed boundaries or armed frontiers. The hierarchical order that most sharply separated men was still widely accepted as the natural form of community. In the words of John of Salisbury, the Christian commonwealth was one in which "the higher members shield the lower, and the lower respond faithfully and fully in like measure to the just demands of their superiors, so that each and all are as it were members one of another by a sort of reciprocity, and each regards his own interest as best served by that which he knows to be most advantageous for the others."

At least the medieval ideal was live and grand enough to make its historic failure a tragic drama of abiding consequence. It inspired most of the greatest men and the greatest works of the age that founded Western civilization. It persisted long after it broke down in practice; it still haunts the imagination of many men even outside the Roman Church. The reasons for its failure, and the issues they raise, are especially pertinent for our own society, which grew out of this failure, set up different ideals, and is no longer so sure of these ideals, while it is trying on a much vaster scale to realize the same dream of a universal order.

Logical, even inescapable, as the breakdown of the medieval order may now appear, it was not simply a human failure. Historical accident played some part, most conspicuously in the Black Death that struck Europe in 1348. The most terrible plague in recorded history, this killed up to a third of the population within a few years, and it continued to break out periodically through the rest of the century. Today it is hard to realize the effects of such disasters in a society that lacked ample reserves of wealth, was unable to marshal quickly what resources it did have, had no scientific means of combating the plagues, and could understand them only as the will of God. We cannot know to what extent men were demoralized, lost heart for the cause of a united Christendom; but we can better understand their obsession with death.

The Black Death also brings up the pardonable limitations of medieval men, in particular their immaturity and ignorance. "A man's will is secure from sinning," wrote St. Thomas Aquinas, "only when his understanding is secured from ignorance and error." Ordinary men enjoyed very little of such security either. Their rank superstition, an unfailing spring of blind hopes, fears, and hatreds, reflected their very limited understanding of natural causes and their vivid sense of the miraculous—of the supernatural as the everyday occurrence, the most probable explanation of affliction and the most reliable solution or cure.

But St. Thomas himself knew that the Devil was a direct cause of tempest and disease, and could as readily transform men into any shape as transport them through the air; so the educated too might be pretty insecure. They were still behind the Greeks and the Arabs in science, or natural knowledge. They were mostly ignorant of their past, including early Christian history, and what they knew was mostly erroneous. Their boldest intellectual enterprise, Scholastic philosophy, was based on a limited understanding or pious misunderstanding of both Aristotle and the Bible, neither of which they could read in the original. Basically uncritical, they were unable to see through the fictions by which they lived. Even St. Thomas failed to detect so gross a fraud as the "Donation of Constantine"—a forgery dating from the time of Charlemagne, full of linguistic, geographical, and historical errors, that conferred on the Church temporal authority over Italy and the western provinces.

True, many men were painfully aware of the gulf between the lofty ideals and the actualities; but they suggest another reason for qualifying and condoning the failures of the Middle Ages. As they despaired of their age, they failed to appreciate the very real advances they had made, materially and intellectually. Peasants and workers were on the whole becoming demonstrably better off, enjoying more freedom and a higher standard of living; scholars had learned a good deal, artists and builders had achieved great feats, technicians had made many inventions; but thinkers remained weak in sizing up both the actual achievements and the problems arising from them. Especially in political affairs they failed to appreciate the most original, impressive achievement of their age, that of the burghers. The greatest thinkers, such as St. Thomas, paid little heed to the revolutionary activities of these burghers —except to worry over the evils of commerce and the charging of interest. The anxieties of the late Middle Ages were in part the natural penalty of growth and creativity.

In philosophy, the supreme achievement of St. Thomas marked the beginning of the end of a daring, necessary, but doomed enterprise. Even as the Church was preparing to accept his grand synthesis other philosophers were busy pointing out basic inconsistencies in it, demonstrating what St. Bonaventure had earlier warned, that it was logically impossible to reconcile Aristotelian philosophy with orthodox Christian faith. (Among other things, this philosophy calls for an eternal universe and dismisses individual immortality as logically absurd.) Above all, they riddled his faith in the power of reason, emphasizing the apparent limits of its power in these high matters. When Duns Scotus and William of Occam showed that none of the fundamental Christian doctrines, even to the existence of God, was rationally demonstrable, they did not deny the truth of these doctrines—they merely argued that the truths were matters of pure faith; but thereby they declared the bankruptcy of the theological enterprise. Hence the brave effort to reconcile faith and reason only deepened the tensions between them and ended by divorcing them, setting up a double standard of truth such as no actual "Age of Faith" would think of.

More immediately disruptive, however, was the growing nationalism. This involved the plain, if ancient evil of war; among the disasters of the Middle Ages was the Hundred Years' War, which devastated France and exhausted England. But one reason why it proved stronger than the ideal of a united Christendom was that it too had an ideal aspect, exemplified most conspicuously by the patriotism of Joan of Arc. As a more closely knit community, with a visible land and a common tongue, the nation could more directly inspire men than could a theoretically catholic Church that was in fact administered from Rome, and sometimes had alien interests; so in the frequent conflicts between kings and popes, most men usually sided with their king. In any case, the racial, linguistic, and cultural diversity of Europe, which was far more heterogeneous than it had been under the Roman Empire, made the growth of nations an almost certain result of the growth of order and prosperity.

At worst, war between the nations was no more unprincipled than war had been in early feudal times, or when the Church was at the zenith of its power. It had always been wanton and brutal, no less on Crusades; pillage and slaughter, treachery and cruelty were routine. It leads us to the basic failings of the Middle Ages: failings that are still understandable, in the ageless terms of selfishness, ambition, and greed, but that are less easy to condone, especially in a Christian society, in an "Age of Faith."

Directly, the wars point to the obvious failure of the feudal nobility. The leaders of this order were clearly incapable of realizing the Christian ideal. Although they numbered some genuinely pious men of the type of Chaucer's knight, their primary virtues remained the military virtues, and these were always accompanied by the military vices of callousness and cruelty. Their pretensions as an aristocracy ("rule by the best") are sufficiently exposed by the late medieval chroniclers, such as Froissart, who celebrated their "fine feats of arms" in the belief that the salvation of society and the preservation of justice depended on their noble virtues, their ideal of chivalry. While recording deeds of valor and honor that testify to the reality of this ideal, they also record in monotonous bloody detail a great deal more evidence of ruthlessness, greed, deceit, infidelity, calculated betrayal of all ideals; and the chroniclers show no understanding whatever of the history their heroes were making. Little more did the heroes themselves, whether high-spirited or cold-blooded. The privileged noble class had contributed very little to the intellectual progress of the Middle Ages, and as it lost political power to the kings it only flaunted its chivalry more flamboyantly, playing at courtly love and tournaments, which by the fourteenth century were all the rage. It bred a "trained incapacity" for any social function except war and conspicuous consumption, while the contemporary invention of gunpowder was outmoding its castles and its picturesque, undisciplined kind of warfare. Since it preserved its social superiority, in a society that would long remain wedded to the medieval ideal of hierarchy, it began to patronize the arts and so to build up the legend that blooded aristocracies have a peculiar passion for culture; but it also preserved an anti-intellectual tradition. True gentlemen were sportsmen and soldiers, not painters, writers, or scholars.

That the feudal aristocracy remained the most honored and pampered class suggests some shortcomings of the more enterprising burghers. For all the practical genius they displayed in learning to govern themselves, they furnished no general political ideas to society at large, and once they had established themselves they also displayed the narrowness and shortsightedness that commonly limit the social enterprise of the business mentality. Many were individualists like the merchant of Prato, a somewhat callous as well as rugged type: wholly engrossed in his business, he never fought for his republic or took part in its government, while his service of God and profit was aided by a flourishing traffic in slaves for domestic use. (His books ranked them with other animals: "He says he has a female slave and a horse and two donkeys and three fifths of an ox. Let us put them down at 70 florins.") But in their associations the burghers did more to strengthen the local, selfish interests that disrupted the unity of Christendom. Their towns ruthlessly exploited the surrounding peasantry. They did their best to shut out all foreign competition; especially in Italy their fierce economic rivalry intensified the fatal parochialism that kept them warring on one another. Similarly their guilds grew as rigid, exclusive, and hierarchical as other medieval orders, losing most of their early democratic spirit. The craft guilds discouraged individual initiative by fixing wages, prices, methods of work, and terms of apprenticeship, primarily in the interests of the masters. The much wealthier merchant guilds, which dominated their lesser brethren as well as their own workers, transcended local interests only to advance their own immediate interests. Together they contributed to an economic slump that set in during the fourteenth century and aggravated the woes of Christendom.

Most portentous were the social problems growing out of the exploitation of workers. Wanting freedom only for themselves, the burghers had always shared the medieval view of rights as exclusive privileges, implying a right to oppress others. Among their earliest creations was a proletariat—the peasants who escaped to the town. There is evidence that these men paid for their freedom by hard work at very low wages, and did not simply rejoice in their new lot. From the outset, moreover, town government was naturally pretty much in the hands of the greater merchants. While this *haute bourgeoisie* must be credited with the remarkable social and political achievements of the medieval town, in time its rule became a purer oligarchy. Its oppressive tendencies, coupled with the recurrence of work stoppages, bred increasing social discontent; we hear of organized strikes by the thirteenth century. Toward the end of that century, and throughout the fourteenth, workers repeatedly rose up in violence, most often in the industrially advanced regions of Italy, Flanders, and France. These uprisings, so rare in Eastern societies, were in a sense another credit to the medieval bourgeois, testifying to the spirit of liberty they had fostered. They did not yet amount to conscious class struggle; the still-unnamed proletariat was at most united by a resentment of "the rich," not by clear democratic principles or any definite political program. Yet there was in fact class war in the late Middle Ages. At this stage the *haute bourgeoisie* seemed little more enlightened in its self-interest than the feudal nobility, had little more to contribute to a healthy social and political order, not to say a Christian one.

Far worse, however, was the contemporary spiritual disorder. We come to the role of the Church in the failure of the medieval ideal. Embarrassing as the subject is, this much seems beyond dispute: the Church had claimed and assumed the leadership of Western Christendom, and by this time its leadership had conspicuously failed, in part because of flagrant abuses now admitted by its followers. As it may be credited with much of the creative achievement inspired by the medieval ideal, so it bore a major responsibility for the failure of this ideal.[2]

Few will dispute either some excuses for the Church. By getting into worldly affairs it incurred all the risks that beset religion when it does not remain aloof and confine itself to the purely spiritual or other-worldly; yet the very genius of Christianity, owing to the great prophets of Israel, calls for it not to remain aloof as the holy men of India did, but to enter the world and seek to regenerate society. In any case, the medieval Church had no real alternative. Representing the City of God, a "kingdom not of this world," it was still perforce a worldly insti-tution, and it was able to accomplish all that it did during the Dark and early Middle Ages chiefly because it was by far the largest, wealthiest kingdom of this world in the West. It had to devote a great deal of its time and effort to the administration of its immense holdings, and could not help getting into business. Neither could it help getting into poli-tics, even apart from the principality of Rome that it inherited from Gregory the Great. It had to deal with a feudal order in which bishops and abbots had become inextricably involved during the confusion of the Dark Ages, and deal as well with warlike monarchs who by tradition got their authority from God. It had to make the hairline distinction between just what things were God's and what were Caesar's. In assum-ing all such responsibilities it bore out the observation of Walter Bagehot: "The whole history of civilization is strewn with creeds and institutions which were invaluable at first, and deadly afterward. Prog-ress would not have been the rarity it is if the early food had not been the late poison."

Still, the early food did become poison. The Church failed to Chris-

---

[2] Catholic historians usually insist on the Augustinian distinction between the True Church, which by definition is incorruptible and infallible, and the historic Church. The latter, to cite Jacques Maritian, was admittedly guilty of "certain excesses" or "impurities arising from the spirit of this world," but the True Church was untouched because it "has never been bound up with or into any temporal regime whatsoever." I have previously remarked one difficulty with this essentially Platonic conception, that Maritain and others offer no clear criterion for distinguishing between the two Churches, or deciding whether a given decree truly represents the True Church. (I suppose, for example, that the many Italian Catholics who continue to vote Communist, in spite of Vatican decrees that so doing makes them liable to excommunication, believe that these decrees have nothing to do with the True Church; but I also suppose that if excommunication means anything the Vatican believes otherwise.) At any rate, a historian is necessarily concerned with the doings of the historic Church, and readers may decide for themselves when or to what extent the record of the medieval Church was in accord with the True one. As for the admitted "excesses" or "impurities," I am dwelling on those stressed by Lord Acton, himself a devout Catholic, in the thousands of notes he accumulated for his unwritten History of Freedom; though I should add that his worry over them was one evident reason why he never managed to write the history to which he devoted most of his life.

tianize politics, as it failed to educate either the feudal aristocracy or the common people, and the plainest reason was its notorious corruption—corruption on a scale seldom paralleled in religious history, and unthinkable in any church in the modern godless world. Early in the thirteenth century Innocent III himself said that "the corruption of the people has its chief source in the clergy," for all the scandalous abuses blamed on the worldly Renaissance had sprung up before his time. The milder forms were business practices that the Church condemned in the burghers, such as the charging of interest; monasteries went into the banking business, while popes employed Jewish moneylenders—"the peculiar sons of the Roman Church," as Innocent IV called them. (Since Mohammed also condemned "usury," Moslem rulers had employed Christians for the same purpose.) The most flagrant abuses developed at the papal court in Rome. "All who have Peter's power are poisoned forever," wrote William Langland, two centuries before Martin Luther; Europe kept ringing with the cry that everything was for sale in Rome. Besides lucrative church offices, the bargains included indulgences for sins, which Urban II had begun granting wholesale as an inducement to join the First Crusade. Later popes drew ever more liberally on this inexhaustible treasury, which was also exploited by underlings; indulgences were retailed by pardoners of the type described by Chaucer, who supplemented their racket by a side line of phony relics. Hence the corruption spread throughout the Church, infecting every branch and order. Within a generation after St. Francis had founded his order, dedicated to poverty, his friars were famous for their greed. Christendom was the more grievously split because the bitterest opposition to the Church came not from ambitious princes, much less from skeptics or infidels, but from the most devout Christians.

No less notorious was the persecution authorized by the Church, even before the Inquisition. One cannot assume that this religious terrorism fatally weakened Christendom, in an age of intolerance when almost all men agreed with St. Thomas Aquinas that heresy was the worst of crimes, properly punished by death. One must doubt, too, the comforting belief that persecution is bound to fail; the Church exterminated the Albigenses so thoroughly that scholars are still uncertain just what their heresy was. Yet the increasingly systematic persecution testifies that Christendom was not really united, and it certainly did not promote unity. Pope Innocent III brought in the state too by making all rulers themselves liable to indictment for heresy unless they swore publicly "to exterminate, from the lands subject to their obedience, all heretics who have been marked out by the Church"; and he punished the Count of Toulouse for refusing to slaughter the Albigenses in his province. The war on heresy stirred up more conflict because the Church was deadliest in its hatred of popular heresies that threatened its power. The Waldensians, for example, preached a simple gospel of fraternity that might have seemed harmless or even saintly were it not, as a contemporary noted, that they "cloaked their madness by saying that it was necessary to obey God rather than man."

Power, not spirituality or the true faith, became the main issue in the conflict that most plainly wrecked the ideal of a united Christendom. This was the battle of the Papacy with the Holy Roman emperors for political supremacy: a drama that unfolded with the inexorable logic of a Greek tragedy, and that also illustrated the favorite medieval moral, the deadly sin of pride. It began on a plane of high principle with Hildebrand, who became Pope Gregory VII (1073–1085). Attacking the institution of simony and denying the traditional right of feudal lords to appoint bishops and abbots, he asserted the necessary principle that spiritual interests should be free from control by the state. His aim, however, was not the traditional ideal of perfect union between church and state. Convinced that either had to be supreme, he plumped for the Church—the Roman Church that "has never erred, and will not err to all eternity according to the witness of Scripture." The pope had the right to depose emperors, he declared, but in turn "was to be judged by no one." By the further claim that the subjects of an emperor excommunicated by the pope no longer owed him fealty, he succeeded in humbling the Emperor Henry IV. And though he himself died a prisoner and an exile, his successors carried on the struggle. The Papacy reached its peak early in the thirteenth century under Innocent III, who commanded the obedience of all the rulers of Europe. "The Lord entrusted to Peter not only the universal Church but the government of the whole world," he announced, and he buttressed his claims with another grandiose fiction, the "Translation of the Empire": the Church had taken the Roman Empire away from the Byzantine Greeks, given it to Charlemagne and the Germans, and so had the right to take it back and give it to somebody else. To maintain such claims, the popes after him made it their chief business to humble Frederick II (1215–1250), by all odds the most able, cultivated, "modern" of the Holy Roman emperors.

Frederick kept the drama ambiguous. Possibly he was sincere when he proposed to other princes that they confiscate the property of the Church for its own good, to protect it against the corruptions of wealth. (At the outset of his reign some Germans had hailed him as a savior, due to prepare the way for the coming Millennium—a hope that remained live enough to get him resurrected as a messiah a generation after his death.) More likely he was somewhat cynical. A distinguished scholar and freethinker, he was intimate with Moslems at his court in Sicily, well versed in Arabic philosophy and science, and he may have been an infidel as the popes charged. In any case, he was no champion of freedom in leading the resistance to their claims. Frederick II ruled as an absolute monarch, declaring that the people had conferred on the emperor the sole right to legislate; outside his court he permitted no freedom of thought and speech, even persecuting heretics. In his pride he could no more have appreciated the tragic irony of the outcome of the power struggle. Innocent IV vowed the complete destruction of not only Frederick but his children; and the vow was made good, the final defeat of the German emperors sealed, by the murder of his grandson Conradin, which was blessed by the reigning pope. Only the Hildebrandine popes had already assured their own defeat.

They had incidentally made reckless use of interdicts and excommunications, damning whole nations in order to humble kings—awful spiritual weapons, but blunted by overuse. In particular they had also resorted to political and military force. As Gregory VII had felt obliged to make good his spiritual authority by calling on other princes for aid, so Innocent III and his successors depended on the aid of French princes, rewarding them with south Italy. By the end of the thirteenth century the real victors in the struggle turned out to be these princes, specifically King Philip the Fair: another modern type of monarch, head of a strong, united nation, who resolved to tax the church holdings that amounted to about a quarter of his land. "We declare, we affirm, we define and pronounce," declared etc. Pope Boniface VIII in a famous bull, "that to be subject to the Roman pontiff is altogether necessary to salvation for every human creature." The ruler of all mankind was then manhandled, imprisoned, and thoroughly humiliated by agents of Philip the Fair.

The rest of Christendom did not arise in his defense. (Presently the greatest Catholic poet took pleasure in torturing him in the *Inferno*.) One reason why the Church failed to dominate the state is that it had nothing new or better to offer by way of social and political order. The popes battled the emperors solely on behalf of their own power and privilege, not the rights of their subjects; they failed to build up a popular following because when in power they did no more for the people than the emperors had done. Hence the aftermath of the humiliation of Boniface was still sorrier. Under French pressure, the Papacy moved its court from Rome to Avignon in France, which became known as a modern Babylon because of its lax and luxurious living, supported by wholesale trafficking in church offices. The "Babylonian captivity" was ended by the return to Rome, but this brought on the Great Schism, as in 1378 the Italians elected one pope and the French another. For forty years the rival popes exchanged anathemas, excommunicated each other's followers, and sold indulgences to finance warring expeditions. Even the ranks of sainthood were split, Catherine of Siena supporting the Italian pope, Vincent Ferrer the French one. Simple worshipers were told (as by St. Vincent) that they were doomed to hell if they supported the wrong pope; so none could be sure of salvation. The councils of churchmen that finally succeeded in picking out an Italian pope acceptable to everyone also tried to limit his power, turn the Papacy into a kind of constitutional, parliamentary monarchy; but the popes soon put down this conciliar movement, which might have averted the Protestant Reformation. Pius II threatened excommunication to anyone appealing from a pope to a council.

Pius also recalled the Crusades, which may sum up the failure of the medieval ideal. The First Crusade had been fired by genuine religious exaltation, if of a murderous kind, and initially had been successful. The victors soon began fighting over the spoils, however, making it easier for the Saracens to win back much of the Holy Land; so there had to be more crusades, all of which failed more or less ingloriously. At the zenith of papal power, Innocent III sent out the Fourth Crusade that settled for the pillage of Constantinople instead of the recovery of the Holy Land, and thereby facilitated the rise of the Ottoman Turks, a much more dangerous threat to Christendom. When they took Constantinople in 1453 Pius II called for another crusade, in anguish and alarm, but in vain. Disunited Europe no longer had the spiritual vigor for such enterprises. "The Turks do not hesitate to die for their most vile faith," lamented Pius, "but we cannot incur the least expense nor endure the smallest hardship for the sake of Christ's gospel." As the Turks continued to advance through the Balkans, into the heart of central Europe, kings took up the cry for another crusade, but now Pope Julius II turned a deaf ear; he was busy trying to arrange a war on Venice. The Papacy had learned nothing from the fate of Boniface

VIII. Shortly it would be rewarded by another humiliation, the ferocious sack of Rome in 1527, by an army of Spaniards and Germans under the colors of another Holy Roman emperor.

2. The Major Implications

One can never be confident that the medieval Church would have succeeded had it extended more rights or granted more freedom; for in view of the long-lived civilizations of the East, the freedoms we know are not clearly essential to social success. One can argue, however, that the despotic tendencies of an authoritarian Church would naturally cause trouble in a society that had some tradition of freedom, and that soon began to recover more of its classical heritage. One may also argue that the whole effort to enforce unity was contrary to the genius of Western civilization, its native tendencies to fluidity and pluralism, its dynamism, its spirit of Quest. At least we must keep ideals of freedom in mind as we assess the failure of the medieval ideal of an ordered, united Christendom. First and last, the truth remains that the society dedicated to this ideal was not a free society by either ancient or modern standards. The growth of freedom was not an inevitable consequence of the breakdown of the medieval order; but in time it was an actual consequence, and a logical one.

We are now dealing, of course, with highly debatable issues, involving moral judgments. Some historians condone the crimes of the Middle Ages as products of "the times," or relics of the Dark Ages. Lord Acton held, on the contrary, that we must judge the past as strictly as the present, so as never to debase our moral currency; he insisted that fraud is fraud, murder is murder, torture is torture—and they are always wrong, always the worse when perpetrated by spiritual leaders. I think it important to remember that "the times" were supposedly the heyday of Christian faith, that many high churchmen were guilty of what almost all civilized men do regard as crimes, and that by any civilized standard the moral record of the Church steadily worsened after the twelfth century.[3] Yet our main concern here is not the admit-

---

[3] The habitual fraud of churchmen is incidentally a further embarrassment to historians. Thus Lord Acton argued against Lea that the Dominicans were largely responsible for the Inquisition, though St. Raymond more so than St. Dominic; but he admitted some uncertainty because forgery was so common. The Benedictines, he noted elsewhere, were the chief specialists in fraud.

ted abuses and corruptions, which may be traced to failings common in all ages. "In the collective affairs of mankind," Tawney wrote, "bad doctrines are always and everywhere more deadly than bad actions," or than the common failings. Medieval churchmen would certainly have agreed with him; a thinker who objected to the celibacy of the priesthood, for instance, was considered more damnable than priests who had wives or popes who had concubines. Our concern is with medieval doctrines, bad by democratic standards, or many would now say by Christian standards, which led to positive restrictions on freedom or denial of human rights, and which may also help to explain the moral failures. They include the holy ends by which the barbarous means were justified.

Jacques Maritain takes us directly to the central issue. The glory of the Middle Ages, he has said, derived from the great human attributes of Freedom and Dignity. The Christian faith may indeed exalt these attributes, as it now commonly tends to, and clearly does in the humane thought of Maritain himself. But Christian tradition also embraces beliefs that are plainly hostile to ideals of Freedom and Dignity; and by and large these were the dominant beliefs in the Middle Ages.

In general, they came down to the tradition of "miracle, mystery, and authority" that Dostoyevsky's Grand Inquisitor held to be the supreme need of all ordinary men, and that in fact dominated the early civilizations. The miracles on which medieval men habitually depended could hearten and inspire them, especially when performed by their beloved patron, the Virgin—Our Lady of mercy and "perpetual succor," who to lowly sinners could seem more than a match for both God and the Devil. Nevertheless, the popular faith of the Middle Ages was compounded of rank credulity, materialism, and idolatry, modes of bondage and indignity. Although some churchmen were troubled by such extravagances as the cult of relics (the authentic relic of the Lord's circumcision, for example, possessed by five different churches in France alone), the Church officially remained much more tolerant of vulgar superstition than of heresy. It had accumulated, after all, some 25,000 saints, whose relics had long been known for their wonder-working powers; it insisted on both the necessity and the efficacy of its sacraments; and it had the highest authority for the tradition of miracle, beginning with Scripture. Gregory the Great had incorporated this whole tradition when laying the spiritual foundations of Western Christendom; among his most popular works was his *Dialogues*, full of tales of miracles, prodigies, and grotesque doings of devils. Before him St. Augustine had written: "Faithful ignorance is better than temerarious knowledge."

The terrorism that helped to protect the faithful against such knowledge was a doubtful aid to freedom and dignity. These attributes were not enjoyed by Jews, of course; Innocent III inaugurated a more systematic persecution of Jews, decreeing that they were doomed to perpetual servitude and must wear on their garments a perpetual badge of infamy. Infidels who escaped slaughter in holy war were likewise outside the pale; Nicholas V issued a bull authorizing the enslavement of Moors. But Christians themselves soon suffered as much, for there was no question whatever of freedom or dignity for heretics. The Church avoided the sin of shedding blood only by burning them. And it was the Church, not the state, that through the Inquisition introduced the judicial method of torture, which was then adopted by almost all countries except England. (Torture had been employed in ancient Rome but only on slaves.) The Inquisition had a wide, enduring effect on principles of justice because its basic procedures became standard for dealing with criminal cases in secular courts. Thus in putting the burden of proof on the accused, and increasing the burden by admitting all witnesses against him but giving him no right to confront them or to introduce witnesses of his own, it established the principle that better a hundred innocent suffer than one guilty man escape. Its files record few acquittals.

It was not simple sadism that instituted the tortures and the burnings, on a scale unprecedented in the history of the higher religions: it was again a matter of doctrine. Chroniclers recorded such popular spectacles as the burning of some 180 heretics before a large gathering of churchmen—"a holocaust very great and pleasing to God." It might well seem pleasing to a God who himself sentenced unbelievers and sinners to an eternity of torture. Medieval theologians all believed in a literal hell-fire; they went to some pains to prove that the damned would retain enough of the flesh to suffer physically as well as spiritually. They agreed, too, that the great majority of men would go to the everlasting fire. Given such doctrines, men would not be disposed to regard torture as an atrocity, or the sight of it as anything but edifying. St. Thomas Aquinas himself declared that the joy of the blessed in heaven would be heightened by the sight of the damned in hell.

The immediate reason for the universal acceptance of these doctrines was belief in the literal, infallible truth of the Bible, which is plain enough on the reality of hell. (Hence men would presently begin burning old women too by the thousands on the authority of as plain a text: "Thou shalt not suffer a witch to live.") But the logic of hell rested on a more fundamental doctrine, that of Original Sin. If it might still seem unfair that most of mankind should be eternally damned for the sin of an unsophisticated pair in Eden, how else could it be justified? Medieval thought accordingly tended to emphasize the natural depravity of man more than his dignity. It followed, too, that such naturally sinful creatures could not be trusted with freedom; original sin was a common argument in defense of serfdom, and against anything like popular government. On all counts, the Church insisted on the primary need of obedience to authority, opposing any idea that men had a right to follow their own lights. It flatly denied freedom of conscience, which the devout Lord Acton considered the very essence of human freedom and dignity, and it became as hostile to the broader principle of freedom of thought and speech. The struggle for such freedom necessarily began as a revolt against ecclesiastical authority.[4]

Short of outright persecution, the Church tended to limit effective freedom of thought by the essential dogmatism underlying all its specific doctrines. If the best minds of the Middle Ages generally enjoyed as much freedom as they wanted or needed, their thought was nevertheless fettered by the premises they were obliged to accept, and by attitudes that discouraged free, disinterested inquiry. Faith remained primary; reason could never openly question the fundamentals of faith, its main business was always to support faith. St. Thomas himself was basically uncritical even as he thought up the thousands of possible objections to the Christian faith; for he answered every one of them, he left no room for doubt on any vital question, and he never really questioned the premises of his faith, the "revealed" truths that dictated his main conclusions in advance. In working Aristotle into Christian theology he left out the essentials of the philosophical spirit: he never proposed that philosophy should be a free, independent activity, as it had been for Aristotle and all other Greek thinkers. Similarly his respect for "science" involved little or nothing of a scientific spirit. No more, despite his formal empiricism, did he habitually look to experience. He could not possibly do so anyhow with most of his concerns, such as the nature and number of angels; but the requirements of the true faith hardly disposed a thinker to put a premium on a respect for fact.

---

[4] An apologist for the Inquisition has argued that religious intolerance bred a disposition to seek truth at any cost, and so explains the distinctive Western passion for the pursuit of truth, in particular the rise of modern science. One may hope he is right, for the sake of the many victims of the Inquisition who in their day were denied the consolations of martyrdom; but if so, it only emphasizes the "bad doctrine" of the medieval Church.

In such a climate of opinion neither science nor the humanities could flourish. The medieval pioneers of science, whom historians are now making much of, stand out because they were so exceptional and had so few followers. Roger Bacon, the most remarkable of them, was hampered not only by trouble with the Church but by many weird beliefs that were more congenial to his age. (He knew from good authority, for example, that no instruction could produce in man such wisdom as could the eating of dragon's flesh, and that the wise men of Ethiopia were the masters in the secret art of catching and saddling dragons, driving them through the air at high speeds to limber their muscles and tenderize their flesh.) More directly he testified to the narrowness of medieval education, lamenting that experimental science was "wholly unknown to the rank and file of students." Now one might add that the students learned no more about art, in spite of the Gothic cathedrals around them. The "liberal arts" at the core of the university curriculum did not include belles-lettres or the fine arts—the latter were ranked with Aristotle's "mechanic arts." The universities had no idea of cultivating imagination or taste because no idea of teaching men to enjoy, to appreciate beauty or truth for its own sake. As their historian Rashdall observed, they had settled down to a discipline that was at once too dogmatic and too disputatious, and these "were but opposite sides of the same fundamental defect—the same fatal indifference to facts, the facts of external nature, the facts of history, and the facts of life."

Common people were perhaps the chief victims of the lack of empirical sense in their betters, for this was nowhere more conspicuous than in social, political thought. Except when thinkers were dealing with the urgent problem of the relations of pope and emperor, they so often seem absent-minded that one might doubt their basic seriousness. The cause might be an unthinking acceptance of authority, an uncritical devotion to the ideal fiction, sometimes the traditional belief that government was at best an evil made necessary by original sin; but in any case the effect was a consistent failure to come to grips with political realities. All the leading thinkers took for granted that monarchy was the natural or best form of government, repeating the stock arguments, such as that of St. Thomas: one God or one queen bee, *ergo* one king. If most agreed that the king's power was limited or that he was under the law, all remained vague about how he should be effectively limited or what to do when he broke the law. None dwelt on the common medieval failure to develop firm institutions to keep rulers responsible. None attempted anything like Aristotle's empirical study of comparative government, though the Church, towns, parliaments, and feudal order or disorder provided diverse enough samples.

In particular, thinkers consistently ignored both the logical and the practical implications of the inherited Roman idea that the community was the sole source of political authority. Outside the towns, which they typically disregarded, medieval government was never in fact a *res publica*, based on free consent of the governed. The "community" idealized in medieval theory was always the same hierarchy, in which the great majority had no political voice and were regarded as inferior by "nature," though those at the top got their privileges by the accident of birth. John of Salisbury, among the most liberal of medieval philosophers, described the common people as the "feet" of the commonwealth, while St. Thomas quoted without comment Aristotle's ideal of peasantry: "men strong of arm, dull of intellect, and so distrustful of each other as to form no menace to the State." Medieval law described them in less flattering terms: the legal term for a serf's progeny was not *familia* but *sequela*—brood or litter. In a society very much concerned about defining and enforcing obligations, the serf alone could not claim the judgment of his peers. No respectable thinker translated the Christian doctrine of equality into social or political equality; this was a proletarian doctrine, sponsored by such wild men as John Ball or such heretics as the Waldensians. The gradual emancipation of the serfs— the most progressive social movement of the Middle Ages—was not anticipated by medieval political theory, any more than it was led by churchmen.

Needless to add, women were not included in the political community. Their status had indeed been elevated by the novel fashion of romantic love introduced by the Provençal poets, then carried to typical extremes in the fashion of courtly love; this put man in the humble position of a wooer, suing on his knees for the favors of his mistress. It was patently an artificial convention, however, which at that conferred no more dignity on wives and mothers, and it was offset by an older convention going back to the early saints who had taken out on woman their morbid fear or hatred of sex: the cause of original sin, she was still the most dangerous temptress of man. If this too was an artificial convention, hardly the feeling of most medieval husbands, official doctrine remained against her. The Christian teaching of equality had ever since St. Paul been outweighed by the myth of Eve: apart from the evil she had brought upon the human race, woman was subject to man "in

every thing" because she had been created for his sake (a divine afterthought that as a bachelor Paul did not really approve). St. Thomas
held that she was naturally weaker in both mind and body, basically
even inferior to a slave: "Woman is in subjection according to the law
of nature, but a slave is not." In the actual law of the Middle Ages
women were not "free and lawful persons"; because of their "frailty"
husbands had a legal right to beat them. And the prestige that some
women were acquiring as saints, queens, or subjects of courtly love was
being countered by the discovery that many others were witches.

Altogether, the political legacy of the Middle Ages included some
high-sounding ideals that centuries later men tried actually to realize,
in a French Revolution that no medieval theologian dreamed of or
would have approved. The bitter struggle against papal pretensions to
supremacy also provided some ammunition for the later struggle against
absolutism, notably the thought of Marsilio, William of Occam, and
Nicholas of Cusa. Immediately, however, this struggle contributed as
much to the growing emphasis on the absolute sovereignty of monarchs.
It drew on another Christian tradition stemming from St. Paul, that
"the powers that be are ordained of God" and resistance to these powers meant damnation; Gregory the Great had declared emphatically
that men must not even judge or criticize their rulers. It still did not
occur to most Christian thinkers that any power that successfully resisted and overthrew a monarch might then claim the Christian duty
of obedience, since God evidently has to ordain whatever powers be.

One reason their logic stopped short was that medieval thinkers, even
to the saints, seldom took seriously the possibility of basic social reform.
They preached charity to the poor the more earnestly because they
assumed that poverty and suffering were also ordained by God, and they
proposed to do little or nothing else about them—not to mention the
medieval idea that the true benefits of charity went to the giver. This
acquiescence in wretchedness is surely understandable, given the long
experience of it and the limited social resources. Possibly it is what
Maritain had in mind when he remarked that medieval men "knew as
no other epoch the worth of human pity and tears." Still, this is a
strange remark, in view of their pitiless cruelty and their pleasure in
burnings. They seemed to know better the natural depravity of man.
This doctrine also helps to explain why there was little passion for
social justice in the Middle Ages, little indignation over the pitiless
treatment of the poor. Such exceptions as the poet William Langland
are conspicuous because of the prevalent callousness that he described:

> The poor may plead and pray in the doorway;
> They may quake for cold and thirst and hunger;
> None receives them rightfully and relieves their suffering.
> They are hooted at like hounds and ordered off.

Much more might be said on behalf of the medieval acquiescence, in terms of piety, humility, "spiritual freedom," possible wisdom. Enough has been said to make plain that modern democracy grew up in a radically different spirit. It began, as it had to, with much more faith in ordinary human nature than the medieval Church had taught. With it grew a humanitarianism that at last tried to realize the Christian doctrine of the dignity of the person, even the person of the common man. The popular cause gained momentum as men came to believe that poverty and misery were remediable social evils, something could and should be done about them. Their hopes were nourished by a broader faith in progress, which would have seemed absurd or even blasphemous to orthodox medieval churchmen.[5]

By now, of course, men are no longer so confident of their progress, or even of the blessings of freedom. Many writers are attacking the optimistic faith in human nature, harping again on original sin; many more are highly critical of the common man, and the common uses of freedom; almost all are given to dismay, sometimes to despair, over our society. Taking for granted the exceptional rights and opportunities they enjoy, they may forget that they are judging our society in the light of higher expectations than men ever had in the past, but even so they have plenty of reason for dismay and alarm—enough to fill another volume. At this point we need consider only the perspective afforded by the Middle Ages. Beset by the deep confusions and uncertainties of a revolutionary world, men may hanker again for the lost

---

[5] In *The New Science of Politics*, Eric Voegelin traces the belief in progress to Joachim of Flora, a twelfth-century "Gnostic," who preached of a forthcoming era of universal peace, justice, and happiness, harking back to the dreams of the prophets of Israel. As Voegelin considers this a blasphemous perversion of the Christian doctrine of salvation, he makes Joachim the primary villain in Western intellectual history, Gnosticism the source of all evils of the modern world. His outline of history strikes me as fantastic, but at least there is no question that the optimistic faith of Joachim was a radical departure from the common faith, another version of the aberrant millenarian movements.

Readers interested in Voegelin's thesis may consult a lengthy, reverential review of his book in the leading article of *Time,* March 9, 1953 (the issue commemorating the thirteenth anniversary of the magazine). The article has some added interest as an example of the current fashion of dressing up the American gospel of business in the trappings of moral and spiritual crusades, thus enabling Americans to enjoy all mammon and heaven too. Somehow it turns out that if we reject Gnosticism, "the opportunity for great progress, especially moral progress, lies before society."

medieval ideal of an ordered society united by a common faith, based on absolute certitudes. Logically it permitted no dissent on fundamentals, or in Maritain's words, it rejected the "dogmatic tolerance" that glorifies "liberty of error"; but forget the tortures and the burnings, this is still a seductive ideal, even outside the Communist world. Many men say that our crying need is a uniform philosophy, a return to the eternal verities, a culture again vitalized by religious faith.

So the Middle Ages might remind us of the conditions of a free society: conditions that by no means guarantee its success, but that are essential to its maintenance or to hopes of its success. Democracy requires a faith in ordinary human nature, the sufficient good sense and good will of common men. Freedom of thought, speech, and conscience logically requires at least a tacit admission of uncertainty about the eternal verities, a tacit rejection of all claims to finality, an open agreement upon the right to disagree peaceably on the first and last questions, and a flat denial of absolute authority to any sect or school of thought. As it inevitably leads to diversity of opinion, it requires a belief that such diversity is a good thing, or at least is preferable to uniformity. It requires some separation of major cultural interests, some independence for each. We could not in any case hope to "Christianize" all art, literature, philosophy, and science, but we must believe that it is better not to have either culture or government dominated by religion, as not to have all society dominated by the state.

If these and other conditions of a free society spell a good deal of confusion and disharmony, and look like spiritual anarchy, we may then recall that the "Age of Faith" never did achieve unity, and that the efforts to impose it resulted in increasing disunity. We may suspect that had the efforts succeeded, and the Church retained its authority, Western Christendom might well have followed Islam into stagnation. One major reason why it escaped the fate of Islam became apparent in the next chapter of its history: it remained truer to its Greek legacy.

PART II

THE GROWTH OF A
REVOLUTIONARY WORLD
(1400 – 1700)

| *Chapter Four* | *T H E   R E N A I S S A N C E* |

1. *The Meanings of the Renaissance*

The once glorious Renaissance of popular imagination—all fine, free, careless Greek rapture—has gone the way of ancient Greece and all other golden ages under the analysis of modern historians. We now have a wide choice in renaissances, typically less exhilarating than the one made famous by Jacob Burckhardt. Some historians have disparaged it by dwelling on its notorious license and corruption, its political and spiritual failures; others by arguing that it was less original and decisive than the less famous, uncapitalized renaissance of the twelfth century; still others by emphasizing that its intellectual leaders were academic, imitative, backward-looking, indifferent or even hostile to science and the revolutionary discoveries and inventions of the time. One school that has restored its respectability by insisting that its ruling ideas were medieval-Christian—i.e., by denying it any historical distinction to speak of—has been offset by another Christian school that sees in it the beginnings of our social, political, and religious woes. Some authorities have therefore wiped the slate clean, dismissing the Renaissance as a mere fiction—not a historical era at all, but an invention of historians.

Now in view of this learned disagreement, the Renaissance is manifestly not a well-defined period. There was no sharp break with the Middle Ages, no revolutionary upheaval. Much that was plainly medieval came through, refusing to fade away as appropriately as devotees of new ages would have it. Much that has been considered distinctive of the Renaissance, especially its humanism, naturalism, and individualism, may be found all over the Middle Ages. Such epochal figures as Dante and Giotto have been placed in both periods. The commonly recognized leaders of the Renaissance were not avowed rebels against authority, least of all against Christianity; they were neither romantics clamoring for freedom of self-expression nor pagans wreathed in vine

leaves. And all historians agree that this was no great popular movement, toward more freedom for the many. Already full of the usual
contradictions, the Renaissance was further confused by a quite different, hostile movement that was also a "rebirth" but was much more
popular—the Protestant Reformation.

Yet a very real, important change unquestionably came over western
Europe during the period roughly dated 1400–1600—a change due to
what I think must still be called the Renaissance. To appreciate it, one
has only to turn from St. Bernard, St. Thomas, and Dante to Machiavelli, Montaigne, and Rabelais; or from the cathedral of Chartres to
St. Peter's and the Sistine Chapel. If it was not a deliberate revolution,
it did involve a great deal of conscious innovation and rejection. If all
the elements of the Renaissance may be found in the Middle Ages, there
was nonetheless a shift of emphasis that amounted to a basically new
spirit. Old ideas were expressed with a new fervor and intensity, and
enlisted much more energy; men were fired by new hopes of the possibilities of earthly life, a new faith in themselves. "Immortal God," cried
Erasmus in 1517, "what a world I see dawning! Why can I not grow
young again?" One can find few glimmers of this spirit in the Middle
Ages. Like most of the men of the Renaissance, Erasmus looked backward too and got his immediate inspiration from antiquity; but he
followed upon an amazing outburst of creative energy that had made
a world essentially different from both the classical and the medieval.
And though the Renaissance was not a movement toward political freedom—though it was marked, indeed, by the rise of tyranny in Italy
and of absolute monarchy over the rest of Europe—it plainly was a
movement toward intellectual and imaginative freedom, and effected
a lasting emancipation of mind and spirit. As it inspired in Jacob Burckhardt the first extensive study in cultural history, so it most clearly
illustrates the need of looking beyond political history.

The Renaissance was also sensual, licentious, and corrupt enough to
look decadent, and no doubt would be labeled so by historians had
Western civilization collapsed or been overwhelmed in the centuries
that followed. In the light of the actual aftermath it looks more like
a period of vigorous growth, the genesis of the modern world. In this
light we may anticipate not only the turbulence but the uncertainty,
complexity, and contradiction that have engendered such widely different accounts of the period.

So considered, the Renaissance got under way in Italy during the
fourteenth century, gathered its full momentum in the fifteenth century, and then spread throughout western Europe, in England cul-

minating in the Elizabethan Age. The Italians were quite conscious of their *rinascita*, or revival of classical culture. By now we can see that their art was essentially original, not truly classical, while scholars have thoroughly discredited the old textbook theory that the main cause of the Renaissance was the influx of Greek scholars upon the fall of Constantinople to the Turks; yet the ancient Greeks did have much to do with it. The rediscovery of their classics in the original was one of the most apparent inspirations of the new spirit, as many writers testified. Classical studies became central in the culture of the period, as never before or since. Artists, poets, and scholars talked continually of "the return of the Muses," the renewal of the "golden age" of classical antiquity, the restoration of its glory and grandeur after centuries of darkness. The conventional name of the period symbolizes at least a half-truth; for if not strictly a rebirth, the Renaissance was in fact distinguished by a resurgence of something like the Greek spirit.

Its most conspicuous sign likewise remains the conventional one—humanism. This was always a Christian humanism in ideal theory, and to a large extent in the actual feeling of its leading spokesmen. In effect, however, it differed profoundly from the humanism of the Middle Ages, or what Maritain calls the "true" humanism of St. Thomas Aquinas. It was centered more on the realization of man's own powers and the values of this life than on the service of God and salvation in the life to come. It stressed much more the possibilities of beauty and delight in the natural world, declaring (in the words of Browning's Fra Lippo Lippi) that "this world's no blot for us, nor blank—it means intensely, and means good." Similarly it was more hospitable to the claims of the natural man, who had been lusty enough in the Middle Ages but was then usually told that he was a sinful man. It laid more emphasis on the "high estate" of man, his "excellent dignity" instead of his depravity. It developed a specific cultural program, based on "studies of humanity," designed to promote this dignity. It led to ideals of civility, beyond chivalry or charity—the ideal type of the rounded gentleman instead of the knight or the saint. In everyday life men became more frankly devoted to the pursuit of worldly pleasure, wealth, power, and fame. Briefly, the pronounced secular quality of Western civilization stems from the Renaissance. The age has therefore been variously described, as "the discovery of the world and of man" (Burckhardt after Michelet) or as the real Fall of Christian man; but for better or worse —for liberty or license—it gave much wider scope and freer play to the human spirit.

With this self-conscious humanism came a growing rationalism, as both art and thought won autonomy from religion. Renaissance men often look naïve because of the flagrant contradictions between their Christian belief and their behavior, contradictions as fantastic as those of the Middle Ages, but they were more open-eyed, sophisticated, critical of both their theory and their practice. If they still did not proclaim an ideal of free inquiry and criticism (any more than the Greeks did), they more freely inquired and judged, in a spirit that anticipated later freethinkers. They rationalized their art, their statecraft, and their ethic as well as their business, often without reference to revealed truth. The self-styled Humanists in particular exalted the powers of "natural" reason rather than faith or grace, as a means to the improvement of man and civic life.[1] The high hopes of a golden age started some men dreaming of utopias, heralding the faith in progress.

Indeed, the men of the early Renaissance tended to be more self-confident than the Greeks had been, and considerably more exuberant. "Men can do anything with themselves if they will," affirmed Leon Battista Alberti; and he proved it by distinguishing himself in athletics, painting, architecture, music, literature, law, philosophy, and mathematics. The self-confidence exhibited by so many versatile artists led Columbus to discover a new world. The exceptional energy, passion, and willfulness that in the Middle Ages had been partially confined by Christian tradition, or obscured by pious fictions, now broke loose. Western civilization was on its singular way, from which there was no return. It would always be more dynamic, and more open, than either medieval or classical theory provided for.

Above all, the "new men" of the Renaissance wanted to be themselves, and many succeeded furiously, if sometimes only in getting beside themselves. There had been plenty of individuality and great personality in the Middle Ages, of course, and sufficient desire for fame and glory even apart from the knights and the kings; medieval artists were not so anonymous as pious tradition has it. But there was little provision for individualism in medieval theory, which emphasized the communal or the corporate body, and like medieval art subordinated the individual to the type. The accepted ideal was holiness, not personal greatness or originality; the principal end was to save oneself, not to know, realize, or express oneself; the primary virtues were humility and obedience, not self-reliance and enterprise. Now individualism

---

[1] I am capitalizing the term whenever I refer to the Italian Humanists, who made up a self-conscious school amounting to a profession.

became unabashed, again franker and prouder than in classical Greece, more vigorous perhaps than in any other historical period. A boundless passion for fame appears as early as Dante, beneath the medieval surface of the *Divine Comedy;* even the damned in hell beg him to keep alive their fame on earth—and as a poet he is very conscious and proud of his power to do so. (We may forget that the hero of the greatest Christian epic is the poet himself, that he has three heavenly ladies—including the Virgin—taking a personal interest in securing his salvation, and that he works himself into the very presence of God.) The Renaissance made a cult of not only the hero but the genius. Benvenuto Cellini wrote his own biography, as no Greek or medieval artist had ever done. Dr. Faustus showed up. So did the Nietzschean superman—another possibly ungodly type, who might nevertheless be worshipped almost as a god.

This highly self-conscious individual takes us to the heart of the Renaissance drama. His liberation is one of the most distinctive achievements of Western civilization, justifying the observation of L. L. Whyte that never before has mankind owed so much to so many. But this individualist obviously can be an egotist, an immoralist, a tyrant; in this age he commonly had little sense of social responsibility; and he contributed his full share to the heavy costs that we must keep in mind as we survey its achievements. Renaissance Italy repeated the tragedy of classical Greece, on a larger, bloodier scale. Here creative energy proved even more turbulent and destructive. All through the period the Italian city-states warred on one another, while they were also racked by internal strife, a legacy of civil war between Guelph and Ghibelline that reached an almost incredible pitch of virulence and frenzy.[2] They failed to unite against the growing menace of France and Spain, as against the constant ambition of the Papacy. All but Venice and Rome finally lost their independence, and with it their creativity.

Hence historians now talk of a "counter-Renaissance," a later phase of disenchantment or revulsion, symbolized by such thinkers as Machiavelli and Montaigne. From the outset, however, a dark pessimistic strain ran through the thought of the Renaissance. It was a natural reflection of the ceaseless violence and corruption of the age. While

---

[2] These famous parties that kept Italy split for two centuries sprang from the struggle between the popes and the German emperors, the Guelphs siding with the popes, the Ghibellines with the emperors. They may be passed over in this history, however, because they soon lost sight of any clear or high political principles. Chiefly they battled over control of their native cities, and in victory offered them nothing better than their own exclusive rule.

hailing the dawn of a golden age, Erasmus had also exclaimed over "this marvellously corrupt world," especially the iniquities of tyranny and avarice; and other celebrants of the age repeatedly lamented its passion for the wrong kind of gold. A deeper reason for the disenchantment was anxiety sprung from the medieval religious conscience, still very much alive. Even apart from their many sins, the classical culture cherished by Renaissance men was secular, naturalistic, pagan—not wholly compatible, after all, with Christian tradition, especially medieval tradition. A Michelangelo was still liable to the old fears that made the aging Petrarch beg the Lord to forgive him for having written the works by which he won his enduring fame.

In any case, the exciting possibilities realized by the Renaissance carried their own penalties. The discovery of man and the world was bound to lead to an apprehension that he is not simply a creature of "excellent dignity," and that his "high estate" is highly uncertain in the natural world, which as it means more intensely means evil too. Dr. Faustus would learn that he could not do or know everything he had a will to. With more critical sense would come more uncertainty about the nature of man, the meaning and purpose of his life, and so a wider range for skepticism and pessimism. With full self-consciousness came Montaigne, and then Hamlet: the complete man of the Renaissance, the most eloquent spokesman of the whole gamut of its emotions— except, perhaps, its Christian hope and faith. Montaigne and Shakespeare had a much more penetrating insight into the nature of man than most formal philosophers have had, and in a history of freedom represent a sufficiently impressive culmination of the Renaissance. But the key to their wisdom is a statement by Montaigne: "I have nothing to say entirely, simply, and with solidity of myself, without confusion, disorder, blending, mingling, nor in one word." This is as far a cry from the exuberant self-confidence of the early Renaissance as from the faith of the Middle Ages.

2. *Florence, the "Second Athens"*

The naturalistic, humanistic culture of the Italian Renaissance had plain enough sources. While Christianity contributed to its inspiration, it grew as obviously out of the spiritual decay or the failures of the Church; Rome played little part in it until toward the end, when

worldly popes set about glorifying their capital. More obviously it grew
out of the worldly interests of the bourgeoisie, who had given Italy the
commercial leadership of Europe. It reflected the rise of this class to
political power, more than they enjoyed elsewhere in Europe; it expressed their enterprise and individualism, the growing power of brains
as well as money; it flourished on the wealth they created, as on their
civic pride. So its most famous patrons, the Medici, were the rulers of
Florence and among the great bankers of Europe.

Italy was also the natural birthplace of the Renaissance as the most
urbanized land in Europe, the farthest removed from the medieval
order of estates. North Italy, that is: southern Italy, which remained
feudal and had no large city except Naples, had very little to do with
the new movement. After a valiant struggle against the German
emperors, the towns in the north had succeeded in getting their freedom recognized by treaty, and then had resisted efforts at papal domination too. They grew into city-states small enough to enjoy an intimate,
vivid life of their own, but prosperous and powerful enough generally
to maintain their independence. They early broke the power of the
feudal nobility; Italy was the one land where the nobility moved into
the cities and took to the ways of the burghers. Always busy in commerce and industry, they had a strong secular bent throughout the
Middle Ages; while the University of Paris became the center of
theology Bologna built up important schools of medicine, mathematics,
and law. In their city-states Italians were likewise closest to classical
tradition. They had more vivid memories of ancient Rome, lived
among more remains of its urban culture; and through trade and
diplomatic relations with Constantinople theirs was the first land to
entertain Greek scholars.

Even so, these conditions do not adequately account for the burst
of creativity, or for the enthusiasm over the discovery of the Greeks.
Venice, the oldest and wealthiest of the Italian city-states, did not take
the lead in the Renaissance; other thriving cities, such as Genoa, contributed little or nothing to it. We are led to the extraordinary role of
Florence. Far and away the most brilliant city of the Renaissance, it
was the main center and recognized leader, becoming known as the
"second Athens." In all history it was indeed second only to Athens in
the astonishing amount and variety of genius it produced—from Dante,
Giotto, Petrarch, and Boccaccio through Ghiberti, Brunelleschi, Donatello, Masaccio, and many other major artists to Machiavelli, Leonardo
da Vinci, and Michelangelo. The story of the Florentine Republic is

one of the most provocative, instructive chapters in the history of human freedom.

Business played a major role here too. Only a small provincial town under the Roman Empire, Florence rose on industry and international commerce much as Athens had. Early in the Middle Ages it became known for its manufactured cloth, and in the thirteenth century renowned for its gold florin; this was accepted as standard all over Europe, matching the prestige of the Athenian owl in the ancient world. A little later, however, Florence began producing such geniuses as Dante and Giotto: men who were scarcely typical bourgeois, and who force some further considerations. The emergence of genius remains unaccountable as unpredictable; we can only say that once a cultural movement gets started it may gather momentum, and stimulate latent genius that otherwise would have been unrealized—as presumably a very great deal is unrealized during ages of torpor or routine life. Nevertheless, we can make out in Florence at least one distinctive factor. It not only won its independence but early developed a tradition of political freedom, which remained alive until the end of its brilliant period. As with Athens, such freedom too is by no means a sufficient explanation of its extraordinary creativity, else the democratic world today would be all aglow; but there is as good reason to believe that it had a good deal to do with this creativity.

Now, Florence was never a full-fledged democracy. Efforts to make it one were invariably short-lived; in effect it was mostly ruled by an oligarchy. Yet it always had an active citizenry, a vigorous public life, and something of a democratic tradition that its rulers were usually careful to heed. Early in the twelfth century we hear of consuls and a citizen assembly. In the middle of the next century a democratic regime made history by giving the city its famous coat of arms (red lily on a white field), issuing its gold florin, starting its tradition of civic architecture by building the Palazzo del Podestà, and battling rival cities with such vigor that Florentines always remembered the year 1254 as "the year of victory." Toward the end of the century another democratic regime issued the Ordinances of Justice, the most celebrated act in its political history, which imposed severe penalties on magnates or nobles guilty of violence against the common people. Thereafter the Florentines kept on running through constitutions, usually resulting from class war, but tending to keep them as politically conscious as the Greeks had been in their *polis,* and as indisposed to stand in awe of their rulers. Conflict between rich and poor did not prevent free and

easy intercourse between them, nor smother the pronounced individuality for which the Florentines were known. When tyrannies arose
all over Italy in the fourteenth century, Florence remained an exception; its tradition was enriched by the impassioned love of liberty expressed by such men as Boccaccio and Salutati, a chancellor of the
republic. When finally the Medici did impose a virtual tyranny in the
following century, they were less despotic than tyrants elsewhere,
established no official court, had much popular support, and kept up
some democratic appearances. At the end of the century democratic
sentiment was still strong enough to drive them out and set up another
republican constitution.

If we can never be certain how inspiring this tradition was, its importance is no matter of mere conjecture either. Much of the vigorous
intellectual activity that made Florence the leader of the Italian Renaissance was directly connected with its active public life, and so too were
some of its major works of art. While elsewhere tyrants soon made a
fashion of patronizing artists and Humanists, thereby contributing
something to the Renaissance, one apparent reason why Florence contributed so much more was that its art, like that of Athens, was more
a civic product, of, by, and for the people. It may be too much to say
that artists again had a great audience, but at least they were repeatedly
stimulated by the civic tradition exemplified early in the fourteenth
century, when Giotto was appointed chief architect and engineer of
the republic, and authorized to design his Campanile in fulfillment of
the public decree: "The Florentine Republic desires that an edifice
should be constructed so magnificent in its height and quality that it
shall surpass anything of the kind produced in the time of their greatest
power by the Greeks and Romans."

The nominal republic of Venice offers the most suggestive contrast,
if still an inconclusive one. The city of St. Mark's and Marco Polo had
been a great city long before Florence, as the only one in Italy that had
preserved its independence since early in the Dark Ages, and it would
remain independent up to the time of Napoleon, long after the republic
of Florence went down. For most of the thousand years of its history
its government was an almost pure aristocracy, on the face of it about
the most vigorous, intelligent, and enlightened of its kind in history.
While professing no democratic nonsense, its rulers succeeded in keeping their subjects contented; throughout the turmoil of the Middle
Ages and the Renaissance, the common people of Venice never rose
up against them. Unlike the feudal aristocracy, they maintained in

their elegant *palazzi* a tradition of high culture. Nevertheless, their dominant motives remained purely commercial, and could look more sordid because of their formal piety; they also made a name for themselves by their addiction to hired murderers, secret trials, and brutal punishments. The patriotism of Venice was linked with no ideal cause, no concern for the freedom of Italy or of man. Its common people were fine craftsmen, and no doubt were more contented than the restless Florentines, but they remained politically passive. And during the ferment of the fourteenth and fifteenth centuries Venice produced very few men to match the great Florentines. Like other Italian cities it hired a Florentine, Verrocchio, when it wanted a public statue. Later it did produce the great school of Titian; but one can scarcely imagine a Dante or a Michelangelo coming out of Venice.

The contrast was accentuated by a little-known but possibly momentous war. In *The Crisis of the Early Italian Renaissance,* Hans Baron argues that the major innovations in art, shortly after 1400, were at least partly inspired by ideals of civic freedom, enflamed by a heroic stand Florence had made comparable to the stand of Athens against the Persian Empire. The crisis came in the closing years of the fourteenth century when Duke Giangaleazzo of Milan, a powerful tyrant, sought dominion over all Italy. Florence led the resistance to him but was unable to build up a united front; Venice refused support, its allies gave way one by one, until finally the city stood alone. Its trade cut off, facing economic as well as military disaster, it nevertheless prepared to defend itself against the all-conquering duke. It was spared the final test by a plague that killed him in 1402; but Baron maintains that the memory of its conduct during the national emergency deeply affected the character and thought of the Florentines in the years that followed, much as Athenians were inspired by the memory of Marathon and Salamis.

This thesis is all too attractive to a student of freedom, even if it gives disagreeable prominence to the role of accident. (Except for that plague, it follows, there might have been no major innovations.) Still, Baron amply documents it. If Florentines overrated their ideal role as defenders of freedom, many evidently did feel this way.[3] Contemporary

---

[3] To cite an unillustrious example, one Gregorio Dati wrote a *History of Florence 1380–1406,* subtitled "History of the long and most important Italian war which took place in our day between the Tyrant of Lombardy and the magnificent Commune of Florence." Dati emphasized that the once free men of Milan had been changed into mere subjects. "And one may say," he concluded, "that all the freedom of Italy lay in the hands of the Florentines alone, that every other power had deserted them." The desertion of Venice he blamed on its oligarchy.

Humanists, notably Leonardo Bruni, handed down to posterity apostrophes to Liberty—"Liberty without which no republic can exist, and without which, the wisest men have held, one should not live." Bruni explicitly drew the parallel of Florence and Athens, the savior of Greece against the Persians, and in a Funeral Oration took over the argument of Pericles, asserting that Florence was the school of culture for all Italy; he added that political freedom was essential to culture, as the Greeks had proved. Correspondingly he introduced a new view of the Roman Republic, glorifying it instead of Julius Caesar; the loss of freedom, he argued (and Machiavelli later agreed), was fatal to Rome. Florentines proceeded to embroider a new theory of their origins, rejecting the fond tradition that Caesar had founded their city in favor of an earlier founding under the Roman Republic, from which they had inherited their love of liberty. This myth helped to inspire such works as Michelangelo's statue of David—wrought during another national crisis, as David was a symbolic champion of freedom.

Italian historians have generally lamented the failure of Milan, which might otherwise have united Italy under its dominion. Most other historians are inclined to believe that the achievements of the Florentine Republic were ample compensation for the loss of another absolute monarchy, especially because still powerful Milan contributed much less to the Renaissance. Florence did in fact become the school of culture for Italy, as Athens had been for Greece; its artists were in demand all over the land, while its workshops drew many other Italians. From Italy its influence radiated over western Europe, with the help of the Florentine invention of metal engraving.[4]

We may then pause to wonder how much difference the art of these Florentines made in Western history. Though as always we can never be sure, we must believe that it counted for something in so far as we are committed to the values of self-realization, the ends of freedom; and at least there is no better case in European history for the possible importance of art as a positive force. This becomes plainer if we look beyond specific, traceable influences to the whole humanistic movement in which the Florentines figured so prominently, and which deeply affected the climate of Western opinion. For art was now more self-conscious and autonomous, more plainly a means to the enhance-

---

[4] Bernard Berenson remarked that one of the most heartening histories yet to be written is this peaceful penetration of Italian art into the rest of Europe. Florentine artists worked in France, Spain, Portugal, and England (where one carved the tomb of Henry VII in Westminster Abbey), even got as far as Moscow and Delhi. Countless European painters, from Dürer to Rembrandt and Velásquez, visited Italy or studied its masterpieces.

mẹnt of earthly life, than it had been since the Greeks. If not the main cause, it was a major expression of the Renaissance spirit—the new awareness of man and nature, the new confidence in man's powers, the sense of new possibilities. It demonstrated most triumphantly the actual freedom of the human spirit. It was intimately connected, as we shall see, with the rise of science, which we all know made a world of difference. At least the change that came over Florentine art in the early 1400's seems more significant than many reigns and wars that have taken up long chapters in histories.

This change was heralded a century earlier by Dante and especially Giotto. In spite of his otherworldly concerns, Dante's epic—the first major work in the vernacular—was filled with the business of this world, rendered with a vivid realism, and in it he paraded all the science and natural philosophy he knew. Giotto, a simple countryman, correspondingly painted his frescoes in a vernacular style. Whereas both Byzantine and Gothic art were designed primarily to inspire a sense of mystery and awe, he pictured man and nature more freely as he saw them, with more attention to human emotion, much less of the conventional symbolism. As Ghiberti wrote a century later, he deserved the "highest praise" for having "brought into being art according to nature." And even apart from the host of imitators he inspired, Giotto set the tradition for the great age of Florence. He was a practical, civic-minded man, who suitably adorned his Campanile with bas-reliefs of Law, Mechanics, Metallurgy, etc. He was as prolific and versatile as most of the greater artists would be, not only a painter but a sculptor, architect, and engineer. He did much to establish the prestige and the independence of the artist, who in medieval tradition was ranked as a mechanic and took orders from prince or bishop, for he won wealth and fame, becoming the most popular citizen of Florence.

The major inspiration as well as the subject matter of Giotto's paint-ing was unmistakably Christian, and it long remained so with his suc-cessors, at the cost of some monotony. (Even the pious tourist may feel a little weary after the hundredth Madonna with Bambino.) Yet it was his naturalistic, humanistic impulse that won the future. Since current fashions in art may make naturalism seem a cramping style, we should note that in the early Renaissance it was spontaneous, unforced, or genuinely "natural," and an emancipation of the mind and the eye. Immediately it signified that men felt more at home in the natural world, freer to enjoy its forms, in the conviction that these were signifi-cant as well as beautiful forms. By 1400 Cennini, a self-conscious disciple of Giotto, explicitly glorified the imaginative freedom and power of the arts, asserting that they were a direct means of apprehending reality, second only to science.

The historic change that then came over art owed much to classical inspiration. Ghiberti collected many marble and bronze relics of antiquity for close study, while Brunelleschi and Donatello spent several years together in Rome poring over its ruins; like most of the artists after them, they thought that classical art was "according to nature" and were fired by a hope of emulating its "noble perfection." As plain a stimulus, however, was the civic pride of republican Florence. The new movement may be dated from a public competition for the honor of decorating a door of its Baptistry, decreed in 1402 (the year when Duke Giangaleazzo of Milan died) and won by Ghiberti. He proceeded to spend most of his life on the world-famous bronze panels that Michelangelo thought worthy of the gates of Paradise, and that were no copy of anything known from antiquity. In his pride he inserted between the panels sculptured heads of his assistants and himself, while he also left his personal signature in an autobiography, the first we have of an artist.

Meanwhile Brunelleschi, a gracious loser in the competition, was stirring as much civic enthusiasm by his still freer, bolder experiments in architecture. "Sent by heaven to revive architecture" as Giotto had painting (so his biographer Vasari thought), he won a later public competition for the honor of crowning the cathedral of Florence with his dome—the first great dome in Europe since antiquity. Not even the ancients, he assured his fellow citizens, had raised a vault as immense as his would be; even so he would build it without columns, without scaffolding, without the help of any other architect; and he did in fact see it through all by himself. If there is some question of the beauty or the heaven-sent inspiration of his dome (which to my taste is less handsome than the domes of Ottoman mosques), there is no question of Brunelleschi's technical mastery and his superb self-confidence, symbolizing a period when artists seem to have paid little in frustration for their exciting sense of opportunity. One may therefore be more impressed by the serener air of his classical churches, such as San Lorenzo and the Pazzi chapel. Since he was a pioneer, initiating the conventional cycle that leads to a peak, his art had reason to be somewhat tentative, awkward, or "archaic"; but even devotees of cycles grant its maturity and sureness. Similarly those who consider the Byzantine and Gothic styles better suited than the classical to the mystery of the Mass may still admire the dignity of these churches, appreciate his aspiration to perfect clarity, symmetry, and order. In any case, Brunelleschi's art was a highly distinctive creation. It was no less original because he boasted of "restoring" the classical style, for he freely adapted this style to new purposes, in new forms.

Donatello had much the same spirit as he "restored" the classical art of sculpture, in as original a style. While he adorned many churches with reliefs, he went on to emancipate sculpture from architecture and to explore its possibilities as an independent art. His David was the first freestanding nude statue modeled since antiquity, the more daring in its nudity because its subject was a biblical hero. It raises once more the question of Christian inspiration, for it has no biblical feeling whatever; David is simply a charming Renaissance youth who looks silly if one tries to cast him in a religious role. Though other of Donatello's works are as pious as one could wish, the essential humanism of his art appears in the prodigal variety of his sculpture, including a great equestrian statue, a cantoria adorned with angels who are lifelike youngsters, a biblical Judith cutting off the head of a tyrant, a tender Annunciation with the most demure of Madonnas, an ultrarealistic, haggard, harrowing Mary Magdalene. This variety might have sprung from restlessness, the tension or torment of a Michelangelo. In Donatello one feels only versatility, ease, freedom, assurance—the self-confidence of his friend Brunelleschi; including a confidence, one supposes, that God approves such pleasure in the bodily forms of his creation.

In the young painter nicknamed Masaccio ("Dirty Tom") one may feel more tension, but of a kind due to the complete absorption in his art that made him careless of his dress. The little Carmine chapel in Florence to which he added a few frescoes, before his premature death, was enough to mark a decisive turning point in the history of art. Here a predecessor, Masolino, had painted Adam and Eve leaving the Garden: figures realistic by fourteenth-century standards, but static, expressionless, and framed by a painted-on landscape. Masaccio painted the same scene: an Adam and Eve with faces distorted by grief, howling, stumbling in flight, against an impressionistic background with a sense of depth. Striking individualized faces and figures in other frescoes likewise appear in movement against backgrounds with depth. Among other things, Masaccio had virtually created the art of perspective. That it now seems obvious—that this is the way we naturally see the world— only emphasizes his originality; for neither classical nor medieval art has perspective. We need not ask the question of the depth of his religious feeling, since Christian inspiration would hardly account for this new technique; whatever he felt, Masaccio was thinking as a painter, concentrating on artistic rather than religious content. Other painters were at once enthralled by his discovery. ("How fair a thing is this perspective!" exclaimed Paolo Uccello.) The Carmine chapel became a school for the celebrated artists of the century, down through Leonardo da Vinci, Michelangelo, and Raphael. "By the perfection of his work," wrote Leonardo, Masaccio showed "how those who took as their standard anything other than nature, the supreme guide of all the masters, were wearying themselves in vain."

According to Vasari, Masaccio's immediate object was to emulate Brunelleschi by giving his figures animation. Together, at any rate, they represent the great animating achievement of the early Renaissance. Although medieval art was full of naïve realism, from gaunt statues to lively carvings of tipplers, its human figures lacked a natural frame, a humanized perspective, a human stage; they were subordinated to supernatural or otherworldly concerns. Now the human scene was rendered more deliberately, coherently, rationally, for its own sake as well. Thus Brunelleschi gave his churches the wall lacking in Gothic cathedrals, clearly defining and ordering space, clearly separating this human scene from the void; Masaccio gave space a comparable order and by perspective added a more obvious human focus, creating an appropriate theater for the natural images of man. This walled, ordered world was a world of man's own, secure, calculable, and controllable. In the words of Bernard Berenson, "Space-composition is the art which humanizes the void, making of it an enclosed Eden." At the same time, the new Eden was not simply an enclosure, for the perspective of Masaccio corresponded to the new sense of horizons, or of an open world. Whether this whole technical advance represented a "spiritual" advance, or brought men closer to God, will depend on one's conception of God and the proper uses of God's world; but at least it helped men to realize more fully their humanity, the essential means to true spirituality. And art itself was open for the further reason that in becoming self-conscious and highly professional it had not yet become genteel or academic, bound by formal rule. It was more liberating than the traditional "liberal arts" because (alas for the academic historian) it was wholly independent of the universities, which directly contributed nothing to it.

This is not the place to evaluate or review in detail the work of the many other celebrated architects, sculptors, and painters of fifteenth-

century Florence—Alberti, Michelozzo, the della Robbias, the Pollaiu-
olos, Botticelli, Fra Angelico, Fra Lippo Lippi, Castagno, Ghirlandaio,
Rossellino, Verrocchio, etc. Suffice it that no cities of its size today could
match even its many lesser known artists. As for the major developments, the most conspicuous was the subordination of religion to
secular or profane interests. (It was typified by Benozzo Gozzoli's
"Procession of the Magi," in which the religious subject is merely an
excuse for a gorgeous pageant, featuring portraits of the Medici and
other Florentines arrayed in all their finery.) But most portentous was
a kind of naturalism that heralded the rise of science.

The long Florentine tradition of fine craftsmanship had involved
much empirical knowledge. Ghiberti asserted that an artist must master
many branches of knowledge, including mathematics, optics, and
anatomy. Brunelleschi, reputed to have studied with Toscanelli, a
famous Florentine mathematician, was much concerned with geometric
space—the objective, measurable, divisible space of science. Alberti, the
first art critic in Europe, wrote scientific treatises on painting, sculpture, and architecture in which he stressed the congruity of the laws
of art and of nature, and drew upon mathematics to formulate his
theories. ("Painting is nothing other than a cross section of a visual
pyramid upon a certain surface.") Both anatomy and geometry were
studied intensively in the workshops of the masters. In general, the
leading artists all assumed what some said in so many words, that art
"according to nature" embodied principles of order, that it truly represented essential reality—in effect that truth is beauty and beauty is
truth, only you needed to know a great deal more about both. In
particular, the workshop of Verrocchio in Florence became a center of
empirical, scientific studies; and in this shop was trained the young
Leonardo da Vinci.

At once painter, sculptor, architect, engineer, inventor, mathematician, naturalist, anatomist, and what have you, Leonardo was not
merely a universal genius but the most striking example of the union
of art and science in a common empirical tradition. Although not a
systematic inquirer, with clear principles by which to order or conclude
his findings, he was a close observer of all natural phenomena, from
fossils to stars, and a thorough dissecter. In the Notebooks in which he
sketched and recorded his observations, he also speculated on everything under the sun, no longer in the a priori terms of the medieval
Schoolmen. "Experiment," he wrote, "is the true interpreter between
nature and man." Out of this tradition came the work of Vesalius,

who discoursed on the "art" of medicine and illustrated it with painstaking drawings. Another line from the thought of Leonardo leads straight to Galileo and Newton; for his studies of perspective, geometric space, anatomy, and mechanics led him to the conclusion that mathematics was the key to reality. "No human inquiry can be called true science," he remarked, "unless it proceeds through mathematical demonstrations."

When nearing death, according to Vasari, Leonardo "made every effort to acquaint himself with the doctrine of the Catholic ritual"—presumably the one subject he had overlooked in the course of his encyclopedic studies. But his secular interests, in particular his studies of such Greek masters as Archimedes, bring up another major contribution of the versatile, many-sided Florentines to the life of the mind. Florence was the earliest and for a long time the main center of Humanism, the first important secular movement to sweep over the Western world. In view of the social, economic, and political realities of the Renaissance, these very academic Humanists may look absurdly ineffectual—until again we take a long view. For they became famous all over Europe, and the movement they started eventually dominated Western thought.

Now, this again was by no means a simple, direct movement toward freedom. Immediately, the Humanists were pious antiquarians, harking back to the ancients for authority. Their classicism generally put a higher premium on rhetoric and learned imitation than on independent thought and original writing; their descendants would saddle poetry and drama with arbitrary rules, set up Aristotle's *Poetics* as the supreme authority just when his authority in philosophy and science was finally overthrown. Outside of Florence they were mostly self-conscious aristocrats, contemptuous of the common people, often of the vernacular; their classicism came down to a classiness that helped to establish the genteel tradition that divorced literature and learning from practical interests and the common life. Many served at the courts of princes or tyrants, whom they flattered to little avail but their own keep as house pets. As many became pedants and snobs, superficial, conceited, arrogant, and as sterile as the medieval Schoolmen they displanted. By the sixteenth century Italians were learning to despise when not to hate them.

Outside of Italy, however, humanism was then embarking on a career more in keeping with its origins. For it had begun as a renewal—a healthy response to the spiritual decay of the Church and the intellectual barrenness of Scholasticism. Petrarch, its traditional "father," had got more than an academic excitement from his discovery of some Greek manuscripts. Weary of dogmatic quibble and strife, angry at ecclesiastical corruption, but still devoted to the world and his art (not to mention Laura), he had found in antiquity the wisdom and virtue wanting in his own time. It was a glorified antiquity, to be sure, all Ciceronian virtue; yet he had more understanding of its actual content than had the pious twelfth-century "dwarfs" seated on the shoulders of the ancients. He could better appreciate its distinctive ideals, its distance from the medieval world (just as he was incidentally the first known man to climb a mountain merely for the fun of it, or the view). He learned just enough Greek to realize, as no one yet had, the importance of the Greek culture that lay behind the Roman, and that had educated his beloved Cicero. In enthroning Cicero he exalted an ethic of civic responsibility that could supplement the medieval ethic of faith, hope, and charity. Similarly Petrarch began popularizing the term "Europe" instead of "Christendom." Though still a devout Christian too, looking rather uneasy in his conventional role as the "first modern man," he nevertheless set up classical studies as an essentially independent cultural program—no longer a servant of theology. His works brought him a fame that inspired or emboldened other men to concentrate on these still suspect "studies of humanity," and so to carry on an intellectual revolution that would go far beyond Petrarch's intentions.

Even as a purely scholarly affair, the new humanism had a significant influence. It initiated a close critical study of ancient texts that immediately led to the exposure of medieval forgeries, for instance Lorenzo Valla's celebrated denunciation of the "Donation of Constantine." Scholars recovered such seminal classics as Lucretius' *On the Nature of Things,* which acquainted thinkers with the Greek atomic theory and the Epicurean philosophy, and Plutarch's *Lives,* for generations the most popular sourcebook of the antique tradition of liberty. By translation they made widely available for the first time almost the whole body of Greek literature. In Florence scholar-patriots like Leonardo Bruni bent this learning to civic interests, made it a means to political education, specifically a schooling in ideals of liberty. Elsewhere the Humanists generally remained academic types, when not supporters of tyrants, but even so they aided the cause of liberty by making the literature of Greece and Rome the core of education. Their curriculum, more truly liberal than the medieval liberal arts, could inspire a humanism broader than their own.

In Florence one important offshoot of the movement was a school of enthusiastic, if half-baked Platonists led by Marsilio Ficino, who translated Plato complete. From the master they derived an optimistic idealism, in which Platonic love and beauty were blended with mathematics, magic, and "heavenly" intelligences; but it effectively stressed man's divine faculty of reason, the power and freedom of his spirit, increasingly a wisdom apart from revelation. With the renowned Pico della Mirandola it became a religion of Humanity, so bold as to reject the doctrine of Original Sin. In his *Discourse on the Dignity of Man* Pico had God give the son of Adam a new revelation: "By the free will of thy spirit thou canst regenerate thyself a godlike being." Meanwhile other Florentines were cultivating earthier modes of humanism. In the fourteenth century Boccaccio, whose *Decameron* became immensely popular by virtue of its frankly secular spirit, wrote a simple life of Dante that was no less a landmark as the first notable example of biography, a new literary form suited to the individualism of the age; the Middle Ages had had only biographies of saints, largely mythical, turned out for religious purposes. Shortly afterward Villani, a still prouder Florentine, inaugurated another major tradition by writing the history of Florence—a mélange of legend and fact that was no work of genius, but was distinguished by more effort to get at the facts than medieval chroniclers had made. Florentine Humanists then took the lead in the development of history as a critical inquiry, an effort at understanding instead of mere chronicling or celebrating. Their endeavors culminated in the works of Machiavelli and Guicciardini, the first European historians of consequence.

With Machiavelli, however, we come to the end of the great days of Florence; and immediately we are forced to reconsider the issues of its freedom. Concerned almost exclusively with political and military events, his *History of Florence* (1525) is a depressing narrative of incessant strife, both civil and foreign war. It expresses little civic pride, none of the republican zeal that appears in his *Discourses;* about the best he has to say for the Florentines here is that "though unable to preserve their liberty they cannot endure slavery." He had plain enough reasons for his disillusionment, as he had himself been jailed and tortured upon the fall of a republican regime, and in a few more years the Florentine Republic would be no more. But he forces the issues of its freedom for other reasons too, which do him less credit as a historian. While he hardly mentions the extraordinary cultural achievement of Florence, he expresses nothing but admiration for the Medici, the popular symbols of its great days; and it was their house that made its last days ignominious, by Machiavelli's own standards.

To a considerable extent these Medici had merited his admiration. Cosimo, who started ruling in 1434, set the style of the dynasty: though a bourgeois parvenu, he was content to rule as a natural aristocrat, without the trappings of rank or royalty. He was as enlightened as generous a patron of letters and the arts, commissioning the likes of Brunelleschi and Donatello, opening the first important public library in Europe, and setting up an academy for Platonic studies, enabling the ardent young Marsilio Ficino to devote his life to Plato. Thirty years of generally statesmanlike rule entitled him to his burial as "Father of his Country." Likewise his grandson Lorenzo the Magnificent—addressed even in letters from his wife as "Magnificent Consort" —earned his title and fame by his personal qualities. He too was an able statesman, devoted to the arts of diplomacy instead of war, sufficiently liberal and public-spirited to be as sincerely mourned upon his death. Himself an ardent Humanist and a writer of talent, he was both an inspired and an inspiring patron of learning and art, perhaps the most illustrious in European history. Among the distinguished company he invited to live as guests in his *palazzo* was a poor boy not yet known as Michelangelo.

But Michelangelo later renounced the Medici as tyrants, for good cause. However enlightened, they belonged to the breed that was arbitrarily ruling other cities; their power finally rested on chicanery, bribery, and force. The illegitimacy of their rule kept them jealous and suspicious of all potential opposition, made them sometimes harsh and cruel. Lorenzo the Magnificent undermined the morale of the Florentines as well by distracting them with pageants and festivals, while setting a brilliant example in the vices of the age. At the end the Magnificent demonstrated the essential weakness of dynastic rule by bequeathing Florence his disgraceful son Piero as his heir. He showed better historical sense by dying in 1492; for the year in which the new world was discovered signaled the end of the old one in Florence.

Two years later Piero was driven out of the city, after signing a humiliating treaty that had permitted the King of France to make a triumphant entry into it. The restored republic was no match, however, for the powers of France, Spain, and the Papacy, now intriguing and battling for control of Italy. Before long the Medici returned under Cardinal Giovanni, another son bequeathed by the Magnificent: Lorenzo had persuaded the pope to make this one a cardinal at the age of fourteen. Giovanni then became Pope Leo X, entering his high office in the spirit of his legendary saying: "Now that God has given us the Papacy, let us enjoy it." Florence did not long share in his pleasure. Leo handed it over to Cardinal Giulio, a Medici bastard, who succeeded him as Clement VII, the most calamitous of the Renaissance popes; Clement dug up two more Medici bastards to serve as rulers of Florence. So the sordid drama went on, until the city found itself facing the forces of both the pope and Charles V, Holy Roman emperor. Finally, in 1530, it surrendered. The next year Clement ended the Florentine Republic forever by abolishing its constitution and appointing still another bastard as hereditary duke. The new regime survived the assassination of its hand-picked lord to become the Grand Duchy of Tuscany, drop all pretense of popular government, and make a history of no further consequence.

We are left, then, with the failure of Florence—and of the whole Italian Renaissance. In the main it is as easy to understand as the failure of ancient Athens. It involves the familiar story of the corruptions of selfish ambition, jealousy, envy, and greed. All were intensified by the rampant individualism of the age and by its enormous energy, the famous *terribilità* apparent even in Dante. Grown more sophisticated, men now knew better than the rude knights and barons before them; yet we have countless examples of incredible barbarity—such as King Ferrante of Naples, showing off as an after-dinner treat his private museum, a choice collection of the stuffed corpses of his enemies. Short of such barbarity, a callous, mercenary spirit pervaded the highest social and cultural circles. Humanists were pleased to agree with Conversino that tyranny was the means to the only "true" freedom for scholars and writers. Leonardo da Vinci himself said simply: "I serve the one who pays me"; and he in fact served as engineer for such enemies of Florence as the Duke of Milan and the King of France, dying in the service of the latter.

The basic familiarity of the story might warn us, however, against some familiar explanations. The sins of the Renaissance were not clearly due to its "paganism," or loss of religious faith. Outside of some learned circles there was as yet little apparent skepticism about the basic Christian doctrines; common people, merchants, and princes alike were mostly as orthodox in belief, as faithful in ceremonial worship, or as devout in superstition. The obvious irreligion was of the sort common in the Middle Ages—the fantastic gap between belief and behavior. (It was typified by Sigismondo Malatesta, who even in this age won a reputation for surpassing wickedness, and who in Rimini built the famous church consecrated to St. Francis and named after himself, where he lies with his mistress, having purchased perpetual Masses to assure the eternal peace of their souls.) Likewise the violence of the Renaissance was a medieval heritage. The tower-houses surviving from thirteenth-century Florence, then a dense forest of such fortresses, are another reminder that the "Age of Faith" was also an age of incessant strife. In this view the Italian Renaissance failed to solve the social, political, and spiritual problems it inherited—the problems that made Dante despair of his age, and made Petrarch look to classical antiquity. The failure looks worse because of the growing rationalism and critical sense, the abundant enterprise displayed in art and thought; certainly the Renaissance was uncreative socially and politically, its rulers were much less enterprising than the early medieval burghers had been. But immediately the most conspicuous failure was again the moral, spiritual failure of the Church.

"We Italians owe it to the Church and the priests that we have become faithless and wicked," Machiavelli wrote, and Guicciardini was even more emphatic about "the tyranny of these vile priests." They perhaps wrote too bitterly, no doubt too simply; but at least the Renaissance popes remain as notorious as they were in their own day for crime and corruption.[5] Apart from their licentiousness, they seemed bent on proving Boccaccio's remark that the Roman Church must be of divine origin to stand the kind of government it had. In the last decades of the Florentine Republic their chief concern was power politics, which they played without scruple. Otherwise the one religious need that the

---

[5] There is no doubt either that many of the lurid stories about them are untrue. Scrupulous historians have sifted the evidence against the most infamous of them, the Borgia Pope Alexander VI, and revealed that he was not actually the monster he was universally reputed to be. Still, the most they can say for him is that his methods and morals were no worse than those of other rulers, which is also to say that he was nothing of a spiritual leader. For the rest, the Renaissance popes themselves made it almost impossible to do them exact justice. Their sins were so blatant that contemporaries were always disposed to believe the worst about them; so charges of fabulous crimes stuck to them as readily as tales of miracles to saints, and it is now often as hard to refute the one as to prove the other.

In poetic justice one might note an indirect contribution that Alexander VI made to the science of medicine. His personal physician wrote the best treatise on syphilis at the time, having had the advantage of treating and studying seventeen cases of it in the pope's family and court.

Church served conscientiously was the popular need for external forms, or for miracle and mystery, symbolized by the SS. Annunziata Church in Florence: the church most venerated by the Florentines, because the most famous for miracle and cure. (It is today a baroque horror, full of gilt splendors, while Brunelleschi's San Lorenzo still lacks a façade.) In Florence too the failure of the Church was dramatized most somberly by Savonarola. A fierce prophet of very literal faith, he denounced at once the tyranny of Lorenzo the Magnificent, the vices of the citizenry, and the corruption of the Church. He was so eloquent that his sermons were read all over Europe, and for a spell the women of Florence even gave up their jewels and finery, while bands of inspired youngsters policed the town in his name as guardians of morality. For his pains he was excommunicated, then arrested, put to the torture, and publicly burned to death.

The martyrdom of Savonarola did no good either, largely because of failings in his own vision. An uncompromising otherworldly medievalist, as opposed to enlightened humanism as to sin, he had given Florence little but a passing emotional excitement. In his own excitement he had delusions as a prophet, and so had helped to bring upon the city the French King Charles VIII, a dwarfish half-wit in whom he saw the Lord's instrument for the salvation of Italy. When he became the political leader of Florence after the fall of the Medici, he was inspired to nothing better than the famous "Burning of the Vanities"—worldly possessions collected by his youthful custodians of morality to serve as fuel for a public bonfire, which thrilled the youngsters more than it edified their elders. Savonarola was unquestionably sincere, not the demagogue Machiavelli thought him; but he demonstrated that Christianity had as yet nothing new to offer political life, beyond the lofty generalities that men had been reciting and disregarding for centuries.

Accordingly he suggests some excuse for the political failures of the Italian Renaissance. "Crime is not always punished in this world," Chateaubriand observed; "faults always are." The crimes of Renaissance men cannot be condoned, especially in view of the gracious, civilized ideals set forth in such popular works as Castiglione's *Courtier*. To some extent their faults may be condoned. For in spite of their apparent sophistication, they were still immature or even naïve in their ardors, like Petrarch by no means so "modern" as they looked to their early admirers, and certainly inexperienced in their new designs for living.

In political life, only Venice entered the Renaissance with a long, settled tradition. Other city-states had lived politically from hand to mouth. As they grew from communes into states with territories they had not correspondingly broadened republican government or enfranchised the surrounding peasantry; they had no precedent anyway for large-scale democracy, but peasants had always been aliens and the democratic spirit weakened once the feudal nobility was no longer a serious menace. The rise of tyranny was prepared for by an ominous but understandable development early in the fourteenth century, when mercenaries began replacing the citizen militia. Merchants and shopkeepers were quick to see the advantage of mercenaries, who relieved them of the military service that interfered with their business and that they could not safely entrust to a disaffected peasantry. Men seeking power were as quick to use them, presently against the little shopkeepers. At that, the *condottiere* or military dictator might be welcomed in times of crisis, which were frequent. One-man government was the oldest political tradition; so a citizenry that still wanted no king might fall back on the strong man, the self-made individual—the "new man" of the coming age. His very illegitimacy might at first prevent hereditary kingship or pure class rule, as it did in early Greece, and make for energetic, efficient government. Outside of Florence, at any rate, tyranny soon became firmly established; and the trouble remained that it deadened the civic sense of the earlier communes, encouraged self-seeking in a no longer independent citizenry.

As for Florence, it too suffered from mercenaries, and from the disaffection of its peasants and its many poor workers; but as the most intellectually active of the Italian cities it most clearly illustrates the deeper reasons for instability, the basic confusions and uncertainties of an age of transition. In art it triumphantly realized the new visions of rational order and harmony, the "beautiful Whole" that Alberti thought the laws of nature and of art conspired to form; only this was a purely formal harmony, a somewhat factitious ideal or artificial front—like the incongruous Renaissance façade that Alberti put on the old Gothic church of Santa Maria Novella. In view of the restless, dynamic, individualistic spirit of the Renaissance, its "classical" art was likely to become rhetorical. There was little sense of mystery and suffering in the bulk of this art, little pity or terror; of the greater Florentines only Michelangelo had a tragic sense of life. The ardent Humanists were still less inclined to any such sense. Their efforts to revive an antique civic tradition reflected a limited understanding of history, past or present, and now seem academic when not nostalgic; they were scarcely acute students of man, society, or the state, or at all "modern" in their think-

ing beyond their paeans to liberty. At the same time, the highly speculative, self-conscious Florentines were likely to suffer from the tensions
between old and new attitudes, which were neither consistently Christian nor consistently rational and secular, and made difficult a whole-
hearted service of either God or man. After the early flush of enthusiasm
the strains grew more apparent. One symptom was the feverish response
to the preaching of Savonarola. Another was the torment of Michelangelo, the mightiest genius of the Italian Renaissance: a magnificent
pagan who glorified the human body, covered the ceiling of the Sistine
Chapel with nudes, and a constant reader of the Bible and Dante, who
in a late sonnet lamented "that fond phantasy which made my soul the
worshiper and thrall of earthly art." Still another symptom was the
emergence of a "modern" type of artist, the eccentric or neurotic.
Among them was Pontormo, who heralded the rise of mannerism: an
uneasy, ambiguous, equivocal style, marked by seemingly arbitrary
distortion and unresolved tension.

Following their brief fling in the puritanism of Savonarola, the Florentines returned to their worldly pleasures and vices, perhaps to deserve
the fate in store for them. Still, virtue could hardly have preserved
their independence. Like the Greek *polis*, Florence suffered from the
relative smallness that had made possible its rich civic life, but the
fault was not only its jealous particularism. It had to contend with more
and greater enemies than Athens had had to, in a world that was growing too big for it. It was simply not strong enough to withstand the
oncoming powers of France and Spain, abetted by popes bent on extending their worldly domains. And at least democracy cannot be
charged with its downfall, as it has been with the downfall of Athens.
The political disorders in the last decades of Florence were due to no
excess of political freedom, but primarily to the intrigues of the Medici
and the popes. As it was, the republic made a brave show as it neared
the end. Although afflicted by a plague that carried off up to a third of
its people, and again turned down by Venice when it appealed for support, it prepared to fight against hopeless odds instead of prudently submitting and sticking to business. It declared its religious independence
by putting up an inscription (still extant) affirming that Jesus Christ
was "King of the Florentine People, Elected by Popular Decree." After
its long dependence on mercenaries, it had followed the advice of
Machiavelli and organized a militia again; and in the final siege citizens
were again fighting on its walls, which Michelangelo had helped to
strengthen.

In this view, finally, we may also do more justice to the works of the severest critic of the Florentine Republic—Niccolò Macchiavelli. A tragic figure who lived to see the defeat of all his hopes, he was at least spared the knowledge that he would be reviled as "Old Nick," the Devil himself—an irony he might not have appreciated. Though now famous as an immoralist, he was all too aware of the moral corruption of his age and felt much as Dante had about it. Supposedly detached and cynical, he was in fact deeply committed to the patriotic cause of the life and liberty of Italy. His works constitute a fitting last testament of the Florentines, who had developed more political awareness and a keener critical sense than any other Europeans of their time. *The Prince* deservedly became one of the political classics of all time.

Plainly it deserves, too, the repute that has made "Machiavellian" a synonym for unprincipled. It is an unabashed argument for pure power politics. Briefly, the only end is the strength and security of the state; this end justifies the use of any means, however immoral; and it positively requires unscrupulous means because men in general are gullible, selfish, ungrateful, inconstant. Machiavelli never talks of original sin, but he assumes on empirical grounds (as did Guicciardini) that common human nature is essentially evil—the assumption implicit in almost all the religious and political thought, before and after him, that has opposed ideals of freedom. His only concern here is freedom for the rulers or the state; with him the modern sovereign state comes into its own. There is no question of justice either, beyond simple prudence or expediency. Machiavelli ironically anticipates the bourgeois gospel of the sanctity of property rights by warning the prince above all to respect the property of his subjects, but merely out of expediency: "men do sooner forget the death of their father than the loss of their patrimony."

Although *The Prince* soon began going through many editions, fascinating rulers while horrifying their Christian subjects, we cannot be sure that it has had so significant an influence on Western history as is commonly assumed. It may have served chiefly to rationalize the practices that monarchs, diplomats, and politicians had come by all by themselves, and would have employed anyway. But whatever direct influence it has had has surely not promoted the cause of justice and freedom as conceived in the modern democracies. Partisans of this cause may therefore point out that in spite of many historical references Machiavelli did not actually derive his theory from a close study of history; it was manifestly a product of his own unhappy time. For this reason it embodied a possibly shortsighted realism, which might well defeat his own purposes, for it tended to undermine the good faith, the public spirit, the capacities for loyalty, responsibility, and self-sacrifice that also seem essential to the maintenance of a strong state. At least it was a poor way of inspiring the patriotism of the Italians to which Machiavelli appealed in his eloquent, forlorn concluding chapter. And in fact it did not work in his own age. Most of the rulers of Italy had long been operating on Machiavellian principles, notably the ruffian Cesare Borgia, whom for a time he secretly idolized as the white hope of Italy; and Borgia failed ignominiously, as in the long run did the Machiavellian popes.

There remain, however, the *Discourses,* which clearly express the genuine idealism and—one may hope—the deeper wisdom of Machiavelli. Here he spoke out of the republican tradition of Florence, which he linked with the great tradition of antiquity. "The common good is regarded nowhere but in republics," he said—a common good that is hardly conceivable if men are naturally as bad as he makes out in *The Prince.* He recognized that tyrants were likely to look first to their own interests, which were safer if their subjects were weak, and he argued that the people are wiser and more constant than princes, even approving the saying "The voice of the people is the voice of God." He had an especially low opinion of aristocracy, condemning the nobility more roundly than any other thinker of his time; these gentlemen who lived idly off their wealth and performed no useful service were "everywhere enemies of all civil government." He believed that the many were more capable of the antique civic virtues he admired, but added that active citizenship was necessary to acquire these virtues. This in turn required freedom to propose and discuss measures for the common good.

If these ideas had much less apparent influence than *The Prince,* at least for a century or so, they make it easier to understand and to honor Machiavelli's much-maligned classic. He never argued for absolutism as an ideal. As he repeatedly insisted, he was not describing an ideal state; it would be much better if Christian princes behaved honorably. He was simply trying to be realistic, recognizing how they actually did behave, and how therefore a wise prince had to behave in order to hold his own. Like Plato's *Republic, The Prince* was an understandable response to the apparent failure of a free society, in some respects possibly a more courageous, independent response. However shortsighted, its realism was remarkable bold and original, a striking advance over all the vague generalities about divinely ordained monarchs and popes that had satisfied medieval thinkers. It showed more insight into the actual drift of the age, the rise of the sovereign state, than Plato had into the political future of his world; as has been said, all history since has been a "running commentary" on Machiavelli. His thesis remains no less pertinent for the democracies. His main point in arguing that the end justified the means was that it should rationally control the means—he despised a mere "brutish greed for power" as senseless; but even in the more common Jesuitical sense that invites abuse his principle has up to some point been accepted by every nation, and must be accepted by anyone who believes that the defense of liberty, justice, or any other ideal cause justifies war. In this respect he made a long-range contribution to the cause of popular government that was probably more important than the direct contribution of his *Discourses*. He put political theory squarely on an empirical basis, where argument might be more profitable than it could be over the will of God or God-fearing princes, and where thinkers might give more realistic consideration to political means and institutions. From this basis other thinkers would arrive at more liberal conclusions.

Immediately the "verdict of history" on Macchiavelli's wisdom was typically equivocal. As he foresaw, there was no hope for the Florentine Republic, but the aftermath under the grand dukes hardly clinched his argument in *The Prince*. While they succeeded in setting up a stabler government and maintaining better order than the republic had, this testified as much to the loss of spirit in their subjects as to their own statesmanship. Granted that Florence could not have gone on indefinitely producing such genius as it had for two centuries, its brilliance faded very rapidly after the end of the republic. Worse, it did not fade appropriately—into the silvery haze, say, of the paintings of Andrea del Sarto. It ran out in a gaudy, grandiose tastelessness. Vasari piously wrote his admirable lives of the great artists of the past, and callously set about desecrating their works, "restoring" them to suit the florid tastes of the dukes and their court; he inaugurated a tradition of destruction and desecration that continued to this century. The dukes adorned the Great Hall of their Palazzo Vecchio, the old civic center, with huge, flamboyant frescoes of Florentine history, commemorating victories in the endless stupid wars with Pisa, Siena, etc. In time they built themselves a mausoleum adjoining the Medici Chapel of Michelangelo, as if to fulfill the anguish in his statue known as the "Dawn": their mausoleum is a tourist wonder, all colored marble and mosaic, perfectly designed to make Michelangelo writhe in his grave, and to accentuate the fact that in two hundred years the grand duchy produced no major artist.

With the decline of Florence, Venice and Rome became the main centers of late Renaissance art, commonly called the "High Renaissance." The aristocrats of Venice were not so idle and unproductive as the nobility pictured by Machiavelli, nor such enemies of civil government; the republic still maintained an independent spirit, resisting papal pressures, permitting considerable freedom of thought, and serving as the chief publishing center in Italy. Here the splendor of the High Renaissance was symbolized by the school of Titian. Individualism reached new peaks with a rising cult of genius, or of art as the creation of great personalities, while the art of the portrait brought the individual into his own as subject too. In Rome the popes sought out the greatest artists of the time—Bramante, Michelangelo, Raphael—to glorify their capital, and made it a cultural capital such as it had never been in the Middle Ages or the early Renaissance. They welcomed the services of Humanists too in much the same spirit as St. Thomas Aquinas had embraced Aristotle; the Medici Pope Leo X, an especially ardent lover of the classics, made his court a brilliant center of literature and learning. The Church at this time succeeded in enlisting the new energies of the Renaissance, assimilating the new interests and values, as it would with no later great movement. At its best it approached a Christian humanism that might have saved it from its conflict with science, and from the inveterate lag behind intellectual advance memorialized by its Index of Prohibited Books.

Yet the High Renaissance was a somewhat dubious peak. Art might seem loftier because it was now more aristocratic and exclusive, the highest form of luxury; the painter-genius worked not so much for the community as for wealthy patrons or connoisseurs, increasingly on easels for galleries instead of frescoed walls open to the public. In Venice art clearly reflected the interests of the nobility it served: richly sensuous, magnificently decorative, it lacked the range and intellectual force it had achieved in Florence. The best-known resident of the city at this time was the notorious Aretino, friend and salesman of Titian, who won prodigious fame as the first professional journalist, publicity man, scandalmonger, and literary blackmailer. And the late flowering of the fine arts coincided with a political and commercial decline, as Venice lost territories to the Ottoman Turks, trade to the Spaniards and Portuguese. Its people were not deeply stirred by these threats, nor by their art or any serious religious or intellectual concern. As a long-established aristocracy, it faded much more gradually and gracefully than Florence did, remaining one of the most enchanting cities in the world; but it had never had the stir or the glow of fifteenth-century Florence.

In Rome the geniuses imported by the popes inspired no independent Roman school or vigorous new movement. Michelangelo strove for the superhuman, with a terrific energy, in a promethean spirit; but conceptions that were sublime in him could easily become grandiose, and did so. St. Peter's remains a monument to papal pomp and power, not to lofty Christian spirituality, much less to simple piety. The wealth and power that made possible the pagan splendors of the largest church in Christendom were gained at the expense of Florence and the rest of Italy, as the popes managed to extend their domains while France and Spain took over large sections of the country. The splendors were also purchased by the wholesale marketing of indulgences, presently farmed out to the Fuggers, at the expense of urgently needed spiritual reforms; one cost of the glorified Rome was the Protestant Reformation. Another cost was increasing persecution, as criticism of papal despotism and corruption grew more intense; Rome now became the supreme headquarters of the Inquisition. In this oppressive atmosphere the High Renaissance soon lost its glow. The death of Michelangelo, in 1564, may be said to mark the end.

By this time, at any rate, the lead in art and thought was passing to other countries. Although Italy would continue to produce some influential geniuses, such as Galileo, hereafter cultural as well as political history was centered farther west. Yet the Renaissance artists and humanists elsewhere all recognized that their inspiration, when not their direct schooling, had come from Italy. It had educated its conquerors much as the Greeks had educated the Romans; the French Renaissance in particular was a discovery of Italy rather than Greece. To the Spaniards the land that had rediscovered man and the world gave a further boon, for a new age of discovery. The Genoese Columbus was another mercenary, willing to serve whoever paid him; but his spirit may also be described as cosmopolitan, emancipated, and he drew upon a common body of knowledge recovered from antiquity, including the idea— still suspect to some of the orthodox—that the earth was a sphere. In a similar spirit the Venetian Cabots served England. And as we leave Florence, it is pleasant to think that the New World got its name from a Florentine explorer who wrote the best account of it—Amerigo Vespucci.

3. *The Spread of the Renaissance*

During the Italian Renaissance the rest of Europe was busy with more than war and politics. All the major lands were evolving a national literature in the vernacular, distinctive art styles of their own. The Portuguese circumnavigated Africa and opened up direct trade by sea with the Far East. Spaniards were exploring and exploiting the New World, bringing into Europe vast quantities of gold and silver, unconsciously starting an economic revolution. Martin Luther set off the Protestant Reformation. Other Germans had distinguished themselves in technology, especially by the invention of the printing press: the most potent means to general education since the invention of the alphabet, which not only enormously expanded intellectual life but transformed the whole cultural environment, in ways that will concern us in every chapter hereafter. Most of these events were more epoch-making and world-shaking than was the spread of the Renaissance through western Europe, and together with political developments they had a much more direct impact on everyday life. Yet this spread had a profound, lasting influence on the mind of Europe. More quietly, it too marked a new epoch in thought.

As a gradual spread, over diverse countries, it was a diffuse movement. It involved less versatility and originality than the early Italian Renaissance; no city of the age rivaled the achievement of Florence. (Elizabethan London came closest.) In general, however, the later European Renaissance led to a riper humanism and a more consistent rationalism, which more directly fostered the growth of intellectual freedom. Its spokesmen produced some books that are still widely read, as the works of the Italian Humanists after Petrarch and Boccaccio are not. For the latecomers had some positive advantages, beginning with all the benefits of the Italian achievement. If they lacked the stimulus of life in an intimate city-state, they might profit from more orderly government and a less parochial society. They might be stimulated by the geographical discoveries, the opening up of a new world. Above all, they had the printing press. By 1550 at least twenty million volumes had come off the presses—a mere trickle by contemporary standards, but an immense flood by contrast with the manuscripts available in the Middle Ages and early Renaissance. Men could and did have a broader, sounder learning than the early humanists, and by the same token they had a much larger audience, a much wider influence.

Our primary concern here is the growth and spread of humanism and rationalism, the conditions of free thought. At the inevitable cost of injustice to the many earnest men who contributed to the movement, it may be surveyed through a few representative figures. They include writers who may still look antiquated or naïve, but whose importance we may underrate because often they express our ideas—ideas now commonplace, but in their time novel, daring, even radical.

So it is fitting to begin with Erasmus of Rotterdam (1466?–1536) : an educator who was world famous in his day and as the first best seller had a more direct influence than any thinker before him; who ended in apparent failure, discredited before his death, overwhelmed by historic disaster; who is little read today, except for academic requirements; and whose living ideals are nevertheless very much alive, if under forms he might not recognize or approve. He won his fame by a program of Christian humanism—an ideal union of a purified Christianity and classical culture, or of "Piety and Erudition." A thorough Greek scholar, Erasmus went behind medieval theology to study the original Bible, and thus got closer to the teaching of Jesus. He sought to purify Christianity by making it more reasonable, ethical, and humane, or truly catholic, attacking not only the abuses of papal power but the excesses of both cult and dogma, and the formal, external schemes of salvation from which the Church derived much of its power and misgotten wealth. But it was mainly the revival of classical learning and culture that fired his hopes of a "golden age" for Christendom.

Finding so much ethical and religious truth in his beloved classics, Erasmus believed that they too must have been in some sense divinely inspired. "St. Socrates, pray for us," he could say. In the spirit of Socrates he exercised his irony on all the barbarism and obscurantism enshrined in medieval tradition. Like the Florentine Platonists, he emphasized the dignity rather than the depravity of man, the essential freedom of the human spirit, and the necessity of liberty to true morality and spirituality. In particular he defended the claims of reason, which in effect he made the judge of all claims to authority. Scripture itself was to be judged by it, and all questions of what was strict truth, what was allegory (such as the fires of hell) ; these matters were not to be settled by the authority of the Church Fathers, who were only men and—as he showed—sometimes mistaken. Such reasonableness made Erasmus one of the first apostles of religious tolerance. Though he did not argue for complete religious freedom, we can hear in him the still, small voice of conscience, which was so seldom heard in the uproar of the Italian Renaissance, and which was only damnable heresy in the Middle Ages. He was among the first apostles of pacifism as well.

As his faith in the power of reason led him to believe that education alone could bring about the golden age, Erasmus was doomed to disappointment. He looks more innocent because he thought it would be enough to enlighten rulers, in an age of such monarchs as Henry VIII of England. Immediately, however, the bright flame of his Christian humanism was put out by the storms of the Protestant Reformation. Although he refused to break with the Roman Church, his mild liberalism was denounced as heresy and his works were put on the Index. He was denounced much more violently by Martin Luther; at first sympathetic to the Protestant cause, he had been repelled by the fierce intolerance of Luther, and objected specifically to his repudiation of free will and reason, the basic conditions of human dignity. It may then be said that Erasmus himself failed to maintain this dignity. By his own confession he was a timid man, lacking the "strength for martyrdom" by which Luther won the immediate future; so he may remind us that the moderate, tolerant, liberal disposition is often not a heroic disposition, and that the line between reasonableness and flabbiness in compromise is always hard to draw. Yet the spirit of Erasmus eventually triumphed. Western thought returned to the firm line he drew before the claims of authority or faith, holding to his position that these claims must be judged by reason. He became a major symbol in the long struggle for tolerance, while others also carried on his effort to recover the gospel of Jesus. His mild, reasonable faith is essentially the faith of most educated Christians today, however they differ on dogma.

His English friend Sir Thomas More, who did have the strength for martyrdom, was a much bolder social critic. While Erasmus hoped to rationalize and Christianize his society, he was an aristocrat by temperament, devoted chiefly to the cause of "good learning," and remained aloof from politics as from popular movements. (He was even unhappy over the swelling flood of printed books, which he thought endangered good learning.) More, schooled in the civic humanism of Florence, was himself a man of affairs, who rose to be Lord Chancellor of Henry VIII. His more active interest in social reform, together with the inspiration of the voyages of Amerigo Vespucci, produced his *Utopia*—a remarkable effort to design a good society by purely rational norms.

Beginning with a satirical criticism of absolute monarchs (which

prevented the immediate publication of his work in England), More
set up a republican form of government for the new land of Utopia. Its
people are devoted to classical learning, of course, having by "natural
reason" developed all the arts and sciences. More surprising, they enjoy
freedom of conscience. Although their author debars heretics from
political office, he refuses to burn them for a simple reason that Christians would learn only after centuries of atrocity: "it is in no man's
power to believe what he list." More's principal concern, however, is
the economic basis of his society. Crime, he declares, is due not so much
to original sin as to poverty and social injustice, "the unreasonable
covetousness of a few." Most surprising to those unacquainted with
early Christianity (or, in other words, to the great majority of Christians) is his proposal to abolish private property and institute a kind of
socialism. The Utopians are thereby able to enjoy a six-hour working
day.

Even so, modern democrats might not enjoy life in this ideal collec-
tivistic state. It has some depressing Spartan features, borrowed from
Plato's *Republic*. These indicate that like Erasmus of Rotterdam, More
still thought primarily in terms of the classical city-state, and did not
foresee that the future belonged to the great nation-state that he would
himself serve. As Lord Chancellor he emphasized how little apparent
influence his thought had in his own time, for he dutifully persecuted
heretics; when he lost his own head for refusing to recognize Henry
VIII as sovereign of the Church of England, he did not clearly die for
his Utopian ideals. His mixed loyalties help to explain why he had to
wait four centuries for canonization by his Roman Church. Nevertheless, the *Utopia* was another work of major symbolical significance. It
was prophetic of the actual future, perhaps to a greater extent than
More himself really hoped for. Above all, it heralded the distinctive
Western tradition of utopianism, a mainspring in the drive to social
and political reform.

With Rabelais such utopianism became both more exuberant and
more openly rebellious. It was still rooted in Christian humanism, if a
much earthier kind. For all the colossal obscenity of Rabelais, the *Gar-
gantua* was a hymn to the "excellent dignity" of man and the goodness
of God's creation. The obscenity itself had an aesthetic, even a philosophical value as a full-throated affirmation of an optimism without
illusion, a love of life that could embrace without flinching its monstrous, disgusting aspects; hence he could satirize all folly and evil, such
as war, with immense gusto. Similarly his ideal curriculum covered all

the arts and the sciences, all the natural sources of goodness, truth, and beauty. It was at once more liberal and more practical than classical education had ever been, more comprehensive in its aim of educating the whole man, body, mind, and soul. If the immortal soul was somewhat slighted, the prayers of thanksgiving at the end of the Gargantuan day were not perfunctory, and this mode of serving God might be as pious as the conventional mode that emphasized rewards in a life to come.

The gusto of Rabelais can hardly be taught or argued, just as none but a giant could cram into a day all that his pupils learn, do, and enjoy. Only by extraordinary energy and vitality could a writer get away with such abundance, without classical limit, order, or form. For the rest, the main issue Rabelais raises is the celebrated motto of his ideal Abbey of Thélème: DO WHAT THOU WILT. This school had no walls, no laws, no authorities, no discipline of any kind; its inmates lived "according to their own free will and pleasure." The only rule was a ban on sourfaced priests, monks, and nuns. (What do you do with a woman who is neither fair nor good? Why, make a nun of her, said Rabelais.) Here, obviously, is a complete rejection of the medieval ascetic ideal; but more significant is a radically different conception of the nature of man. Rabelais was not inviting men to "license"—the kind of lawlessness that was all too common in the Italian Renaissance. Rather, he blamed this lawlessness on the authoritarianism of the Middle Ages, and its stress on natural depravity. He gave his students complete liberty on the assumption that free men "have naturally an instinct and spur that prompteth them unto virtuous actions." In short, he championed the doctrine of "natural goodness," which was due to become popular in the eighteenth century and naturally supported the movement toward freedom.

Needless to say, this conception of human nature now seems much too simple. It is no simpler, however, than the opposite conception of Machiavelli in *The Prince*, or later of Thomas Hobbes; and at any rate it forces an issue that becomes more explicit in Western thought from now on. Any serious thought about the good life, the good society, the good state, must finally rest on some conception of human nature, some assumption about what man is good for or fit for. Such assumptions are no less significant because they are generally unreasoned, or even unconscious. As I have kept remarking from the outset, most civilized societies have implicitly supported the assumption of Dostoyevsky's Grand Inquisitor that man is by nature a sheepish creature, unfit for freedom, who can be made passably good or happy only through "miracle, mystery, and authority." In the Renaissance the growing self-consciousness led to much reflection about the nature of man. Mostly this oscillated between the extremes represented by Machiavelli and Rabelais; but it culminated in the much more complex thought of Montaigne (1533–1592).

With Montaigne we depart from a specifically Christian humanism. Although he habitually professed a conventional piety, out of a decent respect for the public good, Sainte-Beuve's comment is just: "He may have appeared a very good Catholic except for not having been a Christian." Almost all of his countless quotations are from the classics, not the Bible; he never cites Jesus himself. The inventor of the literary form of the personal essay (and essay to him meant "test" or "trial"), Montaigne wrote endlessly about himself, in a lifelong effort to understand himself; his living motto was the Greek motto "Know thyself"— it was not to know and serve God. He knew himself well enough to spot a clue to his religious impulses: "My reason is not framed to bend or stoop; my knees are." It was his unbending reason that distinguished Montaigne, and got his works on the Catholic Index.

His essay "On the Education of Children" represents his furthest departure from the medieval ideal. Like Rabelais and the Greeks, Montaigne wanted to educate the whole man and fit him to enjoy fully the uses of this world. In particular the student should be stimulated to inquire into all things and to think for himself, in complete freedom; he should be "guided only by reason," not faith, and should accept nothing on authority. "Let variety of ideas be set before him; he will choose if he can; if not, he will remain in doubt. Only the fools are certain and assured." For the same reason he should travel, to become acquainted with different customs and beliefs, perhaps even to dabble in foreign vices. Montaigne here followed all the way through the implication that man is naturally good enough to be trusted with such dangerous freedom, anticipating modern "progressive education" by objecting to the universal emphasis on discipline, as to learning by rote. The great end was to learn to be oneself, by oneself. "It is an absolute perfection," Montaigne wrote elsewhere, "and as it were divine for a man to know how to enjoy his being loyally."

The rejection of authority also implied a basic skepticism, however, and this could lead Montaigne to most pessimistic reflections on the natural vanity, stupidity, and folly of man. His *Apology for Raimond de Sebond* is a demonstration, thorough to the point of monotony, of

Detail from Mezquita Cathedral, Córdoba

The Fountain of Lions, Alhambra

Sultan Ahmet Mosque ("Blue Mosque"), Istanbul (p. 14)

OTTOMAN ART

Suleiman Mosque

Sultan Ahmet Mosque

Pagan Saxon art, from the Sutton Hoo Treasury

Megaliths in prehistoric Europe: Stonehenge, England (p. 29)

Charlemagne's Chapel, Aachen (p. 38)

THE NORMANS AS BUILDERS: (p. 43)

(For other examples, see next page)

Durham Cathedral, England

Sicily, Cathedral of Monreale

The Cloister of the
Cathedral of Monreale

Normandy,
St. Etienne at Caen
*French Government
Tourist Office*

Christ Crowning
Emperor Henry II (c. 1002-1014)
(pp. 40-41)

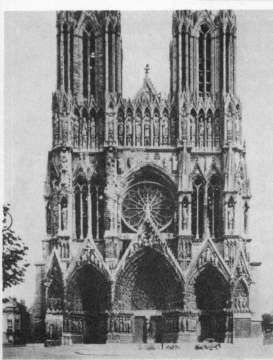

Gothic art:
Rheims Cathedral (p. 53)
*French Government
Tourist Office*

The medieval university: A lecturer on law at Bologna (pp. 60, 65), *The Bettmann Archive*

The medieval bourgeois: Guild Hall at Ypres (p. 77), *Marburg-Art Reference Bureau*

Chartres (p. 53), *French Government Tourist Office*

THE MEDIEVAL TOWN (pp. 75 ff.)

A Flemish town—
detail from Rogier van der Weyden's
St. Luke Drawing a Portrait
of the Virgin
The Bettmann Archive

A Merchant, left (pp. 73 ff.), and A Pardoner (p. 89)—from the first illustrated
Caxton edition of Chaucer's *Canterbury Tales, Courtesy of the Lilly Library*

The Seamy Side of Chivalry, above (p. 67), and A Tournament (p. 86)—
from the *History of Leopold,* 1481, *Courtesy of the Lilly Library*

Country life in the fifteenth century
outside Paris
The Bettmann Archive

Noble beating his wife,
from a manuscript of 1456 (p. 99)

The Danse Macabre
(c. 1500)
(p. 81)

The David of Michelangelo (p. 115)
Alinari-Art Reference Bureau

The David of Donatello (p. 118)
Alinari-Art Reference Bureau

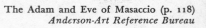

The Adam and Eve of Masaccio (p. 118)
Anderson-Art Reference Bureau

The Adam and Eve of Masolino (p. 118)
Anderson-Art Reference Bureau

Piazza de San Marco

VENICE
(pp. 113-114)

A *palazzo* (The Golden House)

Michelangelo's Dawn, Medici Chapel (p. 132)

View of Florence: at left Brunelleschi's dome; at right the Bargello (p. 117)

Savonarola Preaching—from his *Compendio di Rivelazione* (p. 127)

THE FLORENCE OF
LORENZO DE' MEDICI

Dancing Girls—
from *Ballatette* by Lorenzo and others (p. 124)

the absurd pride of man and the utter incompetence of human reason. "Can anything be imagined so ridiculous as that this miserable and wretched creature, who is not so much as master of himself, but subject to the injuries of all things, should call himself master and emperor of the world, of which he has not power to know the least part, much less to command it?" Montaigne goes on for many pages showing that man is inferior to other animals in intelligence and virtue, and that by his alleged power of reason he only makes a greater fool of himself. He can sound like Pope Innocent III on the misery of the human condition. His ostensible conclusion is a traditional one: given the incompetence of reason to know anything for certain, man must rely on faith alone.

Still, by this argument he undermined faith too, making it seem wholly unreasonable. Why should God be concerned about so absurd a creature? Montaigne explicitly ridiculed the orthodox doctrine that the universe was created for the sake of man and his little earth—a heretical attitude that Galileo would also express. As explicitly he denied the certainties of faith: "The persuasion of certainty is a certain testimony of folly and extreme uncertainty." His doubt was less systematic than that of his follower Descartes, but it was more habitual, resolute, and thoroughgoing. And its sources—the real motives of the *Apology*—are not far to seek. The skepticism of Montaigne may be considered a natural outcome of the critical, rational tendency of the Renaissance, which sooner or later was bound to question the undemonstrable premises of the Christian faith. It was deepened by the growing knowledge of other continents with other customs and faiths, the growing awareness that "our religion, like our dress, is imposed on us by custom." But in particular Montaigne insisted upon it so feelingly because of the religious wars that were now costing many thousands of lives—wars between Catholics and Protestants who were equally certain in their beliefs, and as ferociously inhuman in their behavior. "There is no hatred so absolute as that which is Christian," he wrote; and more wryly he commented: "After all, it is setting a high value upon our opinions to roast men alive on account of them." Another apostle of tolerance, more outspoken than Erasmus, he best illustrates Preserved Smith's remark that it was doubt, not faith, that humanized the Western world.

A further source of Montaigne's skepticism was the self-knowledge he endlessly sought. As he looked into the stream of his consciousness he could see nothing entire, solid, and stable, and so could say nothing "without confusion, disorder, blending, and mingling, nor in one word."

Constantly he was struck by the inconstancies, inconsistencies, incongruities. He saw, too, the invariable mixture of good and ill, sweet and bitter: "we taste nothing pure." The best virtues had some tincture of vice, all faith some tincture of presumption. What, then, could be said of the "essence" of human nature? Certainly nothing so simple as natural goodness or natural depravity: "Man is wholly and throughout but patch and motley." On the whole, Montaigne took a favorable view of the creature, repeatedly telling him to be loyal to his being, somewhere between beast and angel, and not to scorn the world or the flesh; he himself ended as an Epicurean of sorts. But man could make the best of the mixed stuff in him only by following a moderate, middle way; the presumption of trying to live like an angel would merely make him more of a beast. "It is vain to get upon stilts," he concluded, "for if we be upon them, yet must we go with our own legs. And sit we upon the highest throne of the world, yet sit we upon our own tail. The best and most commendable lives and best pleasing men are (in my conceit) those which are fitted to the common mold and human model, without wonder or extravagancy."

This reasonable, humanistic ideal was still not a democratic one, nor wholly "modern." Montaigne's educational program was designed for a young gentleman who would not have to earn his living, and it included no notions about social or political equality. Likewise it included no study of science, which Rabelais had emphasized; himself an aristocratic man of letters, Montaigne had no more interest in science than had most of the Italian Humanists. (He dismissed the Copernican theory as another fad.) Yet his thought represented a major advance toward freedom, and primarily because of his basic skepticism. This incidentally made him one of the first writers to be skeptical of witchcraft, at a time when more and more thousands of old women were being burned, with the sanction of learned churchmen. It freed him from all the illusions and the presumptions that had fired men in the Middle Ages, but had also lit fagots under heretics. Most important, it enabled him to attain the clearest, fullest consciousness to date of complexity, contingency, finiteness, fundamental uncertainty—the essential conditions of freedom of thought and conscience. With Montaigne Western man may be said to have come of age.

Effective freedom, once more, requires at once the free exercise of reason or the power of choice and an awareness of the limits of reason. Westerners have been distinguished both by their boundless faith in reason and by their acuter consciousness of its limitations. Similarly they have been distinguished by their greater respect for the individual, and for the values of individuality or personality; but they have realized more acutely the conditions of these too, even apart from the costs of self-seeking. "Individuality is in itself an element of misery and of littleness," Cousin observed, "because the particular, the contingent, the finite incessantly tend to division, to dissolution, to extinction." This in turn may intensify uncertainty about the whole human condition, the meaning and purpose of man's life. Hence a particular value of Montaigne was not only his mature awareness of limit, flux, and uncertainty, and his freedom from self-deception—it was his demonstration that on these hard terms it was still possible to maintain human dignity and the value of selfhood. He was always able to call cruelty, barbarity, or inhumanity by its right name because he was always devoted to such positive values as good judgment, tolerance, charity, natural piety, a "gay and sociable wisdom"—or the values simply of sanity and decency. One of the first thoroughgoing skeptics in Western civilization, he might be called the perfect skeptic: able to live cheerfully in doubt and suspense, and to hold to an ideal of reasonableness beyond pure rationalism or in defiance of cold logic.

All this is more significant because Montaigne had more evident, lasting influence than other Renaissance humanists. His thought runs all through French literature, from Descartes, Pascal, and Racine down to Gide, Sartre, and Camus; outside of France it soon began cropping up in such writers as Shakespeare and Francis Bacon. In his own time, however, few thoughtful men were either at home in doubt or at ease in faith. The social, political, and religious convulsions stirred the familiar refrains about these "last and most wicked days." Men brooded, too, over the "new disease" of syphilis—a strange malady unknown to the ancients, apparently come in from the New World. Loys le Roy, a contemporary humanist, wrote a typical work: celebrating the "excellence" of the age, reciting the "many fine new things" that had been discovered or invented, but winding up with the thought that the new disease was certainly "the true judgment of God," concluding with a typically medieval prophecy of the violent end of the world. And in England writers now found a more suitable form than Montaigne's essay for the expression of these anxieties, sprung from a coming of age that had meant a loss of innocence, and could look like a fall from grace. Here the late Renaissance was climaxed by another major innovation— Elizabethan tragedy.

The "Age of Faith" had naturally produced no tragedy. It wrote copybook tales of men "fallen out of high degree into misery," but these made only a moral point, not a tragic one, and gave no suggestion of brooding, tormented, rebellious humanity, or of the problem of evil in God's creation. The mystery and miracle plays had no more element of painful uncertainty or actual mystery; their preordained ending was triumph through holiness or miracle. Briefly, through suffering medieval men learned the lesson of their unworthiness that made them worthy of everlasting bliss in heaven. For different reasons the Italian Renaissance had also failed to create tragedy, producing only some academic imitations of Greek tragedy. Florence in its prime was too self-confident for such brooding over the human condition; elsewhere Humanists were typically complacent in their pedantry or their remoteness from the common life. As the Renaissance theater grew up, moreover, it became more a genteel than a civic theater, catering to the tastes of an upper-class audience. Drama was less ambiguous than plastic art, where there was some imitation of a tragic sense of life in the irresolution, distortion, or dissonance of the later "mannerist" style.

By contrast, the Elizabethan theater was a popular, native growth little influenced by formal classicism, except for the gruesome rhetoric and melodrama of Seneca. It was a rowdy, immature theater, a free-for-all crude in its violent action and rant, as crude in its stock characters, stock themes, stock moral lessons; generally it assumed the medieval beliefs about God, man, and the world that still ruled popular thought. But it also reflected the tensions of the late Middle Ages, in particular the horror of death. The wholesale slaughter that overtook the cast in Elizabethan tragedy not only satisfied the taste for crude horrors but fed the obsession with death; death was the very essence of this "Christian" tragedy, as it had never been to the Greeks. In its freedom this drama likewise mirrored the realities of Renaissance life as formal neoclassical drama did not—the lust for life, the swaggering individualism, the violent strife, the unbridled passion for wealth, power, and glory. And when the "university wits" took to playwrighting as a means of livelihood, bringing to the theater their gifts as poets, voicing their deeper thought and feeling, Elizabethan drama became Renaissance tragedy, the most intense expression of the inner conflicts and contradictions of the age.

This tragedy begins with Christopher Marlowe, the first to create the genuinely tragic hero. In his youthful *Tamburlaine* (Part 1), labeled a "Tragical discourse," there is scarcely a suggestion of such discourse;

the mighty lines and the celestial imagery of Marlowe's verse declare the glory of Tamburlaine as the "Scythian shepherd" marches from triumph to triumph in his conquest of Asia. Although known as the Scourge of God, he symbolizes the Renaissance hero, "Fortune's master," vindicating the faith of Alberti—fulfilling the dream of his author —that "men can do anything with themselves if they will." In *Dr. Faustus*, however, the more mature Marlowe knows better. While conventional Christians may read this as the convential morality play that no doubt ordinary Elizabethans saw in it, inasmuch as Faustus is properly damned, others may see something more in it. There is a vivid realization of Faust's damnation—vivid enough to belie Marlowe's reputation as an "atheist"; yet there is no rejoicing at the punishment of this ardent sinner, and no comparably vivid sense of the love of God, the peace of faith, or the bliss of heaven. Like his sad Mephistopheles, who is no conventional spirit of pure evil, Marlowe knows there is a hell, but has no hope of heaven. Having lost only the medieval faith, not the medieval fears, he is incapable of either the lusty humanism of Rabelais or the calm skepticism of Montaigne. Had he lived longer he might have become reconciled to faith or to doubt. As it was, we leave him in the no man's land of Dr. Faustus, between the medieval and the modern world, an "overreacher," still passionately willful, most eloquent in aspiration, dream, and defiance, but unreconciled to his fate, unable to believe that the Faustian life might be its own reward.

Hence Marlowe would scarcely have rejoiced in his historic role as a pioneer, who prepared the way for the much more mature drama of Shakespeare. The most comprehensive, copious dramatist in the world's literature, far superior to his fellow Elizabethans, Shakespeare is not to be pinned down to the Renaissance. It was some generations before readers even discovered the famous problem of Hamlet, beginning the hundreds of different interpretations of a play that has meant more things to more men than any other play in history, and than could ever have been dreamed of in Shakespeare's philosophy. Still, he was no timeless spirit either, but a man of the Renaissance. The very breadth, variety, and abundance of life in his drama were a fulfillment of its humanism, as the amplest and most vivid representation of the human scene. He mirrored the individualism of the age in his host of characters, much more highly individualized than those of Greek or any other drama before him. He mirrored it especially in his many great personalities, above all Hamlet. Read as Renaissance tragedy, *Hamlet* by no means yields its full meaning; but this approach does take one close to the heart of the drama, and to the meanings significant for our present purposes.[6]

Now, the evident humanism of Shakespeare's drama is not clearly a Christian humanism. Although earnest scholars are still busy equipping him with every variety of Christian belief, Catholic and Protestant, both their industry and their disagreement emphasize that he was the most noncommittal of the great poets, in this respect utterly different from Dante before him and Milton after him. Hamlet, the most thoughtful of his heroes, broods over all manner of problems—except the problem of God and the salvation of his immortal soul. In his anguish he never turns to Christ, never seeks the peace or consolation of faith; in his recovery he mentions a divinity that shapes our ends, but without naming the divinity or specifying the ends; and he goes to his death expressing neither Christian hopes nor fears. "The rest is silence." For a historian the main point of the silence is some basic uncertainty: tragedy is not written by men of firm, orthodox faith. The point is confirmed by the contemporary drama of Spain. This too was an indigenous drama, which in Calderón enlisted a great poet, but it never attained to real tragedy; the most somber actions of Calderón led to pious endings, just as "the dark night of the soul" leads mystics to visions of God. Renaissance Spain remained orthodox and Catholic.

Uncertainty, however, is not simple disbelief. Behind Shakespeare's tragedy lay the medieval belief in a universal order, natural, social, and political. In Shakespeare this is still in some sense a moral, if not a divine order: on the face of it mysterious, not clearly rational or just, somehow engendering both good and evil, yet not indifferent to either. Human evil was a corruption or violation of this order—and Shakespeare was very much concerned with such evil, in the judgment of which he committed himself quite plainly. It was the kind of evil denounced all through the Renaissance, in particular the selfish, unscrupulous ambition and the greed that had corrupted the political order, made rotten the state of Denmark. It seemed worse because of the inherited belief in man's high position in the cosmic order, and still more shocking because it no longer seemed natural to a creature of

---

[6] I am recapitulating the interpretation set forth in my chapter on Elizabethan tragedy in *The Spirit of Tragedy*. There I remarked with some pride that I was not offering an original or definitive interpretation of Shakespeare, inasmuch as critics have for generations been announcing the "true" meaning of his plays, and are likely to announce it most dogmatically when it is a meaning that all other critics have managed to overlook.

"excellent dignity." Hence the torment of Hamlet. The all-around man of the Renaissance—soldier, scholar, courtier—he embraced the extremes of its optimism and its pessimism. "What a piece of work is a man!" he had thought as a youthful idealist. "How noble in reason! how infinite in faculties! in form and moving how express and admirable! in action how like an angel! in apprehension how like a god! the beauty of the world! the paragon of animals!" Now he concludes: "And yet, to me, what is this quintessence of dust?" His disillusionment extends to the whole order of things, natural as well as political: "this brave o'erhanging firmament" appears to him no more than "a foul and pestilent congregation of vapors." All the uses of this world were corrupt.

Yet Hamlet could not rest in simple disenchantment or disgust. This world not only made demands on him but still had potentially excellent uses. The most highly individualized, complex, thoughtful of Shakespeare's heroes, he represents the full self-consciousness of the Renaissance. He is Montaigne's man, only much more intense. The many diverse interpretations of his character all illumine some of its many facets, and err chiefly in reducing him to something said "entirely, simply, and with solidity." He is a "sweet prince," noble, gentle, sensitive, "finely attuned to fine issues," who can yet be callous, savage, obscene, reckless, mad—and therefore also heroic. The uncertainties in his own mind, and the inconstancies and incongruities in his behavior, are amplified by an action focused on a clash between "mighty opposites," studded with ironic parallels and contrasts, shot through with questions about the ambiguities of appearance and reality. We need not ponder here the specific mystery of Hamlet's procrastination in carrying out his revenge. He exemplifies the whole mystery of the human condition that he continually broods over, and never resolves.

Finally Hamlet exemplifies the power and the value as well as the curse of self-consciousness by accepting his mortal condition, mastering necessity, and then settling his personal problem. He must die, of course—and not merely to satisfy the conventions of Elizabethan tragedy. In worldly success he could not so triumphantly demonstrate that "the readiness is all," nor bring home so full a realization of at once the mystery, the tragedy, and the glory of the free human spirit. And on these hard but honorable terms, after a period of torment, Shakespeare himself became reconciled to the human condition. He would write *King Lear*, the most terrible of his tragedies, in which evil is most monstrous, disorder most violent, culminating in madness in the hero and civil war in the state, accompanied by awful tempests, convulsions in nature or supernature that raise the darkest doubts about the powers that shape the ends of man; yet also the most compassionate of the tragedies, the most magnificent in orchestration, in which the deadliest evil is set off by the most radiant goodness and beauty of soul. Shakespeare's last plays were all centered on the Renaissance theme of rebirth and regeneration, concluding with *The Tempest*: a "comedy" much more complex and ironic than appears on the surface, not very gay or high-spirited, but ending in harmony, a blessing on a "brave new world" about which the poet has no illusions.

All this may seem a long digression, carrying us far from the history of freedom. One who believes (as I do) that Shakespeare was the greatest poet who ever lived may still believe that he had a negligible influence on the course of history, or even on the course of English literature. Certainly he had no evident influence in his own age. His successors in the tragic theater, notably Webster, dwelt on themes of corruption, dissolution, and decay, often expressing a loathing of man and his works that implied a complete loss of the Renaissance faith, without a return to Christian faith; and the discords were eventually resolved in the grandiloquent affirmations of Restoration drama, the complacent heroics of love-and-honor. Outside of literature the future belonged to such movements as Puritanism, with which Shakespeare had no apparent sympathy, and the rising science trumpeted by Francis Bacon, in which he took no apparent interest. Yet these various currents, which in leading away from him alike led to simplified views of the nature and condition of man, in retrospect lend historical significance to his eminence. He dramatized the intellectual crisis of the Renaissance, the ultimate issues forced by the advance in self-consciousness, in tragedies of unexampled range, depth, and power. He did the fullest justice to the Renaissance individual, the great personality, the more because he still viewed him in relation to the community and the cosmos, as a symbol of the human condition rather than a romantic exception to it. He transcended the profound confusions and uncertainties in a vision that retained the essential values of the Renaissance, earned its faith in the only manner that can make it secure, by going all the way through the reasons for doubt and despair. He pointed to the way, I believe, in which the whole history of human freedom must be read. In the ages that followed, throughout the deep changes in the climate of opinion, he became universally recognized as the greatest of English poets; and we may believe that he made some difference in the thought and feeling of the millions who have come under his spell.

There remains another figure of the late European Renaissance, the most revolutionary and obviously influential, to whose work Shakespeare was indifferent if he was acquainted with it at all. In 1543—two generations before Hamlet began brooding—Copernicus had published his theory about the universe. Shakespeare may be forgiven his indifference. While the Copernican theory deeply impressed a few men of scientific bent, such as Kepler and Galileo, it had otherwise very little influence on sixteenth-century thought. Humanists ignored it, churchmen dismissed it as the obvious nonsense it seemed to men of common sense. Even skeptics might agree with Martin Luther that Copernicus was "an ass who wants to pervert the whole art of astronomy and deny what is said in the book of Joshua, only to make a show of ingenuity and attract attention." The revolutionary consequences of his theory were generally unrecognized until the seventeenth century, the great age of science that will concern us later. Meanwhile we should note that, like Shakespearean tragedy, this extraordinary theory was a natural outcome of the Renaissance.

An audacious thinker, Copernicus still had no heretical or revolutionary purposes. He was a representative man of the age: a good Christian humanist, trained as a painter, who had studied in Italy for ten years and imbibed an enthusiasm for classical learning. The artist as well as the mathematician in him emboldened him to advance his apparently nonsensical theory. Giving cosmic space something like the new dimension that perspective had added to painting, it revealed to him a more perfect "harmony in the motion and magnitude of the orbs," a "wonderful symmetry in the universe"; it was a sublime testimony to the Great Architect, "the Best and Most Orderly workman of all," confirming the marvelous excellence of the creation. So the as pious Kepler told how he contemplated the beauty of this theory with "incredible and ravishing delight." And though Copernicus knew that churchmen might not be ravished by it, withholding it from publication for some twenty years, he was emboldened as well by his reverence for the ancients. He discovered that some Greeks had also concluded that the sun, not the earth, was the center of the universe.

Such independence of spirit was as pronounced in another pioneer of science, Vesalius, who in the same year as Copernicus published his own revolutionary treatise *On the Structure of the Human Body*. This too came out of the naturalism and humanism of the Renaissance, learned by study in Italy; its plates of illustrations were works of art, made under the direction of Vesalius by a pupil of Titian. But his apparently harmless discoveries about anatomy created more stir at the time because of his open defiance of tradition, even of the authority of Galen, whom he greatly admired. Vesalius tried to teach his students to use their own eyes, hands, and heads as they dissected, instead of learning what Galen had taught; and nothing was harder than this. The students were always happier when they found what Galen had— even though he had used apes instead of human beings for dissection. Their progeny in the universities would continue to revere authority, or ignore the evidence of their senses, and as professors would stoutly oppose the great scientific pioneers of the seventeenth century. Nevertheless, the Renaissance—for all its academic humanism—had started the scientific revolution. This would most triumphantly vindicate its faith in the powers of man, inspire still more confident hopes of a "golden age" to come; though let us add (remembering Shakespeare) that it would also revive the worst fears of the Renaissance, and eventually make conceivable the literal end of man's world.

Chapter Five	*THE PROTESTANT*
	REFORMATION

1. The Causes

In 1517 Martin Luther posted in Wittenberg his celebrated 95 theses, attacking the scandalous sale of indulgences by the Papacy. As he defended himself against counterattacks, he soon renounced the authority of the Roman Church and worked out the main articles of his "protestant" faith: the authority of the Bible alone, individual responsibility to God alone, justification by faith alone, man's utter dependence on divine grace. Luther's gospel won immediate popularity among both common people and princes, who were able to protect him against the usual fate of heretics, and with the help of the printing press it spread rapidly over central Europe. He inspired other influential Reformers, above all John Calvin: a much greater theologian and organizer than he, who became something like a Protestant pope. By the time of Luther's death in 1546—only a generation after he had opened war on the Papacy—Protestantism had won not only much of Germany and Switzerland but Scandinavia and England, and it was spreading in the Netherlands and France. Western Christendom was permanently, irreparably split.

Judgments of this tragedy—or this triumph—have naturally tended to be partisan. To an orthodox Catholic it was no mere reformation but a deplorable rebellion against the true faith, essentially perverse, unnecessary, even (according to Hilaire Belloc) accidental. To a devout Protestant it was not only an essential purification but an epochal emancipation, some have said the first major advance in Western freedom and the beginning of modern democracy. There is no reconciling these views, and little hope of maintaining complete impartiality; but at least one may safely venture the remark that both views are considerably oversimplified.

Christendom as a whole had never been really united, of course. Centuries before, the Roman Church had broken with the Holy Orthodox Church of Byzantium, with little anguish or sense of tragedy. In Europe Luther had behind him a long tradition of revolt against the authority of the Papacy; his spiritual forebears included John Wyclif and especially John Huss, who was burned for his dedication to what became the fighting faith of early Protestants: "In the things which pertain to salvation, God is to be obeyed rather than man." But aside from the undeniable corruption of the Church the Reformation was a natural consequence of the whole political, economic, intellectual, cultural development of Europe. Despite its basic hostility to the ideals of the Renaissance, it was connected with this movement as another effort at regeneration, in particular another expression of the surging individualism. It reflected other deep social changes that will concern us in the next chapter. Given the growing nationalism, cultural diversity, and expansiveness, one may doubt that any single "catholic" church could any longer serve the needs of all Europe. In any case the Papacy was clearly not up to the job. Since the thirteenth century it had been steadily losing spiritual authority, and it was still patently unable or unwilling to reform itself. The Protestant Reformation, which in this view looks almost inevitable, turned out to be providential for the Roman Church too, rescuing the Papacy from corruptions that might have proved fatal.

Yet the Reformation was immediately by no means a simple emancipation. Although Luther made it seem so by his bold defiance of authority, once he had broken loose he sought chiefly to impose a stricter, sterner authority. Neither he nor Calvin was a liberal, a democrat, or an apostle of earthly freedom by any ordinary standards. Both were archconservatives, more medieval in spirit than were the Renaissance popes. Both would have been appalled could they have foreseen the belief and behavior of most Protestants today, or simply the innumerable varieties of Protestantism. One cannot begin to understand the Reformation unless one realizes that Protestantism became radically different from what its founders intended.

Now as usual, our concern here is not the question whether early Protestantism was "true" or more "truly" Christian than Catholicism. We need note only that, although it was heretical by contemporary Catholic standards, it had good Christian authority for all its doctrines. Neither Luther nor Calvin introduced any new ideas, or made the slightest pretense of doing so; they merely reverted to early tradition, specifically to the teaching of St. Paul, in effect making a different selection from the dualities or ambiguities of Christian tradition. Our concern remains the effects of Protestantism on the history of Western freedom. But we do have to consider the underlying causes of the Reformation, and the mixed motives of its converts, for these had much to do with its historical consequences.

Only a hidebound cynic or the shallowest of historical materialists will deny that genuinely religious motives gave the Reformation much of its drive. Since early in the Middle Ages sincere Christians had been the most indignant over the Church's abuses of its wealth and power, and Luther now enlisted this indignation in support of a gospel that filled many men with his own fervor. In his revulsion against externals and mere forms, he led the perennial return of the religious spirit to the inner life, the Kingdom or the light within; he offered nothing like a mere "opium for the masses." To recognize the reality and the force of such "ideal" factors is again no naïve idealism; for in many Protestants the fervor swelled into fanaticism—the typically Christian hatred of fellow Christians of different belief, which enflamed the religious wars to come, the most appalling consequence of the Reformation. At the same time, materialistic motives as plainly counted for something. Many simple men were doubtless attracted by a vulgar sort of freedom—freedom from fasts and tithes, the costs of supernatural aid, or freedom from any necessity but faith. Some princes unmistakably supported the Reformation out of ambition and greed; they were quick to confiscate the landed wealth of the Church. In general, most men had the usual mixture of motives, impossible neatly to separate or to weigh, but including worldly ingredients impossible to disregard. These help to explain why the Reformation generated little perceptible moral reform, and more important, why in the long run it perhaps contributed as much to the growth of a secular spirit as the Renaissance did.

Thus a particular reason for its success was its appeal to the urban middle class, engaged in business. This class had long been given to resentment of papal taxation, the immense wealth of the Church, the luxury of bishops and parasitic monks, while churchmen officially frowned on its commercial interests. Luther was far from being a champion of the bourgeois, but he did bring the glad news that the best way to serve the Lord—far better than the way of the useless monk—was to work hard in the Lord's vineyard, "to acquire and preserve property." Calvin made more specific provision for bourgeois interests and values, dignifying as peculiarly Christian the virtues of thrift, prudence, sobriety, diligence, and industry. Although Calvinism was as far from being a religion of business, it was clearly more accommodating than the

Roman Church, and flourished most conspicuously among the middle class.

Another potent factor in the Reformation, and immediately a much more apparent one, was nationalism. Outside of Italy, hostility to the Papacy was embittered simply because it was Italian, and drained off to Rome much of the country's wealth, like as not to support the political ambitions of the popes. Such feeling was especially strong in Germany, which since the defeat of the Holy Roman emperors had been only a chaotic mass of principalities, not a nation powerful enough to keep the pope in his place; Rome drew an immense revenue from the land of Luther. Hence its princes were disposed to rally behind the Reformer, who could not have won without their support, and who soon began appealing to his "fellow Germans." England's break with Rome was purely an act of state, at first involving no real difference in dogma; although its immediate cause, the divorce of Henry VIII, was unpopular even at home, Henry had little trouble getting the country behind him because of the resentment of long interference by foreign popes. Generally Protestantism succeeded only in countries where it was able to win the support of the state, or at least—as in France—to arrange a definite accommodation with the state. Another immediate consequence of the Reformation was that monarchs acquired more power, in both Catholic and Protestant countries, as both sides needed royal support.

More broadly, the Reformation was a response to an age in which change was growing more rapid than ever before. But so considered it was a product of deep unrest, sprung from social and political as well as religious conflict, especially from severe dislocations in the economy. Few men understood these changes at all clearly, and most did not really welcome them. Many felt insecure, frustrated, helpless; they were prey to anxiety and impotent rage. For this reason they might welcome not only the defiance of authority but the seemingly disheartening gospel of Luther and Calvin—the message of their utter unworthiness, even their vileness. Their anxiety was reflected as well in the dreadful superstitions that grew more obsessive with the rise of Protestantism, particularly the superstitions about demons and witches.[1] Altogether, early Protestantism was by no means a simple, serene faith. It was tenser than

---

[1] Today men are likely to regard the witchcraft mania as a symptom chiefly of barbarous ignorance, or perhaps of sadism. They may therefore forget that the sufferers were not only all the women who were tortured and burned, but many of their accusers: other poor women whose children had sickened and died, under the spell of these witches. It is unlikely that a contented populace would have succumbed to this mania, since the existence of witches had been known all through the centuries.

medieval Catholicism, much more insistent on the paradoxes of the Christian faith. It would therefore further the growth of freedom in ways never intended by its founders, and long opposed by their loyal followers. But because of this opposition we must first consider the teachings of the founders, in particular the reasons why Luther dwelt so much on the "spiritual liberty" of Christians—a kind of liberty that denied them claims to freedom for ordinary living purposes.

2. *The Immediate Consequences*

One who cherishes the distinctive values of Western civilization may feel humiliated by the thought that Martin Luther—a man so steeped in crass superstition, so basically irrational and inhuman in his creed, so often coarse in anger and violent in hatred—has been revered as a great spiritual leader. Such a prophet is conceivable only in Christendom, or possibly Islam; he would look grotesque in the company of the wise and holy men of Buddhist, Hindu, and Confucianist societies. So let us try to be fair to a man of great force of personality, who like it or not had a great influence on his age—an age of remarkable adventure. Luther was as distinctively Christian in his torrential passion and his mighty eloquence, his freedom from the possible indolence or self-indulgence of quietism. He was not merely sincere—any fool, bigot, or fanatic may be sincere. In one aspect he was heroic, far more courageous and daring than we can now readily appreciate in his willingness to risk life and soul by open defiance of the most venerable authority in Christendom; he belongs with the Renaissance supermen. In another aspect he touched sublimity by his complete surrender to the will of God, his humble acknowledgment that frail humanity could never be worthy of the divine grace. He was himself aware of the seeming inconsistencies in his teaching: "For what else can our doctrine be in the eyes of the wicked than sheer contradictions, since it both requires and condemns works, abolishes and restores ritual, honors and reproves the magistrates, asserts and denies sin?" He faced up honestly to the ultimate paradox, the unfathomable mystery that was the logic of orthodox Christian faith:

> This is the highest degree of faith—to believe that He is merciful, who saves so few and damns so many; to believe Him just who according to His own will makes us necessarily damnable, that He

may seem, as Erasmus says, "to delight in the torments of the miserable, and to be an object of hatred rather than of love." If, therefore, I could by any means comprehend how that same God can be
merciful and just who carries the appearance of so much wrath and
iniquity, there would be no need of faith.

Still, such faith is scarcely a free man's worship; and Luther's feeling
of absolute dependence on an incomprehensible God—call it sublime,
or call it abject—brings up at once the reasons why he was an enemy of
ordinary freedom. They center in his own torment as a young monk, a
hell such as Christian saints have often had to go through. Despite continual fastings and scourgings, he was hounded by feelings of guilt,
dread, sometimes despair. He suffered more intensely because Satan had
taken an exceptionally tenacious interest in his soul, and was forever
stalking him in his study. (We may have more compassion for Martin
Luther if we keep in mind his casual note about how he was awakened
one night by some sound, but went back to sleep when he realized the
cause: it was only the Devil again.) Finally he experienced some kind
of conversion. After his long experience of desperate effort and miserable failure, he knew that this was not his own doing: it could only be
a gratuitous gift of God.

Even so, the feeling of "spiritual liberty" he now enjoyed fell somewhat short of peace of mind. Luther's gospel was no gospel of peace and
good will, love and joy. For one thing, he retained his vivid sense of
the hellish powers of demons, immediately exemplified by the growing
boldness of witches or women having sexual intercourse with them.
The basic anxiety reflected by his literal belief in such superstitions
appeared in a profoundly ambivalent spiritual posture: on the one hand
an extreme humility, so compulsive that it suggests a morbid humiliation; on the other an overbearing self-righteousness, so fierce that it
suggests a compulsive need to humiliate others. "You are a fool," his old
confessor had told him. "God is not angry with you—it is you who are
angry with God." Luther's saving experience then bred a more dangerous confusion: "The anger of my mouth is not my anger," he cried,
"but God's anger." His anger as naturally bred hatred, which inspired
some of the ugliest passages in all religious literature. (His tirades
against Jews, for example, were as nasty as any that came out of Hitler's
Germany.) Luther's hatred was more savage because again he was prone
in all sincerity to identify his enemies with God's enemies.

In this view, at any rate, his basic doctrines become readily understandable. First and last he insisted on man's utter dependence on God.

Salvation was only by the grace of God, which was a free gift, wholly gratuitous except that it was granted to none but true believers; man's justification was only by faith, never by his own works; and while Luther took for granted that good Christians should and would perform good works, as a sign of grace, they could never claim for them any merit at all. He hated the very word "merit" because it obscured man's crying need of being completely humbled: "For if, as long as he has any persuasion that he can do even the least thing himself towards his own salvation, he retain a confidence in himself and do not utterly despair in himself, so long he is not humbled before God." Luther accordingly denied men free will, since none was free to earn salvation on his own and God made all the crucial choices, with the help of a Satan he had created to take care of the overwhelming majority of souls he had predestined to damnation. It is safe to assume that many followers of Luther were confident enough that they had been granted grace, and as men of true faith were really worthy of it; but the fact remains that he denied man natural dignity, any grounds for claims to freedom and rights.

Hence, too, he was fiercely authoritarian—in practice more so than the Roman Church, whose slackness he despised. Having rejected its authority, he had to base his whole creed on the only other available authority, the Bible. This gave him some difficulties, since the Word of God was not always clear or clearly consistent. Luther had a highhanded way with inconvenient texts, for instance calling the Epistle of James a "mere letter of straw" because it stressed the necessity of good works; and in drawing chiefly on St. Paul, to whom he owed his doctrine of justification by faith, he tended to slight the potentially embarrassing ethical teaching of Jesus. Yet he did not permit others to interpret the Bible as freely as he himself had. Justification was by faith—but only the proper faith; the gospel according to Luther was the only true gospel. He flatly repudiated the principle of freedom of conscience implicit in his initial refusal to violate his own conscience, and his initial teaching that every Christian was his own priest. Having set up his Lutheran Church, with ordained ministers to carry out the forms of worship he prescribed, he soon began warring on not only Catholics but Anabaptists, a more radical sect that anticipated later Protestantism by envisaging the ideal of a "free church in a free state," and electing their own pastors. He had some excuse in that they also anticipated the wayward tendencies of Protestantism by preaching that the Millennium was at hand—another sign of the deep social unrest and discontent; though mostly peaceful, one group set up a reign of holy terror at Münster. Anyway, Lutherans postponed the Millennium by joining Catholics in a persecution of the Anabaptists, pushing through an imperial law that condemned them all to death. For Luther completely justified the use of force, even to the sword, on all enemies of the true faith. He prepared the way for the religious wars and massacres that bloodied Europe for more than a century, and that most thoroughly devastated his own land of Germany in the Thirty Years' War.

Similarly he attacked the claims of reason, the whole effort to maintain rational relations with God. Although he had himself to reason furiously as he expounded and defended his heresies, beginning with his 95 theses, he insisted on the absolute necessity of faith, and faith alone. For him it had to be essentially an unquestioning faith, since the God he worshiped was an arbitrary, unaccountable God, never to be held up to human standards of justice and reasonableness. He was prodigal in epithets to humble "Dame Reason"—that "silly little fool," that "whore," that "Devil's bride," "God's worst enemy," etc. Rejecting more emphatically than Mohammed had the tradition of Hellenism, he accordingly led a revulsion against the Renaissance, especially as represented by Erasmus; at first drawn to Erasmus as a fellow critic of the Church, Luther ended by cursing him as "the greatest of scoundrels," even "the true adversary of Christ." He was naturally hostile as well to the humanism and naturalism of the Renaissance, its faith in human dignity, its interest in the world as a source of beauty, truth, and joy instead of merely a place to work hard in. Art had no serious function in his scheme of things, and it was always dangerous as a mode of idolatry or a source of pride. Science was not yet a serious menace, but in dismissing Copernicus as an arrogant fool he signaled the persistent opposition it would meet from Protestant Fundamentalists.

Most fateful were the political ideas of Luther, as they were crystallized by the Peasants' Revolt in Germany. Here we may discount the common charges that he betrayed the peasants, and his own principles, by full support of the princes who in crushing the revolt slaughtered some hundred thousand of them. Though the poor devils took over from him such slogans as "evangelical freedom" and "divine justice" in asserting their economic grievances, and he at first expressed sympathy with their cause, all along he had argued only for the "spiritual liberty" of Christians, a liberty of the inner life that by no means called for political liberty. If he had some harsh things to say about princes, who shared in the natural depravity of all mankind, he was naturally partial to their rule, since he needed their support against the Papacy, and their divinely ordained powers were a commonplace of Christian tradition, stated most plainly by his spiritual mentor St. Paul. He had never preached a faith in the common people. Like other respectable Christians, accordingly, he was soon frightened by the excesses of the outraged peasants. He was only being characteristically violent when he declared that "the brute populace must be governed by brute force," called upon the "dear lords" to make the civil sword "red and bloody," exhorted them to "stab, slay, and throttle" without mercy. Readers may decide for themselves whether it was pride or humility that led him to assume full responsibility for the slaughter: "Their blood be on my head."

There is no question, at any rate, about Luther's mature political conclusions. He declared the absolute necessity of obedience to "all those who are set over us as superiors," however tyrannical or unjust they might seem; no crime, not even murder, was more heinous than "revolt against established authority" (always excepting, of course, the authority claimed by popes). Likewise he insisted that the permanent division of society into classes was divinely ordained. He stated more emphatically his low opinion of the common people: "The princes of this world are gods, the common people are Satan. . . . I would rather suffer a prince doing wrong than a people doing right." All Christians could still enjoy their precious "spiritual liberty," the more surely if they followed his advice to restrict the Sermon on the Mount to private life; but the outer life he put under the absolute authority of the state. Luther was pleased to say that he had brought the secular state to "the plenitude of its rights and powers." If his boast rather flattered the petty German states, Prussia would eventually vindicate it.

Meanwhile the basic doctrines of Luther were all taken over by John Calvin, who had a considerably greater influence on Protestantism as it spread through western Europe. Trained as a lawyer, Calvin was much more consistent than Luther, remorselessly carrying all his doctrines to their logical extreme. In his *Institutes of the Christian Religion*, which in successive editions he steadily expanded from six to eighty chapters, he provided by all odds the most systematic, comprehensive statement of the Protestant faith. He made Pauline Christianity theologically more respectable by buttressing it with the authority of St. Augustine. More important, he ruled a community in Geneva, where he had consented to remain only on condition that its citizens accept his terms. His theocratic state shortly became the spiritual capital of

the Protestant world, in the words of John Knox "the most perfect
school of Christ that ever was on earth since the days of the apostles."
This godliest of schools made it still plainer that freedom was the least
concern of the Reformers, except as a menace to the monopoly they
claimed on the true faith.

Calvin was more rigorously authoritarian than the impassioned,
sometimes careless Luther, and more insistent on the strict letter of the
law. From first to last he declared the absolute authority of his church.
Having appeared on the scene later than Luther, when such radicals
as the Anabaptists had already stirred up trouble, he was much more
concerned with discipline and organization, and more fearful of freethinking, which he called the supreme heresy. In Geneva he could
stamp out any tendencies to either political or religious individualism
by excommunicating citizens, thereby depriving them of all civil rights.
While enforcing such requirements as churchgoing he also could and
did interfere with private life much more than the Roman Church ever
had, keeping a close eye on the diversions of the godly; among the
characteristic ordinances of Geneva was one prohibiting "treating one
another to drinks." In particular, Calvin could consistently enforce the
intolerance that Luther often could only preach. He made history by
making an example of Servetus, the first Protestant to bring historical
criticism to bear on the Bible they all looked to for authority, and so
to elucidate the early, incorrupt Christianity they sought to return to.
Having published such findings as that the Nicene Creed about the
Trinity is found neither in the Bible nor in the early Church Fathers,
Servetus had to flee the Inquisition in France (which Calvin had
secretly put on to his heresy), and he made the mistake of coming
through Geneva; though he was not a citizen and had no followers,
Calvin had him burned at the stake. Leading Protestants everywhere
applauded with Melanchthon this "signal act of piety."

Likewise Calvin was more literal and thorough than Luther in his
teaching on the absolute sovereignty of God. Not a drop of rain fell,
he declared, not a single hair was lost, not a single word spoken, without the express will of God. Characteristically, he always emphasized
the will and the power of God—not his lawfulness, or the rational
order of his creation—and always with the refrain: "We are not our
own—we are God's." In spelling out the full implications of the doctrine of predestination, he recognized the logical difficulty raised by its
irrefutable logic, for it remains unclear why men should be exhorted
or coerced into serving God, who had predetermined their behavior

down to the last detail, and as unclear why such a God should be called just; but Calvin answered simply that it was unreasonable for men to "scrutinize with impunity those things which the Lord has determined to be hidden in himself." In every edition of the *Institutes* he warned against the dangers of speculating about the divine nature. Indeed, the very obscurity of the Lord's plan was all to the good: the dread it excited was finally "productive of the most delightful benefit." As for justice, whatever God wills is *ipso facto* just. Calvin dismissed more abruptly the objection that the rigid separation of all mankind into the very few Elect and the many Damned violated the Christian principles of equality and brotherhood: "I stop not to notice those fanatics who pretend that grace is offered equally and promiscuously to all." If other fanatics might object that he was destroying the basis of solidarity and community, he had an easy answer for this too: all that mattered was the community of the Elect, as represented by Geneva. The fate of the Damned was no concern of theirs—their business was only to keep the Damned out of the community.

Ultimately, the basic logic of Calvin's creed remained that of Luther —the utter unworthiness of man. Again he was more thoroughgoing (or as Rabelais saw it, "demoniacal"), drawing about the blackest picture of human depravity to be found in the history of religious thought:

> The mind of man is so entirely alienated from the righteousness of God that he cannot conceive, desire, or design anything but what is wicked, distorted, impure, and iniquitous; that his heart is so thoroughly envenomed by sin that it can breathe out nothing but corruption and rottenness; that if some men occasionally make a show of goodness, their mind is ever interwoven with hypocrisy and deceit, their soul inwardly bound with the fetters of wickedness.

Manifestly, such a creature was wholly unfit for freedom of any sort. There was little point either in preaching charity to the monster, or making a point of extending it: to put charity before faith and hope, Calvin said, was "a mere reverie of a distempered imagination." If he neglected to add that the Sermon on the Mount was sheer lunacy, at least he never permitted it to corrupt his regime in Geneva. The only question, then, is why the Genevans voluntarily put up with such a harsh regime; for while they groaned often enough and gave some signs of hating their revered dictator, generally they appeared to believe that his rule was good for them, or at least for their neighbors. Presumably his insistence on their unworthiness and their impotence relieved as it reflected the widespread feelings of insecurity, relieved them more specifically from the burdens of freedom and rational responsibility: "We are not our own." But more obviously gratifying was his assurance that they would come into their own. If he could not prove that they were the Elect, the "most perfect school" of Geneva naturally induced them to assume that they were.[2] Thus Jonathan Edwards in America would find predestination a "delightful doctrine, exceeding bright, pleasant, and sweet." Calvin himself seems not to have been seriously tormented by neurotic doubts about his own predestined fate, any more than by misgivings about the possible "hypocrisy and deceit" in his own "show of goodness."

His political views, lastly, were at bottom the same as Luther's, but here he was somewhat less consistent because of his different experience. Calvin left some loopholes for resistance to tyrannical, wicked, or especially impious kings. Having set up his own independent church, which he wanted to be free from state interference, he was more inclined to remember that the Old Testament was full of examples of resistance to impious kings, noting that Daniel in particular had thereby earned his way into the Bible, and to insist that kings too owed absolute obedience to the Lord—"the King of kings." For all practical purposes, however, Calvin insisted as strongly as Luther on the duty of passive obedience, holding to this whenever the issue was forced (as by his follower John Knox in Scotland). Men had no right to rebel against even the "most iniquitous kings," since God had set them above the people as a punishment of their own iniquity; men should always be on guard against the "seditious" idea that a "king is to be treated according to his merits." Calvin left no loopholes at all for rebellion by the common people, or anything like the Peasants' Revolt, for his immediate purpose in writing the *Institutes* was to prove to the French king that the Protestant faith entailed no such seditious ideas. As a legalist, he took more pains than Luther had in separating the two realms in which Christians had to live—the spiritual kingdom and the political kingdom—and in making clear that "spiritual liberty" should not be "mis-

---

[2] It should also be noted that Calvin did not succeed in making Geneva conform to his standards of virtue. The records of the city indicate that vice became more prevalent after the Reformation, despite increasingly severe punishments. (Two of his own women relatives were convicted of adultery.) His failure may help to explain his obsession with natural depravity, but possibly it was also due to this obsession.

applied to political regulations." As the ruler of Geneva, Calvin was never guilty of any such misapplication himself.

Nevertheless, his theocracy did not outlive him very long. Elsewhere Calvinists soon had to deal with hostile kings—bad kings like those the Israelites had resisted in the name of the True God. It was the followers of the ultra-authoritarian Calvin, indeed, who took the lead in struggles that would eventuate in the growth of both political and religious freedom, ultimately of democracy. We are brought to the ironic consequences of the Protestant Reformation: unintended, unforeseen, yet quite understandable, even predictable, on the whole more logical than the inhuman logic of John Calvin.

3. *The Long-range Consequences*

For the future of Europe, the all-important fact remained that the Protestant Reformation began as a revolt against authority—the oldest, most deeply entrenched authority in Western Christendom. When Rome demanded that Luther recant, he thrilled northern Europe by his reckless refusal to do so, and his public burning of the papal bull. "I cannot and will not recant anything," he told the imperial Diet at Worms, "for it is neither safe nor right to go against conscience." Conservative in his dogma, he was none the less a nonconformist, a radical, a rebel, who at first often used the vocabulary of freedom. "I wish to be free," he said plainly. "I do not wish to become the slave of any authority. . . . I shall proclaim with confidence what I believe to be true, whether it is advanced by a Catholic or a heretic, whether it is authorized or not by I care not what authority." From the outset other Protestants, such as the Anabaptists, began carrying much further the principle of freedom, making much more of the favorite Protestant text: "We ought to obey God rather than men." They could disobey Luther too because he had insisted on the exclusive authority of the Bible, and made the Bible available to ordinary men by his magnificent translation of it into German. As the Roman Church knew in its wisdom, simple men could read many dangerous ideas out of Scripture— ideas of equality, the brotherhood of all men, the evils of wealth, the oppression of the poor, etc. Luther had started something that he could not possibly stop.

If the Roman Church, with its immense organization and its long tradition, conceivably had some chance of maintaining its spiritual authority over western Europe, the Protestant Reformers had not the faintest chance. They may now look more arrogantly, preposterously self-righteous than they were in their assumption that all good Christians should and could agree upon the true faith, and that any disagreement with their own views was not only mistaken but wicked and perverse; for this is what almost all Christian leaders had assumed since Christianity became an established religion. Nevertheless, the Reformers had fatally weakened the principle of religious authority, they had no long common tradition to appeal to, and they could never hope to win universal assent to their personal, partial interpretations of the Bible. Having taken bold liberties, they tried desperately to prevent any further liberties, but they had no means except persecution for maintaining uniformity of belief. From the beginning, moreover, they disagreed among themselves. Luther and Zwingli engaged in a violent controversy over the sacrament of holy communion, each proving his case by arguments from infallible Scripture. A century after Luther's death there were some 180 Protestant sects, almost all dogmatic, all based on the Bible. In defending and propagating their gospel, all perforce appealed to reason, which if not "God's worst enemy" was certainly Martin Luther's.

Protestants were very slow, indeed, to learn the impossibility of agreement upon religious truth, or of the maintenance of any absolute authority. Mostly they learned the hardest way, by incessant conflict, finally through exhaustion; and many never did learn. Yet they themselves had introduced the principle that made agreement impossible, strictly unnecessary—the principle of individual responsibility to God alone. To most Catholic thinkers this still looks like mere egoism; Maritain, for example, has said that Luther exalted individuality, not "true personality," and only degraded personality by freeing "the material individuality . . . the animal man." Those who are less certain what "true" personality is may remark that at least Protestantism gave a kind of spiritual expression to the individualism of the Renaissance, fostering a spirit of personal independence and integrity that seems more human than animal. Eventually some Protestant churches explicitly asserted the right of all men to religious freedom—a right now cherished in the democracies, though not yet formally approved by the Roman Church.

And so with the inseparably related principle of freedom of conscience. This was stated plainly by John Huss, who was martyred primarily because of it rather than any doctrinal heresy.[3] Luther too at first maintained that "faith is free" and cannot be compelled: "Heresy can never be prevented by force." Although he soon repudiated this idea, and Calvin never accepted it, they could not kill it either. Shortly after Luther's death appeared an anonymous work *Concerning Heretics* (generally attributed to Sebastian Castellio) that had a wide influence, sufficient to alarm Calvin. Reminding Christians of all the prophets, apostles, and saints who had been martyred for their religious belief, it argued that "to force the conscience of a man is worse than cruelly to take his life," and asked the pertinent question that Luther had forgotten as completely as the inquisitors: "Would you like to have yours forced?" Persecution was also condemned in the catechism of Socinus, a forerunner of Unitarianism, and toleration to some extent supported by other minority sects, if only because they were exposed to persecution. Again it took most Protestants a long time to learn the obvious truth that granting freedom of conscience was with them a practical necessity, and not necessarily a blasphemy; but again the principle had been implicit in the Reformation from the outset.

In much the same way Protestantism came to advance the broader cause of intellectual enlightenment and the diffusion of knowledge. Despite his antirationalism, Luther had a high regard for learning, including the humanistic learning that had thrown new light on early Christianity and enabled him to translate the Bible. Calvin saw more clearly the need of popular education in a religion that stressed Bible reading instead of liturgy, sacraments, prayers to saints—modes of worship that hardly required literacy. His followers did much more to educate the common people than had the Roman Church; in New England they would take the unprecedented step of making primary schooling not only free but obligatory. Protestantism was likewise more open to new thought, and thence to ideals of freedom of thought, speech, and press, because the Reformers had willy-nilly forced men back to first principles, asserted their right to think for themselves. In

---

[3] Unhappily, it was too much for his own followers in Bohemia. The Hussites defeated papal crusades against them, to the usual accompaniment of heroism and atrocity, but as usual this bred fanaticism and they ended by fighting among themselves. A sect known as Taborites recognized the traditional "signs" preceding the Millennium, and raised the traditional banner: "Accursed be the man who withholds his sword from shedding the blood of the enemies of Christ. Every believer must wash his hands in that blood." One consequence of the fierce struggle was a setback to the cultural advance of Bohemia (modern Czechoslovakia), which thereafter was relatively isolated from western Europe and played a negligible part in the history of freedom until modern times.

exercising this right, some of their followers went on to play a major role in the development of natural philosophy and science that emancipated thought from religious authority. Catholicism, with its long intellectual tradition, could count such pioneers as Galileo and Descartes, but typically they got into trouble with their Church; and thereafter a far greater proportion of the leading philosophers and scientists were Protestants.

In political life, the immediate issue forced by the Reformation was the extent of royal power and the obligation of obedience. Lutheranism remained faithful to its close alliance with monarchy, on whose support it depended in the regions of Germany and Scandinavia where it was firmly established. Calvinism, however, had started as a more independent church, and it was bound for certain trouble as it spread over countries where it was a minority sect. In one digression Calvin had indicated a way of meeting such trouble, suggesting that although private citizens should not take it upon themselves to resist kings, such resistance might be the right, even the duty of lesser magistrates or duly constituted authorities. In Scotland John Knox accordingly exhorted the nobility to uphold God's word whenever kings did anything contrary to it; while he had no more idea of popular rights than Calvin did, arguing only for the religious duty of resistance, he boldly denounced as "blasphemy" the prevailing idea that "God hath commanded kings to be obeyed when they command impiety." In France the Huguenots drew on medieval theory, including the principle of natural law, to argue that the power of kings is properly limited. Protestants got some support, indeed, from Catholics, who might develop an unwonted passion for religious rights in lands where they were a persecuted minority, and elsewhere might be interested in restoring the authority of the Papacy. Up to this point, the basic issues were hardly clear-cut, and the kings generally got the better of the confused struggles.

But Protestants soon began drawing on the more revolutionary democratic principles implicit in their assertion of individual responsibility and right. Thus in Calvin's Geneva Christopher Goodman went so far as to maintain that even the common people had the right to resist if their magistrates failed them: God had not created them to be "bond slaves" or "brute beasts," as they must become if they suffered "all power and liberty to be taken from them." Much more influential was the *Vindiciae contra Tyrannos* (1579), a political classic written by a Huguenot who called himself Junius Brutus. In asserting the people's right to resist unjust rulers, he was careful to point out that by the "people" he meant the magistrates who represented them, not the unruly multitude; yet he also argued that both magistrates and kings derived their authority from the people, and that accordingly "the whole body of the people is above the king." Kings had no "impunity" because they were trustees obligated to maintain "equity and justice," the moral good of the community. Although the interests of "Junius Brutus" were more religious than political, he shifted emphasis from authority and obedience to responsibility, rational consent, and the protection of rights. He was the first important thinker to base political theory on the idea of inalienable rights.

Such ideas gathered force because the Reformers had also willy-nilly stirred up the common people untouched by the Renaissance humanists. However mistaken, the German peasants who revolted against their princes at least thought they had Luther behind them. "All privileges shall be done away," Michael Geismayr proposed, "as they are contrary to the Word of God, and distort the law which declares that no one shall suffer from the misdeeds of others." (Even Luther might have been touched by his conclusion: "This is Geismayr's constitution when he dreams in his chimney corner.") The peasants got positive support from the Anabaptists, who like other radical sects appealed chiefly to the poor, and suffered more because the upper classes were quick to see the connection between these "heresies" and the active social discontent. And the Anabaptists signaled another potent democratic tendency of Protestantism by their practice of electing their own ministers, just as had early Christians. Later Congregationalists or Independents declared the right of any like-minded group to set up its own church, choose its own ministers—in short, to form a voluntary, democratic religious association. More conservative Calvinists at least retained a measure of independence, in spite—or perhaps because—of Calvin's dictatorial regime in Geneva, for thereafter they never allowed their ministry to exercise such power as the hierarchical Catholic priesthood did.

All these tendencies were carried furthest by the Calvinist Puritans, who in England won a revolution that brought out the most radical potentialities of Protestantism, and who in America enjoyed a freedom that before long the orthodox were unable to restrict to their own kind. Some of them quite lost sight of Geneva. Although their story belongs to a later chapter, we may pause to imagine the horror of Calvin's ghost when John Lilburne affirmed that every "individual man and woman," as descendants of Adam and Eve, were "by nature all equal and alike in power, dignity, authority, and majesty"—not merely in damnability. It was "unnatural, irrational, sinful, wicked, unjust, devilish, and tyrannical" for any man—king or minister, Lilburne insisted—to claim the right to rule over "any sort of men in the world without their free consent." That both kings and ministers long fought such ideas, while also fighting one another, only helped to assure the outcome in countries where Calvinism had flourished. The things that were God's, or Calvin's, in Geneva were moved into a private realm, where the individual could not be coerced by either church or state; while the things that were Caesar's were correspondingly limited and made subject to public consent.

The Puritans likewise most fully exemplified the inherent dynamism of Protestantism, sprung from the revolutionary conditions of its birth, which raised as much havoc with the religious law laid down by the Reformers. At first, as in Islam, the doctrine of predestination had fired energy and zeal, inducing nothing like passivity. The Elect were assured that a God of will and power was on their side; or if they had any misgivings they felt impelled to redouble their own efforts, since they could no longer fall back on the Virgin, the saints, the magic of sacraments and relics, or any external aids to salvation, and then they might actually feel the regeneration that was the inner sign of grace. Yet the Pauline Christianity to which Luther and Calvin had reverted was not really suited to an age of vigorous expansion, in which the tendencies to rationalism and independent thought were too strong to be suppressed as they had been in Islam. There was no going back if Protestantism was to remain a driving inspiration. While the spirit of the early Reformers was periodically revivèd in new movements (such as Methodism) that sought to return to early or "pure" Christianity, their basic dogmas became obsolete. The doctrine of predestination was obviously doomed; while it long remained on the books, it was played down, gradually forgotten or quietly dropped, and is today about the deadest of Christian dogmas. The doctrine of justification by faith alone met a similar fate, though its demise has perhaps been more decently veiled. As Luther and Calvin themselves had made a gospel of work in the Lord's vineyard, more and more of their followers openly professed that good works did count for a great deal, and that a man could earn his salvation. The paradoxical outcome was that Puritans especially put more stress on works than Catholicism did, even to the seemingly profane works of business. In this way Protestantism contributed most directly to the secularization of the Western world.

So too it became allied, however uneasily or reluctantly, with all the forces that were revolutionizing this world. Other indirect, belated, ambiguous consequences of the Reformation will therefore keep cropping up in the chapters that follow. At this stage we may note as a final example what it did for the status of women.

Directly, women lost much of the freedom and the prestige that the educated, at least, had achieved in the Italian Renaissance, when without the fanfare of courtly love they mingled as equals with men in such cultivated circles as Castiglione pictured. Early Protestants echoed St. Paul's low opinion of women. "Let them bear children till they die of it," Luther said bluntly, "—that is what they are for"; and others sounded more like the early saints, emphasizing that the Devil had given them a different idea of what they were for. But Protestants were also disposed to a saner view of sex, in keeping with their habit of breeding lustily. The Reformers had abolished the requirement of celibacy for the ministry; while secularizing marriage by making it a civil ceremony, they exalted it above virginity—a heresy that the Inquisition still combated. Now ranked above the nun, the wife might hope for less degrading treatment than was authorized by current law, which still sanctioned wife-beating, at most limiting the thickness of the rod a husband might use or frowning upon the practice of rubbing salt and vinegar into the welts. Puritan New England in fact took a historic step toward restoring her dignity by a law providing that "Every married woman should be free from bodily correction or stripes by her husband, unless it be in his own defence upon her assault." While Catholic countries remained devoted in theory to the ideal of the virgin nun, and in common practice to the mistress, freethinking Protestants would take a much more active part in the struggle for the rights of women.

This was as confused as the earlier political struggles, to be sure, and no more an all-Protestant crusade. All the long-range consequences of the Reformation were no less confused, thoroughly mixed than the motives of its early converts. The spirit of Luther and Calvin was never killed, their legacy of bigotry is still alive in the Fundamentalist sects. Protestantism later bred the most vociferous opposition to science, or more broadly to both moral and intellectual enlightenment, by its emphasis on the literal, infallible truth of the Bible, its only authority. As it lost much of its early fervor it retained much of its tendency to narrowness and harshness, its conviction of an inalienable right to restrict the pursuit of happiness; it put many a blue law on the books, did its best to smother the genial association of holy day and holiday.

Until recent times, few of its sects declared a devotion to political, intellectual, or religious freedom on principle. Altogether, Protestantism was scarcely the main impetus in the revolutionary developments that made over the Western world, for the most part only falling in with these developments more readily than did the Roman Church. Nevertheless, it was on the face of the record a real influence. Protestant countries in northern Europe and their colonists in America indisputably played the leading role in the growth of free thought, the advance of science, the rise of democracy, the Industrial Revolution. Catholic southern and central Europe generally remained aristocratic and monarchical, and its common people more peasant-like. France, the conspicuous exception, had a stronger Protestant tradition than any other Catholic country, and developed a stronger anticlerical tradition. These differences are more significant because the Reformation brought about reforms within the Roman Church—reforms that genuinely renovated it, but without liberalizing it.

4. *The Counter-Reformation*

In spreading so rapidly, and apparently threatening the very existence of the Roman Church, the Protestant Reformation soon revealed that the Church was not so morally and spiritually bankrupt as the many enemies of the Papacy had been proclaiming for centuries. It set about purifying itself of the most obvious corruptions; if political ambition might still lead popes to instigate murder plots (as against Queen Elizabeth of England), Rome would never again be the seat of such scandals as it long had been. Elsewhere the spiritual resources of Catholicism were demonstrated by a remarkable gallery of saints, including Thomas More, François de Sales, Philip Neri, Teresa, John of the Cross, and Ignatius Loyola, founder of the Jesuit order. Within a few years after the death of Luther the Church halted the surge of Protestantism. The only country it lost thereafter was the Dutch Republic, while it permanently recovered much greater territories that Protestantism had been winning—south Germany, Poland, Bohemia, and Hungary.

Its success was due most conspicuously to Loyola's Society of Jesus, formally approved in 1540. In the belief of the pope who canonized him, Loyola was raised by divine providence to combat that "foulest of monsters," Martin Luther. A romantic soldier, he too had been blessed by a saving experience, which made him a Soldier of the Cross, wholly dedicated to the task of restoring the true faith. His spiritual travail taught him that man indeed had the free will denied by Luther, but he brought it under the thorough discipline set forth in his *Spiritual Exercises.* His militant order became the most efficient organization in Christendom, and worked tirelessly all over Europe. In the spirit of its founder it remained highly imaginative, tempering a discipline as rigorous as Calvin's with much more tact. It developed the best schools in Europe, employing the methods of the humanists and exposing students to such subjects as science and philosophy, but always with the aim of inoculating them against the dangers of heresy and free thought. It was both more rational and more humane than Calvin's "most perfect school of Christ," teaching that naturally sinful man could nevertheless earn salvation, because a merciful Christ did not demand perfection. "God asks nothing impossible," declared St. Ignatius. In China its missionaries had spectacular success—success that might have had momentous consequences were it not that a pope infuriated the Chinese emperor by ordering an end to their toleration of heathenish Chinese customs.

At some risk of possible injustice, I shall not dwell here on this impressive achievement, for the usual simple reason: the regenerated Church did not foster the growth of freedom. Many might applaud its refusal to make any concessions to the "modern spirit," which no longer seems so salutary as it once did. In successfully holding to its traditional dogma, rejecting the heretical notion of "progress," the Church proved that a conservative, authoritarian religion could survive in a dynamic, revolutionary society, and intimates that such a religion might satisfy the deepest needs of most men in such a society. In any case, it is indisputable that after the Counter-Reformation the Catholic Church was distinctly less liberal than the medieval Church had been.

Its spirit was exemplified by the Jesuits. We may discount the evil reputation they won, which led to the suppression of their order in the eighteenth century. Although they were unquestionably given to the casuistry denounced by Pascal, and might stoop to murder in their war on heretics, their declared mission was chiefly to propagandize, not to deepen or purify the faith; they naturally paid some price for the quick results they sought. More pertinent here is the essential nature of the Jesuit order: a militarist organization, ruled by a general, trained to absolute, unquestioning obedience, not in the least concerned with ideals of freedom, dedicated rather to the creed of Dostoyevsky's Grand Inquisitor. "Laying aside all private judgment," Loyola had said, "we ought to keep our minds prepared and ready to obey in all things the true Spouse of Christ our Lord, which is our Holy Mother, the Hierarchical Church." Private judgment should not even distinguish black from white: "what seems black is white if the Hierarchical Church so orders." When Jesuit thinkers tried to set limits to the power of monarchs they were by no means trying to assure the rights of subjects, or of ordinary Christians. Their primary object—which made them feared and hated by many Catholics too—was to maintain the authority of the pope, the generalissimo of the Hierarchical Church. Their cult of the Papacy made it impossible for them to consider the most feasible means of maintaining the independence of the Church—separating it from the state.

Meanwhile their basic ideals had governed the Council of Trent, which first met in 1545, completed its work in 1563, and fixed the future course of the no longer truly "catholic" Church. The hopes of some bishops and monarchs that the Council might reunite Christendom, and of more that it might limit the power of the Papacy, were soon shattered. Although the doctrinal differences between Protestants and Catholics were no more serious than those among medieval Schoolmen, and now seem much less significant than all the traditional beliefs about the Creation, the Fall, the Redemption, the Trinity, etc., that both sides agreed on, both had become intransigent, the more so because the most fundamental issue at stake was the authority of the Papacy. The popes, who at first disapproved the idea of a council as a threat to their authority, generally dominated its proceedings from the outset, packing it with Italians and later bringing in a battalion of Jesuits to outmaneuver the opposition. Affirming that authority was lodged in both the Bible and the tradition of the Church, the Council agreed that the principle of hierarchy was divinely ordained, even though the Holy Ghost had neglected to mention the word in the Bible. Regulations were approved to eliminate such plain abuses as simony and the sale of indulgences, but otherwise no basic constitutional limits were set on the pope; his powers of excommunication were strengthened, all the bishops were sworn to complete obedience of him. In effect, the Council of Trent assured papal absolutism, which eventually culminated in the dogma of Papal Infallibility.

The one drawback so far as the Papacy was concerned was that its temporal powers could not be assured. Philip II of Spain accepted the decrees of the Council with the proviso "saving the royal rights," the French king was as careful to accept only its decrees on dogma, and the Holy Roman emperor never officially recognized its work at all. The triumph of the secular power was sealed for all time by the great European congress that in 1648 drew up the Treaty of Westphalia, which in ending the Thirty Years' War also ended the religious wars (and incidentally ended the Holy Roman Empire in all but name). The treaty was made wholly by and for the sovereign states, on terms disapproved by the current pope. In matters of faith, however, the basic decisions of the Council of Trent were generally acceptable to the Catholic world, and they remained final. The Council not only emphatically reaffirmed but more sharply defined the absolute, infallible truth of Catholic dogma, especially the dogmas questioned by Protestants. It decreed once and for all that outside the Catholic Church there is no salvation.[4] At the same time it paid an involuntary tribute to the Reformers by likewise reverting to early Christian tradition, as plainly repudiating the spirit of Peter Abelard and St. Thomas Aquinas. It condemned all "inquisitive curiosity" about Catholic dogma: "Faith excludes not only doubt, but even the desire of subjecting its truth to demonstration." The renovated Church proceeded to take stronger measures to suppress all doubt and discourage all such desire, in particular by its Inquisition and its Index of Prohibited Books—instruments far more efficient than any the Reformers had devised.

Although the Inquisition had been revived before the Council of Trent gathered, its persecution now became much more thorough and systematic. It made a name for itself above all in Spain, the homeland of St. Ignatius Loyola and the greatest Catholic power. Here it had a record of almost no acquittals, in keeping with a strategy summed up by one inquisitor: "It is no great matter whether they that die on account of religion be guilty or innocent, provided we terrify the people by such examples." There remains some question about just how many thousands it racked and burned, and how unpopular it actually was, since the auto-da-fé was always a gala occasion, but in any case it effectually eliminated all traces of Protestantism at home. In 1568 Spain gave singular proof of its Catholic zeal by a decree condemning to death as heretics the entire population of the Netherlands. As for the Roman

---

[4] In view of popular mentality, this decree later gave the Church a practical advantage that some Jesuits exploited. While many Protestants came to admit that Catholics might be saved, Catholics still insisted that no Protestant could be; so simple men might be persuaded that it was safer to bet on the Roman Church.

Index of Prohibited Books, this too had been anticipated by censorship but it was established more formally by the Council of Trent, and then put in charge of a special committee in the College of Cardinals. Among its immediate victims were Catholic humanists, first of all Erasmus, who had been immensely popular in Spain. Although the censors presently relented to the extent of putting Erasmus, Dante, and other suspects on a separate Index, allowing their works to be published after a thorough expurgation, an increasing number of famous works were listed among the Prohibited Books, which the faithful could read only on pain of excommunication. The Church turned literally reactionary just as Europe was about to enter the great age of science and philosophy, and then the Enlightenment. To appear on the Roman Index was almost a proof of intellectual distinction, and the complete roster would serve as a sufficient index to the intellectual history of Europe.

There remains more question about how effective the Index was, or whether it deserved the name Father Sarpi gave it at the time—"the finest secret ever discovered for applying religion to the purpose of making men idiotic." On the record, it was not the utter blight on literature and thought that many of its critics have assumed. Spain, where it was most thoroughly enforced, went on to enjoy its golden age in literature, in Cervantes and Calderón producing its greatest writers; writers in other Catholic countries managed to publish works of distinction, sometimes liberal in tendency; and the most fruitful of the heretical ideas in prohibited books (such as Galileo's, which remained on the Index until 1835) generally became well enough known to educated Catholics. But on the record, too, the Church at least succeeded in discouraging free inquiry, searching criticism, or original speculation. Italy went into a cultural decline, the seventeenth century was the most barren age of Germany (both Catholic and Lutheran), and the whole Catholic world except France plainly lagged behind the Protestant world in creativity. As for the Catholic masses, they remained unlettered and servile. They were denied the free public discussion needed to fit them for self-government, given little opportunity or incentive for self-realization except through obedience or blind faith.

Needless to add, important changes have come over Catholicism too, as it perforce adapted itself to the revolutionary changes that kept transforming the Western world anyway. Especially in America, most Catholics do not actually subscribe to the decrees of the Council of Trent, if they ever heard of it at all, and are as devoted as most Protestants to ideals of freedom. The Church itself tacitly acknowledged a change in spirit as it dropped the Inquisition, began removing famous works from its Index of Prohibited Books. Formally, however, it has never renounced the dogmas laid down at Trent; and the spirit of the Counter-Reformation dominated its official policies during the history covered in this volume.

| # *THE GROWTH OF POWER*

1. *The Explorations and Discoveries*

In 1494 Spain and Portugal signed the Treaty of Tordesillas, which in effect divided between them the whole world except Europe; Portugal got the Eastern Hemisphere, Spain the Western. To the Spanish kings the possession of only one hemisphere meant a grudging concession, since in the preceding year Pope Alexander VI had issued bulls granting them sovereignty over any new lands they wanted, east or west. To the peoples of Asia, however, it meant nothing at all—they of course never heard of these ridiculous arrangements. By 1500 the best informed among them knew only that a few of the "Franks," rude people who centuries before had tried to wrest a strip of land from Islam, had recently shown up in India. And had there been a farsighted, universal historian, acquainted with the whole civilized world, he would have been more amused by the preposterous conceit of these Europeans; for the history of preceding centuries clearly indicated that the future belonged to Asiatic peoples.

Islam had long since thrown the Frankish infidels out of the Holy Land. In the thirteenth century the Mongols had swept over most of the civilized world, building an empire that reached from Poland to the Pacific—by far the greatest empire yet known to history. No mere horde of barbarians, they were vastly superior to the Europeans in military discipline and strategy; they drove as far as Vienna and could almost certainly have conquered the rest of Europe had they had a mind to. Although their empire soon broke up, their descendants still dominated large regions (including southern Russia), and in the fourteenth century Tamerlane had again demonstrated their power by conquests such as no European people had yet achieved. Now Turkish peoples were on the march, dominating most of the civilized world from Mongolia to Algiers. Babur was about to set up the great Mogul Empire in India; the Ottoman Turks had added the Balkan region to their growing empire and within a few decades they too would reach Vienna. For a long time the Ottomans had been adding to the woes of the wretched Europeans by disrupting their commerce with Asia.

Yet the explorations of the Portuguese and the Spaniards in fact inaugurated the movement that eventually culminated in Western domination of almost the entire world. Portugal had led the way under Prince Henry the Navigator (1394–1460), who laid out a systematic program. Defying the ancient fears of a tropical boiling sea, and a tropical sun that might turn them into Negroes, successive expeditions explored the west coast of Africa, rounded the Cape of Good Hope, then explored the east coast; and in 1498 Vasco da Gama finally reached India, thus opening up direct communications with the East by sea. Within a few years the Portuguese proceeded to establish bases in India, capture the great Malayan port of Malacca, and put in at Canton in China. Seeking a shorter route to the East, Christopher Columbus had meanwhile sailed into the Atlantic and found America, a land reached centuries before him by the Vikings but for all practical purposes discovered by him. Before long Magellan would round South America and head into the vast Pacific, from which one of his ships managed to complete the first circumnavigation of the globe. And this whole enterprise—beginning with the program of Henry the Navigator, the first monarch in history to devote himself primarily to fostering geographical exploration—was characteristically Western. Contemporary China, India, and Islam embarked on no such adventures, even though the Arabs had had a superior fleet. The self-confident Europeans not only hit upon new opportunities but carried them through with remarkable promptness and daring, developing another unique type—the professional explorer. The heroic spirit recorded in an old inscription, "Seafaring is necessary, living is not necessary," found epical expression in *The Lusiads* of Camoëns, who proudly announced that his Muse celebrated no "mere national aggrandizement," as it indulged in no mere "flights of fancy."

The Portuguese poet concluded his epic on a different note, however, lamenting that those to whom he sang were already become "hard of hearing and hard of heart." The whole enterprise was as characteristic in its anomalies. It was essentially a very worldly undertaking, which nevertheless had got off the ground on the wings of fancy. It had an immense effect on Europe, beginning with an obvious shift of power to the Atlantic countries, but leading to other changes that could no more have been foreseen by the most farsighted European historian of the

time. Its major consequences were largely unintended, even contrary
to the hopes and aims of the explorers and their royal patrons. Ultimately the discoveries contributed a great deal to the cause of freedom,
in which none of the pioneers expressed the least interest. We are
dealing with one of the epoch-making adventures of history, but as
usual one that is far from simple.

It began in medieval ignorance and fantasy. Knowing almost nothing
about the East beyond the little Holy Land, except that exotic spices,
jewels, and textiles came out of it, medieval men typically filled the
void with fabulous legends. The literary romance of Alexander the
Great was one handy medium, as about all they knew about him was
that he had conquered Asia. Imagination ran wilder when Marco Polo,
the "millions" man, came back to tell of the wonders and the immense
wealth of the East. His report that Kublai Khan had evinced some
curiosity about the Christian faith bred the exciting illusion that the
East was panting for conversion; Europeans never forgot the Great
Khan, the "King of Kings," cherishing the hope of saving his soul and
sharing his wealth long after the Chinese had overthrown his Mongol
dynasty. Most inspiring, perhaps, was the myth of Prester John: a
mighty Christian monarch in Asia, somewhere behind Islam, who in
the twelfth century sent Western Christians a letter telling of his desire
to join them in crushing the infidels. (The forger of this letter, presumably a churchman, is still unknown.) Prester John was taken very
seriously for some centuries, even though his dynasty mysteriously
neglected to send further signs or any aid against the advancing Moslems, and he was finally moved from Asia to Abyssinia. A primary
objective of the early Portuguese explorers was to get in touch with him
and exploit his Abyssinian empire as a base in the rear of Islam.
Chroniclers represented the undertaking of Henry the Navigator as a
continuation of the Crusades.

There is little question that religious zeal helped to inspire the early
explorations, especially because the Portuguese and Spaniards had long
been engaged in struggles with the Moors. But there is less question
that religion helped chiefly to rationalize the stronger economic motives, inasmuch as Europe had pretty much lost its fervor for crusades.
Christopher Columbus best exemplifies the confusions and delusions
that generated the enterprise. In his journals he kept remarking his
intention to make Christians of the Indians, perhaps to enlist the
Great Khan in the defense against "the abominable sect of Mahomet,"
while reminding Ferdinand and Isabella of the profit that would

thereby accrue to Spain and Christendom: "this was the beginning and end of the undertaking, namely, the increase and glory of the Christian religion." In between, however, he dwelt on the riches Spain could expect, if only to justify the high rewards he expected for himself (for example, the position of "Admiral-in-Chief of the Ocean Sea and Viceroy and Perpetual Governor of all the islands and mainlands I should discover"). He was especially eager to find Zipangu (Japan), which Marco Polo had reported on hearsay was especially rich in gold; so the gold trinkets worn by the natives in Haiti convinced him that this was indeed the land of Zipangu. Columbus had a frank passion for gold. "It is the most estimable of all materials," he told Isabella, perhaps needlessly. "With it one may establish a fortune and obtain everything desirable in the world of wishes. One can with it even get his soul into paradise." The Spanish *conquistadores* who followed in his wake might have a high sense of mission, but certainly they were unabashed in their greed for gold.

If simple greed animated other explorers too, it may be fairer and more illuminating to say that the ruling motives of the epoch-making enterprise were essentially practical, in keeping with the tradition and the economic development of Europe. Long greedy enough, Europeans were now roused because the Ottoman Empire sat on the overland trade route to the East and its spices, treasured as both condiments and preservatives, nor were they appeased by the monopoly on this trade that the uncommercial Turks granted their fellow Christians, the Venetians. Hence the Portuguese sought a sea route to the spices, then Columbus a more direct route. In particular the Europeans displayed their genius for technology as they mastered the new skills needed for voyaging far from shore. At the outset of the fifteenth century their ships were distinctly inferior to those of the Arabs, from whom they had much to learn about practical navigation as well; in setting up his program for exploration, Henry the Navigator called in not only sailors but shipbuilders and instrument makers, astronomers and chart makers. By the end of the century the Europeans had the best ships in the world, as they would have ever after. They had also developed the novel art of naval gunnery; da Gama demonstrated their lasting superiority in naval warfare by destroying an Arab fleet in the Indian Ocean. By this time, too, long-distance seafaring had become a widespread enterprise proceeding on its own momentum. If Columbus had not discovered America, somebody else would surely have done so within a few years. There was no missing it—and then no pause in the effort to get through it or around it once it was recognized as a new continent, a barrier to the East.

In a broader retrospect, the explorations signaled a major theme of European history in the sixteenth and seventeenth centuries—the drive for power. They led to an immense expansion of trade, which in turn contributed to a marked industrial progress; the outcome was as marked a growth in money-power. They were both cause and effect of the related growth of the nation-state, henceforth to be the sovereign power in Europe, and to make large-scale power politics the sovereign concern of its rulers. Power likewise became a major theme in the world of thought. Thomas Hobbes based his political philosophy on the premise that the mainspring of human nature was "a perpetual and restless desire of Power"; he reduced all other passions—as "for riches, knowledge, and honor"—to this ruling passion. Spinoza, who in some passages held up a lofty ethical purpose for the state, in other passages argued that might makes right: "The big fish devour the little fish by natural right." And it is no coincidence that modern science was born in the seventeenth century. The great pioneers of science, from Copernicus and Kepler to Galileo and Newton, were indeed inspired by different motives, or in the words of Thomas Sprat, they sought to breathe "a purer air"; so their epoch-making achievement belongs in a separate chapter. Still, science was to give Western man tremendous power, far beyond the dreams of ancient men or contemporary men in the East; and some pioneers, especially Francis Bacon, were dazzled by visions of these potentialities. Whereas Socrates had valued knowledge as a means to wisdom and virtue, to Bacon it meant first of all power.

The uses and abuses of power—a basic theme of all human history since the beginning of civilization—will accordingly become a more pressing concern in Western history from now on. For the other peoples of the world the discoveries meant the beginning of European imperialism, which would break up some half dozen civilizations. In the East the threat to native independence was not yet serious because the Western nations still lacked the power to master this new kind of imperialism, involving scattered territorial possessions many thousands of miles from home. Nevertheless, the Portuguese, and after them the Dutch, merely exploited the natives. They were interested mainly in quick profits, not in long-range programs of development, still less in any mission to spread the blessings of Western culture; and if their rule was no harsher than the natives were accustomed to, it in any case

brought no compensations to speak of. In the New World the Spanish
conquistadores quickly reduced to servitude the natives they did not
exterminate. Here the royal government, prodded by some high-minded
missionaries, tried to assure the Indians justice and a measure of freedom, but colonists were more interested in exploiting them; chiefly
the Indians were assured the consolations of the Christian faith, which
they had especial need of because they had little earthly opportunity
or hope. And here, too, colonists welcomed the Negro slaves that the
Portuguese had early begun importing from Africa. Slaves had long
been common in southern Europe but chiefly as domestic servants; in
the Spanish Indies they were used for more purely economic purposes,
working the sugar plantations. The traffic in African Negroes became
so lucrative—enriching first the Portuguese, then the Dutch, then the
English and Americans—that men overlooked the economic evils of
slavery, not to mention the scandal to Christendom.

Immediately it brings up the ambiguous consequences of the discoveries, in keeping with the mixed motives of the explorers. The
Christian religion gained very little beyond its converts in Spanish
America, who brought it the "increase" predicted by Columbus but
less clearly the "glory"; their faith remained essentially primitive (as
with most it still is), patron saints replacing their pagan deities and
magicians. In the Portuguese possessions in India, Ceylon, and Malaya
such missionaries as St. Francis Xavier made some converts whose
descendants have remained loyal to Catholicism to this day, but they
represented a minute fraction of the population. The later Dutch made
no effort to convert the East Indies they won control of, by their un-
welcome intrusion tending rather to strengthen the hold of Islam in
the region. Both Portuguese and Dutch concentrated mainly on efforts
to monopolize the spice trade, which in the East was the actual "beginning and end of the undertaking." Otherwise the Spaniards had the
most spectacular success in their naked greed, finding not merely the
gold promised by Columbus but a vaster wealth of silver. A flood of
bullion poured in on Spain, presently on all western Europe. Only it
did not simply enrich Europe, much less relieve the want of the common people. Before long it accentuated the costs of imperial success.

Portugal and Spain dazzled the rest of western Europe by their apparent wealth, but thereby aroused the Dutch and the English, who were
to profit much more from the discoveries. Epical as its achievement was,
little Portugal was never strong enough to dominate India or control
the trade routes. The costs of maintaining its "empire"—a 10,000-mile

chain of trading posts and forts—ate away most of its profits; its spice trade was soon enriching chiefly the city of Antwerp, much better situated than Lisbon as a central market; and by 1580 Portugal came under the domination of Spain, to begin reverting to its natural status as a minor power. Except for its African colonies and several outposts, about the only enduring result of its achievement is *The Lusiads.* Proud Spain fared much beter, becoming the greatest power in Europe through the riches it had won by exceptional daring, fervor, cruelty, and luck; yet by the end of the sixteenth century it too was on the decline, headed for a fate more painful and inglorious because it clung to its pride and its delusions of glory. It had squandered much of its wealth in costly, fruitless wars, culminating in the disaster of the Spanish Armada; as early as 1557 King Philip II began declaring himself insolvent. But from the outset Spain suffered more insidiously from its rich colonial empire, which was destined to impoverish it.

All moral considerations aside, the gold for which the Spaniards had such a passion was literally a curse. It served primarily to support an absolute monarchy and an obsolete nobility that were alike distinguished by bigotry and obtuseness, an exalted incapacity for enlightened rule. So far from being enriched by the loot from the New World, the common people had to pay for the holy wars and the extravagances of their betters by heavier taxes. They suffered more because little of the loot went to the development of industry either, in a land lacking a substantial middle class, dominated by a nobility that disdained commerce and the manual arts; the Spaniards neglected even to produce the goods eagerly sought by their colonies, which therefore helped to enrich foreign smugglers. The gold only galvanized the ineptitude of the rulers, who mistook it for the real wealth of the nation. By their bigotry and cruelty they succeeded in stirring their Dutch subjects to rebel and win their independence; with the loss of the busy Netherlands Spain lost a primary source of its real wealth (as a contemporary Italian observed). It proceeded to expel from the homeland the thrifty, industrious Moors, under whose rule in the past agriculture and industry had flourished as they never did under Spanish kings. The upshot was a disastrous economic as well as political decline in the seventeenth century, during which only the parasitical Church prospered.

In a history of freedom, the decline of Spain was a pure boon to the West. We may pause to do honor to its quixotic idealism, immortalized by Cervantes, exemplified even by the most bigoted King Philip II. Reputed to have laughed only once in his life, at the news of the great massacre of St. Bartholomew, Philip was indeed selfless in the service of his God, conceiving kingship as a high responsibility, not a personal privilege. He reminds us how Spain suffered from its long struggle to drive out the infidel Moors, for in the course of this crusade it developed its tradition of fanaticism. But such tributes and excuses finally accentuate the fact that at its zenith it did nothing to promote the growth of freedom, and except for a few writers gave not the least promise of furthering any such cause. Even before the final expulsion of the Moors from Granada, in 1492, Ferdinand and Isabella had set up the Spanish Inquisition, which thereafter assured a relentless hostility to all the basic freedoms, religious, intellectual, political. Had Philip II been able to carry out his exalted mission he would have crushed freedom in the Netherlands and England too. Otherwise, Spain's waste of its wealth was significant only as a portent. The recurrent paradox of civilization was to become pronounced in western Europe: as the nations gained in wealth and power, many of their people were worse off, enjoyed less effective freedom.

To begin with, all the colonial powers adopted the policy of Portugal and Spain, seeking to achieve monopoly in the interest of "national aggrandizement." For this purpose they gave exclusive privileges to closed stock companies, such as the Dutch East India Company, which might develop more refined techniques. (Whereas the Portuguese had destroyed spices in order to keep prices high, the Dutch took pains as well to limit production, chopping down trees and chopping off the heads of recalcitrant producers.) Similarly all the powers took to mercantilism, strictly regulating trade, putting up high tariffs in order to protect domestic manufactures and to restrict if not ruin the trade of rival powers. They used their colonies as pawns in this commercial war, drastically curtailing their economic freedom; colonists were typically required to trade with the mother country alone, told what they must buy and what they must produce for export. These policies, let us add, were natural enough, at this stage perhaps necessary. The effort at monopoly was only an extension on a larger scale of the practice of medieval towns, guilds, and trading companies, now with a clearer eye to the power politics befitting the rise of great nations; privileged stock companies may well have been the most feasible means for supplying the large amount of capital and bearing the risks entailed in building up trade over such enormous distances; and the failure to trust to *laissez faire,* or a self-regulating market, was no simple perversity—the mercantilists had almost all history behind them in their refusal to believe that private gain automatically promotes the public good, and in their insistence on putting the national interest first. Still, there remains considerable question about what this "national interest" is, and how best to promote it. Aside from the royal exchequers, the profits of the age of discovery in fact went chiefly to merchants, bankers, middlemen, and a few stockholders. Consumers paid the costs.

The costs grew higher because statesmen agreed with the Spaniards that gold was the primary index to the wealth or prosperity of a nation.[1] The most marked, though generally unremarked result of the bullion that poured in on Europe, in quantities much greater than were needed for ordinary monetary purposes, was a steady inflation that went fast and far enough to revolutionize the price structure, disrupt the whole society. It impoverished many men, since there was nothing like a comparable rise in wages or in returns to peasants. Its victims, no doubt, were liable to shortsightedness. Generally they believed that gains by merchants were necessarily at the people's expense, only a proof of gouging or cheating; and workers failed to realize that the lag of wages behind prices was the chief cause (or so economists now say) of the industrial progress of the age. The mercantilists themselves, however, shared the popular idea that "one man's gain is another man's loss," applying it to whole nations, and the victims had better excuse for succumbing to economic fallacies, as well as for resenting the great gains by the few. At any rate, the widespread discontent was embittered because hardly anyone had any clear understanding of the basic causes of the economic and social disruption.[2] For at least two centuries more, all the leading powers would remain stubbornly devoted to the ends and means that became standard in the age of discovery.

Yet in the long run the by-products of the discoveries were to count for much more than these immediate costs. Although all popular uprisings were quickly put down, the social discontent remained an active ferment, yeast for the more radical ideas of Protestantism. The lust for power could not be confined to rulers. In spite of all the regulation and effort at monopoly, the new opportunities called out much individual enterprise and independence of spirit, as the explorations themselves

---

[1] This still familiar belief incidentally generated the rather odd, if staple idea of a "favorable balance of trade"—one in which the value of exports exceeds the value of imports. That is, the nation prospers by selling away more of its material goods or tangible wealth for the sake of more money or gold.

[2] One of the few thinkers to perceive the serious dangers of inflation was, strangely, Copernicus. The still uncelebrated stargazer took time off to write a little treatise on the subject, a potential classic in economics except that it was little noticed and soon forgotten.

had from the outset. In the New World colonists soon began to misbe-
have, refusing to buy and sell solely in the interests of the mother
country; smugglers compensated for the shortsightedness of statesmen,
doing a flourishing business that promoted wider trade. Piracy, dignified by patriotic or even religious fervor, kept redistributing the wealth
of Spain and building up the power of England.

No less significant was the growth of scientific interests. This was no
mere by-product but among the means and the causes of the explorations, beginning with the interest in Greek and Arabic science. Henry
the Navigator had set up a staff of scientists to carry on research in
geography, mathematics, and astronomy, and though his motives were
primarily practical, they included something of simple curiosity. With
the help of the printing press, such curiosity—so natural, yet not too
common in the great societies of the past—became almost a rage.
Amerigo Vespucci, the best geographer of the time, published letters
about the New World that were read eagerly all over Europe. By the
middle of the sixteenth century Mercator was producing his celebrated
maps of the world and his globes. The explorations revolutionized the
common picture of the world, spreading the idea hitherto known only
to the learned that the earth is a sphere. They helped to prepare men
for other implausible ideas, such as the Copernican theory. In general,
the mind of Europe was expanded, to some extent emancipated, by the
new knowledge that came in with the bullion—knowledge of a world
much vaster and more various than had been reckoned with in medieval
philosophy.

So men gave an ironic twist to the pious statement of Columbus that
his sole inspiration had been "the prophecy of Isaiah about a new
heaven and a new earth." They began indeed to contemplate a new
heaven and earth, and then to entertain new ideas about man and
society that would have shocked the God-fearing, gold-loving discoverer
of America. The emancipated mind indulged in a good deal of fantasy
and romance, creating such images as the Noble Savage—a standing
reproach to Christendom. It also grew more critical and skeptical, in
the manner of Montaigne; more aware of the diversity of custom and
belief, men could realize that their own belief might be custom, and
were somewhat less disposed to accept it on unreasoned or unconscious
faith. But the most significant result of the discoveries was perhaps the
simplest—just the wonder, the thrill of the unprecedented achievement.
Tending to forget (as Columbus himself did) that pride was the deadliest of sins, men felt freer to dream and to dare, to speculate and to

adventure, in both the physical world and the world of the mind. Thus in his *Novum Organum* (1620) Francis Bacon hailed the discovery of a marvelous "New Intellectual World" to be explored: "I publish and set forth these conjectures of mine just as Columbus acted, before that wonderful voyage of his across the Atlantic, when he gave the reasons for his conviction that new lands and continents might be discovered."

For there remains the most obvious fact: men had discovered a new world, opened up a new frontier. Like Portugal and Spain, all the major powers were interested primarily in exploiting it, never realizing that their colonial empires were by no means so profitable as they took for granted. In North America, however, colonists came with different motives, if still far from purely idealistic ones, and they enjoyed considerably more freedom than all other colonists elsewhere. Here the potentialities of a new life in a new world would finally be realized.

2. *The Rise of Money-Power*

Although historians commonly talk now of the "economic revolution" in the sixteenth century, at first glance this hardly looks very revolutionary. True, there was a great expansion in business, due immediately to the geographical explorations, but business had long since evolved large-scale capitalistic enterprise. Now one might see only more of the same, at that still lacking such essentials as a gospel of free private enterprise and a self-regulating market. Europe still looked much more like the medieval world than the modern world. There were no giant industries, nor giant strides in technology; the great nations had only a few million inhabitants, the great cities rarely more than a hundred thousand; communication and transportation were as slow as ever, the fastest post covering only some eighty miles a day. In one aspect a much smaller, cozier world than it is today, sixteenth-century Europe was in another aspect a much larger, wilder one. And certainly it was in no mood for revolutionary change. If men were excited by the geographical discoveries, stirred by a growing sense of power, they were not yet given to dreams of a brave new world of material abundance, nor did they assume that change was natural and naturally for the better.

Nevertheless, their world was being transformed, more rapidly than ever before, more profoundly than they realized. The extent of the change may be as hard for us to realize, since it led to customs, beliefs, and attitudes that now seem practically instinctive; but this is to say that the sixteenth century was indeed becoming "modern." If "revolution" is perhaps too strong a word for the immediate changes in its economy, these unquestionably marked the beginning of a new era. They foreshadowed the reign of economic interests, which were to grow much more powerful than they had been in any previous civilization—so much so that Europeans would even find plausible an effort to explain all history by a theory of economic determinism, while in the New World leaders would say proudly that the business of America was business.

The most famous businessmen of the sixteenth century, the Fuggers, were suitably farsighted, preserving for posterity the letters of their correspondents. In the panorama of the age afforded by these newsletters, one may at first be struck by its medieval appearance: the routine violence and misery, the royal conspiracies, murders, and executions, the piracy, plagues, and peasant wars, and especially the ubiquity of religious interests, as in the recurrent massacres, the autos-da-fés, the persecutions of the Jews, the trials of witches, the driving out of demons, the prodigies, the miracles, the magic—even to the papal anathematizing of a "conglomeration of dolphins" that were interfering with shipping and fishing. But then one may wonder at the scope and the detail of these reports, all of apparent interest to the Fuggers. The correspondents write in from Lisbon, Madrid, Paris, Antwerp, London, Venice, Florence, Rome, Vienna, Prague, Danzig, Warsaw—from all the leading centers of Europe—and they give news as well of America, India, Japan, and the Ottoman Empire. They were not writing to entertain or to preserve a record for posterity: everything that went on in the world of affairs was of some concern to their employers, who maintained branches in all these cities. The House of Fugger had wider interests than almost any royal house.

Built up by Jacob Fugger (1459–1525), it was much more than an international banking house. On thousands of looms it continued to manufacture cloth, by which Jacob's ancestors had begun to make the family fortune. It had lucrative commercial interests in Italy and especially in Antwerp, carrying on an extensive trade in spices. It had also entered the mining industry, owning copper mines in Hungary, silver mines in the Tyrol, both silver and mercury mines in Spain; through a cartel it almost won a European monopoly on mercury. Its main interest, however, remained finance: the House of Fugger served as banker for the rulers of Europe, including the popes. Accordingly, it had its finger in many a political pie too. Jacob Fugger had enabled Charles V to become Holy Roman emperor by providing the immense sums of money needed to bribe the Electors into choosing him instead of Francis I of France; he could speak down pretty haughtily to the emperor as to other royal debtors. But he did not aspire to political power, the role either of a Medici or of a king behind the throne. First and last he was a capitalist, almost selfless in his dedication to the acquisition of wealth, who might be called the first great apostle of the religion of business. In his last years, the family tradition had it, he refused to heed the relatives who suggested that it was time to retire and enjoy his wealth; he said that he preferred to keep on making a profit as long as he could. In noting that his profit was a good steady 54 per cent over the last sixteen years of his life, let us add that apostles seldom retire.

At any rate, he was not without honor in his own country and age, and had a sufficient following. Other great international banking houses competed with the House of Fugger, occasionally combined with it in efforts to control an industry or obtain a monopoly. They engaged in as diverse activities, a range of enterprise much greater than the merchant bankers before them had attempted. While they still concentrated on financial or commercial more than industrial capitalism, they were organizing private business on a larger scale than history had yet known, achieving an awesome concentration of money-power in the literal sense—massed capital rather than landed wealth. As they grew into something like family corporations they helped to suggest another major innovation, the joint stock company. With such unprecedented organization of economic power sixteenth-century Europe was also achieving a more systematic commercialization of economic life, represented by the Bourse. Whereas the medieval fair had been a seasonal market for the exchange of tangible goods, the Bourse was a daily market for the exchange of paper bills or securities. These more purely speculative activities were attended by much more extensive use of such earlier inventions as insurance, while landed property began serving similar purposes through the development of the mortgage. Men could operate more freely and fully on the principle of calculated risk.

More revolutionary were the broader social consequences of the growth of business and money-power. First we may discount the fashion of invoking a new "Spirit of Capitalism" to explain the changes, and also the fashion of reducing them to the old story of simple greed, as many outraged contemporaries did. There was nothing wholly new about the spirit of Jacob Fugger, nor was he any greedier than his medieval predecessors—he was only more successful. Yet the most important changes were indeed changes in attitude and belief. Although they were gradual, at first more or less unconscious, in the long run they did amount to a new spirit. To appreciate the world of difference they made, we need only to look back to the Middle Ages.

Under the heading "Cheating Which is Committed in Buying and Selling," St. Thomas Aquinas took up such questions as these: "Whether it is lawful to sell a thing for more than its worth. . . . Whether the seller is bound to state the defects of the things sold. . . . Whether in trading it is lawful to sell a thing at a higher price than what was paid for it." In practice, of course, medieval merchants did not habitually worry over such questions, sticking to the first principle of good business—buying cheap and selling dear. Still, all medieval thinkers agreed with St. Thomas in condemning this principle; none supported the practices by which Jacob Fugger made his 54 per cent profit, with no apparent twinge of conscience. Similarly they agreed that while commerce was always a spiritually dangerous business, finance was positively sinful; they all branded as "usury" the charging of interest on loans, the main source of Jacob's fortune. He testified that this was still a live issue by financing the expedition of a German churchman to the University of Bologna, to seek support of the thesis that charging interest was lawful—only he was thereby declaring his freedom from sin. In the same spirit the "Commercial Arithmetics" published during the century—the main technical education offered businessmen—dropped all apology for including problems of interest. Toward the end of the century Queen Elizabeth of England legalized "usury" up to 10 per cent per annum, repealing a law against it that had proved "the utter undoing of many gentlemen."

Quite apart from the misfortune of these worthies, the new law plainly made sense. However unchristian the charging of interest, it was not only universal practice, thousands of years old, but indispensable to large-scale business. But again the change had a deeper significance: it marked the coming divorce of business from religion, the frank secularization of both its theory and its practice. Businessmen were not yet seeking autonomy, inasmuch as they mostly took for granted the mercantile policies of the state, and they would always pay lip service to Christian ideals; yet they were achieving an open emancipation from the traditional constraints on business. Theory was approaching practice in making the primary consideration expediency, not morality, or at best service of the state, not of God. In the intellectual world one sign was the rise of the science of economics, christened "political economy" early in the seventeenth century. Still weak in theory, economic thinkers were at least scientific in their effort at a purely empirical study; they no longer began or ended with considerations of God's will in matters of the economy. Political thinkers came closer to God when they took up the rights of private property, but not for clearly religious reasons: rights that medieval thinkers had tended to regard as matters of social convenience now began to acquire an aura of sanctity. A century before John Locke argued that the main end of the state was to preserve property, the French jurist Bodin qualified or confused his argument for the absolute sovereignty of the state by declaring that rulers could not touch property without the owner's consent. And in the world of affairs, where the generally unphilosophical businessmen operated, there were intimations of the proverbs of the future: Business is business, Business and sentiment don't mix.[3]

Since commerce and finance had never actually been governed by sentiment, the new spirit was most conspicuous in the venerable realm of agriculture. Land had not been generally conceived as a commodity to be bought and sold, for the sake of profit, but now wealthy merchants took to buying it, when not to acquiring it by foreclosure. They were a new kind of landlord, indifferent to traditions of tenure, copyhold, and manorial obligation; interested in making money out of their estates, they introduced business methods and stimulated large-scale agriculture. In England especially, agricultural capitalism induced the conversion of arable land into sheep pasture, the enclosure of village common lands, and the dispossession of yeomen, who were replaced by hired laborers. The outcry over the many who remained unemployed —by the middle of the sixteenth century up to 10 per cent of the populace—was met by a plainer statement of the new creed. Property was an absolute right, entailing no absolute social obligations; its owner was

---

[3] Among the unconscious witnesses to the transition was Fra Luca Paciolo, who about 1500 perfected the key invention of double-entry bookkeeping. He advised that every businessman "must always commence his affairs in the name of God, whose name must appear at the beginning of every manuscript" (as it did in the ledgers of the merchant of Prato) ; but when he got down to business he emphasized that the most important thing was "cash, or any other substantial power." And how the prospects of cash might reconcile merchants to the grievous religious disorders of the century was indicated by one of the Fugger correspondents. Reporting the uprisings of Belgian Calvinists, who pulled down all the pictures and altars in the churches of Brussels, he observed that such commotions "ill serve the promotion of commerce." A few days later he casually noted that some merchants had salvaged four shiploads of statues, bells, effigies of saints, etc. for dispatch to Russia: "The consigners hope to do good business with them."

free to use it as he saw fit. Still more novel were the implications of this creed. Although self-interest was nothing new and exploitation had been common to medieval as to all other past societies, economic activity had always been subordinated to noneconomic ends, some notion of the common good. Sixteenth-century Europe was beginning to evolve a predominantly economic society, governed by the struggle for wealth. Business was on its way to achieving not only autonomy but primacy. In the next century Christopher Wren symbolized the new spirit in his plan for the City of London after the great fire, putting at the center the Bank of England—not St. Paul's.

Now, all this has an evil sound, possibly unbecoming to historical exposition, but hard to avoid. The economic revolution in fact bred some universally admitted social evils, of particular concern in a history of freedom. No reputable historian, to my knowledge, has described the gains in wealth and power as pure social gains, or simply a growth in freedom. Yet neither has any student of economic history described them as pure evils or simple losses. The problems they generated or aggravated were due in part to a plain measure of economic progress, which as plainly involved further possibilities of social progress.

Even Marxist historians agree that the callous bourgeois were developing by far the most expansive, productive economy yet known to history. Immediately, the big merchants were introducing some rational uniformity into the vast confusion of the medieval economy, with its innumerable different standards and local regulations. (In the vicinity of Baden alone, for instance, there were by the sixteenth century 112 different measures of length, 123 for liquids, 163 for cereals, etc.) Similarly they helped to break down traditional practices that hindered growth or possible improvement. While the medieval guilds maintained high standards of workmanship, they also maintained rigid routines, discouraged individual initiative, and fortified the common hostility to innovation and invention—a disposition exemplified by an English order in 1623 that not only denied a patent for a new stocking frame but commanded that it be done away with. We may now be weary of the endless hymns to the efficiency of private enterprise, so we may forget that the rising capitalism unquestionably was more efficient. Its benefits were not going merely to capitalists either; their profits were no more simply squeezed out of consumers than were the profits of the guild masters. One obvious reason for the growing power of money was the creation of wealth, at best the constructive use of this power. It was producing more goods.

This unheroic, unromantic business class did have its reputed virtues

of industry, enterprise, resourcefulness, imaginativeness—virtues that
showed to clearer advantage by contrast with the ways of the titled
aristocracy. While the Spanish nobility in particular merely squandered
the wealth of America, businessmen were opening and building up a
new world of opportunity in Europe, providing more scope and incentive for able individuals; in the Netherlands they proved their social
worth by draining marshes, digging canals, and building dikes. Most
significant for the long run, however, were the less tangible influences
of their ruling principle of calculated risk. This promoted a spirit of
venture, since it entailed real risks, but above all an essential rationality, typified by the perfection of double-entry bookkeeping. With the
help of another bourgeois invention, the printing press, the habit or
the spirit of rational calculation began pervading the whole society. In
government it helped to offset the tradition of feudal heroics (though
the monarchies characteristically neglected to adopt rational bookkeeping until the eighteenth century). In thought generally it both fortified
and supplemented the classical tradition of rationalism by more empirical sense, or concern with fact. Accordingly, it had much to do with
the revolutionary developments to come, notably the rise of science and
of democracy. The Industrial Revolution then gave only the clearest
surface evidence of the deep ways in which capitalism may be said to
have fathered modern civilization—and in the process bred its own
critics.

Such potentialities became apparent in the sixteenth century. If the
business class aspired chiefly to wealth and money-power, not to freedom—as yet not even to economic freedom—it was nevertheless more
open to new interests and new ideas than was the aristocracy, and its
kind of rationalism might grow more conscious and philosophical. Thus
Antwerp, the economic capital of the century, was a famous center of
learning too, noted for its cosmopolitanism and its vigorous intellectual
life. As Holland then took the commercial lead in western Europe it
became the freest nation of the seventeeth century, and the principal
asylum for victims of persecutions; its sensible burghers could see that
religious conflict was bad for business, bad for the whole community.
When England worsted the Dutch Republic in trade wars, while also
carrying through a political revolution, it succeeded to the ideal role
of the bourgeois. Early in the next century Montesquieu observed that
England was the great land of the middle class, pre-eminent in "piety,
commerce, and freedom."

That "piety" got into this union should remind us that greed alone

could never have generated such an expansion of business, for it had
failed to do so in the Roman Empire, Islam, and other great societies
that had a sufficient love of gold. The expansion was due more to the
sustained energy, the genius for organization, the vision, and the kind
of dedication typified by Jacob Fugger. And one reason why business
then succeeded in winning a divorce from religion is that first, through
the Protestant Reformation, it was legitimately wedded to religion.
This marriage—without precedent in history—gave it not only a higher
social prestige but much of its drive and sense of dedication. It made
business no mere occupation but a "calling," as by acquiring wealth
the Christian could do more good. With the gospel of work it produced
the gospel of wealth, stimulating in the middling ranks of society the
ambition to make a good living. It begot an odd, historically unique
type—the God-fearing businessman.[4]

   Initially, at least, this offspring of the Reformation was no bastard.
While preaching the gospel of work, Luther abhorred "Fuggerism"
and denounced the charging of interest as violently as he denounced
all the other abuses tolerated by the Roman Church. Calvin, who gave
considerably more play to business (incidentally starting Geneva on
watchmaking), not only insisted first and last on its Christian obligations to the community, but in Geneva enforced stringent regulation
of it. When he accepted as lawful a reasonable charge on loans, he was
merely recognizing a necessity of economic life, seeking to avoid the
shocking contradictions between medieval theory and practice. In giving
his blessing to the economic virtues of enterprise and industry he likewise sought to dedicate them to the service of God. His followers were
generally quite sincere as they "labored busily for grace," made a
"Christian gaining." The Huguenots in France became known for their
exceptional diligence, sobriety, and honesty; to their bankers Cardinal
Richelieu entrusted his personal fortune. The early Puritans, who were
still more zealous in spiritualizing their business, could innocently use
economic metaphors even in their prayers and their diaries—as John

---

[4] This seemingly impious thesis, first developed by Max Weber in *The Protestant Ethic
and the Spirit of Capitalism* and later amplified by R. H. Tawney, has been widely
criticized, and it obviously comes out too simple in the cruder Marxist or economic interpretations of history. Neither Weber nor Tawney, however, argued that Protestantism was
the "cause" of the rise of capitalism. They merely dwelt on connections that are quite
plain, written all over the works of Calvinists in particular. Tawney also stressed that
the business spirit was by no means confined to Protestants. Like Jacob Fugger, most of
the big bankers of the sixteenth century were Catholic, as were most of the chief commercial cities; and Catholic Portugal and Spain had taken the lead in economic imperialism.

Janeway (to cite but one of innumerable examples) "every night made even his accounts," took note of "what income and profit he received in his spiritual traffique." Altogether, Calvinism was in this respect true to the genius of Christianity, which has ever refused to renounce the world or keep aloof from it, to commit itself to a pure unworldly spirituality; and the effort to Christianize the Earthly City was especially needful in sixteenth-century Europe, a society already dedicated to the pursuit of worldly wealth and power.

Still, the later union of "piety, commerce, and freedom" was not actually harmonious. The growing power of commerce was a menace to both piety and freedom, which were only beginning to learn to get along with one another. Commerce was having an easier time—it could get along well enough by itself. Meanwhile many people continued to suffer from the hangovers of the economic revolution.

Inevitably slow in adjusting themselves to a changing world, as slow in understanding it, men had been more exasperated because of the peculiar problems of a capitalistic economy. They began to experience a cycle of boom and bust unlike the customary kind of hard times, due to scarcity; the latter half of the sixteenth century saw a series of crises, brought on immediately by the bankruptcies of both royal houses and big banking houses while wealth kept pouring in. By then, too, inflation had become more rapid, and more ruinous to the many who lacked capital, credit, or access to royal favors; among its victims were the lesser gentry. But those who suffered most, naturally, were the common people. They tended to feel worse because of a widening gap between rich and poor, as the great banking houses made great fortunes for some while encouraging a royal extravagance in war and courtly ostentation that laid heavier burdens on most.

The conspicuous victims at the time were the many dispossessed peasants in England. Although eventually they might find their way into industry in towns or mines, they made up what amounted to a new class—the permanently unemployed. Hence a by-product of the increasing national prosperity was a marked increase in vagrancy and pauperism. As the medieval system of charity broke down under this new burden, the emergency might be met by poor-laws, but the relief these provided was conditioned by harsh regulations. Agitation only intensified the fears of the prosperous. Would-be reformers or defenders of the peasants, like the uncelebrated John Hales, called out the conservative theme of the future: they were angrily denounced as fomenters of class hatred. Parliament's dispassionate idea of social reform was an act authorizing collections in church for the benefit of the poor, and providing that confirmed vagrants might be sold into slavery.

More portentous, however, was the wider impact of the economic revolution on the working class. The proletariat grew larger with the expansion of industry, the more so as its ranks were swollen by crafts-men from guilds unable to meet the competition of the big new com-panies. Workmen had had very little chance of getting rich, but now they had a real chance of getting poorer. Wages always lagged behind the rising prices, including the higher rents in cities getting more con-gested. One sign of the increasing poverty was the disappearance of meat and wine from the worker's table; common in 1500, these were luxuries in 1600. Another sign was many a fruitless strike, embittered by resentment of absentee owners. Workers found no champion like John Hales, no effective sympathy among writers and thinkers, while employers grew more powerful. Mineowners got together in agreements not to raise wages, or to employ miners who had left home in search of better jobs. They also had the support of government; the increasing regulation of industry almost invariably favored employers. Thus in Belgium the lace industry was protected by a law providing that no girl over twelve should be allowed to make lace, as the owners had found it profitable to employ only children.

Such apparent exploitation was facilitated by the growth of monop-oly, an old medieval practice now feasible on a larger, more efficient scale. Although businessmen were competing vigorously for the increas-ing wealth, they were not yet exalting in theory the virtues of free competition, but rather were anticipating the tendency of big business to use its power to eliminate competition. The monopolies excited a great deal of public indignation, inasmuch as all consumers were hurt by them; they were repeatedly denounced as an outrage against both God and the commonwealth. Nevertheless, the indignation had little effect. In England the same Parliament that sealed the defeat of John Hales, in part by prohibiting any public assembly met to incite opposi-tion to enclosure, also repealed an act that prohibited conspiracies of capitalists to raise prices. How the wind was blowing was indicated most clearly by a declaration issued as early as 1522 by the Town Council of Augsburg, Jacob Fugger's native city. Trade, it began, was "unequivocally beneficial" to the whole community, adding to "the wealth of everybody"; it followed that the more trade the better for everybody, and the wealthier the merchants the bigger the beneficial transactions; and since regulation of these transactions would only discourage the merchants, maybe even induce them to take their business elsewhere, it would be a great harm to the community. "To place limits on the earnings of investments would be absolutely unbearable," concluded the Town Council, adding that it would be a particular injustice to "widows, orphans, and other sufferers" who derived their income from these sources.

These widows and orphans may well have been brought into the argument in good conscience, even though limits were regularly placed on the wages of workers, whose widows and orphans had no income. The significant point is that the councilors had become so devoted to business that they could take for granted its benefits to the entire community, despite plain evidence that there were many sufferers from it. They were anticipating the novel theory that unregulated self-interest is the best means to social good—the self-interest, that is, of owners and employers. In effect, they were already arguing that economic considerations should come first. While no doubt as pious as Jacob Fugger himself was, they were heralding the materialism that would permanently confuse goods with the good life, obscure the question of ends by a triumphant concentration on material means, and so confuse both the means and the ends of communal freedom.

Granted its productivity (in spite of a good deal of unproductive speculation), the emerging capitalistic society was not a genuine community. The big trading companies and banking houses, forerunners of the industrial corporations to come, naturally lacked the corporate sense of the Middle Ages. Apart from all considerations of greed and tendencies to exploitation, they simply bought human labor; though they doubtless had faithful retainers, ordinary workers could not enjoy the feeling of belonging, much less any sense of partnership, that craftsmen might enjoy in their guilds or even serfs on the feudal manor. The power they exercised was essentially naked economic power, which might be accorded the respect due to money but not the reverence stirred by natural authority or great leadership. They rationalized their activities in the disagreeable sense of reducing human relations to a purely economic nexus. Generally they were indifferent to public opinion; while the news correspondents of the Fuggers reported at length on all kinds of goings on, they hardly ever mentioned public opinion except in matters of religious strife. The values of the community had to be realized by other social means. So did the values of civility and high culture; another significant omission in the voluminous Fugger newsletters is any reference to the greater writers and thinkers of the century. And to all such values the growing money-power and money-spirit were a natural menace.

If the Protestant effort to Christianize economic life was not doomed to failure, its failure is at least easy to understand. The gospel of work and wealth was obviously liable to corruption; men who helped God by helping themselves were apt to forget God as they succeeded in helping themselves to a good deal, more especially because large-scale, impersonal business does not make for refinement of conscience. A deeper source of corruption, however, was the admirable Protestant principle of individualism, best exemplified by the "inner-directed" Puritan. To early Puritans this was a principle of individual responsibility, always backed by insistence on Christian duty to one's fellows. With success it was insensibly transformed into a principle of individual right to do as one pleased, especially with the property one had acquired. The inner-directed man was turning into the proud self-made man—a type, it has been remarked, that relieves God of a considerable responsibility. At the same time, he often behaved as if he had a God-given right to charge all that the market would bear. In time he would proclaim that capitalism was God's own plan for Christendom, and so become more self-righteous on principle than businessmen had ever been in any previous society.

The obvious victims, as ever, were the poor; but again they were beginning to suffer more especially from the twisting of the Protestant ethic. The poor had always been blessed by Christian tradition, if in ways they might not always have reason to appreciate; they were an accepted class, properly objects of charity, by which the wealthy could help to get themselves through the eye of the heavenly needle. Now they were becoming the "idle, shiftless poor." Success in business—the "Christian calling"—was a proof of God's blessing; so it followed that poverty or failure was due to a lack of Christian virtue. This attitude helps to explain why another seemingly contradictory idea began to spread in the seventeenth century—the positive utility of poverty in the working class. (Among its advocates in England was Sir William Petty, a self-made man whom Marx called the founder of economics.) Workers kept poor and ignorant might work more industriously, and thereby contribute more to national prosperity while also escaping the sin of indolence. Proposals to raise wages and to educate workers were now condemned as both economically unsound and morally reprehensible.

But many businessmen also suffered, if less grievously, from their Calvinistic heritage. This intensified the odd kind of asceticism typified by old Jacob Fugger, the compulsion to keep on to the end making profits instead of retiring to enjoy them. Businessmen remained builders or creators of sorts and manifestly were engrossed in their work, apart from the wealth it brought them—their compulsion was not mere avarice; yet one may wonder how much joy they felt in building and making, how much aesthetic pleasure they got from their work. Their driving will was most obviously a will to power, or specifically to possession more than creation; and they could look like slaves to it. There was less apparent freedom of spirit in the rising capitalist class than the Medici had enjoyed, or the medieval burghers. By their economic individualism they were creating a new aristocracy of wealth, but one that would not be distinguished for either individuality or aristocratic spirit.

At this stage, however, the business class was still far from being the ruling class. Outside of Italy it was sharply separated from the nobility, which continued to enjoy much more social prestige and privilege. The unheroic, unromantic businessmen could look a little pathetic in their aspirations to respectability. (In the latter half of the sixteenth-century Commercial Arithmetics were adorned with prefatory poems, fancy dedications, and other such trappings of belles-lettres.) While most of the greater writers and artists came out of the bourgeoisie, almost none directly expressed or catered to its distinctive interests except in Holland, where it was served by a great school of painting, and to a lesser extent in England, where it made do with the countless sermons, journals, and biographies of the Puritan saints. Nor did capitalism rule the state. Its eventual triumph inspired the theory that economic power is primary, the main source of political, military, and all other power; but if so, this was still a benighted age. Typically both disinclined and unfitted to be political leaders, the capitalists were in fact the servants of an aristocratic society, ruled by kings. Because the kings depended on loans from the big bankers, Tawney described them as "puppets dancing on wires held by a money-power to which political struggles were irrelevant except as an opportunity for gain"; only the fact remains that the puppets called the tune, which was often ruinous to the holders of money-power. When Philip II of Spain hit on the idea of declaring his kingdom bankrupt, as an excuse for refusing to repay his loans, the House of Fugger lost some millions of florins and never recouped its loss. Thereafter it staggered periodically under more such blows, as did rival banking houses; none had any legal recourse against the kings, who remained their biggest customers. States could survive the royal bankruptcies, but capitalists might not; while the House of Fugger declined, some other houses went bankrupt for good. The dominant power at this time was plainly the nation-state.

3. *The Emergence of the Nation-State*

Modern history, it is commonly said, begins with the appearance of the nation-state: a state that traditionally has declared itself under God but has always acted as a secular, autonomous institution, putting the avowed national interest or "reasons of state" above all other interests, and in its conflicts with other nations—the substance of recorded European history from Machiavelli to recent times—recognizing no higher authority. This kind of state is now so familiar that it seems the most natural kind, even to many who no longer idolize it. It has indeed an obvious natural basis in tribalism, one of the universals of human history. Yet as a large-scale affair, embracing some millions of people with a common culture, it was another new development that came into its own in the sixteenth century; it first emerged clearly in the Atlantic powers—Portugal, Spain, France, and England. And it was another characteristically Western institution, comparable to states found in all civilizations, especially homogeneous Egypt, but in almost no other attaining so full a development.

To appreciate its novelty we have only to recall the Middle Ages again. In the welter of feudal principalities there were at first no nations with definite borders, clearly recognized sovereignty, cherished traditions, or common consciousness of nationality. (England came closest, but under alien Norman rule.) Instead of states there were "estates," or classes. Law was chiefly custom, something already there —not something deliberately made by a centralized government. The main reason why Christendom was never really united was that authority was everywhere divided between kingdom and Church, in the secular realm between king and feudal lords. In the incessant conflicts the only considerable national war was the Hundred Years' War between England and France, which at that was largely due to confused boundaries, the English king claiming possession of some lands in France. Outside the Church the major political entity was the Holy Roman

Empire, and this was an amorphous affair both geographically and politically, no real "land." As a fiction inspired by memories of Rome it amounted to an effort to revive about the only kind of large state known in the past—empire. Empire was essentially different from the nation-state in that it embraced peoples of different tongues, creeds, and traditions, united only by conquest.

The weakness of the Holy Roman Empire gives an immediate clue to the rise of the nation-state. In the early sixteenth century, under Charles V, the Empire was on paper the greatest power in Europe, at the peak of its strength. Since the thirteenth century it had been ruled by the dynasty of the Hapsburgs (originally minor Swiss lords), and it had grown by virtue of the Hapsburg genius for shrewd or lucky marriages. Through the marriages of his grandfather and father Charles V inherited widely scattered territories, in particular the Netherlands and Spain. Nevertheless, it was only on paper that he was above all the other kings of Christendom. While he was handicapped by having to fight the Turks and contend with the Protestants in his realm, his main trouble was that his dynastic empire was a ramshackle, wholly artificial kind of state, lacking any real unity; he was worn out by his lifelong effort simply to hold it together. Charles tacitly admitted that it was no match for the rising nation-states by splitting the Empire in two, bequeathing the Spanish half together with the Netherlands to his son Philip II; and even so Philip proved unable to retain control of the Netherlands. Out of the other half emerged Austria, which became another mongrel state ruling over diverse peoples—Germans, Czechs, Hungarians, Italians—and never achieved the power of the Atlantic states.

Now, in view of the evil reputation that the nation-state has recently acquired among many thinkers, we need first of all to understand why this new institution acquired such great power. It was not a factitious contrivance of evil ambition in a Christendom that had lost its innocence, but the outcome of a long, gradual, organic process. It had such medieval antecedents as the Italian city-states. While its development was often punctuated by violent episodes, it did not result either from any deliberate plan to overthrow "feudalism"—a concept still unknown. The most conscious effort it involved was the effort of temporal rulers everywhere to keep the pope in his place, outside their realm. Fanatically Catholic Spain was in this respect as independent as any other nation; the ultrapious Philip II inaugurated his reign by a war with Rome. The Church, indeed, unintentionally contributed a great deal to the growth of the nation-state, for it provided a model of centralized government, while the Papacy made plainer the objections to such a government from afar, in the interests of Rome rather than the national community.

More to the point, there now were such communities. As has already been noted, the nation-state may appear to be an almost inevitable outcome of the cultural, social, economic development of Europe. The plainest reason for it, again, was the linguistic diversity of Europe; the first nations to emerge were united by a common language, and their common consciousness was soon heightened by national literatures in the vernacular. At the same time, the feudal system was unable to accommodate the expansion of commerce and industry, provide for the interests of the growing urban middle class; businessmen in particular wanted an end to feudal confusion. The most apparent need of Europe at this stage was law, order, and security, which could be provided only by a strong centralized government with clear authority. The nation-state that met this need was not strictly an inevitable development, inasmuch as it failed to develop in some lands, but these lands illustrated its value. Thus Germany remained a congeries of principalities, whose independence was guaranteed by the Peace of Westphalia that ended the Thirty Years' War; until Prussia became a strong nation its people had little voice in European affairs. Similarly Italy remained split, largely dominated by greater powers that brought it more peace than it had known in its heyday, perhaps saved the country from tearing itself to pieces, but in any case deprived it of the independent national life that might have enabled it to maintain a more vigorous cultural life, become less of a museum.

All in all, the nation-state was by no means the simple power structure pictured by Machiavelli and later realists. Although perpetually addicted to the use of military force, it was not created or sustained by force alone. Its power rested on a community of interest and need, a genuine commonwealth; it represented a people who for all their internal differences were united by a shared experience of achievement, prospect, and danger. It channeled the energy of the age, offered a clearer purpose for the drive to power. Nor was devotion to it the mere narrowing of interest that may appear by contrast with the universalism of medieval Christendom. The "catholic" ideal, always confused by local, factional interests and cramped by bigotry or religious conceit, had become pretty nominal or fictitious by the late Middle Ages. The emerging nation-state signified an actual widening of consciousness, a transcendence of parochialism, an extension of feudal or civic loyalty to a much larger group. Appropriately, if unwittingly, it brought about the immense expansion of the intellectual horizons of Europe by sending out the explorers.

More consciously, its rulers introduced more rationality into government. They extended law and order by means of a more businesslike administration, in keeping with the growth of organization in business and the embryonic science of "political economy." In foreign affairs *raison d'état* tended to confine the lust for personal glory or revenge, the high spirits or the low passions, which medieval and early Renaissance rulers were wont to indulge. It encouraged the growth of statesmanship and diplomacy, or policy Machiavellian in the best sense of the end rationally controlling the means. Such policy now found a remarkable practitioner in Cardinal Richelieu. A servant of the state, wholly dedicated to the national interest as he saw it, the cardinal was by no means a high-minded idealist, but he was as far from being a self-seeking politician or irresponsible adventurer. Among other things he illustrated one of the clearest gains flowing from *raison d'état,* the curbing of religious passion or prejudice: in the heyday of the religious wars he upheld the official toleration of the Huguenots at home—again not as a matter of high principle, but out of simple realism or expediency. By contrast, the nation-state that was least rational and enlightened in its policy was Spain—the most medieval, in a sense the most idealistic.

For the long run, the nation-state had further potentialities that its early rulers were generally unaware of. Shortly becoming an inspiration to literature and a patron of the arts, it would help to enrich European culture by cross-fertilization, to an extent never approached by the Roman Empire or any other great empire; the different nations were so many centers of new possibility. It provided more scope and incentive for individual enterprise than could the manor, the monastery, or even the free town, which was given to stringent local regulation. In England the rise of the nation was both cause and effect of extraordinary enterprise by daring, gifted individuals, but Spain too rose on the exploits of its *conquistadores* and then enjoyed a golden age. And apart from the ideal of self-determination for peoples having a common tongue and tradition—an ideal that is now stirring the whole non-Western world—the nation-state could promote the ideal of liberty more readily than could either an empire or a hierarchical church. Given more actual unity and community, and a kind of equality in citizenship as a born right, the ancient idea of the sovereignty of the people could become more meaningful. The slogan that the voice of the people is the voice of God—an idea scarcely popular with the high priests of God—in fact began to ring out in the ungodly nations.

Such possibilities for freedom, however, were realized by only a few nation-states, pretty late in their history. In the sixteenth and seventeenth centuries the political actualities were mostly quite different. We have now to guard against some dubious inferences commonly drawn from the sound enough assumption that the rise of the nation-state was a natural, logical development. Realists may then conclude that its rise was a "historical necessity," if not a supreme culmination, and that moral judgment of it is accordingly irrelevant, even impertinent. Actually it forces moral issues, which a historian cannot evade no matter how conscientiously he tries to refrain from moral judgment, and which directly concern a student of freedom because they involve issues of justice and rights, the means and ends of freedom. For whether or not its rulers consciously followed the advice of Machiavelli, they felt free to use means that were immoral by any civilized standards, often unprincipled on cynical principle.

True, the behavior of the nations was no worse than that of most kingdoms and empires before them, not to mention the Renaissance Papacy. But simply because of the growth of rationality it entailed a more explicit repudiation of the Christian ethic, or freedom from higher obligations. The nation-state practiced on a much larger scale the selfish individualism of the Renaissance, without the restraints to which individuals were subject; there was no higher court above it, no legal or institutional means of holding it responsible or making it conform to ordinary standards of decency. Hence confusion about the good life was deepened by another radical dualism, between public and private morality. "Reasons of state" could justify dishonesty, infidelity, treachery, robbery, ruthless violence—behavior that would shame most ordinary men in their relations with their neighbors; while the crimes of nations might be compounded by an egregious vanity that would seem ridiculous in an individual. The "natural depravity" of man—the traditional excuse for denying freedom to common men—was most glaring in the behavior of states that still denied them freedom.

In particular the nations amplified the feudal custom of war. Having grown out of efforts to put down unruly feudal aggressiveness, they remained as aggressive and kept Europe more continually embroiled in war than most civilized societies had been. War, not peace, was the

normal state of affairs; in the seventeenth century there were only
seven scattered years in which European states were not fighting one
another. Although a major reason was still religious hatred, aggressiveness was intensified because the rising nations tacitly subscribed to the
thesis of Machiavelli: "The State is an organic structure whose full
power can be maintained only by allowing it in some way to continue
growing." War was now completely justified, no longer deplored as it
sometimes was in early medieval theory. Commonly it was glorified,
since it was a means to both individual and national aggrandizement.
And as always, the prevalence of war signified a much more serious
menace to freedom than the possible subjection of vanquished peoples.
Common people on both sides were liable to pillage and slaughter,
easier prey because they were noncombatants. (As yet relatively few
men were killed on the battlefield.) Everywhere they suffered in militant states administered largely in the interest of building up the
national power, thereby distracted from such causes as social reform.

More insidiously they were menaced by the spreading ideal of patriotism. This was not yet the supreme ideal, at least among the common
people; the notion that there was no greater good than to die for one's
country would take some time to seep down to men who still had no
voice in their country's affairs. But the glorification of the nation-state
was under way, embryonic Hegels were on the scene. Spain was again
prophetic, for its imperial despotism throve on a sense of messianic
mission, a fervor that was more clearly nationalistic than Christian
—as Catholic Portugal could testify. Everywhere in Europe nationalism
was at least strong enough to obscure an elementary question. All
nations acted on the principle that their ends justified the use of violent or unscrupulous means; but what end should the state serve?

In any rational view, the state too is a means to some end, some notion of the well-being of its people. In practice, it was an end in itself.
More precisely, its end was material power. If it naturally sought material prosperity as well, this was another means to aggrandizement, or
immediately to maintaining the power of rulers; mercantilism was
hardly devoted to raising standards of living among the common people. There was as yet little idea—and none at all in such statesmen as
Cardinal Richelieu—that the primary end of the state might be to promote the welfare of the common people, much less to secure and extend
the blessings of liberty. Except for a narrow, partial, when not nominal
devotion to the cause of Christianity, there was as little idea of promot-

ing the communal well-being through the diffusion of any "higher" goods, enabling the people to realize the values of beauty, truth, and goodness. The state was not yet rooted deeply enough in the national culture to proclaim any cultural mission; patronage of the arts and sciences was inspired mainly by the exclusive interests of the ruling class, or was a means of flaunting royal power. The capital city was symbolic as it grew bigger, more imposing, and more congested, with more slums to offset the palaces and imperial squares that were not civic centers. And the whole issue of ends was further obscured by the revival of the ancient confusion of the state with society. While religious strife led to a gradual separation of the things that were God's from the things that were Caesar's, otherwise the interests of the national state were in effect considered identical with the interests of society or the community as a whole. Its rulers were free not only to censor the press but to intrude on economic and all other social activities, even to matters of dress and diet; thus laws attempted to preserve class distinctions by regulating what people in different ranks should wear and eat. The nation-state at this time lacked the physical means to exercise the power that the modern totalitarian state does, but it contained the seeds of totalitarianism inasmuch as its good was considered the supreme good, the first and last end.

More specifically, it forced another basic political issue—the problem of sovereignty. In 1576 the political philosopher Jean Bodin, the first to use the word, defined sovereignty as "the absolute and perpetual power of the state," which was "unrestrained by law." He emphasized that there could be no human authority above the ruler of the state: "Only he is absolutely sovereign who, after God, acknowledges no one greater than himself." Bodin proceeded to confuse the issue hopelessly by arguing that the sovereign was nevertheless bound by the laws both of God and of nature; respecting ancient usage, he still adhered to the medieval theory of constitutional government, while as a bourgeois he was also concerned to safeguard private property. But thinkers after him seized chiefly on his principle that a well-ordered state must have the sovereign power "to lay down the law to all subjects without their consent." They found as congenial another of his arguments, that this supreme power was best exercised by a monarch; he confused as well the indivisible rights of the state with the rights of majesty. For everywhere the nation-state had risen to power under kings, who by this time were either ruling or aspiring to rule as absolute monarchs. This related development was as natural, perhaps necessary, in some respects clearly salutary; but it was a more apparent setback to the cause of freedom.

4. Absolute Monarchy: The Age of Louis XIV

Once considered a "reactionary" development, and now sometimes given the more fashionable label of "revolutionary," the rise of absolute monarchy was at least another break with medieval tradition. Once more Spain set the example as it became the leading power in Europe. Beginning with Ferdinand and Isabella, who united the country, its kings consciously sought autocratic power. They still had to deal with the Cortes, a parliament that was convened more or less regularly, especially for purposes of taxation; but its power steadily declined, an appointive Royal Council took over its political functions, and by the seventeenth century the sovereign won the right of taxation without the consent of any representative body. Meanwhile the kings kept the Church subservient, retaining jurisdiction over ecclesiastical appointments as all other internal affairs. In like manner autocracy became the prevailing rule elsewhere in Europe. In England, where Parliament survived, the Tudors used it to strengthen their power and maintain their independence of Rome; throughout the sixteenth century writers emphasized, as never before or since, the necessity of obedience to kings. In France the Estates-General met for the last time in 1614, to distinguish itself by a seemingly odd insistence on the same theme: the Third Estate demanded that the right of resistance to royal authority, "on any pretext whatsoever," be expressly condemned. Latecomers on the national scene almost uniformly followed the political fashion. Sweden enjoyed a brilliant, if brief period of military glory under Gustavus Adolphus; Frederick William of Brandenburg, the "Great Elector," virtually created the state of Prussia singlehanded; and Peter the Great was most despotic when he deliberately set out to Westernize Russia.

As an outmoded form of government, absolute monarchy may now look like a temporary, even "unnatural" phase of Western political history. Nevertheless, it remains a highly significant phase. It dominated European history for several centuries, after all, as its baroque architecture still dominates the European scene; until some hundred years ago it was the basic form of government in most countries. Its tradition survives in the common hankering for the rule of the strong man, if not the Führer. It calls for understanding no less if it is labeled "reactionary," for it was a reversion to by all odds the oldest, commonest, most persistent form of government in recorded history.

Kings came to power in Europe pretty much as they had in all previous civilizations, and for as good reasons.[5] While the establishment and maintenance of their power entailed plenty of blood and iron, they seldom exercised and never represented "naked" power; essentially monarchy rested on an authority that their subjects considered legitimate and were pleased to dignify as "majesty." They drew immediately on the feudal tradition of personal loyalty to the lord, which harked back to the immemorial tradition of personal loyalty to the tribal chieftain, the immemorial custom—in communities as in families—of investing leadership in one man, not many. Through Christianity they drew as well on the universal tradition that lent sacredness to the monarch, since medieval thinkers had taken for granted that kingship was ordained by God. Reverence for the "crown"—the ancient symbol of continuity, consummation, completeness—was deepened as kings became father symbols for peoples growing conscious of their national identity. (Thus Henry VIII was soon honored by a synthetic legend that Constantine the Great had conferred dominion over the British Isles upon his ancestor King Arthur.) All but the sorriest kings had greatness thrust upon them, and even these might inspire a high devotion because of their high office—as Joan of Arc met martyrdom in the holy cause of getting crowned the contemptible Charles VII of France.

Or put their case at its worst, say that in the last analysis the kings maintained their sovereignty by sheer force, even this strengthened their claims to legitimacy, sometimes to greatness. Given feudal tradition, they had had to use force to command obedience, establish their supremacy, and strengthen the nation. In however selfish a spirit they had responded to the crying need of Europe at the time, which was not liberty but law and order. Yearning for this, men welcomed the "King's Peace," the "King's Justice." At worst, the tyranny of one seemed more tolerable than the tyranny of many.

Because of the advantages of hindsight we are always likely to forget the most obvious question: In a given society at a given time, what were the choices actually open to men? Specifically, what at this stage in Europe were the feasible alternatives to kingship? In the large national

---

[5] On the rise of kingship in early civilizations see *Freedom in the Ancient World*, pp. 51-54.

communities, democratic government was hardly conceivable; the common people had never been represented in the parliaments, and outside some towns had been given no preparation for self-government. England would demonstrate that an approach to constitutional monarchy was feasible, but its Parliament would remain unrepresentative until well into the nineteenth century; and first it demonstrated the incapacity of aristocracy, the only real competitor with monarchy. The Tudors came into power as the saviors of England, putting an end to the disastrous Wars of the Roses between noble houses. In France the lesson was spelled out more plainly by the Fronde, an uprising by the great nobles, who exploited popular discontent over taxation; having no ideal of constitutional government, only a selfish interest in recovering their feudal privileges, the nobles succeeded only in prolonging for some years a civil war that devastated France and by its failure strengthened absolute monarchy, to the relief of most Frenchmen. As for hindsight, still another demonstration was provided by Poland. Here the nobility did succeed in controlling the government, reducing the king to impotence; it proceeded to subject the peasantry to an oppression worse than any in western Europe, while also holding down the middle class whose commercial activities it disdained; so it managed to keep Poland medieval, and to facilitate the eventual partition of the country by its neighboring monarchies.

The most apparent reason for the ascendancy of kingship remains its immediate practical success, attested by the increasing wealth, power, and stability of the monarchical states. By and large the kings were a progressive force, the leaders in more rational government. Ideally representing all classes in the nation, to a reputable extent they did in fact serve the interests of all but the most ambitious nobles. Even the common people, who everywhere bore the brunt of royal taxation, had reason to prefer their rule; together with the King's Peace, royal justice seemed their best hope for protection against the powerful and wealthy. The bourgeoisie had plainer reason for supporting the kings, the possibly shortsighted but not unfounded assumption that they were good for business. Gifted individuals from all ranks could profit by the opportunities and incentives offered by monarchy, under which the individualism of the Renaissance continued to flourish. Hence the learned humanists were mostly pleased to support the kings, if at first with provisos about their traditional obligations, and artists and poets offered more enduring evidence of their immediate success, in the flowering of national cultures. The despotic Philip II is still revered by many Spaniards as their greatest king, while Queen Elizabeth gave her name to the first great age of English literature.

Most widely influential at the time, however, was the Age of Louis XIV. This calls for close attention because under King Louis the modern nation-state fully emerged and absolute monarchy reached its peak; France became the major power in Europe. It took over as well the cultural leadership of Europe, setting the standards of judgment and taste, making French the international language of the cultivated. Hence even the skeptical Voltaire looked back on the Age of Louis XIV with admiration verging on awe, viewing it as one of the few great ages in the history of civilization, worthy of rank with Periclean Athens and Augustan Rome. But Voltaire brings us to another obvious reason for taking a hard look at it. By its aftermath it revealed most clearly the basic weaknesses of absolute monarchy, the reasons why this was only a transitional phase in western Europe even though it had remained the basic form of government in almost all other great societies in the past. The aftermath culminated in the French Revolution.

The reign of the "Sun King" at Versailles was foreshadowed early in the sixteenth century by the dashing Francis I, who inaugurated the cult of regal splendor by building Fontainebleau. Toward the end of the century Henry IV founded the Bourbon dynasty and gave it an auspicious start by ending the bloody religious wars in France: he issued the Edict of Nantes (1598) that granted the Huguenots toleration. But Louis XIV owed most to the work of Cardinal Richelieu, the Bismarck of the age. As chief minister of Louis XIII (1624–1642), Richelieu devoted all his remarkable energy and ability to making the king the supreme power in France, and France the supreme power in Europe. Completely ignoring the traditional Estates-General, he set up in its stead a council appointed by the king, and made both taxation and legislation the royal prerogative. He took particular pains to weaken the fractious nobility, keeping close watch on them through spies, ruthlessly punishing any appearance of conspiracy. For administrative agents he turned to the bourgeoisie, laying the foundations of a centralized bureaucracy, while to strengthen the king both at home and abroad he built up a large standing army, also responsible to the crown alone. In foreign policy Richelieu never allowed religious principles to interfere with *raison d'état;* though a prince of the Church, he made no bones about supporting Protestants in Germany against the

Catholic Hapsburgs. As the contemporary pope remarked upon his death, "If God exists, he will probably have to atone; if not, he was a good man."

On earth God appeared to approve his work. A year after Richelieu's death Louis XIV succeeded to the throne at the age of four, to begin the longest reign in recorded history (1643–1715). During his minority France was ruled by Cardinal Mazarin, who carried on Richelieu's Machiavellian policies in a more shameless spirit and by his extravagance touched off the rebellion of the Fronde, but this made young Louis an apter pupil. When Mazarin died, the king at once announced to his ministers that he alone was going to rule the state, henceforth their duty would be only to advise and to carry out his orders; or in the words immortalized by Voltaire, "L'état, c'est moi." He in fact ruled as an absolute sovereign, doing without a prime minister, uniting all power and authority in his own person, and completing the work of Richelieu by systematically eliminating all possible opposition to his will, beginning with the complete subjection of the nobility. Louis transformed the once proud, independent warrior-aristocrats into servile courtiers at Versailles, wholly dependent upon the royal favor, concerned chiefly with precedence in the endless ceremonies; the courtiers soon learned that to retain his favor they must never be caught discussing affairs of state. He kept them out of such affairs by staffing his government from the ranks of the bourgeois, commoners surer to realize the need of absolute obedience to the will of the sovereign. (As Colbert, the greatest of his ministers, wrote to the son who succeeded him, "Never as long as you live send out anything in the king's name without his express approval.") His clergy dutifully recognized their place in the royal scheme: "We accordingly declare that kings and sovereigns are subjected by the ordinance of God to no ecclesiastical power in temporal things." From the Sun King alone emanated the radiance of France. God himself, it has been suggested, came to be conceived in the image of Louis XIV.

Contemporaries had some excuse for such confusion. Although historians are still debating the Sun King's claims to greatness, they differ chiefly over the weighting of his admitted qualities: on the one hand, his selfishness, callousness, prodigality, overweening pride, and limited intellectual reach; on the other, his courage, energy, conscientiousness, tireless industry, and ability to recognize great ability in others. They are generally agreed that no king ever worked harder at being every inch a king, and that he long played the part with very considerable success. At home his subjects greeted with enthusiasm his determination to rule instead of merely reign; he was unquestionably popular until toward the end of his reign—and is still revered by conservatives in France. Abroad he made an immense impression as the very model of a sovereign; other monarchs imitated his style, his court, his palace. The fact remains that under Louis XIV France became the dominant power in Europe.

If he owed much of his success to his ministers, he had the wit not only to employ them but to approve their counsels. Public administration he turned over largely to Colbert, who had a bourgeois genius for it. Colbert controlled the state finances, closely regulated commerce, established the first office to collect statistics, superintended the development of national industries, built roads and canals—organized the entire economy to strengthen the state. If his very businesslike administration may be given the less agreeable name of bureaucracy, which feudal society had managed without, this society had therefore had to manage without extensive public works or an orderly economy either. At any rate, Colbert made France the first really modern state. For his military purposes Louis XIV found another genius in Louvois, who created the first modern army. France had had a typical feudal army, untrained, undisciplined, often unpaid, addicted to plunder of Frenchmen too. Louvois made it a professional military machine, efficiently drilled, well equipped, serviced by experts in artillery and the science of fortification. Although widely hated because of his brutal methods, he was wholeheartedly supported by the king, who in return got by far the best army in Europe. In the first half of his reign it won him more territory and still more diplomatic influence.

Less credit is due Louis himself for the most enduring achievements of his age, which were cultural rather than political. Yet he remains the symbol of the *grand siècle,* and in a real sense he presided over it from Versailles, built to his orders in the "grand style." His elegant palace is no longer so greatly admired, of course, nor is the baroque art of the period, which elsewhere in Europe was less chaste than Versailles; the very name for this style now connotes decadence, since to many it seems rhetorical, ostentatious, hollow—at best not grand but grandiose. Still, one who is no lover of it (as I am not) may appreciate the kind of freedom that others still admire in it: the restless movement, the fertility of invention, the bold defiance of conventional form or order, the courage of flamboyance or license. As Geoffrey Scott has insisted, "decadent" is not clearly the word for an art that displays such energy, self-confidence, and resourcefulness. Neither Gothic nor classical, never sublime nor serene, it was at least genuine as an expression of the contemporary sense of drama and power. Similarly the regal accompaniments of the baroque—the formal garden, the palatial square, the avenue—created a sense at once of openness and order or control.

The neoclassical ideals that governed the literature of the *grand siècle* were rather different from the baroque, if also matter for critical dispute. They sprang from the ruling principle of obedience to authority—a principle formulated by Renaissance critics, but now become more obviously suited to the climate of an authoritarian regime; thus both drama and poetry were bound by rigid rules that today seem patently artificial. Nevertheless, such formal discipline bred admirable qualities of clarity, precision, economy, restraint. Together with the tradition of rationalism it helped to produce a truly sophisticated literature, reflecting a clearer artistic mastery of experience. In a historical perspective, the ideals of propriety and dignity signified a timely effort at good taste and good sense, a salutary phase in the development of European culture as a mature effort at consolidation. There is no reason to wonder why the Age of Louis XIV set the literary standards for all western Europe. And though Louis himself considered literature at best an elegant pastime, he was at least pleased to be the patron of the likes of Molière, Racine, and Boileau.[6]

The king was also persuaded by Colbert to establish the French Academy of Sciences, a sequel to the informal gatherings of such luminaries as Descartes and Pascal. This he lent more financial support than the Royal Society in England was getting, subsidizing its researches in the natural sciences. Louis XIV accordingly contributed to another movement far more significant than the affairs of state that to him were all-important. It gave some pith and moment to an academic excitement of his reign—the battle between the Ancients and the Moderns. Although the Moderns were so proud, or silly, as to argue that

---

[6] An incidental expression of the growing civility of the age was the school of St. Cyr, opened by Mme. de Maintenon, the last wife of Louis XIV. The first boarding school for girls in France, it amounted to the first serious effort to educate women; and it was immediately popular, flooded by many more applications for admission than it could accommodate. St. Cyr calls for no more than a footnote here, however, for it was hardly a landmark in the emancipation of women. It inspired no national effort to found more such schools, and at that the education it offered was designed primarily to improve the manners and morals of the young ladies, not to open or train their minds. That women had or were entitled to have independent minds would not be generally recognized in educational theory until well after the French Revolution, which ended the history of aristocratic St. Cyr.

the literature of the Age of Louis was superior to the whole literature of Greece and Rome, they nominally won the battle; their more distinguished opponents were inclined to agree that moderns were indeed superior in natural philosophy and science. Writers were growing aware of a revolution in thought, which was in turn generating the revolutionary idea of progress. Toward the end of the Sun King's reign appeared Fontenelle and Bayle, forerunners of the Age of Enlightenment.

But this whole movement obviously went on in spite of Louis XIV, not because of his works. Though at first fairly tolerant so long as his autocratic rule was not questioned, he was naturally no friend of free thought; he kept the press under severe censorship. The formal gardens of Versailles—not to mention its slavish routines—symbolized a kind of regimentation that pervaded cultural as well as economic and political activity, and grew more oppressive. Colbert directly superintended the Royal Academy of Painting and Sculpture, bending art to the service of the state, or specifically to the glorification of the monarch; as Louis graciously told the members of the Academy, "I entrust to you the most precious thing on earth—my fame." Even so, this precious trust failed to inspire creativity. The latter half of the Sun King's reign was much less radiant than the first half. Few writers of note emerged to replace the major writers now dead or silent, and of these La Bruyère began his literary career by observing, "All has been said." By this time Louis was fast losing the popularity he had at first enjoyed.

His reign ended in utter failure, the worse for being in no sense whatever a great failure. Immediately it was a failure in war, which had taken up more than half of his reign, cost the lives of hundreds of thousands of his subjects, and served no purpose higher than aggrandizement—"the worthiest and most beautiful aim of a prince," he had written a fellow monarch. Had he realized his dream of becoming master of Europe he would have had nothing to offer it except alien rule, an artificial unity imposed by force. As it was, his initial victories united other powers in opposition, and in his later years he met chiefly defeat, at most succeeding only in holding his own. What he held was an impoverished kingdom, whose finances he had wrecked. Despite terrific taxation, which brought misery or even famine to the peasantry, his treasury was no longer able to meet the costs of his wars. The Grand Monarch was too vain or myopic ever to remark what his successor, Louis XV, said, "Après nous le déluge"; yet it was he who brought on the deluge. He went to his grave to a chorus of jeering and rejoicing by his subjects.

What had begun as absolute monarchy, resting on the glad consent of the governed, ended as despotism, resting on mute habit when not force. Though Louis was never so malignant or cruel as some despots, he took quite literally his divine right to rule as he saw fit, and his word was as literally law. He made it plain that the decent respect he showed for custom or traditional privilege involved no constitutional rights to oppose his will. He explicitly denied elementary rights, as to property, that in practice he might graciously allow: "Being absolute rulers, kings have naturally full and free liberty to dispose of all property." There were never any effective checks on his power, beyond simple prudence. And his prudence was among the casualties of the early triumphs won by the armies of Louvois. In going to his head, these incidentally fed a conceit that helped to shatter his imperial dreams; fancying himself as a generalissimo, he began dictating from Versailles orders to his generals in the field. A more fateful sign of his delusions of grandeur was his Revocation of the Edict of Nantes (1685), followed by a barbarous persecution of the Huguenots.

A plain sign of his growing bigotry too, this was still not due to pure fanaticism. In the spirit of Cardinal Richelieu, Louis XIV himself admitted that religious conscience had nothing to do with his conduct of foreign affairs, writing that he made treaties only to "plaster over" the "permanent hostility" to the Catholic Hapsburgs; nobody took seriously "whatever precious articles one may include about union, friendship, and the seeking of common advantages." As for his piety at home, his devout wife Mme. de Maintenon aptly defined its quality when she told a cardinal that he would never miss a fast day but could never understand what repentance or humility meant. By the same token, however, he did have a vivid idea of what it meant to be an absolute sovereign. To him it seemed that the rule of one man called for one church, one faith; he fancied it an insult to his majesty that a million of his subjects should have a different faith. At any rate, the consequences of the Revocation were disastrous enough to mark the turning point in his reign. Although Louis forbade emigration under penalty of life sentence to the galleys, up to 200,000 or more Huguenots succeeded in fleeing. The loss to France was much greater than the number suggests, for they were among the most industrious, skilled of its people, a mainstay of its economy. (Their flight ruined, for instance, the silk industry of Tours.) With the talents and skills they brought to

England, Holland, and Prussia, they carried tales of atrocities that intensified the hatred of Protestant Europe for Louis.[7]

For the long run, Louis was as fatally successful in suppressing all open opposition at home. The nobility he made worse than useless, for in depriving them of all political power he made a point of allowing them to retain all their other feudal privileges, in particular exemption from direct taxation. They provided him with some generals and officers, but mainly they served to ornament his court and by servile flattery to maintain his majesty. To the Church they passed on some of their surplus offspring, at some expense to its spirituality; a second son might get a bishopric and lesser children could be comfortably set up in abbeys and convents, whether or not they had a religious vocation. Otherwise the chief function of the nobility for the nation was conspicuous consumption, of wealth they had not created. Enjoying privilege without any responsibility, they could hardly be expected to maintain a high tradition of either patriotism or *noblesse oblige*. The livest element in their aristocratic tradition helped to doom to ineffectuality the lesser gentry who were unable to afford life at Versailles: the little *seigneur* was debarred from engaging in trade, an occupation fit only for the "vile bourgeoisie."

These vile folk fared somewhat better under Louis XIV, even apart from those who rose in his service. They might prosper as merchants and in towns enjoy semblances of their medieval privileges or "liberties"; although Louis characteristically tried to do away with municipal government, some towns maintained a surprisingly independent spirit. On the whole, however, he kept them under firm enough control, and municipal liberties declined into little but a show, purchased by money payments to the king. Furthermore, he naturally had no idea of increasing the power of the bourgeoisie as a class; the wealthy were still denied the prestige and the privileges of the nobility. They were accordingly disposed to a smoldering resentment, which would flare up in the French Revolution, but also to some affectation of gentility, which lessened their usefulness: they might aspire chiefly to living like

---

[7] Because the French clergy egged him on, it should be noted that the Revocation was not due to pressure from Rome. Publicly, Pope Innocent XI celebrated the "glorious religious spirit" Louis had shown, "that extraordinary zeal, never sufficiently commended by any praises," for safeguarding and extending the Catholic religion; and the Catholic world rejoiced sufficiently. But privately the pope deplored the zeal of Louis as impolitic, or too extraordinary. Louis O'Brien, an apologist, explains that he could not formally reprove it because the powerful French clergy might well have declared him a heretic and broken away from Rome.

seigneurs, disdaining any "gainful occupation." The business class in France displayed much less enterprise than its freer brethren in England and Holland, or than the Huguenots driven out by Louis.

Neither was it inspired by the achievement of its most honored son, Colbert. The first great apostle of efficiency in government, Colbert nevertheless failed to build a sound economic foundation for the French state. Immediately, his dedication to mercantilism led him to start a trade war with the Dutch, which then led his royal master to embark on endless, fruitless campaigns to conquer Holland. At all times, the trouble remained that his policies were designed primarily for the short-run interest of the state, or more especially the king. He had to provide for the notorious extravagance of Louis, who outdid other monarchs in this respect too; the upkeep of the huge royal court at Versailles—built at a cost still unknown—took more than half of the national revenue. He had to contend as well with a rotten fiscal system inherited from Richelieu, who had not worried over the deficits he piled up for the sake of national aggrandizement. Although he attempted reforms, the system of taxation remained not only flagrantly inequitable, bearing most heavily on those least able to pay, but hopelessly confused and inefficient; with some taxes the costs of collection ate away up to half the proceeds. One reason for the almost incredible stupidity of these arrangements was that Colbert never realized the economic need of a prosperous peasantry, in a country predominantly agricultural. Another reason was simply that he was not much concerned about the state of the common people.

Cardinal Richelieu had set the example as a servant of the state—not the people. He observed casually that the people should be treated like mules, always kept hard at work, so as not to be spoiled by rest or ease. Louis XIV had more Christian sentiments, occasionally declaring that it was a king's duty to ease the burdens of his people, and making some sincere efforts to do so; yet by the nature of his autocratic regime he did nothing effectual, even before the more crushing burdens imposed in the last decades of his reign. He had done his best to centralize power in his own hands, and he exercised it by remote control from his palace of Versailles, built to augment his majesty, insulate him from his subjects. As his orders passed down from the top, he could have little idea of their effects at the bottom; communications from the bottom up were much poorer, while censorship discouraged open criticism or complaint. Hence his Christian sentiments amounted to sentimentality—an indulgence of pleasurable feelings without the pain of intellectual or moral commitments to make them good. The common people paid for his wars, by the preposterously inequitable taxes that he did nothing about. Countless thousands died of hardship and hunger while the superficial splendors of Versailles were kept up without stint.

To devotees of the *ancien régime* (Louis Bertrand, for instance) such observations smack of democratic sentimentality; and it is possible to argue that the glory of the Age of Louis XIV was worth the human costs. It is impossible to deny the costs. The common people were indeed not ground down into abject servility, retaining enough spirit to put up some resistance to tax collectors, but essentially theirs was only to do and die. They enjoyed little freedom or opportunity, as little justice by Christian or democratic standards. Certainly they did not share in the glory of the age. And the glory, once more, was fading before the Sun King's reign came to its dismal end.

Versailles hardly inspired the most creative thought of the age, the growth of modern philosophy and science. Most directly it inspired fine art and belles-lettres, which now became most purely the property of a ruling class. While the reigning ideals of regularity and propriety naturally discouraged tendencies to spontaneity, gusto, exuberance, or abundance, literature suffered directly because the court of Louis XIV largely fixed both its style and its content. Versailles was a highly artificial indoor world, insulated alike from the commonwealth and the cosmos. Debarring the writer from political or civic interests, it tended as well to discourage any free-ranging imagination, any concern with the elemental realities of the common life, the good earth, the heavens above, the all-encompassing darkness—the natural conditions of both freedom and necessity, and in drama the natural sources of amplitude, magnitude, and resonance. Hence the costs were most apparent in serious or tragic drama, which by definition was concerned exclusively with the affairs of royalty and nobility. Molière maintained the independence of the comic spirit, aided by the convention that defined comedy as an affair of ordinary life, but writers of tragedy concentrated on the genteel themes of love and intrigue, while scrupulously observing the taboo against the introduction of common people or any reference to the vulgar objects of everyday life.[8]

---

[8] In *The Spirit of Tragedy* I remarked that Anglo-American critics have typically had a rather low regard for Corneille and Racine, and may therefore be suspected of provinciality: the French, whose literature is by general consent one of the great literatures of the Western world, still rank them among their greatest writers. We may better appreciate the dignity of French neoclassical drama by reconsidering the sprawl, extravagance, and crude horrors of popular Elizabethan drama. Nevertheless, I should still maintain that as tragic poets Corneille and Racine hardly belong in the same class with the

Since many literary men (such as T. S. Eliot) still cherish the notion that a blooded aristocracy provides the ideal conditions for the nourishment of high culture, it should be remarked again that Louis XIV and his court patronized literature in the disagreeable sense of condescending to it. It was a polite fashion, by no means so vital a concern as the affairs of the court, the issues of precedence, the burning question of who was in, who out of the royal favor. Even the highly cultivated Mme. de Sévigné dismissed the popularity of Racine as "a passing craze, like that for coffee"; and when he retired and gave up writing, though only thirty-eight years old, no one publicly lamented the loss of the greatest dramatist and poet of the day. Previously Corneille had suffered from another tendency of genteel literature that now became pronounced—the reign of superficial, transient fashion, or a seeming freedom that signified an actual tyranny comparable to that of the latest style in women's dress. A soldier of the old aristocratic school, Corneille wrote a triumphant kind of tragedy, rendering in the grand style the struggle of heroic will against passion, seeking to excite "admiration" instead of mere pity or terror: a drama without shadow, uncertainty, or sense of mystery, which would seem ideally suited to the Grand Monarchy in an age of power. Yet it went out of fashion; and the old soldier morosely gave in, wrote mediocre love plays in a vain effort to compete with the more popular Racine.

The retirement of Racine himself brings up an uglier, more ominous fashion. It was due immediately to vicious attacks on him, the remarkably virulent malice that so often cropped out in an age supposedly devoted to propriety, decorum, and restraint. The malice was an apparent by-product of the prevailing servility and hypocrisy, an outlet for frustration, or for revulsion against the ineffable tedium and triviality of life at Versailles. Though men of fashion like Nicholas Breton might rhapsodize over "the gallant life of the Court," all "the choices of contentment" that made it "the Paradise of the World," there was actually as little free choice as lasting contentment on the royal assembly line; the Memoirs of Saint-Simon make plain how weary, stale, flat, and unprofitable the uses of this courtly life became.[9] But the malaise

---

Greeks and Shakespeare, if only because the Age of Louis XIV was not conducive to great tragic drama. Versailles could provide no theater for an *Oresteia* or *Oedipus Rex*, *Hamlet* or *King Lear*.

[9] Since literary men also tend to be rather supercilious about plumbing and other physical conveniences they take for granted, it might be added that Versailles was as unsanitary as spiritually unwholesome. Courtiers had some excuse for using its elegant corridors as urinals.

points as well to a profounder disillusionment beneath the apparent complacence and the glitter of the Age of Louis XIV. Most of its serious literature has a somber, melancholy cast; from Pascal to La Rochefoucauld, Racine, and La Bruyère, its greater writers typically express a pessimistic or even cynical view of human nature. This was not by any means an age of radiant faith. One reason why the heroic drama of Corneille went out of fashion was that to sophisticates his simple faith rang hollow.

So in time did the celebration of absolute rule by divine right—the literally absurd pretensions of the Sun King. These were most thoroughly exposed by Saint-Simon, who knew that his royal master should be treated "like a god, like a father, like a mistress," but kept recording how he had demoralized the court, ruined the nation, brought on a state of utter "decadence, confusion, and chaos." Though on his deathbed Louis XIV expressed some repentance for the abuses of his power, he was scarcely aware of the crowning irony of his overlong reign. The greatest monarch of the day, he did most to rouse the political and intellectual forces that would doom absolute monarchy. He never succeeded in conquering the little Dutch Republic, a haven of free thought at the time, and he was defeated most signally by England, which by then had dethroned James II and firmly established a constitutional monarchy. The success of England suggested that parliamentary government was not necessarily so confused and indecisive, rule by one not so essential to efficiency and strength, as thinkers commonly assumed. Frenchmen were slow to draw this conclusion, mostly blaming the failure of Louis on his vanity and arrogance, not on the principle of absolutism; but the sophistication of the *ancien régime* steadily continued to erode its foundations.

The immediate aftermath of his reign was obscene. The regency that ruled France in the name of the youngster who succeeded to his throne made a mockery of his majesty. His will was set aside; the government was turned over to ministers again; the bigoted piety of his later years gave way to a notorious license. When Louis XV grew up he was pleased to reign instead of rule, enjoy the privileges of absolute monarchy without assuming its responsibilities. So the worst of Louis XIV lived after him, under the appearances of revulsion against him. The royal court was as recklessly extravagant as ever; although noblemen were now allowed by law to engage in commerce, most were too proud to do so, while with the clergy they continued to claim exemption from all direct taxes; the whole fiscal system remained hopelessly inequitable and inefficient, assuring economic and social disorder; and wars went on as a matter of royal routine, mostly as inconsequential as costly except for one in which France lost its immense possessions in America— an empire that Louis XIV had neglected to develop in his intentness on winning supremacy in Europe. Yet this was the Age of Enlightenment. Under a censorship more fitful or halfhearted than Louis had exercised, writers were attacking both religious and political absolutism, preparing the ground for the French Revolution. From the tradition of rationalism that had come through his age, and from the example of England, the men of the Enlightenment now drew a more positive faith than had the writers oppressed, bored, or disillusioned by the court of the Sun King at Versailles. And because his fame had helped to make French the international language of Europe, their radical ideas spread all over the world he had vainly tried to master.

5. *The Philosophy of Political Power*

"Apart from the universal consent of peoples and nations," declared the Bishop of Chartres in the days of Richelieu, "the prophets announce, the apostles confirm, and the martyrs confess that kings are ordained by God, and not only that they are so ordained, but also that they are gods themselves . . . not by nature but by grace." Such god-kings, it followed, were hardly subject to the will or the judgment of ordinary mortals. By this time the ancient idea of rule by divine right had been given a further twist: kings got their authority directly from God, not through the people or the commonwealth, and they were responsible only to God. The most eminent Bishop Bossuet spelled out the whole argument on behalf of Louis XIV. In the king rested the "power and will, even the reason of the State"; popular consent had nothing to do with it. The people must obey him even if he were wicked and persecuted them: "Subjects have only the right to oppose the prince's violence with respectful remonstrances, or with prayers for his conversion, but not with rebellion nor murmuring." God alone could judge the judgment of princes, if with some respectful assistance from his bishops.

Now, the divine right of kings to govern wrong seems so obviously absurd that again we might pause to understand why the doctrine was so long accepted, by men who were neither fools nor scoundrels. The most thoughtful felt a need of legitimatizing the absolute authority that kings were in fact exercising, and that seemed to many—as it did to Bodin—an absolute necessity of political order; resistance to the claims of the monarch generally resulted in civil war, threats of feudal anarchy. The common disorder only confirmed the natural depravity of the race, which called for iron rule. Always autocracy was the "true pattern of divinity," as King James I of England observed—heaven is never a republic. Thinkers knew well enough that kings could govern badly, but they had good biblical authority for insisting on the necessity of obedience even so; God himself had said as much when he gave Israel the king the people clamored for, reminding them of the despotic ways of kings, warning them that if they would have one this was what they were in for. And though Jesuits might deny the absolute sovereignty of kings, men knew enough to discount their arguments: they were only trying to restore the power of Rome. The municipal parlement of Paris cited the Bishop of Chartres in condemning these subversive papists.

Yet the doctrine of divine right plainly could not do for the long run, in a society growing more secular and sophisticated. As we have seen, it was weakened immediately by religious conflict. When Protestants began citing the prophets who opposed the kings of Israel, the arbitrary choice in biblical texts accentuated the essential weakness of the doctrine: it seemed plausible only on the grounds of a literal faith, which at that (as King James admitted) required an acknowledgment of "mystery" in the divine will. Once men began to appeal to reason instead of authority, it was bound to seem as absurd as it now does. Hence even in the heyday of absolute monarchy, the divine right of Louis XIV came down to a pious fiction, something like the reverence for the "crown" in England today. Bishop Bossuet had to argue for it at length because it had not won absolute belief, was not really enshrined among the eternal verities. The Machiavellian principles on which Louis conducted his foreign policy made it plainer that the fiction was not very pious either.

So we are brought to the historical importance of Thomas Hobbes, the philosopher *par excellence* of the age of power. Much more systematic and philosophical than the pragmatic Machiavelli, Hobbes offered in his *Leviathan* (1651) a purely rational defense of absolute sovereignty, on wholly naturalistic grounds. His thought had no immediate influence on political life, indeed, merely providing another possible justification for what rulers were doing anyway; at this stage political theory was a product, not a cause of political development. But at least it led to a clearer awareness of the actual development— the growth of a mighty, purely secular state. It heralded the domination of thought by frankly secular, utilitarian principles. In particular Hobbes paved the way for thinkers, notably John Locke, who did have a considerable influence on political life. It is no fluke that political theory became most active and fully developed in England, France, and America, the nations that underwent major revolutions and henceforth shared the major role in the history of Western freedom.

The gist of the *Leviathan* is simple. The "state of nature," before the institution of government, had been a state of endless war of all against all, "and the life of man, solitary, poor, nasty, brutish, and short." To end this bloody anarchy, men had made a social contract by which they conferred all power upon a sovereign or sovereign body, surrendering their freedom in return for security and order. Hobbes set a few limits on the power of the sovereign, for example declaring that subjects could not be compelled to injure themselves or to confess to their crimes, but for all practical purposes he argued for absolutism. The sovereign had the "incommunicable and inseparable" rights to make war and peace, levy taxes, determine property arrangements, decide all controversies over law, reward and punish subjects, control the press and public meetings, suppress any dangerous opinions—in general all the rights that Louis XIV exercised, and that any ruler short of a monster could wish for. The one serious proviso was that the sovereign must protect his subjects: if he lost the power to do this, as by defeat in war, their obligations ceased. As for the nature of the sovereign, he did not have to be a king; Hobbes held that monarchy was the stablest, most efficient form of government, but his theory applied to the ruler or ruling body in whatever form. In any case, the important thing was that the subjects were absolutely bound by the terms of the social contract, and had no right whatever to rebel against rulers they considered tyrannical. The sovereign, on the other hand, was not so bound, having been granted unconditional power: "He that is made sovereign maketh no covenant with his subject beforehand."

For Hobbes this social contract was not necessarily an actual historic occurrence, but essentially only a convenient way of representing the logic of the state, explaining why rulers in all viable states did have sovereign power and commanded obedience. Although his "covenant" may now seem arbitrary as a one-way affair, binding only on the ruled, at the time it made both historical and philosophical sense. Having lived through the Civil War in England, he had reason to share the common belief that only absolute sovereignty could prevent disorder; though not disposed to illusions about the superior virtue of kings, who had for him no aura of divinity, he thought that at worst tyranny was preferable to anarchy. Logically, his one-way contract came straight out of his major premise, that the ruling passion of mankind was self-interest, specifically a "perpetual and restless desire of power after power, that ceaseth only in death." To give men the right of resistance to the sovereign was therefore only to invite turmoil or anarchy. There could be no hope of stable government unless subjects were kept in complete subjection by force and fear, "the terror of some common power."

For his time, in fact, Hobbes was too remorselessly logical. He was unpopular not only with the men who made the English Revolution but with the royalist party of the Stuarts he was trying to support; the king's followers could see that in rejecting the traditional idea of legitimacy he undermined the reverence on which the monarch depended. The more acute might see, too, that he neglected to support the basic principle of aristocracy, for he did not argue that the ruling class was "naturally" superior; his theory rested on an assumption of equality in the state of nature, in that all men had the same lust for power, and those inferior in brawn or brain power might compensate by cunning or deceit. But this brings us back to the lasting importance of Hobbes, the reasons why he is ranked among the great political philosophers. Like Machiavelli, he helped to emancipate thought from the inveterate appeal to authority, immediately to the will of God— argument about which is especially futile in political theory because the authors of Scripture had no interest in such theory. More clearly than Machiavelli, he forced the basic issues of political philosophy, beyond practical politics. Thereby he facilitated the rise of more liberal philosophy in his own century.

Those who do not consider Hobbes so clearheaded as he seems to logicians may still welcome his revival of the ancient idea of the social contract. This idea would indeed long confuse thought by mythical ideas about a state of nature, fallacious ideas about how society and the state developed, since it implies that self-conscious individuals got together to form a government, whereas such individuals came late in history, long after government; yet it at least focused thought on the human purposes served by the state, the empirical problem of how best to achieve these purposes, and it also implied the idea of government by popular consent. Hobbes accordingly opened the door to different interpretations of the social contract, in particular John Locke's seemingly more reasonable theory of a contract binding on both rulers and ruled. Likewise his insistent realism might call attention to possible deficiencies in his empirical sense. For his whole theory was in fact a purely deductive affair, not derived from an empirical study of history or even of contemporary politics; else he might have noticed the evident power of sentiment, the common reverence for kings. As for his relentless logic, one might wonder how men so selfish and power-hungry as he assumes ever got together in the first place—and then wonder why they should believe that they have no right to resist the sovereign, must obey the covenant made by their unknown ancestors.

Today the issues forced by Hobbes are still more pertinent because recent history may appear to have vindicated him. Not only has his Leviathan acquired a monstrous power, under such as Hitler, but "power" has become a still more fashionable term in current political theory—ostensibly more realistic, scientific, precise than such terms as "freedom" and "justice." Yet one may still wonder. Are men so simply selfish as he premised? Do they obey rulers only out of fear? Or in his more specific terms of a "perpetual and restless desire of power after power," is this actually the dominant motive of "man"? Even of most men? Even in our highly competitive society? While the assumptions of Hobbes have become the common sense of ordinary Americans, these Americans do not look like the anarchic individualists he pictures. In both the democracies and the dictatorships men may look more like sheep than wolves, or in other words, more like the creatures described by the Grand Inquisitor; their most apparent passion is not for power but for security—they seem content to enjoy power vicariously. As for Hitler, he was very much aware of the power of sentiment, and millions worshiped him as they never would the absolute sovereign described and defended by Hobbes. At the same time, the sentiments of freedom and justice appear to have counted for something in the struggle against Hitler.

One cannot give a categorical answer to the questions raised by Hobbes. By the same token, however, one can say that he himself was too categorical, and like most rigorous logicians took too simple a view of man. He overlooked the important differences that culture makes in human nature, and that history may make. Nor was he, after all, a reliable guide to the history of his own age. His overriding concern was stability and order, not justice or the rights of subjects; but under a limited monarchy with guaranteed rights his own country would become the stablest, strongest nation in Europe. Meanwhile Hobbes had neglected to take into account perhaps the most remarkable achievement of the century, one much more astounding than that of the Grand Monarchy of Louis XIV—the achievement of the Dutch Republic.

6. *Postscript: The Dutch Republic*

"What other country," wrote Descartes of Holland, "where you can enjoy such perfect liberty, where you can sleep with more security . . . where poisoning, treacheries, calumnies are less known, and where there has survived more of the innocence of our forefathers?" "Innocence" was not quite the word for the busy Dutch, among whom the philosopher had found haven. At the time he wrote, in the early decades of the seventeenth century, they were the wealthiest commercial community to date, the greatest naval power in Europe, owners of most of the shipping in Atlantic waters, and exploiters of a colonial empire. Yet Descartes was speaking for many Westerners in his praise of the Dutch Republic. Little as it was, numbering only two million people, it led Europe in not only business but art and learning, and was as widely admired for its culture as envied for its wealth. Above all, it was indeed a land of liberty, the freest of the age. Among others to find haven in it were the parents of Spinoza, Jewish refugees from Portugal; various English Puritans, including the congregation that sent the Pilgrims to America, and later John Locke; and the French philosopher Bayle, a Huguenot refugee from Louis XIV, who published here his revolutionary *Historical and Critical Dictionary*. The presses of Holland were the mainstays of intellectual freedom in Europe, printing works that authors could not or dared not publish in their own countries. Altogether, the Dutch composed one of the most notable chapters in the history of Western freedom.

The key to their achievement was no more pure idealism than it was innocence. Although their republic was born of a heroic struggle for independence from Spain, it was not clearly due to any passion for liberty engrained in the "national character" or tradition of the Dutch; they became proud, self-conscious Dutchmen only after they had won their independence. The most apparent key was rather their character as bourgeois. They had started coming up in the world as businessmen,

and in their heyday in the seventeenth century they were the most
thoroughly bourgeois country in Europe, with the most systematically
commercialized economy. Their republic was ruled by men like the
"Masters of the Cloth Hall" painted by Rembrandt, known to European diplomats as Their High Mightinesses the Estates-General of the
United Provinces. The quality of their virtue was accordingly somewhat strained. They always kept a shrewd eye to business, making
money by trade with Spain even while patriots were fighting to win
their independence; their sobriety could be coarse or callous, especially
where "natives" were concerned, or European rivals for their trade in
spices and slaves (they tortured some Englishmen they ran across in
the Spice Islands) ; at home they put five-year-olds to work; and as
High Mightinesses they were not free from vanity and ostentation.
Nevertheless, they displayed not only the intelligence and enterprise
but the civility and all the decent virtues that the bourgeois were
ideally capable of. Their history is important in its own right, for all
they achieved and all they meant to other Europeans in the seventeenth
century; but it serves as well to round out our whole story to this time,
illumining the more civilized uses of power, in particular the potentialities for the growth of freedom.

The Dutch entered history as inhabitants not of Holland but of the
"Low Countries," embracing the land of modern Belgium too, and
peoples speaking a French dialect instead of their German dialect. In
the early Middle Ages this was a major center of the revival of commerce and civilization. The many towns that grew up, such as Ghent,
Bruges, Antwerp, Utrecht, Delft, and Rotterdam, wrung charters from
the feudal lords roundabout and so became semi-independent city-
states, governed to some extent under democratic institutions. No
nation, they settled down as provinces that eventually came under the
control of the dukes of Burgundy and then of the Hapsburgs, but they
retained considerable local autonomy. Hence it was not merely the
Protestantism of many of the burghers that led them to revolt against
Philip II of Spain; Catholics too resented his interference with their
liberties, no less his determination to install the Spanish Inquisition in
the Netherlands. In 1576 all the provinces united under William of
Orange (William the Silent) , an uncommonly wise statesman who had
agreed to lead them on condition that freedom of worship be guaranteed to both Catholics and Protestants. The guarantee was not observed
in the bitter war that followed, as hatred grew more virulent and
William was assassinated by a Catholic agent; so the rebellion became

primarily Protestant. Thereby it enlisted the aid of England, now alarmed by Philip's dream of bringing all Europe back under Catholic hegemony, and with this aid the Dutch finally won their independence in 1609.

By this time they were the Dutch. The Spanish had early won back the southern provinces, and the truce that ended the war permanently partitioned the Low Countries. The line of partition was not drawn neatly, however, by race, language, or religion. Spanish Netherlands, the Belgium to be, included about a third of the Dutch-speaking people as well as many Protestants, while a third of the Hollanders remained Catholic. What determined the borders of Holland was the great rivers —the Ysel, Rhine, and Meuse—behind which its defenders had been able to entrench themselves and beat back the Spanish armies.[10] At any rate, the Hollanders made the most of their strategic advantages. They took over the commerce of Spanish Netherlands, ruined by a generation of war and oppression, and secured it by blockading the river leading to Antwerp and Ghent; Amsterdam replaced Antwerp as the financial capital of Europe. Even before they won their independence they organized their East India Company and started building their colonial empire. Presently they established themselves in Indonesia, drove the Portuguese out of Malaya and Ceylon too, planted colonies in India, Japan, South Africa, and Manhattan, and discovered Australia and New Zealand. Meanwhile they virtually finished Spain as a major power by destroying a treasure fleet off Cuba, then another Spanish armada off the coasts of England. Holland took its place in the concert or conflict with England and France as the leading powers in western Europe.

It was too small, of course, to compete indefinitely in such company. The English learned much from it about commerce and banking, but were ungrateful as well as apt pupils; the Navigation Act of Oliver Cromwell, which crippled its carrying trade, led to open wars for what another Puritan called "the fairest mistress in the world—trade." The Dutch then had to contend with Louis XIV, who initiated his grand

[10] The Dutch historian Pieter Geyl had to wage a long scholarly campaign to discredit the fiction of an intrinsically Catholic Belgium and Protestant Holland, each with a distinctive national character to match, which became popular after the two nations went their separate ways. The Dutch refused to entertain the idea that mere geography and accident of war had marked out "the land of the Dutch"; Belgian historians (including the distinguished Henri Pirenne) likewise overlooked the centuries of common culture, not to mention their many Dutch-speaking compatriots, in order to make out a "Belgium" that was in being from the outset. As Geyl remarks, both strikingly illustrate how the writing of history has been influenced by the worship of the modern nation-state.

design of becoming master of Europe by overrunning the Spanish
Netherlands. Another William of Orange—William III—was from
first to last his most determined opponent, and succeeded in maintaining the national independence, again with the aid of the English; but
again the English profited most from the joint success. Thereafter
Holland receded into its natural role as a minor power, while Britannia
ruled the waves. The Dutch retained the bulk of their colonial empire,
however, and continued to prosper—not to mention the satisfaction of
seeing their William ascend the throne of England by invitation.

Now, Protestantism unquestionably aided their rise in the world.
Calvinists largely made up the zealous minority that ordinarily leads
rebellions or makes revolutions; the moderate William the Silent increasingly depended on them as his toughest, most determined fighters.
With the success of the revolution Calvinism became the national
religion of Holland, known as the Dutch Reformed Church. It helped
to shape the national image of an industrious, sober, thrifty, honest,
immaculate people—godly men of white starch and iron. But it helped
much less in the distinctive contribution of the Dutch to the cause of
religious freedom. The victorious Calvinists promptly condemned the
liberal teachings of Arminius, who granted men some freedom of will,
and it was not their piety that presently induced the formal toleration
of both Arminians and Catholics. One reason was simple weariness
with long, bitter experience of persecution. Another was the tradition
stemming from Erasmus of Rotterdam, restated by William the Silent:
"Who in this world is sufficiently courageous to touch another's conscience?" Still another was simple prudence or good sense, in a people
given to diverse religious views but common habits of industry, with
plenty of business on hand; persecution was not only inhuman but
uneconomical, wasteful. On all counts an unsung burgomaster of
Amsterdam, Pieter van Hooft, belongs among the great Dutchmen for
a letter he wrote in 1596, on behalf of a poor artisan who was reading
the Bible in some simple way not approved by the godly Calvinists:

> I hear that he is being excommunicated. Now let the Church be
> content with that, and cease persecuting him and his family any
> further. These people live in the fear of the Lord, they worship
> him as far as their insight reaches, and that ought to be enough. A
> man's life should not be dependent on learned subtleties.

Similarly the burghers had acquired their progressive spirit long
before some took to Calvinism. In the sixteenth century their fellows

made Antwerp the bourse of Europe by doing away with medieval restrictions, putting up in its own Bourse the famous inscription "For the use of all merchants of whatever land or language"; in the face of the rising mercantilism they maintained an unprecedented freedom in trade. Upon winning their independence the Dutch promptly founded the Bank of Amsterdam, which became as progressive a fiscal school in handling the chaotic currency of Europe and assuring full solvency at home. Most important, they offered an object lesson—immediately to the English—as a people who had deposed their king, formed a republic, and then prospered exceedingly. Their government was a loose federal system, hard to describe because the United Provinces were too jealous of their independence to entrust it to any national executive or clear national system, and because they nevertheless found room for a landed aristocracy; in national emergencies they depended on the princes of Orange, who were both noblemen and elected stadholders. But if such a government could hardly do for a large nation, the important point remained that it gave the Dutch more freedom than any other people of the time enjoyed. The princes of Orange could be strong rulers without putting on royal airs; as the great William the Silent had mingled freely with the burghers, so William III lived plainly and hated pomp, differing from his mighty opposite Louis XIV in all but diligence. English thinkers noted the contrast between the prosperous democratic republic of Holland and the fading despotic republic of Venice.

Modern thinkers might be more impressed by a rare blend of private and public enterprise, harking back to the early medieval town. Individualistic, competitive, and adventurous, the Dutch distinguished themselves no less by their co-operative enterprises and their strong communal spirit. They literally created much of their land by building dikes and canals, founding cities on reclaimed mud flats. Amsterdam adopted a model city plan of concentric canals that provided for orderly, uncongested growth, and that is still the envy of professional city planners today. All the cities took care to provide for orphans, the aged, and disabled soldiers; it was not merely prosperity but civic enterprise that kept them almost free from the beggars who infested the royal capitals of Europe. All were as far in advance of aristocratic Europe in the amenities of clean, comfortable living—amenities unknown at Versailles. In their neat brick homes, on canal streets or on farms that were models of progressive agriculture, the Dutch did develop a distinctive national character, a style of their own. No mere merchants

230 THE GROWTH OF POWER

busy in getting and spending, they cultivated a civil way of life that was most clearly and fully represented by their most typical artistic achievement—painting.

In so far as Dutch painting was religious it was Protestant, but by the same token it did not adorn churches. Essentially it was a secular art, celebrating the everyday life of the burghers rather than their Sabbath expectations of the life to come—portraying one big happy or busy family. It is especially significant because artists elsewhere in Europe, though coming chiefly from the middle class, expressed chiefly the interests and values of the court or the nobility. In Holland painting was of, by, and for the bourgeoisie. Here for the first time in Europe the middle class was served by a distinctive art all its own.

This ultrabourgeois, realistic art was accordingly limited in range, perhaps in depth. It no doubt suffered somewhat from its popularity, as every solid burgher had to adorn his home with paintings; it became another flourishing industry, a form of investment, managed by dealers and liable to the ills of mass production or overproduction. (Already in sixteenth-century Antwerp there had been many more master painters than butchers or bakers.) We may have some doubts, too, about the taste of the burghers, the level of appreciation, especially because most of the greater painters—Steen, Hobbema, de Hooch, van Ruisdael, Vermeer, Hals, Rembrandt—had money troubles, when they were not actually poor. Rembrandt, the greatest of them, suffered most from a decline in popularity, a neglect such as no great artist had to fear in the Italian Renaissance; the rejection of the picture he submitted for the Amsterdam Town Hall portended the plight of much genius in the bourgeois society of the future. Yet the Dutch Republic produced all these admittedly great painters. If it did not give them security, it did give them ample incentive and ample freedom, within limits they found congenial.[11] Likewise the Dutch school of painting ranks by general consent among the great schools. In portrait and still life, landscape, street, and home, it represented the real values of its society: values not wholly unspiritual, which may seem as lofty as those of the courtly Rubens, may show to better advantage by contrast with the baroque art of the age. Unstrained, if also less tense, Dutch art expressed a clear mastery of the world it knew, one in which its patrons

---

[11] Of Rembrandt one may say that he was too spiritual for the burghers, but one should add that he was the periodic type of the lonely giant, the towering genius like Shakespeare —whose supreme greatness was no more appreciated by the Elizabethans. At least the failure to appreciate his genius was not confined to dealers and their customers, for the greatest Dutch poet, Vondel, ranked him lower than a painter named Flinck. And even so one may find it hard to imagine Rembrandt outside of Holland, least of all at Versailles.

felt thoroughly at home, freer than the middle class would when it became the ruling class in a much greater world.

Another reason for believing that ordinary Dutch burghers had some true appreciation of their paintings is that almost all could read or write, and many showed a fondness for thinking too. Holland had the highest rate of literacy in Europe. Its University of Leiden (founded by William the Silent in the critical early days of the revolution) soon became the most illustrious international center of learning, attracting the most famous scholars of the century. With their international trade the Dutch had picked up some idea of the possible advantages of a free trade in ideas, and their government was more disposed than any other to tolerate if not to welcome it. Hence Holland became an asylum for freethinkers at a critical time in the intellectual history of Europe, when modern science was on the rise. Amsterdam and Leiden served as the main publishing centers for the revolutionary thought of the future. The many foreign works printed by Dutch presses included Galileo's *Dialogue on the New Sciences,* the treatises of Socinus and Descartes, Locke's *Letter concerning Toleration,* and the first English newspapers.

On their own Dutchmen contributed much more to the advance of knowledge than can be properly recognized here. On behalf of the innumerable forgotten men, known to few but scholars, we might piously note one Isaac Beeckman, who got Descartes interested in mathematics and physics; Jan Swammerdam, who studied the anatomy of insects with a loving care, technical resourcefulness, and fine art suggestive of the painters; Balthasar Bekker, whose *World Bewitched* helped to kill the ugly superstition of witchcraft; and Anna Maria van Schuurman, once famous as a scholar, now remembered chiefly because she was a woman. When we come to the rise of science other names will crop up, such as the inventors of the telescope, the microscope, and the pendulum clock—the last-named an incidental work of Christian Huygens, one of the geniuses of the age. But there remains another major thinker who serves better to round out this chapter, in a piety suitably tinged with irony. "The Dutch commonwealth," wrote Hugo Grotius, "is such that no one who is at all wise should have anything to do with it." Exiled from this commonwealth in the early days of religious strife, Grotius was no hearty bourgeois and was not at home in the world rendered so masterfully by the painters; yet no man of its golden age was more important than he in the history of Western freedom.

The greatest pupil of Erasmus, he was another apostle of an ideal

Christian humanism. While his scholarly *Annotations* on the Bible prepared the way for the critical researches of the next century, he won wide acclaim in his day for his efforts to achieve peace between the churches by minimizing their dogmatic differences, stressing the essentials of Christian piety. He also won the enmity of the Elect in the Dutch Reformed Church; like Erasmus, he defended human freedom against the doctrine of predestination, asserting that freedom was man's principal characteristic and privilege. His major concern with freedom, however, derived from his work as a jurist, specifically his theory of natural law. Though devoted to the ancients, Grotius was as enthusiastic about the rising science of his own day; the works of Galileo, he wrote, surpassed all previous human effort, even made the ancients superfluous. In the spirit of Galileo, he gave natural law an autonomy that it had never had in medieval theory, declaring that propositions about it would be no less valid if one did not assume the authority of God. Above all, he directly applied it to the behavior of nation-states. On its bearings within the state he was inconsistent by liberal standards, rejecting the traditional theory of the sovereignty of the people (and he was therefore severely criticized by one Gronovius, another Dutch thinker of the century); but his chief interest was in proper relations between the sovereign states. He sought to regulate the unavoidable competition between them, at least to keep strife within the bounds of "civilized warfare," by rules that would make possible a just peace afterwards. In his masterpiece, *On the Law of War and Peace* (1625), he laid the foundations of international law.

The bitterness of Grotius in exile may be viewed as a symptom of failure, since Europe in his century made no·progress toward either Christian unity or international peace. At that, he was himself more deeply attached to Holland, less international in spirit, than had been his master Erasmus, an avowed citizen of the world who chose to spend his last years in Switzerland; so he might have grieved had he known that the golden age of Holland would end in his century, and with it the great school of painting that had glorified its life. Yet he had not simply failed, of course—any more than had the Dutch commonwealth or its painters. Though he was ahead of his time, he lived long enough to see Holland attain religious peace and a considerable measure of religious freedom. Science was advancing too, even though the Roman Church had silenced the unsurpassed Galileo. In the next century the rational, humanistic ideals of Grotius would become the reigning ideals. With the decline of religious fanaticism war would at least become relatively civilized, and little Holland would no longer have to fight for its life; it could prosper without being a great naval power. And our own century, in which war has again become frightful, has also honored his major bequest, sought to realize his vision of an international community of states founded on law.

We might well conclude, then, with a glance at another enlightened little state, the land in which his master chose to die. Switzerland had anticipated the political achievement of Holland, without the advantage of sea power and despite the internal obstacles of mountain barriers and the lack of a common language. Winning independence from the Holy Roman Empire by 1500, its people were soon fortified, and distracted, by the militant faith of Protestantism, to which they contributed one of the major Reformers, Zwingli, while among them Calvin built his state at Geneva; like other peoples, the Swiss began fighting furiously among themselves. Alone, however, they had the wit to put aside their irreconcilable religious differences, soon agreeing that each canton should worship as it pleased, so long as it made no foreign alliances and pledged itself to support all the other cantons in defense of their liberties. The Swiss Confederation, already established when Erasmus settled in Basel, was like the Dutch Republic a loose affair, its members being as unwilling to trust a central government with much power; and it later got into some trouble because its rulers were mostly oligarchs. Nevertheless, the Swiss held together, maintained their independence, and prospered. In their mountain fastness they also set an example by adopting a policy of neutrality, keeping out of the wars of their neighbors. Their history would call for much more attention here were it not that it had little influence on the rest of Europe, which did not follow their example. They exported Swiss Guards, who for pay served states less wise, and they produced writers, scholars, and thinkers of some note, though none so well known as their legendary hero William Tell. Otherwise the germinal ideas that came out of Switzerland were sown chiefly by foreign settlers or exiles, from Erasmus through Voltaire to Lenin.

Chapter Seven | # *THE SCIENTIFIC REVOLUTION*

1. *The Genesis of Modern Science*

Once upon a time "revolution" meant only regular motion round a center, or a harmless rotation. The basic reason why it now means irregular, radical, commonly violent change is a quiet, undramatic affair that at the time was neither called nor intended as a revolution—the growth of science in the seventeenth century. Although men have since made historic drama out of the silencing of Galileo by the Church, this created nothing like the stir that Luther had made, not to mention whatever wars were then going on. Few men heeded the event, nor were the still fewer who shared Galileo's interests embattled by it; they quietly went on with his work. Yet the growth of science was a literally extraordinary affair. It introduced the most momentous change in human history since the "Axial period" that had given birth to philosophy and the higher religions, more than two thousand years before.[1] It began revolutionizing not only men's ideas about the universe and themselves but their ways of thinking. It would profoundly transform their whole society as science had never done in ancient Greece, Islam, or any other society, directly by making possible an industrial revolution, indirectly by helping to inspire political revolutions. It would assure constant and ever more rapid change, force men to live in a continuously revolutionary world. By now many are accordingly indisposed to applaud all the thought and energy that science has liberated, more disposed to sympathize with the churchmen who tried to suppress Galileo; yet the most hostile thought has been no less deeply, irrevocably affected by it, and the kind of knowledge it has brought cannot possibly be ignored or discarded. Misgivings about its works only heighten the need of understanding how the scientific revolution came about; and its quiet beginnings might prepare us for a story as complex, ambiguous, and easy to misunderstand as any in Western history.

---

[1] For this period see *Freedom in the Ancient World,* pp. 106-113.

"You can't scratch if you don't itch," Einstein was fond of saying by way of explaining scientific research. This may now appear to be an itch for power, the obvious utility for which most men value science; historians are dwelling on its connections with the economic development of Europe, the rise of the bourgeois, the growth of capitalism —connections that clearly help to explain why no other society developed science as we know it. But as clearly utility is not the immediate key to the scientific revolution. It is rather the reason why most men, particularly businessmen, have never really understood the scientific spirit—the essential itch. The pioneers in astronomy, from Copernicus to Newton, were hardly inspired by economic motives as they achieved the first great triumph of modern science. No sensible bourgeois would have ventured such dangerous speculations as Galileo's, or even such seemingly harmless ones as William Harvey's about the circulation of the blood; in publishing his discovery Harvey confessed that he "trembled" because it defied venerable belief, and in fact his medical practice thereupon "fell mightily." Men seeking power were still haunted by alchemy and especially astrology, which had become the vogue among the rulers of Europe. Science began revolutionizing thought precisely because it was not materialistic, but had got free from merely practical concerns. As it turned out to be the greatest power that man had yet discovered it became the supreme demonstration of the value of "mere" theory, which hardheaded men continued to scorn. (So a secretary of defense in America defined basic research as "when you don't know what you're doing.") One cannot begin to understand the scientific spirit until one appreciates what Kepler wrote after he discovered his third law of planetary motion: "Let nothing confine me: I will indulge my sacred ecstasy."

Beginning as the simple itch of natural curiosity, this passion owed much to the Greeks. Directly the pioneers of modern science built on the foundations of Greek science. With a wealth of mathematics they took over the idea of applying it to astronomy; Kepler had previously grown ecstatic over the Copernican theory, an elegant mathematical representation of the planetary system. First and last, however, they had caught the scientific spirit—the spirit of free, disinterested curiosity that had led Thales, the "father" of natural philosophy, to venture the astonishing, idle speculation that all things were made of water. This was historically a rare spirit, lacking in the Romans as in the Eastern peoples before the Greeks; it explains why the very practical Romans made no contributions to science. Granted the natural vanity of the pioneers—the pride all men take in their brain children—it was essentially a selfless spirit that could become a kind of religious passion, a more truly "sacred" calling than ordinary sinners and churchgoers knew.

Something of this spirit had come through the medieval Schoolmen, who in poring over the classics had transmitted the academic, unexciting, but indispensable habit of patient industry. A few thinkers, such as Roger Bacon, had more exciting glimmers of the possibilities of mathematics and science. Nicholas of Oresme even suggested that the universe might be running on its own like a clock—a notion derived from the all-important Greek idea of a lawful universe, now guaranteed by God. This idea, so much more wonderful than all the piddling, transient miracles that medieval men prayed for or sought through holy relics, became a virtually unconscious premise of scientists, but at first it was a positive inspiration to them. It accordingly throws a melancholy light on the notorious conflict between science and religion that the Church disastrously initiated: the great pioneers were almost uniformly devout men, who like Copernicus felt "infinitely grateful" to God because he had been pleased to permit their discovery of the "great marvels" of his handiwork. Still, the Church was by no means betraying its principles when it tried to silence Galileo. It was loyal to its basic principle of authority, and to the theological concerns that had dominated medieval thought. Roger Bacon himself agreed that "science" was important only as an aid to theology, clarifying the true faith. The new science represented a sharp break with tradition, which the Royal Society of London accentuated by adopting as its motto *Nullius in verba*—"We accept nothing on authority." Its spirit, which was as contrary to Protestant orthodoxy, owed more to the Renaissance.

The Royal Society did accept a great deal on authority, of course —the authority of independent reason, as upheld by Erasmus and Montaigne. The discoveries of the pioneers heightened their confidence in the powers of reason, both unaided and unhampered by the authority of Scripture and Aristotle that had constrained medieval rationalism. Similarly scientists were indebted to the frank naturalism and humanism of the Renaissance. They studied nature for its own sake, as serious thinkers in the Middle Ages had rarely done; they took to "natural" philosophy instead of theology, looked for natural causes instead of supernatural ones. Or more precisely, they studied nature for man's sake. Science became popular among cultivated men because it seemed an essentially humanistic study, much more genial than Scholasticism.

In view of what followed upon its triumph—the growing abstractness, the narrow specialization, the divorce from the humanities, eventually the hostility of literary men—it should be emphasized that the birth of Galileo on the very day that Michelangelo died symbolized no break with the Renaissance, but immediately a deep continuity with its art. Leonardo da Vinci explicitly declared the painters' faith in the evidence of the senses as a means to true knowledge. "If you say that sight is apt to impede the steady and subtle thinking of the mind," he wrote, "I answer that such eye, as lord of the senses, does its duty in giving a fall to those confused and lying discourses—not sciences—through which men are always disputing with noise." Still more to the point, the pioneers of science took for granted the Renaissance idea that the world was a "perfect work of art," whose secrets were obviously to be found in principles of symmetry and harmony. Their theories not only were works of high imagination, as all great scientific theories are, but typically were announced in the language of poetry.[2] They rhapsodized over their discoveries of a wondrous simplicity that it took a scientist's eye to perceive. They were sure that so beautiful a theory as the Copernican simply must be true, even though it had not yet been properly verified.

Indeed, they more freely indulged their enthusiasm than Greek scientists had. Although Europe appeared to be sobering down as it entered upon its neoclassical era in art and letters, its scientists still had a lust for intellectual adventure. Stimulated by the geographical discoveries, they enjoyed a purer exhilaration as they explored the new world they had discovered, and had more of the epical spirit of Camoëns than did the gold seekers. Yet at the same time their thought was more disciplined by a respect for empirical fact—the nasty, stubborn facts that had too seldom troubled seriously enough all the philosophers before them. The fundamental, all-important difference between Greek and modern science remains the obvious one: the European pioneers discovered scientific method.

Its beginnings are most striking in Kepler, a thinker deeply religious and wildly imaginative, still attuned to the ancient music of the

---

[2] For that matter, plenty of aesthetic terms may still be found in scientific discourse today. Short of Einstein's pleasure in the "pre-established harmonies" revealed by physics, mathematicians and scientists habitually talk of the "beauty" or "elegance" of their demonstrations. One need only remember that the scientist is a human being—not an impersonal monster or magician—to perceive that he gets a simple aesthetic pleasure out of his work, especially when he succeeds in making the stubborn facts fall into some shape, which is then called a "theory."

spheres. In studying the motions of the planets, he tried over and over again to keep them moving uniformly in circles, since the circle was traditionally the "perfect" figure and therefore the only one becoming heavenly bodies; but it was no go. His observations kept indicating that they moved in ellipses and at that did not even move uniformly, speeding up as they got closer to the sun, as if in unseemly haste. Kepler finally stuck to the disreputable facts, and thereby discovered his laws of planetary motion. His successors developed not only the habit of checking their thought against experience but methods of verifying it by experiment. While thinkers from Roger Bacon to da Vinci had talked of "experiment," they meant by it essentially only "experience"; now Galileo gave it the modern meaning, describing it as "the ordeal of experience"—the kind of ordeal known to Kepler. Likewise the pioneers gave the modern meaning to the word "science," which the Greeks had never distinguished clearly from philosophy. They established standards of reliability lacking in Greek science, definite means of choice between conflicting theories. These means were not infallible, as scientists would ever after keep scrapping once accepted theories; yet their scientific methods were sure enough to make possible the unprecedented steady, cumulative advance in knowledge, and application of this knowledge, that mark the scientific revolution as the greatest revolution in the history of thought.

It is in this deeper sense—beyond merely economic motives or hopes of material reward—that a practical spirit stimulated the rise of modern science. Greek science had been hedged by an aristocratic tradition of aloofness from considerations of utility, as merely sordid, and by a more positive contempt for the "base mechanic arts": attitudes that were perhaps high-minded, perhaps supercilious, but that in any case kept science an intellectual pastime, useless for social purposes. The European pioneers had no such scorn of useful knowledge. Thus when Joseph Glanvill defended the Royal Society against charges of being un-Aristotelian, he declared that the inventor of the compass deserved more gratitude than ten thousand Aristotles. Again, the classical tradition had fortified the "inveterate conceit" remarked by Francis Bacon, "that the dignity of the human mind is lowered by long and frequent intercourse with experiments and particulars, which are the objects of sense and confined to matter." Galileo and others readily swallowed any such pride as they turned to the stuffy world of sense, and used their hands as well as their heads in experiments on matter. Perhaps the chief contribution of Christianity to science was the dignity it had conferred on manual labor, exemplified by the contributions of its monks to the mechanic arts.

Immediately science owed a good deal to the technological progress of Europe, beginning with the printing press that facilitated the dissemination of scientific discoveries and formation of a scientific community. Although no major inventions were made in the sixteenth century, men then began gathering and publishing the technical knowledge that had accumulated. Treatises on mining and metallurgy, for example, led to the classic *De re metallica* of Agricola (1556). In making a point of direct observation and precise description Agricola not only provided trustworthy data but illustrated the value of the intimate, firsthand, unacademic kind of knowledge acquired by artisans and technicians—types to whom Francis Bacon and Galileo would own their debt. "Pure" science would make possible the applied science or technology of the future, but at this stage it was the pupil; the inventions came first, advances in theory were made possible by data and systematic methods developed in technological practice. In particular scientists were indebted to instrument makers, who were drumming up business for their ingenious wares; thus Galileo improved a telescope that some Dutchman (probably Hans Lippershey) had made as a curiosity. The scientific progress of the seventeenth century depended on the invention of such instruments as the telescope, the microscope, the thermometer, the barometer, the pendulum clock, and the air pump.[3] For the first time men were able to measure such things as heat, air pressure, and small intervals of time.

Thereby they bring up a more mysterious development in the European mentality—a new kind of itch. Why in the world should men want to measure such things precisely, as they had not in the past? The great mechanical clocks of the medieval cathedrals were chiefly showpieces, which incidentally told time, and more lately Rabelais, for all his interest in the sciences, seems not to have known how old he was or much cared to know; but by the end of the sixteenth century men had somehow developed the itch to know exact times, distances, rates, quantities. They made a favorite quotation of a text in the Wisdom of Solomon: "But you have ordered everything according to measure,

---

[3] The thermometer is a happy reminder that Florence was still intellectually alive: its Grand Duke Ferdinand II perfected a liquid one that was widely used. He was also one of the founders of the Florentine *Accademia del Cimento* (1657), in which disciples of Galileo carried on research. Unhappily, and perhaps not by coincidence, this Academy of Experiments folded up after ten years, when the brother of Ferdinand was made a cardinal. One of its members then committed suicide, to escape torture by the Inquisition.

number, and weight"—a wisdom surely unheeded by the Israelites, and the Greeks too. It was at this time that a churchman figured out the exact date of the Creation (9 A.M. of October 23, 4004 B.C.). Presumably the new interest was connected with the growing interest in technical knowledge, or more broadly with the spread of business habits of close reckoning. These gave some impetus to correspondingly useful developments in mathematics, notably such inventions as decimals and logarithms; Simon Stevin, the inventor of decimals, was also the first to publish tables for the calculation of interest. And as an engineer, who independently helped Galileo to lay the foundations of modern mechanics, Stevin points to a related aspect of the new mentality. Men were growing more interested in pure mechanism, studying its operations. The exploitation of mechanical power in industry (as by bigger and better pumps), the progress in engineering, the improvement of mechanical clocks, the felt need of precision, the regimentation of the countinghouse, the impersonal order of capitalism—all such circumstances were disposing men to regard the universe as a clockwork mechanism, and to glorify God as the supreme Clockmaker.

So we might pause to consider the paradoxical relations between the rise of science and the rise of business. Capitalists were concerned with material goods and definite quantities, in a world in which time and space were very real and very important; yet these materialists were constantly dealing in the abstractions of money, mathematical symbols, hypothetical futures. On both counts they unconsciously anticipated the power of abstraction, isolation, and measurement that science would exploit. Scientists concentrated on the quantitative aspects of the material world ignored by the medieval Schoolmen, as by almost all the wise men in all past societies; they succeeded so brilliantly because they dropped the questions of final causes and essences, confined themselves to the humdrum question of how things operated, began to count, measure, and weigh. Thus Galileo noted that although philosophers had always been aware of the acceleration of falling bodies, he was the first to ask how much faster they fell and then to measure the rate of acceleration. Still and all, science was far from being primarily a bourgeois interest. The pioneers came from all classes, in fact numbering more gentlemen than businessmen. Despite the practical interests that stimulated it, and that it richly rewarded, theoretical science was above class interest—much more so than were literature and the fine arts.

In like fashion science may be related to the rise of the nation-state.

The state gave it more positive support than it ever got from the big banking houses or trading companies; kings and their ministers served as its patrons. However ironical, it was not simply strange that science grew up in the age of absolute monarchy. Scientists were generally permitted as much freedom as they needed, except in countries dominated by the Inquisition (true to form, Spain produced no scientists of note) ; most kings had enough wit to tolerate the advance of such potentially useful knowledge, while none had the wit to foresee that the scientific spirit would prove fatal to their claims of divine right. But again science was by its nature a supranational interest. Very soon it became an international co-operative enterprise, in a Europe split by political and religious strife. More truly catholic than medieval Christianity, it more clearly transcended all the differences that separate men—racial, tribal, social, cultural, religious. For it was not just another philosophy either, but a mode of knowledge that all informed men could agree upon, and that the whole non-Western world would eventually welcome, as it would not the Christian religion.

In short, the growth of modern science was connected with all the major social and cultural developments in western Europe. To understand it, we need to take into account all these diverse influences, but also to qualify every one of them; for to ignore any, or to insist that any one was the "real" or "ultimate" cause, may induce not only a limited but a distorted view.[4] If in this broad view the genesis of science is neither so miraculous nor so pure as some might like it, at least it is in keeping with the genius of Western civilization for multifarious life and growth, and with the Faustian aspiration to realize all man's powers, in the pursuit of all possible goods. And we may then do fuller justice to science as a product of free creative imagination,

---

[4] One example is the thesis popularized by Werner Sombart, that science and technology—like everything else modern—grew out of nationalistic warfare. The needs of warfare were in fact a stimulus, and involved some connections that were much plainer to early scientists than to some later historians; thus studies of motion grew out of an interest in the path of projectiles, which may be traced to the invention of gunpowder, etc. But once started on this kind of thinking, a historian can trace anything to almost anything else, and stop at whatever chicken or egg he has a mind to. As for warfare, one obvious question remains why it failed to breed science in any other civilization.

While on the subject of anomalies, we might note that the seventeenth century made almost no advance in the very practical science of medicine, despite important discoveries in anatomy and chemistry. Here utility was unable to compete against hallowed tradition, as well as the aristocratic taboo on the use of the hands. It took as bold a doctor to venture to doubt that castration was an infallible cure for leprosy as to venture upon any surgery. Perhaps the greatest doctor of the age was the sensible Thomas Suydenham of England, who saved many lives by merely sparing his patients much of the customary treatment.

which like the work of Michelangelo and Shakespeare was conditioned
by the state of society but not absolutely determined or compelled by
it. The scientific revolution was no response to a challenge that had
to be mastered, no necessity for survival. Even in the intellectual realm
the new theories were not forced by new data—the great theories came
first, stimulating the search for more data.

In this light we can better appreciate, lastly, the importance of
Francis Bacon, the famous herald of the scientific revolution. It has
become easy to belittle his work. No scientist himself, he contributed
nothing to scientific knowledge, and even as a publicity man failed to
herald the great theories of his time, rejecting the Copernican theory,
ignoring the work of Kepler and Harvey. Likewise he failed to realize
the primary role of theory, as he had a naïve idea of the inductive
method for which he became famous: he conceived it as a simple mechanical process, a way of grinding generalizations out of a mass of
data. His innocence of the metaphysical mysteries of induction may
now be attributed to a vulgar gospel of "utility and power," which
blinded him as well to the potential abuses of science.

But this is to judge Bacon by sophisticated modern standards, with
the benefit of hindsight. (At that, let the sophisticate ponder a casual
remark by Whitehead: "It is at once evident that the concept of simple
location is going to make great difficulties for induction.") His own
century rightly saw much more in him. The Royal Society of London
proudly declared itself his offspring, modeling itself on the House of
Solomon in his *New Atlantis;* and a century later the men of the French
Enlightenment dedicated their *Encyclopedia* to him, avowing that they
owed most to the "extraordinary genius" who had laid out the program
for a "universal dictionary of sciences and arts" at a time when these
scarcely existed. For Bacon was indeed the Columbus of modern
science, the discoverer of the "New Intellectual World" he mapped
out. More clearly than any thinker before him he foresaw the real
possibilities of the future, and the real need of a new way of thinking
to realize them. And in trumpeting them he was by no means a simple
vulgarian, but an Elizabethan: a highly imaginative man of the Renaissance, who incidentally wrote with such a wealth of metaphor that
eccentrics are still trying to identify him with Shakespeare, and who
had a vision of epical adventure beyond the apparent reach of Shakespeare. He so greatly inspired other thinkers because he insisted that
the matter in hand was not mere economic or political power, personal
or national ambition, but "the real business and fortune of the human

race, and all power of operation." The Lord Chancellor of England was another "overreacher" like young Christopher Marlowe, dedicated to "the effecting of all things possible." The men of Renaissance Florence would have applauded his superb assurances: "I stake all on the victory of art over nature in the race."

In habitually stressing power, Bacon was not only speaking the language of his day but attacking the major barriers to the advance of science. Men were still obsessed with magical means to power, still needed to be told first of all that they might realize their dreams by their own natural powers of mind; and even so he spoke as a true scientist when he added that "the very contemplation of things as they are, without superstition or imposture, error or confusion, is in itself more worthy than all the fruit of inventions." On this philosophical level Bacon emphasized the potential power of science as a means of discrediting the authority of Aristotle, proving the superiority of the inductive method. However crude his conception of this method, he had hit upon the essential truth that it was the most positive means to discovery; whereas the philosophy of Aristotle—the metaphysician and logician idolized by the Schoolmen—was barren of works, its deductive logic permitting no discovery of new knowledge, its syllogisms only proving verbal propositions drawn from unproved premises. So the Schoolmen had gone round and round, spinning cobwebs that obscured the facts of nature, the source of all reliable knowledge. There was only one solution: "to begin the whole work of the mind over again from the beginning." If this has a naïve ring (even though ultrasophisticated positivists have made the same noise over again in our own generation), Bacon spotted for all time the major sources of prejudice and error in his justly celebrated account of the Idols: the "idols of the tribe" common to all mankind, such as wishful thinking and anthropomorphism; the "idols of the cave" peculiar to the individual, due to his temperament or circumstances; the "idols of the market-place" deriving from social intercourse or particularly the nature of language, as in the inveterate confusion of names with things; and the "idols of the theater," the grand systems of philosophy that come down to so many elegant "stage-plays, representing worlds of their own creation after an unreal and scenic fashion."

These grand systems force the immediate issue for a student of freedom. They are creations of "reason," exemplify the "rationalism" that has been cropping up in every chapter, in the guise of an essential means to human freedom. Bacon, the great iconoclast, won his large

following by attacking primarily the rigorous rationalism of the Schoolmen. Whitehead accordingly described the scientific revolution as
"through and through an anti-intellectualist movement." The celebrated emancipation of mind, it would appear, was a denial of the
sovereignty of reason, as in another aspect it was a surrender to the
claims of brute fact; and one might wonder at the value or even
the reality of such "freedom." Modern positivists—scientific analysts
of the "idols of the market-place"—have in fact called all these key
words "meaningless."

Still, we cannot drop them, vague and ambiguous though they are.
By "reason" we can and we must make at least rough distinctions, in
order to size up a revolution in thought that was meaningful enough
to be literally epoch-making. To begin with, Bacon himself was by no
means essentially "anti-intellectual." He was only formulating a *Novum
Organum,* or New Logic, insisting that thought must start out from
observed facts, hold to the axiom that "Nature cannot be commanded
except by being obeyed." If to a devotee of "pure" reason this looks
like bondage to the world of vulgar sense, or mere particulars, by ordinary standards of reasonableness a respect for fact would seem as necessary as a respect for logic—madmen can be quite logical. By contrast
the apparently thoroughgoing rationalism of the Schoolmen was actually limited by the arbitrary authority of Scripture, which generated
some beliefs about the world that were positively false. And as science
developed it became at once more strictly empirical and more philosophical or "rational." It built up a tradition of close observation and
systematic fact-finding that could be pedestrian or unphilosophical,
but that provided the necessary basis for a kind of public truth that all
rational men could agree upon, as they never can upon the higher
religions or the grand philosophical systems. At the same time, scientific inquirers had to interpret the facts, judge their relevance or significance, generalize them into laws. Newton not only leaped to a grand
theory but formulated philosophically the theory implicit in scientific
method, which Bacon had stated more crudely. That scientists then
tended to grow unconscious of the philosophy or the rationale they
were operating on was due immediately to its indisputable success.

There remains the plain truth that science immeasurably increased
the real power of the human mind over the natural world, the real
freedom of operation. Bacon stands out as the pioneer who most clearly
saw in science not merely a revolutionary way of thinking but a means
of revolutionizing society. He dreamed of armies of research specialists,

banded in an international organization, co-operating in an epic conquest of nature for the benefit of all mankind. Another reason why he did not commit himself to a narrow, shortsighted view of utility, but specifically warned against the "unseasonable and puerile hurry" to snatch fruits, was his intoxicating vision of long-range prospects, which made him a pioneer in science fiction too. In his last work, *The New Atlantis,* he sketched a Utopia in which scientists would take the place of the philosopher-kings in Plato's *Republic.* The brave new world envisaged by the Lord Chancellor may entrance us no more than Plato's ideal state, which it resembles in its government exclusively by experts; but in any case his dreams were made on more solid stuff. He foresaw the many inventions, such as airplanes and submarines, that would come out of the conquest of nature. He anticipated as well the organization of science, the systematic research, the professional publications, the international congresses. He himself did more than any other one man to socialize science, lay out a program of action, and form a community transcending class, nation, and church.

2. *The Century of Genius*

In labeling the seventeenth century the "Century of Genius," Whitehead remarked truly that we are still living upon "the accumulated capital of ideas" provided by its genius. We might therefore suspect, as he went on to argue, that these ideas are inadequate for our intellectual purposes in the twentieth century, if only because there has been another scientific revolution, and the world of Einstein is profoundly different from the world of Newton. But simply to understand the problems created by science, the new "ordeals of experience" that lay ahead, we must first try to appreciate the extraordinary creative genius of the seventeenth century; and we might also suspect that it requires a considerable effort of historical imagination. Let us consider the symbolic story of Galileo, his telescope, and the professors. When he discovered four moons circling around Jupiter, his colleagues—including the foremost philosopher of his university—refused to believe him. When he told them to look through his telescope and see for themselves, they refused even to look. They were typical academics, we might say, just old fossils; but at that their attitude seems almost incredible—as it did to Galileo, who in a letter to Kepler fumed over their "extraordinary stupidity." Nevertheless, there is much to be said on behalf of these professors.

They were not defending merely their personal opinions, dear though these always are. Their immediate stake in the controversy was their Christian faith, the proper belief upon which depended the salvation of their immortal souls. If the moons of Jupiter would seem quite harmless (as good Christians now take calmly the knowledge that there are in fact eleven of them), still there was no room for them in the stellar universe that had been mapped out in orthodox doctrine. Why should the professors risk their souls by looking through Galileo's newfangled tube? Trusting the evidence of the notoriously fallible senses? As thoughtful men, they did not ask themselves the question what are the facts—they asked a profounder question: What is the *truth?* And they knew all the essential truths about God, man, and the universe, on the very best authority. No more were they behind the times. They represented precisely the most respectable, informed opinion, held by the great majority of educated men. They stood not only for beliefs centuries old but for ways of thinking much older, the immemorial wisdom of the race in looking first and last to venerable authority. They were maintaining the integrity of a universal tradition, sanctified by the idols alike of the market place, the theater, and the tribe.

For the same reasons the pioneers of science were themselves full of antique beliefs, odd relics of an essentially supernatural or magical view of nature. The brilliant Kepler incidentally believed in witchcraft and practiced astrology on the side, but as an astronomer he was much concerned over the question why God had made just six planets, and much excited by his discovery that the "five regular solids" (whatever they are) could be fitted into the space between their orbits. Likewise most of the pioneers were not yet disposed to consider new ideas naturally better than old ones, or instantly to cry up discoveries like the principle of the barometer, which defied the axiom that "nature abhors a vacuum." They could understand another outraged professor, one Jacques Pierius, who defended nature against Pascal by arguing that mercury was a "crazy bastard" that didn't know how to behave, but God had avoided the scandal of a vacuum by attaching certain vapors to it, and these had filled the end of Pascal's tube. Only by understanding this climate of opinion can we appreciate the wonderful originality of such theories as Harvey's about the circulation of the blood—a discovery that now seems so elementary that we may only wonder why anatomists had never hit on it before, yet that aroused the scorn he anticipated. It required exceptional daring and genius for the Columbuses of science to set out on their explorations of the natural world, without compass, in the face of storm signals, and to report what they had seen with their own eyes.

Or often what they had not seen—what instead they had reasoned out for themselves, in defiance of common sense as well as revered authority. Their genius was most apparent in their triumph over common sense, beginning with the preposterous theory that the earth traveled around the sun. Galileo expressed a boundless marvel over the feat of Copernicus, whose reason was able to commit such a "rape upon his sense." Other ideas made commonplace by the pioneers were as extraordinary and absurd at the time—that the little ball of the sun was much greater than the earth, that the stars were incredibly remote from us, that light traveled to us from these twinkling stars, etc.[5] Galileo himself afforded a brilliant example of uncommon sense, far more impressive than his discovery of the four moons, when he formulated his first law of motion, that the natural motion of a body is in a straight line at a uniform speed; for he had never seen such motion, nor could any man ever see it—it was a pure abstraction, not a fact of observation. To realize how far science departed from ordinary common sense may help us when we come to the still queerer nonsense of twentieth-century physics (and are told, for example, that to understand the quantum theory we must conceive a clock whose mechanism has vanished, leaving only the ticks). Immediately it may help us to do more justice both to Galileo and to the professors who refused to trust the evidence of their senses. In building on such evidence scientists soon made out that there was much more—or much less—than meets the eye. The physical "reality" they pictured would become as unlike the appearances of the world as the spiritual realities of religion and the grand philosophical systems.

Yet the scientific revolution cannot be understood as the work of genius alone. Even as Bacon wrote, it was becoming a broad cultural movement, an intellectual style comparable to new styles in art. Despite the sharp break with tradition, it had a deep continuity with intellec-

---

[5] Let us consider, too, the observation of Carlyle as he contemplated these stars two centuries later: "A sad spectacle! If they be inhabited, what a scope for misery and folly; if they be *na* inhabited, what a waste of space!" Conservatives were once concerned over the reckless extravagance of the Creator, whose administration of the universe hardly seemed businesslike.

tual history, reaching back to ancient Greece; Bacon's appropriate name for the "Century of Genius" was the "Great Renewal." Once under way it developed a kind of automatic momentum, every discovery and invention giving a new impetus. The pioneers inaugurated a striking phenomenon in the history of science and technology from now on, as men working independently often made the same major discoveries; thus the pendulum clock was invented by both Galileo and Huygens, analytical geometry by Fermat and Descartes, the infinitesimal calculus by Leibniz and Newton. They accordingly raise some question about the credit due even to the greatest genius. Mathematicians and philosophers of science still regard Newton's theory of gravitation as the supreme work of genius in all history to his time, and certainly he had very great qualities of mind, far more exceptional than Christopher Columbus had; yet it seems likely that some man was bound to propose such a theory sooner or later. Scientists might be humbled by the thought that no other man could have done the work of Michelangelo or Shakespeare, and that great achievement in art is more individual, irreplaceable, unsurpassable. Or they might better take pride in the nature of science, which honors its greatest men by improving upon their work, often junking their conclusions, thereby achieving a steady progress unmatched in art, as in religion or philosophy.

At any rate, Newton was born at precisely the right time (fortuitously in the year of Galileo's death) ; for all the necessary preparatory work had been done for his grand synthesis. As a synthesis, his theory of gravitation was a classic example of international co-operation. The initial astronomical theory of Copernicus, a Pole, was open to serious scientific objections if only because he had worked with incomplete, faulty data; his brilliant hunch was right for the wrong reasons. Tycho Brahe, a Danish nobleman, then met the primary need of accurate data by devoting his life to astronomical observation. In carrying on his work, his young German assistant Kepler succeeded in getting down to the uniformities underlying the eccentric behavior of planets, formulating the laws of their motion. The Italian Galileo made further contributions to Copernican theory, with the aid of his Dutch-invented telescope, but went on to study earthly motion, as in freely falling bodies. The laws of motion that he formulated raised a new problem for astronomers: not how the planets kept moving around the sun, or why they did not move in perfect circles, but why they kept revolving at all instead of shooting off into outer space in straight lines—the

"natural" motion of bodies. The French philosopher Descartes amplified the mathematical principles employed by these discoverers, making
them the key to the entire physical universe. Finally Newton of England comprehended all the discoveries in his universal principle of
gravitation, a mathematical formula that applied alike to pebbles and
planets, falling apples and rising tides.

Such co-operation became more systematic under the aegis of scientific academies, as in Florence, France, and England. These were established deliberately in order to promote experimental science, which for
a long time would get little or no encouragement in the universities,
typically dominated by professors of the kind that exasperated Galileo,
and which was hardly understood by men more favorably disposed.
(Charles II was amused when he heard that his Royal Society was busy
weighing air.) They soon started publishing papers, like the *Philosophical Transactions* of the Royal Society, thereby making their findings promptly available to inquirers elsewhere. Incidentally they made
it harder to assign individual credit for discoveries, as ideas were tossed
around in lively meetings, but chiefly they helped to form the scientific
mentality and character. "Whereas the individual man of science may
be easily tempted to dogmatize," Laplace later remarked, "a scientific
society would very soon come to grief through the clash of dogmatic
views." The community introduced a novel discipline, impersonal
means of settling differences of opinion, while recognizing when agreement was impossible or controversy unprofitable; thus the Royal Society agreed to exclude theology and politics from its wide-ranging
discussions. Scientists began to acquire some reputation for the virtues
of simplicity, seriousness, and selflessness. Such merits, Fontenelle
observed, pertained "rather more to our sciences than to our savants";
for the express aim of the societies was the disinterested pursuit of
truth, for the benefit of mankind, and success required conformity to
a discipline that imposed a scrupulous regard for truth. No saint by
nature, the scientist in his professional capacity could never be so
dishonest as many a successful statesman, businessman, or churchman.

Above all, the scientific revolution resulted from the discovery of
science itself—the method of truth-seeking. As formally perfected by
Newton, this was a method of verifying by experiment inductions
formulated in mathematical terms, enabling positive prediction. In
most ordinary practice it involved rougher methods of observation,
measurement, and experimentation, guided and controlled by the
simple question that men must always have asked in some fashion, but

never before had asked so deliberately and persistently: What are the facts? Bacon was quite right when he boasted that scientific methods would enable ordinary intelligence to make notable discoveries and inventions. If the seventeenth century stands out in European history for the many geniuses in science and mathematics, many other little-known men were doing important pioneering work, as they had been before the geniuses went to work. They greatly enlarged the scope of scientific inquiry, which ranged over all natural phenomena. While study of the stellar universe held the spotlight, Leeuwenhoek was as dazzled as he peered through his microscope and discovered "living atoms," now called bacteria. Gilbert's earlier investigations of magnetism and electricity, which Bacon understandably dismissed as fables, prepared for Newton's fantastic idea of forces operating at a distance.

Now, we can do nothing like justice here to either the brilliance or the range of the scientific achievements of the seventeenth century. We need consider only some implications necessary to a proper understanding of this revolutionary force, or more especially some cautions against popular inferences. And first another word on behalf of the many obscure men, known only to specialists, who did the unspectacular but necessary spade work of fact-finding. While establishing the habit of scientific inquiry, sometimes contributing finer techniques, they provided the foundations of the comprehensive theories to come. Elementary studies of natural history possibly did more in their day to promote the growth of the scientific spirit than did the geniuses in mathematics and physics. Among the forgotten pioneers was Francesco Redi of the Florentine Academy, who set about refuting by simple experiments the popular idea of spontaneous generation of life, and so helped to dispel the "spirits" that since the beginning of history had fortified ignorance by doing the work of natural causes.

Yet it still needs to be said that the facts alone are never enough, never speak for themselves. Particularly in the social sciences all too many workers shy away from significant generalization or theory, stick to the relatively safe, easy business of fact-finding, in the apparent illusion that once a sufficiently great mass of data has been accumulated a great law or theory will somehow emerge all by itself; whereas theory is essential to not only the interpretation of facts but the initial decision as to what facts to look for. Thus chemistry before Robert Boyle was no science even though much empirical knowledge had been accumulated through metallurgy, medicine, and for that matter alchemy. Boyle made it a science by introducing clearer concepts, or theory. In *The Sceptical Chemist* (1661) he began by insisting that it should be studied as a branch of natural philosophy, not a useful art, and he proceeded to analyze its vocabulary, in particular its assumed "elements"—the four traditional elements of earth, air, water, and fire, and the currently more fashionable salt, sulphur, and mercury. Following his lead, chemists eventually worked out the atomic theory; and on this basis they built up an immense amount of knowledge about an astonishing variety of substances, incidentally acquiring a power far greater than alchemists would have by turning everything into gold.

Even so, the atomic theory was much less elegant than Newton's theory of gravitation. It lacked a comprehensive formula, leaving chemists with some ninety-odd kinds of matter—not to mention what physicists have now done to the once substantial atom, breaking it down into electrons, neutrons, positrons, and an ever-increasing litter of particles. By contrast, Newton embraced the whole cosmos in one grand generalization, a principle of universal order that applied to every particular motion in it. By all odds the greatest, most influential single achievement of the century, his theory remained the model for all other sciences, and the dream—or the despair—of historians and social philosophers aspiring to introduce a comparable law and order into human affairs. Now we may add that after reigning for two centuries as the supreme achievement of science it suffered the same fate as the inelegant atomic theory: it was superseded by Einstein's theory of relativity. But we must then understand why this fate is by no means a reflection on the greatness or the enduring importance of Newton's work.

Contemporaries were dazzled by his "mathematical" principles of natural philosophy, fulfilling the modern development of mathematics as a universal method of analysis. As this original, free creation of the human mind had revealed the wonderful order of the universe, some leaped to the conclusion not only that man had penetrated to the essential "reality" but that this reality was necessarily mathematical —an identity that would seem at once more plausible and more mysterious when the arbitrary invention of non-Euclidean geometries, in defiance of common-sense notions of space, provided a better key to the universe. Newton was more modest. In making his celebrated remark that he did not frame hypotheses, he was not asserting that he was offering the gospel truth about the universe, the handiwork of the Great Mathematician. He was merely distinguishing between speculative hypotheses and experimentally verifiable theories. Mathematics was a convenient shorthand for stating such theories, not the guarantor of their truth. His final appeal was to experiment or observed fact; so new data might force a revision of his theory, as in time happened.

As a mathematician Newton had also invented calculus, which applied algebra to motion, and his ideas about motion involved another philosophical revolution of sorts that in subtler ways helped to keep science open and thought free. One reason why thinkers in the past had never got deeply interested in motion, or bothered to measure it, was their common-sense assumption that the "natural" condition of bodies was rest, just as the "essence" of things is immutable. As for the spheres, they were kept rolling by pressing into service the celestial Spirits or Intelligences of yore. Galileo had done away with the logical need of such spirits by his singularly original idea of extending to motion the principle of inertia: bodies in motion always tended to keep moving uniformly, and came to rest only because some force acted upon them. The reason why men never observed such "natural" motion was that such forces were forever at work. The earth itself was forever in motion—it was not so static or staid as philosophers would have it. "The Earth is very noble and admirable by reason of so many and so different alterations, mutations, generations, etc.," Galileo observed, and he added that if it were immutable, "I should have esteemed it a lump of no great benefit to the World, full of idleness, and in a word, superfluous." As conceived by Newton, it was not yet an evolutionary world, but it was more dynamic than the world of classical science. It featured concepts of mass and force rather than inert matter and form; it was better suited to the exceptional energy and willfulness of Western men.

Such dynamic concepts would accordingly generate a good deal of popular confusion. In particular Newton's apparently absurd idea of forces that somehow acted directly, instantaneously, at a distance led to the still common notion that the law of gravitation is a physical something that "makes" things fall, instead of a formula that merely states how they uniformly do fall. But it brings up another major contribution of Newton, in that he felt no imperious need of explaining how or why forces acted at a distance—enough that they appeared to do so. He put aside the whole question of final causes, which thinkers since Aristotle had made so much of, or so little for purposes of empirical knowledge, and which could not be investigated by scientific methods, demonstrated conclusively by any method. He gave science complete autonomy within its realm not only by formulating its methods but by carefully restricting this realm, defining the grounds of inquiry. He emancipated it from the ultimately futile controversies of the Schoolmen. There would be continual controversy in science after him, because always unsolved problems; he himself left such problems as the nature of light, not ruling out the wave theory of Huygens even though he was strongly inclined to a corpuscular theory; but his procedure made it possible for scientists to resolve their problems and continually to advance, instead of going round and round.

Quite possibly, then, Newton might not have been much surprised or dismayed by the fate of his grand synthesis. In any case, scientific inquiry as he formulated its method and scope logically precluded any claim to the final truth, the whole truth, and nothing but the truth. While its factual basis and its empirical laws were being solidly established (as his own law of gravitation still works satisfactorily for ordinary earthly calculations), all its comprehensive theories were due to be modified or supplemented. All current theories, including Einstein's, face the same fate as scientists come up with new data; they can never be sure that all the pertinent returns are in. Herein is the peculiar distinction of the orthodoxy that Newton did so much to establish: the one orthodoxy that welcomes innovation and heresy, keeps thought free as a matter of vital principle, and honors its greatest geniuses by aspiring to antiquate their work.

3. *The Emancipation of Thought*

"Come then, excellent Sir, and banish all fear of stirring up the pygmies of our time," wrote Henry Oldenburg to Spinoza in 1662; "long enough have sacrifices been made to ignorance and absurdity; let us spread the sails of true knowledge." By this time there was apparent reason for his breezy assurance. Oldenburg was reporting that the Royal Society, of which he was secretary, had received its charter. A few years later, when Thomas Sprat was already commemorating the Society by writing its history, he observed that the love of natural science was the ruling fashion in Europe. Hence Newton's *Principia* (1687) was everywhere hailed as a masterwork, hardly a pygmy standing up to protest this apotheosis of Galileo's heresy; in all intellectual history no genius had met prompter recognition. Nor was the enthusiasm over science yet due to its utility for practical or indus-

trial purposes. The reasons for its social success were summed up by
Fontenelle—a man of letters who had popularized its discoveries, and
in 1699 was appointed secretary of the revived French Academy of
Sciences.

Since one reason why the Academy had languished was that Versailles had saddled it with studies of military problems, Fontenelle
remarked in his inaugural address that utility was a mere by-product of
science, and even ventured to say that science had better be kept apart
from the royal court. Its allegiance was simply to the cause of true
knowledge. This still risky allegiance illustrated its almost religious
sense of dedication, in spite of its purely secular interests; Fontenelle
pointed out that scientists pursued the truth without regard for self-
interest, profit, or any but spiritual rewards. He accordingly celebrated
the scientist pretty much as the Middle Ages had the saint, or as the
Renaissance had the artist. He emphasized the liberal, humanistic
values of science, noting that good literature had the same qualities of
clarity, order, and precision. But in particular he emphasized its most
obvious value, as an emancipation from ignorance and error.

No less obviously, this emancipation had been achieved against the
opposition of the Church; so it brings us to the too familiar, tiresome
theme of the conflict between science and religion. We now realize
(or ought to) that the "victory" of science was not won by a glorious,
hard-fought campaign, nor was it simply a victory of right over wrong.
The early champions of science were defending ideas only half true, or
right for the wrong reason; the Church had good logical reasons to
oppose them apart from its concern for the faith. In fairness to both,
we may conclude that there is no necessary conflict between science
and religion rightly understood. Yet there is no getting away from the
historic importance of the actual conflict.

At the beginning of the century Bruno was burned at the stake for
his vision of an infinite universe: a vision more imaginative than reasoned, scientifically immature, but nonetheless prophetic of the im-
mensities, bold and lofty—a sufficiently noble cause for a martyrdom
consciously risked and courageously accepted, rightly commemorated in
the history of freedom. The less heroic Galileo at least served to define
clearly the basic issue. The Holy Office decreed that his Copernican
beliefs were both "philosophically false and utterly heretical, because
contrary to Holy Scripture." Under threat of torture Galileo made his
historic recantation: "I bend my knee before the honorable Inquisitor-
General, I touch the holy Gospel and give assurance that I believe, and

always will believe, what the Church recognizes and teaches as true. . . . Now, in order to remove every Catholic Christian's just suspicion of me, I abjure and curse the stated errors and heresies, and every other error and every opinion that is contrary to the teaching of the Church." The "spiritual" power had won—by the method of compulsion, not persuasion. In maintaining a defensible theory about the universe, the Church had not only condemned a more fruitful theory but denied the freedom to theorize. It had committed itself to a policy of opposing instead of welcoming new knowledge about God's creation, initiated an aggressive warfare that assured its long, humiliating retreat. It had made the victory of science essential to the cause both of truth and of freedom.

After Galileo's retraction, legend suitably has it, he muttered to himself "but the Earth does move." It kept on moving, the new "natural philosophy" kept spreading. Its spread frightened all the major sects, which joined in the persecution of its followers. Lutherans hounded the pious Kepler, Calvinists exiled Grotius, Jews excommunicated Spinoza, Anglicans silenced Hobbes and burned his books, Jesuits got the works of Descartes put on the Index. Even so, the battle lines were not at first clearly drawn. Although the terrorism of the pious strengthened a growing tendency to skepticism, the pioneers were typically not yet skeptical of the claims of faith per se; few thinkers opposed the authority of the churches on the grounds that men can have no certain knowledge in matters of religion. (Hobbes was an exception as an apparent atheist.) No scientist called outright for complete freedom of speech and press, any more than Galileo himself had.

Yet few if any now agreed with the expressed belief of Copernicus that science was a dangerous activity, properly confined to initiates, whose findings should not be made freely available to laymen. As his theory won acceptance, some men began drawing the evident moral from the Church's misguided effort to suppress it—thought must be kept free. Pascal reminded the Jesuits of their futile success in getting Galileo condemned: "It will never be proved by such arguments as this that the earth remains stationary." John Milton went much further in his classic plea for freedom of the press, the *Areopagitica*. Having visited the aging Galileo, he told the Parliament how the learned men in the land of the Inquisition "did nothing but bemoan the servile condition into which learning amongst them was brought; that this was it which had damped the glory of Italian wits; that nothing had been there written now these many years but flattery and fustian."

Milton rang out the conclusion: "Give me the liberty to know, to utter, and to argue freely according to conscience, above all other liberties." Spinoza then offered the most comprehensive philosophical defense of such liberty. His pantheistic God logically favored natural knowledge and the "natural light of reason," which were the essential means of emancipation from the "human bondage" to passion and irrational desire; so he concluded that both religious and civil order suffered when "liberty of philosophizing" was denied.

We are much more impressed by these writers, it is true, than their contemporaries were. The ringing words of Milton did not reverberate through the seventeenth century; the works of Spinoza won just enough notoriety to get on the Index, the intellectual honor roll of the future; and everywhere outside of Holland the press was kept under royal censorship too. This censorship was notably ineffectual, however, in preventing the growth and spread of free thinking in western Europe. Soon orthodox thinkers like Bishop Boussuet were no longer merely expounding the true faith—they were defending it. If the censorship was managed as inefficiently as much else of the royal business, one reason was that it was sometimes perfunctory or halfhearted. Rulers themselves might feel something of the confused allegiances of the age, typified by Henry More of the Cambridge Platonists: a deeply religious man, given to mysticism, still a believer in ghosts and witches, but also a Fellow of the Royal Society, who defended the claims of reason in religion and opposed the dogmatic intolerance that laid down the terms of a single allegiance. Most important at this time was the pervasive, indirect, often unconscious influence of the "new philosophy," or more broadly of the scientific spirit.

Perhaps the clearest example of this influence was the gradual disappearance of the witchcraft mania. At the outset of the seventeenth century the belief in witches was virtually universal, shared by such scientists as Kepler and Harvey, and it was defended well into the eighteenth century, for the good reason asserted by John Wesley: to disbelieve it was to disbelieve in the Bible. Nevertheless, the superstition lost its hold, very few witches were tried after 1700, and presently the laws against them were repealed—all this not so much because of any concerted attack on the laws as because in the new climate of opinion the belief seemed stupid. Meanwhile some thinkers had been analyzing the sources of such beliefs. Richard Simon published in Holland his *Critical History of the Old Testament,* subjecting it to the same methods of textual criticism applied to other ancient documents; Spinoza more explicitly treated Scripture as a historical document, and in particular rejected the miracles it made so much of, deeming them unbecoming the author of a lawful universe; and in his *History of Oracles* Fontenelle offered a critical survey of supernatural fables in general. Such tendencies culminated in Bayle's *Historical and Critical Dictionary*, the most devastating attack on the "ignorance and absurdity" challenged by Henry Oldenburg. Convinced that superstition was a worse evil than atheism, because a spring of both crime and folly, Bayle relentlessly hunted down and exposed all that was dubious in holy tradition. As he often found its sources in the Bible itself, he said flatly: "Any literal sense that contains an obligation to commit crime is false." Similarly he rejected any dogma that clashed with "natural understanding." Insisting on the absolute independence of philosophy, he asserted that morals and religion too "are completely independent of each other"; atheists, he noted, commonly led more virtuous lives than Christians. Most fiercely he attacked the crime of persecution, which the Church still justified by a perversion of the simple biblical parable "Compel them to come in." His initial defense of the Huguenots broadened out into another argument for freedom of religion as a universal philosophical principle.

The "art of doubt" that Voltaire said he learned from the *Dictionary* was more like a science in Bayle's painstaking researches, but at any rate it reflected a basic skepticism in the scientific spirit. This demanded evidence for belief, looked to the facts; it was implicitly hostile to an unreasoned faith, or to belief supported only by the authority of custom or tradition. Hence both Fontenelle and Bayle insisted that the fact of universal belief in a fable, over no matter how many centuries, proved nothing whatever about its truth. And by their time men were growing aware of another apparent paradox, a saving skepticism promoted by the very success of science. Its success had been won in part by confining inquiry, ruling out such questions as final causes, in effect recognizing the inescapable limits of positive knowledge. It demonstrated that men might achieve more real freedom and power if they gave up the illusion of "the omnipotence of thought" (as Freud would call it) —an illusion that may be seen alike in primitive magic and in metaphysics or theology. Though science was already notorious in pious quarters for its intellectual pride, as its disciples maintained its standards in defiance of hallowed authority, in another aspect it was much humbler than orthodox piety, which professed so intimate an acquaintance with the Creator and his designs: humbler in its acknowledgment of finiteness, its respect both for fact and for mystery.

Still, there was no mistaking its pride. The kind of skepticism it helped to inspire, which today is much more widely diffused, may obscure the positive faith it upheld, the main source of its immense influence on thought. Basically this was the faith in reason come down through the classical tradition. As Galileo put it, the human understanding is "infinitely surpassed by the Divine Wisdom," yet the mind of man is "one of the works of God, yea, one of the most excellent"; and out of respect for God men should respect the claims of their understanding. It was now a more militant faith, however, less sober or classical in spirit, because derived from a new mode of understanding. Against the authority of the Church Galileo set up no mere skepticism but the authority of positive knowledge, and a positive means to more truth. Likewise Bayle, who at times verged on utter skepticism, crusaded against error with a passion that presupposed the truth that could be got by "natural understanding." Scientists had established a new kind of authority, backed by incontestable works, up to a point logically impossible to deny, the more compelling because it involved no compulsion or threat. In so doing they built a solid basis for claims to freedom of thought and speech, as not merely a private right of individuals but a proved means to truth and therefore to public good.

Such implications of the scientific revolution were not widely or fully realized until the eighteenth century, the Age of Enlightenment, when they formed the gospel of the *philosophes* who championed the cause of freedom. Yet almost all the radical ideas of these thinkers were abroad before they went to work. The Century of Genius had begot philosophers to match the pioneers in science—in particular René Descartes and John Locke. This pair took up quite different positions, accentuating the duality or ambiguity of the scientific rationale; but alike they were much bolder than they now seem, because most influential in transforming the climate of opinion.

Descartes (1596–1650) was a literal, old-fashioned rationalist, up to a point squarely in the tradition of the medieval Schoolmen. Although he admired Bacon's *Novum Organum,* he did not adopt the method of induction or put his trust in factual knowledge, arguing instead that real certainty could be got only by deduction from established first principles. His basic criterion of truth was "clear and distinct ideas," as best exemplified by mathematics. His aim was a full explanation of the universe, no mere description of it; he criticized Galileo for having explained only "particular effects," neglecting the "first causes of nature." Hence he constructed a metaphysics, another grand system of thought, which might have struck Bacon as only another stage play of the mind, a strut of the Idols. (Among other things he explained why clouds could rain blood, not bothering to check up first on the facts.) Based on a dualism of matter and mind, it came down to a restatement of the familiar Christian dualism, with the sanction of the Christian God. Because Descartes was indifferent to history too he could more easily conclude that the clear and distinct idea he thought he had of God must be innate, God-given, not the cultural product it looks like to historians.[6] His most popular disciple, Malebranche, always insisted that "religion is the true philosophy."

Nevertheless, Descartes had reached these conventional conclusions by a highly unconventional method of systematic doubt, because of which he ended on the Index and lived on in history as the founder of formal modern philosophy. As a student at one of the best Jesuit schools in Europe he had "learned all that others had learned," only to become increasingly embarrassed by "doubts and errors," the discovery of his ignorance—and all the ignorance disguised as learning; so he resolved to doubt everything, accept nothing on authority, start thinking all over again from scratch. When by pure reason he arrived at his metaphysical dualism of matter and mind, he dutifully turned over the realm of mind to theologians, as piously bowed to the authority of Scripture and the Church in questions of faith, but churchmen were properly alarmed: he was teaching men to accept only what they clearly understood. "I see," wrote Bishop Bossuet toward the end of the century, "that under the name of Cartesianism a great battle against the Church is preparing." By this time Descartes had won something like the authority Aristotle once had, and his method had deeply impressed many other thinkers, such as Spinoza and Bayle, who did not accept his metaphysics. However sincere his piety, moreover, his primary interest was unquestionably the world of matter. This he reserved for mathematics and science, to which he gave complete authority; as an absolutely lawful world, it left no real room for miracles or Providence, needing God only as a First Cause. (Once he was careless enough to remark, "Whenever I use the term 'God' you can substitute 'the mathematical order of nature.' ") Chiefly his authority went into the propagation of the scientific view of the universe.

---

[6] By an odd twist of his logic he had to have God before he could believe in the existence of the world explored by scientists. Our senses may deceive us, life may be but a dream; but his ideas about a world seemed to be forced by something outside him, God was no dream, and a good God would never deceive his creatures. *Cogito, ergo* heaven and earth —everything the mind could wish for.

By contrast, Locke (1632–1704) remained loyal to the empirical tradition stemming from Bacon. Though much impressed by Descartes, he was more impressed by the "incomparable Mr. Newton," and from Newton's triumph drew the epistemological moral. All knowledge came from experience, specifically from the operation of the mind on sensations; limited by their senses, men could never know the whole of reality, or such matters as ultimate causes; but they could learn much more if they clearly recognized the limits of their knowledge, stopped wasting time in fruitless controversy. The moral was simple:

> It is of great use to the sailor to know the length of his line, though he cannot with it fathom all the depths of the ocean. It is well he knows that it is long enough to reach the bottom at such places as are necessary to direct his voyage, and caution him against shoals that may ruin him. Our business here is not to know all things, but those which concern our conduct.

Because Locke's empirical theory of knowledge has become the common sense of Anglo-Americans, we might suspect that it was no model of logical rigor and clarity. Thus in rejecting the Cartesian doctrine of innate ideas, describing the mind at birth as a blank sheet on which experience wrote, he failed to see clearly that the operations of the mind implied something like innate faculties, beyond the properties of blank sheets, and he failed to deal adequately with the problem of the validity of its operations, or the correspondence of its ideas with external reality. Especially characteristic was his treatment of the key idea of "substance" or "matter," the supposed source of our sensations. Locke was acute enough to recognize it as a problem, remarking that we do not directly perceive any such thing, or have a clear and distinct idea of it apart from its sensed attributes (an idea of the "substance," say, behind the redness, roundness, ripeness, etc. of the apple); he granted that all we know for certain is ideas in our own minds, which conceivably might be dreams; and then he blandly walked away from the problem, observing that pleasure and pain are sufficient proof that there is some solid matter out there, and "beyond this we have no concernment to know." It is accordingly easy to ridicule his British habit of muddling through logical difficulties. It is also possible to describe his policy as wisdom, the good sense of recognizing the inescapable limitations of logic and of refusing to be logically consistent at any human cost. But all that concerns us here is that his empirical theory of knowledge was in its day a radical theory, and served as the foundation of a liberal philosophy that directly did more than the Cartesian to stimulate the growth of freedom.

Although we can hardly say that the appeal to experience necessarily makes for liberalism (remembering Dostoyevsky's Grand Inquisitor), in Locke's time it did naturally have such a tendency. Aristotle and St. Thomas Aquinas had also held that knowledge comes from experience, but his theory drew fire because it was now more likely to menace the principle of authority and to sow the scientific spirit than was the abstract rationalism of Descartes. The practical difference it made was shown in Locke's refutation of the ancient doctrine of innate ideas. While pointing out the empirical objections—that infants seem to lack such ideas, that men know them only when they come to the use of reason, that even so the idea of God does not actually command universal assent, etc.—he noted as well that this doctrine was too convenient a way of keeping traditional beliefs from being questioned, putting them beyond rational inquiry and judgment. It was because of the "historical, plain method" he maintained against Descartes that Voltaire and French Encyclopedists hailed him instead as the creator of "scientific philosophy." At least Locke's plain method was more effective for combating the absolute authority claimed by church and state.

In religious matters he made a typically prudent, or illogical, exception to his empirical theory by admitting revealed knowledge, the assent to which he called faith; only by divine revelation could we know such things as the existence of angels and an immortal soul. Nevertheless, Locke weakened the certainty of religion by possibly imprudent reservations: we must be sure that the matter of our faith is indeed a revelation from God, we must be careful to interpret it correctly, and if faith and reason conflict, reason should prevail—we should believe nothing plainly contrary to our knowledge or our God-given faculty of understanding. As typically he failed to foresee that on these grounds angels and souls might lead a precarious existence. At any rate, he struck the keynote of the immediate future in *The Reasonableness of Christianity*, an exposition of his own faith, and in his famous *Letter concerning Toleration*, which argued that compulsion in matters of faith is absurd.

The political liberalism for which Locke is best known had more to do with the distinctive political history of England, the subject of the next chapter. His admirers on the continent, however, drew out its connections with "scientific philosophy" as they attacked the *ancien régime*. They also made plainer a wider connection that Bacon had indicated in *The New Atlantis*. While Bacon's Utopia was an engineer's dream, his program more technological than political, he heralded the distinctive Western impulse to put ideas to work, use ideas to make over both society and the natural environment. He had not only a livelier sense than any thinker before him of new possibilities but more confidence that they could actually be realized by his empirical methods. In other words, he was fired by the hope of progress—the most novel social idea to come out of the scientific revolution. Though a considerably cooler type, Descartes also promised that by his method men could become "the lords and possessors of nature." The sensible Locke set limits to man's certain knowledge only to promote the cause of natural knowledge, improve the conduct that was the real business of the human race. All lent support to the growing belief that the Moderns were superior to the Ancients, the present was better than the past, and thence to the belief that the future was going to be still better. "We are now in an age," said Fontenelle, "that bids fair to become daily more and more enlightened, so much so that all preceding ages when compared with this will seem to be plunged in darkness." And if behind such feeling lay the Christian spirit of quest, science was now the obvious source of the faith that Europe was acquiring in itself. Confident that science itself would always keep advancing, men were hailing it as the main agent for the advance of all civilization, the promotion of well-being on earth.

In the *philosophes* this hope would inspire an aggressive use of reason to question, criticize, and protest rather than to moderate and harmonize. In the Century of Genius it reflected a purer, more immediate kind of emancipation. Jaded by the new wonders discovered or invented every day, we may see only crass materialism in Bacon's enraptured vision of such wonders, and at best find rather quaint the enthusiasm of Kepler and Bruno over the revelation of a cosmos so much worthier of God—a cosmos whose inconceivable immensity we take for granted. Yet nothing was more important to most of the pioneers than such exhilaration. The biographies of the century repeatedly note the sense of freedom that men felt as they passed from academic to scientific studies. At the end of the century Leibniz—a more spiritual type than either Descartes or Locke—reported how he had felt "transported to another world" when he began studying science. Thereupon he characteristically proceeded to spend many years planning and propagandizing for the Berlin Academy he founded, so that natural knowledge might be systematically accumulated and applied in the service of humanity.

Altogether, none of the pioneers wished or foresaw the political revolutions that would follow upon the spread of the new faith, the new hopes. At this point the connection between these revolutions and the scientific revolution may be sufficiently indicated by the "great Trinity" revered by Thomas Jefferson—Bacon, Newton, and Locke.

4. *The Costs*

Early in the sixteenth century, before Copernicus published his theory, the artist Dürer printed two celebrated, prophetic engravings. One shows St. Jerome working serenely in a tidy study, with animals sleeping peacefully in the foreground. The other, *Melancholy,* is a scene of hopeless confusion—a heavy, dejected figure surrounded by dismal animals, a scribbling infant, and a litter of mathematical symbols and scientific instruments. A century later, when out of this litter had come the work of Galileo, the poet John Donne was more explicit. The "new philosophy," he wrote, "calls *all* in doubt":

'Tis all in pieces, all coherence gone,
All just supply, and all relation.

So far the rise of science has been treated here as a success story, a purer triumph than the rise of Protestantism, nationalism, and capitalism— and rightly so: in this history it represented a much clearer gain, involving little immediate abuse of power, no direct threats to the freedom of the many. Yet it may be as rightly viewed as another crisis in Western history: not desperate, not insurmountable, but painful enough to many men, and eventually costly in less obvious ways. The conflict with the Church was only the beginning of a deeper disruption, disharmony, disunity sensed by Donne, though not by Galileo. At best, the triumph of science inevitably created new problems, involving the usual costs of freedom.

Now, we must keep in mind that the pioneers by no means attacked religion, but did their best to avert all possibility of conflict. When most militant, like Galileo and Bacon, they warred only on Aristotle and the Schoolmen. At that, Bacon borrowed from the later Schoolmen his doctrine of twofold truth: he sharply separated the natural from the supernatural, the truth got by observation of God's works from the truth based on faith in God's word, and he emphasized man's obligation "to render unto faith the things that are faith's." Descartes sought the same end by his absolute separation of matter and mind or soul. In theory scientists could therefore go about their study of the physical world without harm to religion, and in practice the more philosophical ones, such as Boyle and Newton, took pains to keep their science and their religion apart. Newton had the least thought of religious offense when he gave science complete operational autonomy by formulating its method, indeed showing more interest thereafter in God than in gravitation. Knowing now that this whole effort at separation did not work very well, and is scarcely an ideal philosophical solution, we may forget that it not only stemmed from the Middle Ages but by this time had become much more necessary. The necessity was at once practical and logical: practical in view of the authoritarianism of Christian tradition, logical in order to distinguish positive, verifiable knowledge from perhaps more exalted but unverifiable beliefs. Moreover, other philosophers soon set out to restore a unified view of the world, without sacrificing either God or science. If the grand pantheistic system of Spinoza would never do for the orthodox, Leibniz gave no serious offense when he transformed atoms into dynamic "monads" and spiritualized the world of matter and motion.

Still, the new scientific account of the universe called for a profound spiritual readjustment. Christians had always lived at the very center of the universe, on an earth that had often enough been degraded, described as a sink, but that nonetheless was the reason for the creation of the universe. It was a considerable jolt to be moved to a mere planet. Unlike Bruno, most Christians were not exhilarated by the idea of a "plurality of worlds," nor did they feel simply emancipated from vain hopes and fears when they began hearing (as from Galileo) how absurd it was to suppose that God had created the whole stellar universe just for their sake. Rather they might feel insignificant, lost—as fearful of the known as of the unknown. And since men had evidently misinterpreted the revealed word of God, the basis of Christian faith, they might be prey to other gnawing uncertainties about their faith. Science had launched them on a great adventure, with promises of more wonders to come; but it did not clearly make for peace of mind, the familiar kind of "spiritual freedom."

In the seventeenth century such underlying anxiety found most eloquent expression in the *Pensées* of Pascal, who has haunted French thought down to this day of Existentialism. "If we begin with certainties, we shall end in doubts," Bacon had warned; but he added buoyantly that "if we begin with doubts, and are patient in them, we

shall end in certainties." Pascal knew better. A devout Hamlet, a child
of Montaigne who was also a brilliant mathematician and scientist, he
was terrified as he contemplated the "infinite immensity" of the "whole
dumb universe" revealed by science, and brooded over the paradoxical
condition of man, caught between the extremes of the infinitely great
and the infinitely small, which man alone in the universe was conscious of, but could not comprehend: a torment still worse for Pascal
because he believed that only by faith in God could men find happiness
or peace, and because he knew that by the triumphant methods of
mathematics and science one could prove nothing whatever about the
existence of God. A student of the world's religions may remark that
Pascal's desperate need of certainty was a product of a particular cultural tradition, not an absolute need of "human nature," and that
historically considered, religion too is a spiritual adventure, a quest, a
vision of ultimate good rather than a possession of absolute truth.
Nevertheless, acquired needs may be as vital as any other, and as hard
to modify. For the great majority of men, particularly in Christian
cultures, religion has never meant a spiritual quest or adventure, but
has served as the abiding means to certainty, the ancient rock amid the
shifting sands and tides. And Pascal sensed another disturbing thing
about the "dumb universe" that would become more apparent as time
went on. The new world revealed by science was not really designed
for the human spirit, even apart from the fact that it was no longer a
man-centered world. It might discourage the uses of freedom.

Because of Newton's triumph, physics dominated scientific thought
in the Century of Genius. One name for it was "celestial mechanics"—
a rather odd marriage of ideas, more especially because the ruling
principle was the once despised "mechanics." Newton sealed the mechanistic theory of the universe implied in the work of Galileo and explicitly formulated in the philosophy of Descartes. While he offered
it as strictly a theory, possibly a means to "some truer method of
philosophy," he also expressed the hope that "we could derive the rest
of the phenomena of nature by the same kind of reasoning from mechanical principles." These were indeed very fruitful principles, as
Harvey had demonstrated when he put aside the soulful functions of
the heart and conceived it as a pump; yet they created a grave problem: How could one fit the human spirit into a machine world? How
reconcile its presumed freedom and spontaneity with invariable mechanical laws? How account for thought, for will, for life itself?

"Give me extension and motion," Descartes said confidently, "and I

will construct the universe"; but on this further problem he was much
less confident. With the help of the French word "âme," which means
both mind and soul, he began by absolutely separating mind from
matter, making it by definition immaterial. Hence it could not logically
affect matter or be affected by it, and was ideally free—except that it
had no means of translating its will into physical action; while all experience testified that mind and matter unmistakably do affect one
another. Although Descartes tried to get them back into relation, by
devices ranging from "animal spirits" and pineal glands to the will of
God, none came up to his own standard of "clear and distinct" ideas.
His followers accentuated his failure by continuing to wrestle with the
problem, with no more success. There was no satisfactory way of fitting
an immaterial mind into his mechanistic scheme.[7]

Hobbes then simplified the whole problem by getting rid of this
misty mind: there was nothing in the world but matter in motion. As
human beings are obviously composed of matter, and all matter was
governed by mechanical laws, it logically followed that men too were
machines. Sensations were only deceptions caused by the pressure of
external bodies on our senses; desires, feelings, thoughts were only
motions in the corporeal mind. "Imagination is nothing but decaying
sense," ran a typical dictum by Hobbes, who displayed considerable
imagination in explaining its deceptions, but whose method came down
to the simple idea *is nothing but*. Thus he concluded that good and
evil were nothing but names for pleasure and pain, and all that passed
for idealism was but a mask for selfish desire, the perpetual lust for
power that made political freedom impossible in "Leviathan"—the
great animal that was the state. In particular he did away with the
problem of "free will" by denying that there was any such thing,
affirming that the behavior of man was as rigidly determined as the
motion of all other matter. Although he kept up appearances by
retaining God as the First Mover (characteristically describing religion as a "pill which it is better to swallow without chewing"), he
consistently maintained that the so-called human spirit was mere appearance. Thereby he introduced a major paradox of modern science.

---

[7] In this generalization I am expecting men of ordinary common sense, who are still mostly
Cartesians of a naïve sort. As practical men (especially in America) they may distrust
"mere theory," but as unconscious metaphysicians they typically couple a crude materialism with a vague notion that they have souls. I should add that about other forms of life
Descartes was unequivocal: animals were only extended matter, hence machines. This
idea gave no trouble, since Christian tradition had denied animals anything like souls;
though it still might disturb lovers or observers of the more intelligent animals.

The plainest demonstration of the power or effective freedom of the human mind, science would provide thinkers with their main arguments for denying that man had any real freedom, substituting a more rigorous determinism for the fading doctrine of predestination.

In his own day the bald materialism of Hobbes had little influence, being denounced as simple atheism. Few men were seriously troubled by the mechanistic, deterministic implications of physics for human behavior, as most thinkers continued to take for granted the sovereign reality of mind or soul. Neither were they much troubled by the apparent failure of the Cartesians to bridge the gap between matter and mind, or by the double standard of truth that scientific thinkers were operating on; for ever since St. Paul Christians had been accustomed to a radical dualism of body and soul, and they were growing accustomed to the virtual separation of religion from the practical concerns of business and "reasons of state." The deeply split personality of Pascal was an exception. If men of two minds are liable to be half-hearted, the disciples of the "new philosophy" were mostly whole-hearted in their enthusiasm over its possibilities, and at worst seemed only somewhat absent-minded in their piety—as when Bacon remarked, in a spirit reminiscent of Pope Gregory the Great, that "the more absurd and incredible any divine mystery is, the greater honor we do to God in believing it, and so much the more noble the victory of faith." Few men felt with Donne that all was in pieces, "all coherence gone"; few were aware of the now-familiar "dissociation of sensibility" apparent in the strained metaphors by which Donne sought to unite his thought and feeling. At this stage we are dealing chiefly with portents of the troubles to come. The chief reason for bringing them up now is that the troubles were aggravated because men for a long time were not deeply concerned about them, or seemed unaware of them. A split sensibility became engrained in common sense.

So we might take a closer look at Sir Isaac Newton: the supreme genius of the century, the sovereign of "celestial mechanics," who in the century to come was revered in the spirit of Edmund Halley's prefatory ode in the *Principia Mathematica*—"Nearer the Gods no mortal may approach." In middle age Newton suffered a nervous breakdown verging on paranoia, involving delusions of persecution by friends and fellow scientists supposedly trying to steal the credit for his achievements; for the rest of his long life he did no scientific work. A Freudian may suspect that he came too near the gods, or suffered something like the anxiety of Pascal because of an unconscious sense of guilt over his handiwork. If so, however, it was quite unconscious; and what we know of the man gives a stranger idea of him. This mathematical genius spent more time poring over the works of alchemists and computing the generations since Adam than he did in working out his universal theory of gravitation. He avoided discussion of the philosophical and religious implications of his theory, but not because of any apparent fear; he seemed simply indifferent to them. To all appearances he was a good solid bourgeois, except that he showed as little interest in the practical uses of science. He wrote nothing about its possible service or disservice of humanity. When, full of honors, he became a member of Parliament, he sat there in silence. It is hard to think of him as a scientific saint either, since he evinced no more passion for truth than for any social cause.

Newton may accordingly recall Gilbert Chesterton's description of scientists, as innocent old gentlemen who incidentally revolutionize the world while pursuing their hobby: "When a man splits a grain of sand and the universe is turned upside down in consequence, it is difficult to realize that to the man who did it, the splitting of the grain is the great affair, and the capsizing of the universe quite a small one." Now that physicists have succeeded in splitting the atom, making possible hydrogen bombs, they have acquired a terribly urgent sense of social responsibility; but in Newton's day there were already some intimations of the possibly frightful abuses of the power that science would give men. Some supporters of the scientific academies were emphasizing their utility to the nation, rather than their service of humanity, and among the immediate fruits of applied science were the improvement and greatly increased use of artillery. Gunpowder was celebrated as one of the great discoveries of the Moderns, proving their superiority over the Ancients. About such matters Newton had nothing to say.

They were none of his business, let us add at once: he was devoted to pure science, basic research. Neither he nor the great company of devoted men after him can justly be held responsible for the use other men made of their findings, in particular because science itself never instigated conflict between nations, as religion had; the dispassionate, disinterested scientific spirit would always remain much too rare in the realm of social and political problems. As for Bacon, who hailed the power to come as simply a blessing, heralds can hardly be expected—any more than religious prophets—to anticipate all the costs of victory, or to provide complete blueprints for the society of the future. Yet the fact remains that Bacon's faith was much too simple. Science as such offered no guide to wise, humane uses of the power or freedom it conferred. Newton also revealed that scientific training is no assurance that the scientific spirit will be carried over into thinking about social, political, ethical, or religious problems. Indeed, his triumph involved a way of thinking that could menace human values, or hopes of wisdom. He won autonomy for science by carefully hedging its realm, concentrating on the measurable aspects of the natural world that could be reduced to mathematical principles; so among other things he concluded, "Nature is pleased with simplicity." Actually, of course, it was man who was pleased. Because thinkers must always seek simplicity in order to cope with multiplicity, and are never happier than when they have reduced everything to a single principle, they always tend to forget that they are simplifying and reducing, and that the terms of man's life are never simple.

Newton showed no interest in the sciences of life and man, which do not lend themselves readily to mathematical principles or the scientific method as he defined it. Given the thralldom to "celestial mechanics," psychology and the social sciences would not emerge as recognized sciences until the nineteenth century—and would then overcompensate for their dubious scientific status. The latecomers often sought respectability by taking over atomistic or mechanistic concepts that are not clearly suited to their different subject matter, shying away from such untidy or unverifiable notions as "purpose" and "value," piling up measurements and statistics that might give the illusion of mathematical precision and certainty, and in general accentuating a tendency to belittle man and dehumanize his world in the interest of intellectual economy and efficiency.[8] In Newton's day this tendency took a subtler form. While scientists repeatedly talked of "saving the phenomena" by heeding observed fact, they were discrediting the phenomena in another sense—the appearances of the world as directly, concretely experienced.

---

[8] Behaviorist psychologists set a conspicuous example when they not only disregarded but denied the reality of anything, such as consciousness itself, that cannot be directly observed or measured. But an anthropologist has as proudly stated that "the most realistic and scientifically adequate interpretation of culture is one that proceeds *as if* human beings did not exist." Like the Newtonian universe, culture has it own inviolable laws and goes all by itself; human beings would be simply a nuisance were it not that man—except as a scientist—is denied autonomy. On popular levels the habit of drastically reducing all kinds of human experience to its physical or physiological basis, and then regarding this basis as its "essence," appears in the pseudosophisticates who are pleased to say that love is really nothing but a biological urge to reproduce the species. It might be noted that thereby they give an inaccurate description even of their lust, since when they have their eye on a pretty girl they have no desire whatever to reproduce, nor the faintest thought of the species.

Newton seemed to agree with Hobbes that sensations were "deceptions"; he wrote that to speak of light as colored was to speak "grossly," in the manner of "vulgar people." Locke then helped men to avoid such vulgarity by distinguishing between the "primary" qualities of matter, such as weight and size, and the "secondary" qualities of color, smell, feel, etc. that were dependent on our senses. Science dealt with the primary qualities, which could be measured and weighed, and which in spite of his puzzlement over the idea of "matter" Locke somehow knew existed independently of man and his senses. The secondary qualities were purely subjective, and as their name implied, were of an inferior grade of reality, if they could be called real at all. In this view the world of nature—seemingly so vivid, once so instinct with purpose—was actually only a whirl of matter, soundless, colorless, odorless, seemingly pointless; and should all life disappear from earth (as science now tells us that in time it must), the great mechanism would go on in the endless dark, without a tick. And this view, oddly, came to be regarded as the *concrete* reality. Among the "capital of ideas" inherited from the Century of Genius is the idea that the physicist's partial description of the universe is not only the essential but the literal truth about it. Hobbes's "is nothing but" way of thinking has got into much common sense.

Hence Newton's habit of keeping his scientific thought strictly apart from his thought about life and man proved ominous. Understandable, even necessary though it was, it pointed the way toward the eventual divorce of science and the humanities. This meant another characteristic split in Western life, another major impediment to the goal of liberal education, or of full, harmonious self-realization. With it came perhaps the most grievous intellectual costs of the triumph of science. Scientific methods of inquiry have by now produced an immense store of knowledge in every field of thought; and thereby they have compelled a narrow specialization, fractured the intellectual community into professional societies separated both from one another and from the great society, fractured language itself into professional dialects or varieties of learned jargon, so that to most men the "poetry of science" makes no more sense than the science of poetry. Here we may get a better perspective from Newton's more philosophical contemporary Leibniz. Habitually thinking as a whole man, Leibniz aspired to an ideal union of thought and feeling. "Happiness, joy, love, perfection, being, force, freedom, harmony, order, and beauty—all," he wrote, "are linked together." His lifelong project of an encyclopedia was accordingly to him a very vital matter, for he believed that to preserve civilization men had to organize and unify all the knowledge then available; else "in the end disorder will become nearly insurmountable," and the multitude of writers all face the fate of "general oblivion." Now we have whole shelves of encyclopedias, alphabetizing a much vaster stock of knowledge; but the alphabet scarcely imposes unity, the sum looks more like insurmountable disorder—not to mention the available means to universal oblivion.

Leibniz also reminds us that there was considerably less tension in the thought and feeling of men as Europe entered the eighteenth century, the Age of Enlightenment. Newton did not at all look like Dürer's figure Melancholy. Except for the conflict with religion there was as yet no deep split between science and the humanities, no serious quarrel over the intellectual uses of freedom. Literary men were no more jealous or suspicious of science than Fontenelle was. Alexander Pope would celebrate in verse the "new philosophy" that troubled Donne: "See Mystery to Mathematics fly!" In France other writers would produce a famous Encyclopedia, propagating the knowledge and the spirit of science, grounding on the new philosophy the liberal faith that became the ruling faith of the Western democracies. Their age, which saw the social and political fruition of the Century of Genius, made much plainer that the scientific revolution was indeed a great emancipation of thought, a supremely important episode in the history of Western freedom. It accordingly represents a more popular success story, a triumph of more general consequence. But as we read this story, with due reverence, we had better keep in mind that its heroes were disposed to believe that Nature was pleased with the simplicity of their faith, that the Newton they revered had become something of a mythical figure, that the science they knew was rather different from ours, and that our living faith can never be absolutely proved by scientific or any other methods.

PART III
THE RISE OF
DEMOCRACY (1700–1800)

Chapter Eight | *PRELUDE: THE*
HISTORY OF ENGLAND

1. The Muddling Mother of Parliaments

It is not England that made her Parliament, the saying goes, but Parliament that made England. Englishmen are wont to add that the key to this process was not intellect but character, not theory but sentiment. Like most "not-but" statements these are half-truths, of course; yet they are suitable prefaces to a singular history, full of anomalies, embarrassing to both historical materialists and idealists. Parliament is unquestionably the main reason why England calls for a separate chapter in a history of freedom. As unquestionably its growth was unplanned, largely unguided by conscious theory, still less by any aspiration to become the "mother of parliaments." Its success was due most obviously to traits of public spirit, good humor, a sense of fair play, a respect for law, a willingness to compromise, or what may be called a want of logic —to attitudes essential for the maintenance of any free society, but especially needful under the British system of government, which to orderly thinkers may look like a hopeless muddle, or absence of system. Its influence, which produced an unruly child in America, was on the continent heightened by misunderstanding, due in part to the political thinkers of England, whose theory—from Hobbes and Locke to Burke and Mill—often misrepresented its living tradition. "What kind of people do they think we are?" cried Winston Churchill as the English fought alone against the all-conquering Hitler. In his shrewdness Hitler had badly underrated them, or perhaps overrated their prudence; but he had some excuse, given a people who had acquired a reputation as shopkeepers while developing a tradition of freedom by a remarkable combination of illogic and good sense.

In justice to the celebrated British character, however, we must view it as a product of their own efforts—again not simply of race or blood. As they grew addicted to a conscious ideal of freedom they grew fond of attributing it to their Anglo-Saxon forefathers, who later were endowed with the alleged Teutonic genius for freedom.[1] In fact, the Anglo-Saxons had only some rudiments of tribal democracy, common to barbarians, and they failed to cultivate these as they settled down in England and became a simple agricultural people. They lost their old sea habits, which the English would not recover for some centuries. Although they showed considerable promise as they grew literate, they made perhaps their most enduring contribution by losing the battle of Hastings in 1066, succumbing to William the Conqueror.

Having to rule over a conquered people, William succeeded in setting up a stronger, more orderly administration than was readily possible in the feudal confusion on the continent. England got an earlier start to becoming a nation. At the same time, William did not wield or claim absolute royal power, being bound not only by feudal law but by the old Saxon law that he had tactfully sworn to observe. His sons had no automatic right to succeed him as the king of the English but had to be elected, in keeping with Saxon custom; to win the election against a brother, Henry I made sworn promises in a charter that anticipated Magna Carta. And as the Normans settled down they added the possible advantages of mixed blood, then the clearer advantages of an enriched language. An unstable blend of Anglo-Saxon and Norman French, English was more susceptible to new influences than were the purer languages of the continent, so it later borrowed much more extensively from Latin and Greek, acquiring by far the largest vocabulary (if also the most irregular phonetics and grammar). It became a wonderfully copious language for such muddlers as poets.

As the last foreign invasion of England to this day, the Norman Conquest also accentuated a particular advantage of the "sceptred isle." It was a small land with definite borders, close enough to the continent always to be part of the Western community, open to all the stimulating influences of the rising civilization, yet remote from Rome and the Holy Roman Empire, protected by its straits, relatively secure. On their tight little island the English could more easily become united and work out an independent destiny. Sufficiently warlike, they still did not have to maintain a large military establishment, worry over the threat of warlike neighbors, or recover from periodic devastations. Of their own will they entered upon the Hundred Years' War with France, the first great national war, and as stupid and needless as any; but the Eng-

---

[1] Since the world wars, the forefathers accordingly had to be distinguished from other Germanic peoples. One don who dwelt on the "ineradicable barbarism" of the Germans described the Anglo-Saxons as "virile."

lish gained something even from this. While it heightened their self-consciousness and public spirit, the victories won by English archers over the mounted French nobles inspired one of the popular themes in their history—the democratic theme of the "sturdy yeomen." For such reasons their nobility tended to become less exclusive and parasitical than the nobility of France, Spain, and Germany, eventually taking to the commerce and industry disdained by its peers abroad.

Otherwise medieval England sowed much the same kind of mixed seeds as the rest of western Europe. Christianity inspired or sponsored the bulk of its art and learning, and in John Wyclif produced the one great English heretic; an early champion of the individual conscience against the authority of the Church, Wyclif also became the prophet of a more democratic gospel than he intended, as John Ball declared himself a disciple when leading the Peasants' Revolt of 1381. London emerged as the great city, with a charter of medieval liberties like those enjoyed by the free towns everywhere. Though merchants were less enterprising than their fellows in Italy and the Low Countries, clothmakers in the fourteenth century began contributing more than their share to the future greatness of England, with the aid of Flemish weavers brought in by Edward III. English kings, who included the usual assortment of statesmen, warriors, and blunderers, were on the whole stronger than their counterparts elsewhere, but their power was hedged both by feudal custom and by the principle of constitutionalism come down from Roman tradition; they were expected to obey the law of the land. And like other kings they ruled with the aid of a parliament.

No British invention, the Parliament that was to become the major political creation of England was at first no more designed as a citadel of liberty. It never met by initiative of the governed or by regular institutional procedure. Kings summoned it from time to time to suit their own convenience; the most ambitious ones had especial need of it to raise the armies and moneys they needed. Down to the sixteenth century representation in it was commonly considered more a burden than an honor. In England as elsewhere there was no clear theory of sovereignty, no clear line between executive and legislative powers, no regular means of holding the king strictly to the law he was supposed to obey. The basic idea that the king could do no wrong was ambiguous enough to suit his purposes, and the clearest custom supported his supreme authority; while he shared with Parliament uncertain powers of making laws, it remained certain that no statute was valid without his assent. What English kings made of kingship depended pretty much upon them, or upon changing circumstances more than changing principle or parliamentary statute.

Yet there were differences between English and continental practice, which in the event were to prove most important. To begin with, there was only one parliament instead of many. On the continent some local parliaments survived the rise of monarchy but the royal ones withered away; only in England did this national body persist all along and become Parliament—a permanent capitalized institution. If this outcome was hardly assured in the Middle Ages, it was heralded by events that at the time caused more stir than Magna Carta. One was the deposition of a lazy, feeble king, Edward II; Parliament forced him to give up the throne to his son. Another deposition, that of Richard II in 1399, was more revolutionary because Parliament charged the king with not merely incompetence but violation of the law of the land. Richard, it declared, had said "that the laws were in his own mouth and often in his own breast, that he by himself could change and frame the laws of the kingdom . . . and he has acted on these sayings." In other words, it explicitly condemned the idea of absolute monarchy; and having forced Richard formally to renounce all his royal rights, it proceeded to choose his successor, in effect holding that the new dynasty ruled by parliamentary title.

By this time, too, the English Parliament had acquired something unique—a House of Commons, representing burghers and yeomen. As elsewhere, the early parliaments had comprised the three feudal estates, but only in England did they split up into Lords and Commons. Characteristically, this institution did not originate by plan or statute, nor in response to popular demand; precisely when and how the two bodies came to sit, debate, and vote apart is unknown. By the end of the fourteenth century, at any rate, the Commons had acquired considerable power and prestige. It was a party to majestic acts of state, such as the deposition of kings; its consent was necessary for all statutes and extraordinary taxation; its independent petitions were often granted by the kings. The reasons for its increasing importance are clear enough, though again not a matter of high political principle or passion for liberty: both the kings and the great barons sought its support in their continual struggles. With the growth of a money economy the burghers also acquired more authority as the makers of money, more knowing about such matters than the lords; early in the fifteenth century it became established that all money grants were to be initiated in the House of Commons, thus preparing the way for its eventual claim of exclusive control of taxation.

The composition of the Lower House was in keeping with its hap-hazard growth, amounting to a medley of middle-class Englishmen. Its members were not elected in accordance with any national law, nor by uniformly democratic procedures; each borough chose its representa-tives in its own way, usually to suit oligarchic interests. Nevertheless, this messiness reflected a decent tradition of local self-government that nurtured an independent spirit. The medley made for respectability and strength because it included not only town burghers but landed gentry, the knights of the shire. The Lords found it easier to co-operate with the Commons because their lesser brethren sat in it; they did not habitually view commoners with the contempt that became the insignia of aristocratic pride on the continent. Until this century the English have had little sentiment of equality, dearly loving their lords, and to democrats they looked class-ridden; yet they were the first nation in Europe to begin realizing a measure of equality in political life, where it counted most, and their class feeling was tempered by a measure of mutual respect that bred in commoners more self-respect. When they developed political parties these would become more or less national parties, not irreconcilable class factions. So the English early began muddling through to one of the miracles of political history: a quite simple idea, indispensable to the success of democratic government, but never clearly or fully realized in the Greco-Roman world or the Italian city-states—the idea of a "loyal opposition."

A related distinction of the English was that they alone retained their native common law. Their pride in it, which had much to do with their uncommon respect for law, was as usual somewhat foggy. They owed much more than they realized to Roman law, which had not only con-tributed to their notions of constitutional government but helped their eminent jurists, beginning with Bracton, to rationalize their law. One of their most prized institutions, trial by jury, was not an English inven-tion; the idea came from the Franks, and it then evolved in typically unpremeditated ways. Still, this democratic mode of judgment by neigh-bors was in keeping with the spirit of their common law. It was a law suited to the interests of commoners, protective of their basic liberties. Edward I (1272–1307) won his fame as the greatest English lawgiver by calling in representative advisers and legislating primarily in the national interest, rather than the royal interest that would govern the thought of lawyers on the continent. The significant point remains that trial by jury became firmly established in England, while it disappeared from France—returning centuries later as an English importation.

In the fifteenth century Sir John Fortescue, chief justice, bequeathed a lasting memorial to a law that had made England the land of liberty. He contrasted English with French courts, where there was no trial by jury and torture was a common procedure. From his own observation he described the misery of the French common people, continually insulted and robbed by servants or soldiers of the king; whereas in the realm of England "no man sojourneth in another man's house without the love and the leave of the good man of the same house." He boasted that the English common law rejected the idea prevailing in other countries given to Roman law, that "the Prince his pleasure hath the force of a law." Fortescue was no political philosopher, no thinker at all to speak of, only a sensible man appealing to experience, as English thinkers would characteristically do; but common sense already told him that the people were sovereign, the best monarchy was limited or "politic," for no people would ever form a kingdom except to enjoy more securely the natural goods of life. By no means a revolutionary either, Fortescue was constantly cited by the men who later made the English Revolution.

He could scarcely have foreseen the interim. In his day England suffered from protracted struggles between the noble houses of Lancaster and York, whose badges gave these civil wars the name of the Wars of the Roses. A few years after his death the wars were ended by the reign of Henry VII (1485–1509), founder of the Tudor dynasty; and England entered upon a century of absolute monarchy, an apparent setback to "politic" government. The setback was real enough to give James I the delusion that he ruled by divine right, and so to start the troubles that ended in revolution. Yet under the Tudors there was actually no sharp break with tradition. Rather, their rule accentuated the underlying continuity, the basic logic—or illogic—of English political history. Tudor England underwent the impact of all the forces that were transforming western Europe—the Renaissance, the Reformation, the explorations and discoveries, the economic revolution, the rising nationalism, the emerging science; and these forces had freer play under its monarchs than they did in any other major state, substantially aiding the growth of both its power and its freedom.

2. The Tudors and the Elizabethan Age

There is no blinking the fact of personal rule under the great Tudors —Henry VII, Henry VIII, and Queen Elizabeth. Now more than ever before we hear of the divinity that hedges a king, the necessity of obedience to kings. In 1528 William Tyndale, translator of the New Testament, declared the theme when he wrote, "For God hath made the king in every realm judge over all, and over him there is no judge"; Cardinal Wolsey declared the costs when he cried, "Had I but served my God as I have served my King"; and both joined Thomas More, Thomas Cranmer, Hugh Latimer, and others on a celebrated roll of martyrs to the royal interests. We hear nothing of Magna Carta, which is not even mentioned in Shakespeare's *King John*. Parliament, obviously subordinate to the monarch, was to Queen Elizabeth a kind of antique nuisance; in her reign of forty-five years (1558–1603) there were only ten Parliaments, meeting usually for only a few weeks, and to one of them her lord chancellor apologized for the necessary evil of summoning it. The lord chancellor spoke for the main governing body of the kingdom— the Privy Council. Henry VII had made over the ancient royal council into a convenient agent of his will, or register of his decisions; Thomas Cromwell greatly strengthened it for Henry VIII, creating a bureaucracy through which it could supervise the whole work of government; and thereafter it acted like a modern cabinet, but with no pretense of independence or representativeness. Similarly the Tudors created the Star Chamber, a supreme court of justice responsible to the king alone.

Under Henry VIII in particular the absolute monarchy often had the ugly look of despotism. Although historians are still disputing his qualities, he was plainly an egotist who behaved like a Machiavellian prince, and ruthlessly sacrificed his servants (including Thomas Cromwell) whenever it suited his interests. No one can claim for him the role of prophet in his most famous, enduring work, the break with Rome and founding of the Anglican Church—immediately to get the first of his divorces, then to lay hands on the wealth of the monasteries. As head of the Church of England he was pleased to boast that he was at once King, Emperor, and Pope, and to call England his "imperial realm." On his deathbed he professed his faith in God, which may well have been sincere according to the lights of kings in his time, but first he had demonstrated his sovereign indifference to the niceties of religious principle by burning or hanging both Protestants and Catholics—initiating a dubious distinction for England, which at one time or another would persecute all the major Christian sects. Needless to add, he initiated no real reformation.

Yet the Anglican Church, founded for purely political reasons, leads to the heart of the ambiguities of English history, and immediately of Tudor rule. However unseemly its origins, it was a truly national

church; the many Englishmen who disapproved of Henry's divorce
were mostly united in resentment of the Italian pope and the steady
Roman drain on the wealth of England.[2] If only because it stood on no
firm doctrinal ground, and stood for no fervent religious principle, it
soon began to exhibit the English genius for compromise, or sensible
muddle. Immediately it spared England the religious wars that tore
other Protestant countries, avoiding the systematic persecution by which
Henry's daughter, "Bloody Mary," had tried to restore Catholicism.
Under Queen Elizabeth it grew more disposed to tolerance than any
other major established church, partly as a matter of policy in a country
still divided by religious differences, partly too out of sentiment or
principle. (She herself said majestically that she would not "make windows into men's souls.") Its lenience was set off by the religious tyranny
in Calvinistic Scotland. While compensating the pious with the great
English Bible and Prayer Book, the Church of England continued to
permit considerable latitude in thought as it settled down into the conservatism befitting a respectable, well-established church.

For the long run, moreover, the break with Rome did not simply
strengthen absolute monarchy or enable Henry VIII to play either
emperor or pope. Parliament gained more. At this juncture the king
had especial need of it, to pass all the necessary laws and assure the
support of the nation; the Reformation Parliament, which was neither
bribed nor coerced, broke all records by sitting for seven years, gaining
invaluable experience in continuous government. Henry VIII expressed
his royal pleasure in it by assuring its members the right of freedom
from arrest. He did more than any king before him, indeed, to make
Parliament a consciously national body, to assure its privileges as an
essential arm of the government, to extend its authority and sphere of
action—to fit it for its eventual job of overthrowing the monarchy. The
House of Commons in particular now grew markedly in both size and
prestige. More and more gentry and lawyers sought the honor of sitting
in it, many became old hands at its business, and with growing experience it developed more regular and efficient procedures, as by a committee system for considering bills.

Such gains were consolidated during the reign of Queen Elizabeth,

---

[2] It should be added that Pope Clement VII did not act on high principle either in refusing Henry VIII a divorce. Shortly before this he had granted a divorce to Henry's
sister, Queen Margaret of Scotland, on flimsier grounds, as popes were wont to do for
reasons of state. He turned Henry down rather than risk the displeasure of the Holy Roman
Emperor Charles V, at the time master of Italy.

whose relatively few Parliaments made a point of getting as much done as possible in their short sessions. While she showed much less respect for them, especially when they stubbornly kept calling on her to get married and give England an heir, it was significant that she always did have some trouble with them. The Spanish ambassador, who in his Philip II knew an honest-to-God absolute monarch, was prophetic. "These heretics neither fear God nor obey their betters," he wrote of one parliament. "I said what they wanted was simple liberty, and if kings did not look out for themselves and combine together to check them, it was easy to see how the license that these people had taken would end." Still blunter was Peter Wentworth, speaking out in the House of Commons itself. "Sweet is the name of liberty," he declaimed, "but the thing itself a value beyond all inestimable treasure. . . . Liberty of free speech is the only salve to heal all the sores of this common-wealth . . . and without, it is a scorn and mockery to call it a Parliament house, for in truth it is none, but a very school of flattery and dissimulation." Queen Elizabeth thereupon violated the right assured by Henry VIII, having Wentworth arrested and imprisoned; but at least she felt obliged to pretend that his arrest was not for the words spoken in the Commons, and one can scarcely imagine any Spanish commoner addressing such words to Philip II, or any French one to Louis XIV a century later.

Even so the queen was popular. Few English kings were more popular than the Tudor "tyrants," as by ordinary worldly standards few were more successful. Beginning with Henry VII, they had rescued England from the feudal anarchy of civil wars fought over no civil principle. With stability they had brought generally efficient government, and a prosperity that survived the severe economic dislocations of the sixteenth century. They kept taxes low on principle; the subjects of Elizabeth were proud of being the least taxed people in Europe. And the Tudor monarchs themselves made no claim to divine rights, as none to unlimited power or supremacy over the law, if only because they had no need of such claims to buttress their natural authority. They governed by consent of the governed: possibly a mistaken consent, but not simply an unreasoned one. The respect they elicited was no cowering subservience, or simple awe of the trappings of pseudodivinity, but in part was earned by the respect they showed for the people. They felt no need either to put on majesty, or hold themselves aloof, by building a Versailles. At the time of the Spanish Armada Queen Elizabeth spoke truly enough to the men who were preparing to meet the expected invasion: "Let tyrants fear. I have always so behaved myself that, under God, I have placed my chiefest strength and safeguard in the loyal hearts and good will of my subjects."

Hence all the old institutions and the old ideas that went with them came through the century of Tudor rule. In this century England produced its first notable political philosophers since John of Salisbury in Thomas More and Richard Hooker, who were alike liberal; John Locke would acknowledge his indebtedness to "the judicious Hooker," a proponent of the ideal medieval theory of government limited by law derived from the community. Likewise Thomas Smith, secretary of state under Queen Elizabeth, stated the ideal theory of Parliament as representative of the whole realm: "For every Englishman is intended to be there present . . . and the consent of the Parliament is taken to be every man's consent." Actually, it was by no means so representative, as Smith himself admitted when he noted that the "proletarii" had "no voice nor authority in our commonwealth"; but he also noted that even this poorest class was not wholly neglected, since "in cities and corporate towns, for default of yeomen, inquests and juries are impanelled of such manner of people." This element of freedom—the tradition of local self-government—flourished under the Tudors, who reduced the costs of the royal bureaucracy by entrusting more duties to local officials. Even the Star Chamber was not unpopular, as it was at first a device for holding to account powerful men who might intimidate ordinary courts of justice; and when it began to acquire its modern notoriety it heightened reverence for the common law. By the end of Queen Elizabeth's reign jurists like Edward Coke were proclaiming the supremacy of this law of the people, describing it as the very constitution of the rights of Englishmen.

Meanwhile new ideas had been coming in, new forces were at work, of more lasting consequence than the sporadic despotism of the Tudor monarchs. The humanism of Erasmus remained an active ferment. Hugh Latimer kept denouncing the abuses of the Royal Reformation, calling for more popular education, preaching that a "true Commonwealth" must be based on the equality and dignity of men. Other men spread the classical ideas of "natural reason" and "natural law" that would crop up in such defenders of the Tudor monarchy as Francis Bacon. English humanists typically gave the Renaissance creed a practical English turn by seeking to educate the aristocracy for political life. Thus Sir Thomas Elyot wrote *The boke named the Governour*: an unoriginal, rather crude version of Castiglione's *Courtier*, but well adapted to the needs of his less refined society, highly influential in popularizing the idea that gentlemen and noblemen should maintain their prestige by acquiring learning, and that aristocracy meant responsibility, not mere privilege. The humanists helped to build up the tradition of a cultivated, public-spirited ruling class, setting the ideal embodied by Sir Philip Sidney—poet, scholar, courtier, soldier, statesman. As the English nobility contributed far more to government than the French nobility could under Louis XIV, so did the lesser gentry—a rising class, as it was not in France. It in turn helped to stimulate a rising yeomanry as well as a rising bourgeoisie. The poorer class too was helped by the wealthy, who in the reign of Queen Elizabeth made a fashion of endowing or founding not only hospitals and almshouses but grammar schools and colleges. The social mobility at this time most sharply accentuated the paradox of English society. No theme in serious thought was more popular than the necessity of hierarchy, place, order, degree; as Shakespeare wrote, "Take but degree away" and all is anarchy; while all through the society ambitious men were seeking by their wits to improve their fortunes and rise above their degree—as Shakespeare got himself a coat of arms.

The dismayed conservatives were right: these restless individualists and upstarts were causing trouble, and sowing the seeds of much more. Still, they were harvesting a wonderful crop of achievements, realizing the glory that we know as the Elizabethan Age. Generally considered the greatest age of England, it at least marked her emergence into greatness, and remains among the most brilliant ages in history. And though it was by no means wholly indigenous, also marking the culmination of the Renaissance in England, it came as an extraordinary burst of energy and creativity, carried faster and further than the Renaissance did elsewhere in western Europe, resulting in an immense expansion alike in wealth, power, and culture. We may better appreciate its spontaneity and freedom of spirit if we keep an eye on Spain, the chief rival of Elizabethan England.

It took the English a long time—more than half a century—to catch on to the opportunities opened up by the Portuguese and the Spaniards, and to the added advantages of their island, "bound in with the triumphant sea," now that the Atlantic seaboard had replaced the Mediterranean as the main sphere of enterprise. Henry VIII made a start by building a navy and encouraging the fishing industry in order to build up a merchant marine.[3] Once the English did take to sea they caught up with remarkable rapidity. Soon their merchants, privateers, and explorers were all over the world that Drake sailed around, performing the feats celebrated in Hakluyt's prose epic *The Principal Navigations, Traffics and Discoveries of the English Nation.* Both the individual enterprise and the camaraderie for which the English seadogs became famous might seem natural to maritime life, but Spain indicated that the connection is not automatic; under Philip II it developed no such vigorous merchant and maritime class. Philip helped by trying to keep all foreigners out of the New World that the pope had obligingly assigned to Spain, for the English retaliated by piratical raids on his ships and colonies. The lure of Spanish gold inspired in them all the daring of the *conquistadores,* and somewhat more gusto.

That the plunder was only a fraction of this gold was also to the good. While Spain squandered its wealth, the much poorer English went to work to create wealth by commerce and industry. They had been behind the continent in technology until the Tudors started catching up here too by importing foreign craftsmen. An unsung achievement of the Elizabethan Age was an exceptionally vigorous industrial growth, spurred by a great increase in coal production, which made England the leader of Europe in industry and technology, and prepared for the revolution of two centuries later. This too was chiefly the work of individual enterprise, aided by social mobility and freedom from class constraints. The gentry were commonly as energetic as the burghers, lords might set up glassworks or ironworks. Together with its seadogs and its M.P.'s, the entrepreneurs of England were proving the spirit of an essentially free society on the rise.

The dazzling cultural achievement of Elizabethan England as clearly reflected this spirit. In Spain the Golden Age of Cervantes, Lope de Vega, and Calderón came late, after the peak of national glory, when Philip II had gone into the shades, and it was much more limited in range, much less exuberant and abundant; it produced no such pioneers as Gilbert and Bacon, no such rebels as Marlowe—no such diversified a galaxy as these and Spenser, Sidney, Hakluyt, Raleigh, Chapman, Jonson, Shakespeare. All questions of relative genius aside, Spain could

---

[3] The discovery of the North Atlantic fisheries was perhaps as significant for Europe as the more spectacular discovery of gold and silver in Spanish America, since fish were a staple of commerce. In England an act of 1548 prescribed two fish days a week, not for religious reasons, and presently a third was added. Add Lent, and Englishmen were putting flesh on the future mistress of the seas by eating fish about half the days of the year.

hardly create a drama like Shakespeare's, with its host of highly individualized characters, its many great personalities, its ampleness, its brooding depths, and its intensity; for the ruling ideals of Spain, under its
absolute monarchy and authoritarian Church, naturally tended to pre-
clude such freedom and abundance. And however exceptional the
genius of Shakespeare, he was representative of a popular indigenous
literature. The gentry and nobility contributed their full share to
literature, while the queen herself was a child of Renaissance humanism, fluent in Italian, Latin, and Greek; but the stirring Elizabethan
theater was a spontaneous national affair—served by poets come out
of the lower ranks of society, thronged by men from all but the highest
ranks, closer to the great communal theater of ancient Athens than was
the neoclassical theater to come.

The inspiration of all this creativity was primarily secular. Although
the English were increasingly conscious of their Protestantism, their
zeal for it was more patriotic than religious—their Church was the
Church of *England*—nor did the rising Puritans as yet set the tone of
the national life. The Elizabethans built no churches to speak of, as
they created no great religious art or literature; their explorers and
buccaneers went out with no higher sense of Christian mission than
their merchants and manufacturers; their Parliament and their queen
were engrossed in affairs of state, to which religion was subordinated.
National self-consciousness was the most apparent spring of their enthusiasm and creative energy; patriotism was the sovereign ideal, the
focus and sometimes the curb of their rugged individualism, their lust
for wealth, power, and fame. The Elizabethan Age was accordingly no
more serene than the Italian Renaissance. Worldly ambition or simple
greed generated internal strife, more profoundly the tensions reflected
in Shakespearian tragedy, as men continued to assume the supreme
importance of order and degree, under God. But for the time being the
Elizabethans maintained something like an ideal tension. They had an
advantage over the men of the Italian Renaissance in a longer tradition
of rights under law, a deeper aversion to tyranny or arbitrary rule,
coupled with a clearer national purpose and more public spirit.

They also had a considerable advantage in their monarch. Without
absolving Queen Elizabeth, we may discount somewhat the common
charges of feminine caprice, niggardliness, procrastination, irresolution.
There was some wisdom in her policy of not regally doing and spending
(except on her wardrobe), but trusting to the initiative of her subjects, giving a freer rein to their energy and talent. Another name

for her notorious parsimony was prudence or economy, in a country much poorer than Spain; at least her government was almost the only royal one in Europe that never went bankrupt. And for all her shifty tactics, she did not falter in times of crisis. Even her enemies paid her tribute. "Just look how well she governs," exclaimed Pope Sixtus V (one of whose predecessors, the sainted Pius V, had tried to get her murdered) : "she is only a woman, only mistress of half an island, and yet she makes herself feared by Spain, by France, by the Emperor, by all." At home Edward Coke, the champion of the common law, expressed the common sentiment when he was Speaker of the House: "We have cause daily to praise God that ever you were given us."

This was said in 1592, after the defeat of the Spanish Armada; and it brings us to the crucial war with Spain, which in a history of freedom has a significance somewhat like the stand of ancient Athens against the Persian Empire. In Philip II Queen Elizabeth had indeed a "mighty opposite." Bigoted, pitiless, despotic, Philip was even so wholly dedicated to the high cause of restoring Europe to the Catholic faith. He was a worthy symbol of the idealism of Spain, which was no less real because—like the idealism of England—it was shot through with a love of gold, and stooped without compunction to power politics. No such zealot herself, Elizabeth long appeared to disadvantage in her reluctance squarely to oppose him. Not until her hand was forced by the fall of Antwerp and the assassination of William the Silent, threatening the collapse of the Dutch rebellion, did she go to the aid of the Dutch and thus bring on open war with Spain. But then England willy-nilly became the leader of Protestant Europe against the grand designs of Philip. If Elizabeth did not relish this costly role, she at least adhered to it for the rest of her reign, and her people rose to it. All Europe watched in suspense as Philip assembled the mightiest armada in history to invade England.

Historians have since made out other major factors, especially economic ones, that reduce this great war (a war never even declared) to something considerably less than an all-out struggle between freedom and tyranny. The defeat of the Spanish Armada itself soon became matter of legend, or myth, much more glorious than the historic fact. Garrett Mattingly has given a vivid account of the monumental confusion in the assembling of the Armada, and then of the sea battles—the first great naval battles in modern history, which neither side had any clear idea how to fight. The battles were by no means so decisive as the ensuing storms, which dispersed and wrecked the Armada; both sides agreed that God settled the issue by sending winds and waves. At that, the disaster failed to crush either the spirit of Philip or the power of Spain. Like a good Christian, Philip observed that kings "must submit to being used by God's will without knowing what it is—they must never seek to use it." The war went on for well over a decade, and at its end Spain still had its whole colonial empire, while England was mistress of neither an empire nor the seas. It is not demonstrable—least of all from the masterpieces of Shakespeare—that the glow of victory inspired the glory of Elizabethan literature.

Yet no debunking can do away with the actual consequences of the defeat of the Spanish Armada, which included the ideal meanings it had for contemporaries. To the men who fought this war it was no mere phase in power politics, but a showdown struggle between the powers of good and evil; call them naïve, deluded, this is only to emphasize the reality of their patriotic and religious motives. Queen Elizabeth and her relatively free subjects were at their best during the national crisis. Despite God's mysterious will, the Spaniards might well have succeeded in invading and conquering England had not the English had better ships and guns, and better seamen to fight them—all their own doing. Philip II might have dominated Europe and done much more to stamp out Protestantism, with incalculable consequences. As it was, his defeat made it certain that no one nation or church was then to be master of Europe. Other countries no longer looked on mighty Spain—hopefully or fearfully—as the irresistible wave of the future. Protestant countries felt freer to make their own future, as the Dutch in particular set about doing. Above all, Englishmen were left free. The very legends they promptly began weaving about the defeat of the Spanish Armada, as a God-willed triumph over the powers of tyranny and darkness, strengthened their confidence in their ideals and their own powers. Among the indirect, unforeseen, unintended, but supremely important consequences of their victory were the revolutions of the seventeenth century that clinched their basic liberties.

3. *The Puritan Revolution*

For feminine reasons unclear, possibly unwholesome, Elizabeth refused to marry and give England a Tudor heir; but thereby the Virgin Queen helped immeasurably to make it the mother of parliaments. She was succeeded by the Stuart King James I (1603–1625), son of Mary Queen of Scots. James had an idea of kingship more like that of Philip II, if a less clear awareness that kings are instruments, not commanders of God's mysterious will. He set out to rule as the absolute monarch that Queen Elizabeth may have been in practice but was too politic to say so, or to claim a God-given right to be. At once he stirred up a conflict with Parliament, which ended by giving his son Charles a unique distinction: Charles was the first European king to have his head cut off by his subjects.

Although there had been innumerable rebellions in Europe and even revolutions of sorts, the English Revolution was the first major one of lasting consequence. Earlier ones had generally been more like spontaneous uprisings against oppression, limited in scope and aim, lacking a clear political program; none resulted in a lasting new political order that might serve as a model for other peoples. The English Revolution too was a very confused affair, no more purely rational or ideal than collective action ever is. No party deliberately planned it or guided it to its outcome; instead one thing led to another, in ways unintended and mostly unwanted. Yet it remains the prototype of the great political revolutions that have made Western civilization so radically different from all the Eastern civilizations. It grew out of a conflict over clearly stated principles; it led to fuller, more explicit assertions of the rights of the ruled against their rulers; it was won by a people's army, some of whose officers were devoted to the still more revolutionary ideas of the future; and after its apparent failure in victory it was followed by another revolution, this time bloodless, which assured the triumph of parliamentary government, with a bill of rights—the triumph of the main principles asserted by the men who had started the struggle against James I. This outcome, which set England squarely in opposition to the tendencies prevailing in all the monarchies on the continent, was certainly its pre-eminent contribution to the history of Western freedom.

Now, in recent times the English Revolution has gone the way of all others, being reduced to an economic conflict. No historian today, I take it, would deny that economic or class interests had much to do with it, as was plain to many men of the time even though they had no Karl Marx. Such material motives added mightily to the confusion, in particular the conflicting aims of the rebels; one reason why they failed in victory was that many had a clearer idea of their grievances than of their ends. But here in particular I should say that a purely economic interpretation of history is too easy a way of evading the complexities of human conflict, and that it chiefly obscures the uniqueness and the historical importance of the English Revolution.[4] All over Europe men had much the same economic and class interests, but neglected to make a revolution. The plain influence that the English had on subsequent political history, particularly in France and America, was due most obviously to the principles they thought they were fighting for.

As obviously the struggle began over the issue of royal prerogatives. Before ascending the throne James I had written his *True Law of Free Monarchies,* maintaining that monarchs ruled by divine right and were responsible only to God, and he made it clear to his first Parliament that none should "presume to meddle with anything concerning our government mysteries of State." The House of Commons "derived all matters of privilege" from him, sitting not by any right of its own but by his grace; so too all the liberties of the people were by "grace and permission of our ancestors and us." Though never so despotic or brutal as Henry VIII was on occasion, he proceeded to give more offense by exercising his discretionary powers to set a new high in extravagance and corruption, reducing his "government mysteries of State" to a system of jobbery, lavishing sinecures and pensions on royal favorites while selling high offices in both church and state. But the House of Commons had defined the basic issue at the outset. It told the Stuart king that he had been "misinformed": its privileges were matters of right, not of royal favor, and included the right to debate freely such questions as the limits of his prerogative. When James dismissed it and for some years ruled without a Parliament, Chief Justice Coke strode forth as its champion. Flourishing the long-forgotten Magna Carta, he upheld the absolute supremacy of the common law as the source of both the powers of the king and the rights of his subjects, and said flatly that any royal decree contrary to the law of the land was null and void. When James dismissed him too, he carried on the struggle from the floor of the next House of Commons.

Although the opposition to the king was no doubt intensified by

---

[4] I should also note that economic causes turn out to be no clearer than other ones. The conventional Marxist interpretation of the revolution, for example, is that it represented the triumph of the bourgeoisie, or more precisely of "capitalism"; it marked the "decisive shift" from a feudal to a capitalistic society. One who doubts the precision of this vocabularly may now consider a rival economic interpretation supported by Professor Trevor-Roper. Whereas the Marxists have assumed that the English gentry supported the bourgeoisie because they too were a prosperous rising class, he offers substantial evidence to prove that they were actually in serious economic difficulties, and therefore as hostile to the capitalists of London as to the royal court; he makes out their distress as the basic cause of the Revolution. He concludes, however, that the revolt of the gentry was not only "blind" but a failure, in effect more postively denying the whole affair any political or ideal significance to speak of; so one who still wishes to speak of such possibilities may doubt whether he has got down to the "real" cause either.

economic distress, especially among the many lesser gentry still suffering from the inflation that had set in in the sixteenth century, the Revolution did not grow out of a severe depression, or anything like intolerable misery. The country at large was still uncommonly prosperous, much better off than contemporary Spain, France, and Germany, and the many poor who failed to share in this prosperity failed as well to provide tinder for riot or rebellion; in the countryside they were if anything inclined to be pro-royalist. Neither was the struggle primarily a class struggle. Although the bourgeois took a leading part, the opposition to King James cut across class lines; the early leaders (like Coke) came chiefly from the gentry and nobility. As the struggle went on, class lines indeed became clearer. The king drew his support chiefly from the aristocracy and its natural allies, the Anglican clergy and the inveterately conservative universities; the opposition was centered in the middle classes, including the lesser gentry; and eventually the conflict settled down into the familiar alignment of the Civil War—Cavaliers versus Roundheads. But this emphasized a further complication that we must shortly return to. What had worked up the middle classes to a fighting pitch was not clearly their distinctive interests as bourgeois, still less as "capitalists"; businessmen as such were no more disposed to man the barricades than they are today. Their fervor came most plainly from their Puritan religion—another "ideal" factor that it is now fashionable to minimize.

With the accession of Charles I, at any rate, the principles at stake became more sharply defined. Although Charles may now look fatuous in his disregard of public opinion (for example, sacrificing his initial popularity by at once marrying a Catholic princess of Spain), he was nevertheless acting on principle in his refusal to make any concessions. A more conscientious ruler than James I, he was more deeply convinced that "a sovereign and a subject are clean different things," more highly resolved to maintain the true law of a free monarchy. Hence the issue was soon forced. The House of Commons drew up the celebrated Petition of Right (1628), which asserted that the royal prerogative could not touch the person or the property of an Englishman. King Charles defied it by trying to raise money on his own, dismissing judges who would not interpret the law to suit him, imprisoning some leaders of the House, making a martyr of the high-minded Sir John Eliot. For eleven years he managed to rule without a Parliament. Finally, in 1640, he was obliged to summon one again in order to raise money for his war with the Scots; and the struggle then came to a head.

Instead of taxes the "Short Parliament" voted for a redress of its grievances, so it was abruptly sent home. A few months later the successes
of the Scots forced Charles to try again, this time to a quite different effect: the "Long Parliament" virtually took over the government, refusing ever to go home. Led by the House of Commons, it
secured the arrest and execution of his fearless chief councilor, the Earl
of Strafford ("Black Tom Tyrant"), on a charge of treason against the
nation; it pushed through acts providing for regular meetings of Parliament and prohibiting its own dissolution; it abolished the Star Chamber and other seats of royal power; it demanded control of the Militia,
which by law and custom had always been commanded by the king—
it went so far and so fast that Charles might be forgiven his attempt to
arrest its leaders. Only this act was as ill-advised as strictly illegal: it
brought on open civil war. The Long Parliament then won its way
with the aid of Oliver Cromwell's New Model Army. Charles had no
reason to rejoice when the army finally sent home many of its members, expelling them, for the remaining Rump Parliament set up a
court that tried and sentenced him for treason; and in 1649 he was
duly beheaded.

By this time the Revolution had carried far beyond the purposes of
the men who started it. Typically British, Coke and others had not
thought of themselves as revolutionaries at all, but had stood out as
conservatives. The House of Commons was only trying to preserve the
traditional rights of Englishmen, only resisting a misguided king, not
attacking the crown itself. When the Long Parliament went to work,
however, a new note was sounded. Henry Marten remarked that he
did not think one man was wise enough to govern all—"the first word
I ever heard man speak to that purpose," noted Clarendon, the royal
historian. (So sensible men always greet ideas destined to be the common sense of the future: "I never heard of such a thing in my life.")
New elections to Parliament in 1645 brought in men who were to join
Marten in forming the "Commonwealth party"; this held that monarchy was "neither good in itself nor for us." The House of Commons
opened the fateful year 1649 by passing three resolutions: that the people were the source of all just power, that as representatives of the
people the Commons held supreme power, and that whatever laws it
enacted needed the consent of neither the king nor the House of Lords.
A month later it finished the job of making England a republic by
abolishing the monarchy and the House of Lords.

By this time even more radical ideas were abroad. For the most part these came directly out of Puritanism, which had been realizing the logic or the license of Protestantism by steadily breeding new modes of dissent and revolt; so we are brought back to the major role of the Puritans from the outset.[5] Outspoken and aggressive enough to earn the dislike of Queen Elizabeth, they became ever more troublesome under the Stuarts, in Parliament and out, intensifying the political struggle against the monarch by making it a religious struggle against the state church too. They provided most of the drive that led to open rebellion, and then made it an out-and-out revolution by beheading King Charles. Their role was quite plain, positive, easy to understand. It was also highly confused and ambiguous, as easy to misunderstand or misjudge. For although the Puritans were generally of the middle class, they were at this time no more typically bourgeois than typically English, but immoderate men of unwonted religious fervor, because of whom the first great revolution in the Western world was the last in which religion was a major factor. Mostly intolerant and illiberal on self-righteous principle, scarcely devoted to any disinterested ideal of freedom, they nevertheless did most to make the conflict a struggle for freedom. As they all sought religious freedom for themselves, some began to realize the practical if not the logical necessity of conceding it to others, even to demand an absolute separation of church and state; then some others were led to assert a democratic creed as foreign to the intent of Coke as of Calvin, shocking to the orthodox among them; while all along even the orthodox were committed to attitudes potentially more revolutionary than they knew, contradictions that helped to overthrow absolutism in both church and state.

In spite of the many and increasing differences among these offspring of Calvinism, they were akin in being literally "puritans": men unwilling to compromise or muddle, unhappy over the sensible or impure middle way taken by the Anglican Church, bent on making the English Reformation a real reformation by establishing the "holy community" here and now. They were united in a common dynamic faith, dramatized by preachers who had more apparent influence than the ministry had ever had before them, or has ever had since. It was most conspicuously a grim faith that may now seem morbid in its obsession with

---

[5] Catholic opposition to the king was a negligible factor, as the Catholic cause had been discredited by the exposure of the Gunpowder Plot in 1605; this virtually ended the heroic, subversive efforts of the Jesuit fifth columnists in England. In taking over the religious opposition, the Puritans gave little comfort to the Jesuits when they acted on their teaching that orthodox subjects have a right to depose heretical kings.

natural depravity, worldly temptation, and the dangers of hellfire, which earned its description as "the haunting fear that someone, somewhere, may be happy." It made the Christian life no mere pilgrimage but an unremitting warfare against the Devil in his manifold guises; preachers constantly drew on military metaphors in exhorting their followers to keep in spiritual fighting trim, while many of the "fighting saints" kept diaries in which they daily notched their victories and their setbacks. If good works alone could never save the Puritan, they were nonetheless essential in this "Christian warfare"; for only by strenuous experience could he know that by the grace of God he was one of the Elect.

Yet he could know. The historical record of the Puritans makes it plain that they lived no more in fear and trembling than in a spirit of resignation to their predestined fate, but had been filled with courage and self-confidence. Their vivid awareness that salvation was always a "tough work" was as invigorating an awareness that it was always possible; the preachers who girded them for the daily battle were bound to intimate that all men who strove hard enough might be saved, but they also told "how a man may know whether he be the child of God or no," and then grow in purity and grace. The countless volumes of sermons included such suggestive titles as *The New Covenant, The New Birth*—a new hope for Christendom. In effect, the preachers finally stressed not so much the fall of man as the possibility of redemption, not so much his natural depravity as his perfectibility. Some went on specifically to preach a gospel of universal grace, but the Puritans as a whole foreshadowed the modern faith in progress.

At the same time they realized most fully the revolutionary implications of the Protestant spirit of individualism and nonconformity. Lacking the political power to lay down the law, the preachers had to stress the responsibility of the individual, and thus tended to make him more independent than most of them really wanted. However obscurantist their dogma, they likewise strengthened a tendency to rationalism, for ancient custom or tradition was no sign of truth to the Puritan. As Milton insisted, custom was allied rather with error; the whole past looked to him like no march of Providence but a puddle of error and evil—pretty much as it looked to the men of the Enlightenment. And some of the embattled reformers also anticipated the Enlightenment by concluding that the "Christian liberty" all Puritans harped on included liberty of conscience. In their self-righteous zeal to impose righteousness, most of them long agreed that such liberty was "spiritual

whoredom"; but from their experience, by their faith, others learned
that a Christian must be responsible to his own conscience, against
whatever human authority or institution.

For such reasons, too, the Puritan gospel was basically democratic
even though few expressed any desire for political democracy. In the
spirit of early Christianity, the preachers were consciously democratic
in their style of speech. As one observed, the Holy Ghost in Scripture
"hath used great simplicity and wonderful plainness" instead of a lofty
or learned style, writing in a manner "fit for the capacity of all because
it was for the use of all"; hence they made a point of speaking in plain
English. By their endless sermons they also intimated the idea of equality, if only in depravity—the ordinary man was no worse than the noble;
what counted was not birth or rank but character built by "tough
work." And the Puritan congregation was itself a school of democracy.
Necessarily a voluntary association based on free consent, it bred a
habit of free and equal discussion corresponding to the tradition of
parliamentary debate. Its members could and did withstand the oppressive tendencies of their ministers by freely withdrawing, forming new
congregations of their own. A true church, said John Milton, might
consist of a single member.

On English earth, accordingly, Puritanism ran something like a predestined course, beginning with the fate of the Presbyterians, its main
body. Good Calvinists, they were devoted to the ideal of a theocracy
headed by "presbyters," or elders, and so fought to replace the Anglican
Church with their own established church, like the Church of Scotland.
As they controlled the Long Parliament they won their way, proclaiming Presbyterianism the state religion; but already they had lost control
of Puritanism. Left-wingers known as Independents or Congregationalists had been rapidly gaining influence, especially in the New Model
Army. These agreed with Milton: "*New Presbyter* is but *Old Priest*
writ large"; they wanted independent congregations, each free to manage its own affairs without interference by either ecclesiastical or political authority. They were therefore more open to republican principles,
joining the Commonwealth party while the Presbyterians grew friend-
lier to the principle of monarchy. In the victorious army they held the
famous free debates that issued in the Agreements of the People, and
they then broke up the Long Parliament, which was no longer clearly
representative of the will of the people.

The Independents in turn soon went the way of nonconformity, impelled to various kinds and degrees of independence in belief. We

need not dwell here on the many sects into which Puritanism kept splintering, from Separatists, Baptists, Arminians, and Millennarians to Dippers, Salmonists, Bidellians, Traskites, Philadelphians, and Christadelphians. Suffice it that as the independent spirit of the Puritans led. many to radicalism, so their confidence led many others to varieties of utopianism far beyond the dreams of Calvin's Geneva. Otherwise the very confusion helped to impress the more moderate among them and their allies with the necessity of tolerance, and of more secular arguments for political and religious freedom. Such eminent opponents of the Stuarts as John Pym, John Goodwin, Henry Parker, John Selden, and Sir Henry Vane drew on the older tradition of Renaissance humanism and rationalism, stemming from Erasmus.[6] Similarly the Anglican opponents of Puritanism included some liberal men who were repelled by its narrowness and harshness. Even Archbishop Laud, due to be executed as the archpersecutor, was no inquisitor but a well-meaning little man, more rash than cruel in his efforts to enforce good manners and good sense in religion; while his godson William Chillingworth wrote an admirable book on behalf of a reasonable Christian faith, decrying the traditional belief that there was only one true way to heaven. These saner voices were mostly drowned out in the contemporary uproar; yet they are the voices that continued to sound long after the Revolution, the more persuasively because they had lost the ring of novelty, become the muted common sense of Englishmen.

So we might pause over John Milton, the greatest of the Puritan writers, and in his own day one of the least effectual. Beginning as an ardent Presbyterian, dreaming of a godly new commonwealth, he came by his republican principles with the aid of the classical tradition he reverenced. (He incidentally owed much to the Machiavelli of the republican *Discourses*.) Though he was hardly consistent as a political thinker, he kept sounding a cry for liberty impassioned enough to earn him some reputation as a godless "libertine." When the Long Parliament decreed that all books and tracts had to be licensed, he promptly

---

[6] One sign of this spirit was the translation of the *Satanae Stratagemata* of Acontius, an early champion of freedom of conscience who had been favored by Queen Elizabeth; it maintained that no man or party was infallible, and that Satan had no more powerful ally than intellectual and spiritual pride. Another such almost forgotten work—a reminder again of the innumerable obscure men of good will who in their day labored for unpopular causes we now take for granted—was *The Last Book of John Smyth Called the Retraction of his Errors, and the Confirmation of the Truth*. Written by a Puritan preacher, an exile in Holland, this was a moving confession of a lifetime spent in ardent, bitter, futile controversy, from which he had at last learned the wisdom of charity, the virtue of tolerance.

published—without license—his *Areopagitica*. Freedom of thought and speech, he maintained, was essential to the cause both of truth and of virtue, which required the knowledge of good and evil learned by Adam. Though his classic plea for a free press was not celebrated at the time, or heeded at all by those in power, Milton had drawn to a head a fundamental issue of modern history, which the Puritans were the first to dramatize on a national scale.

Like all European monarchs, Queen Elizabeth had taken for granted the necessity of keeping the press under royal censorship (one printer was hanged, drawn, and quartered for publishing a seditious book), and the Stuarts naturally tried to tighten the censorship. Nevertheless, the market was soon flooded with books and pamphlets, a great many of them by Puritan preachers. The punitive efforts of the authorities only swelled the popularity of such men as John Lilburne, a demagogue-saint who in the pillory kept on declaiming, and from prison managed to keep issuing a stream of manifestoes. When the Long Parliament assembled, still more tracts came seething off the presses of London. (One farsighted bookseller who tried to collect a copy of everything that came out managed to gather about a thousand items a year.) The Puritans thus built up a habit of reading that enormously increased the power of the press. They launched what amounted to the first major effort at popular education by open discussion—an indispensable preliminary of popular government. Once in power, their leaders soon made it clear that their volubility was no belief in freedom of the press; but as censors they were no more effectual than the Stuarts had been. While they might gag or intimidate some men, they were unable to prevent the most earnest from speaking out, as Milton did, or to discourage their congregations from continuing to read for themselves. Again Protestantism had started something it could not stop.

The most remarkable outcome of all this popular agitation was the emergence of the Levellers, from the ranks of the common soldiers who won the Revolution—men representing another lost cause, which was to be the great cause of the future. Whereas the men who started the revolution wanted only constitutional government, or rule by law, the Levellers called for popular government, rule by the majority. Mostly devout Puritans, they wanted an essentially Christian kind of democracy rather different from the modern kind, with more stress on equality than freedom. Yet this principle of equality was indeed revolutionary when translated into political terms, and they at least made clear its imtimate connection with freedom, even its necessity to secure real freedom for the many.

Immediately they exposed the hollowness of all the cloudy, abstract talk about the "sovereignty of the people" from the Middle Ages down. Medieval theologians had been quite unconcerned over the fact that the sovereign people mostly had no actual voice in their government, and had not chosen their serfdom; Renaissance humanists usually had little respect for the common people, no desire at all to enfranchise them; and now that the Puritan Revolution was won its leaders talked like Marxist bourgeois, revealing that by the sovereign "English people" they meant the people of property. The Levellers were the first to demand not only equal justice before the law but equal suffrage. Colonel Rainborough (the one senior officer among them) put their case simply: "Really I think that the poorest he that is in England hath a life to live as the greatest he; and therefore truly, Sir, I think it is clear that every man that is to live under a Government ought first by his own consent to put himself under that Government." When told that only the landed and trading interests had a permanent interest in government, and therefore a right to participate in it, Rainborough replied, "I do hear nothing at all that can convince me why any man that is born in England ought not to have his voice in election of Burgesses." As the conservatives also pointed out that the historic rights of Englishmen had never included such equality, the Levellers gave a new interpretation to the traditional doctrine of natural law: by this still unwritten law of God, all men were born with natural rights, equal and inalienable, which it was the main duty of government to protect. And as they were a minority, they anticipated another fundamental principle of modern democracy, seeking to restrain the possible tyranny of the majority too: they asserted that Parliament itself had no right to infringe on the "native rights" of all men.

Puritan leaders, alarmed as respectable Christians have always been by men who took seriously the Christian doctrine of equality, were as modern in denouncing the Levellers as communists. Actually the dissidents did not call for equalization of property, leveling of all class distinction, or any such communism as the early followers of Jesus indulged in. But this possible implication of their creed was seized on by the much smaller sect known as the Diggers, represented in print by Gerrard Winstanley. Called by Jesus Christ, the "head Leveller," these men began digging up enclosed land, sowing it with vegetables, and in a manifesto explained that all landlords were violating the commandment "Thou shalt not steal" by expropriating the common treasury God had created for beasts and man. In *The Law of Freedom,* dedicated to "All the Nations of the Earth," Winstanley argued that poverty was the root of all tyranny and injustice. In proposing to do something about it, he attacked the ministers who had been telling the poor that what Jesus meant when he said they shall inherit the earth was "inward satisfaction of mind," or spiritual freedom. We need not go into the details of the new social system he proposed, in which the land would belong to all and buying and selling would be replaced by communistic exchange; modern socialists studied him no more than his contemporaries did. Yet Winstanley stands out as one of the most significant thinkers of the time, the more because he stood alone. He was the only one who was deeply concerned about poverty, the actual condition of ordinary men in the "holy community" of Puritanism. If his proletarian utopia has a quaint air, he was more realistic than all his hardheaded or roundheaded contemporaries in recognizing that talk about political liberty and equality meant little unless one took seriously the social economy, the well-being of the common man. The talk went on; so it turned out that his was the prophetic voice crying in the wilderness.

At the time, of course, the Diggers were promptly suppressed. Unfortunately, the time was 1649—the very beginning of the Puritan Commonwealth. In victory the fighting saints were establishing neither a holy nor a republican community. We must now consider the consequences of the first major political revolution in Western history.

Having grown accustomed to revolutions since then, and recently less disposed to idealize them, we all know the pat story. The moderate, reasonable party loses control; zealots and extremists take over, usually by violence; the ideals that inspired the revolution go down with its enemies, usually in a reign of terror; and the usual end is tyranny or dictatorship. Up to a point, this was indeed the story of the English Revolution. The execution of King Charles was clearly the work of extremists, deplored by the great majority of Englishmen. In the aftermath the ideal cause of the revolution was as clearly betrayed by his executioners; Oliver Cromwell, the man in armor, soon dissolved Parliament and set up his Protectorate, a military dictatorship that anticipated Napoleon. Still, the English did not wholly abide by the as yet unwritten book on revolution. There was no bloody reign of terror, just as there had been little atrocity during the Civil War. In one sense the moderates came out on top—the party of the center, represented by Cromwell, who put down both the Presbyterians on the right and the Levellers on the left. That in another aspect both zealots and moderates were disappointed by the outcome suggests some typical confusion, and the usual need of wariness against pat conclusions.

Thus the Revolution hardly sealed the triumph of the bourgeoisie. It was no victory for "capitalism": the City of London—purged more than once because of its royalist tendencies—was not the power behind Cromwell's throne. Neither was the aristocracy crushed by its defeat, for it became considerably stronger in the aftermath and the century following. What triumphed immediately was the broader interest of property, dear alike to the nobility and the upper middle class. The famous debates held by the New Model Army, made famous especially by the arguments of the Levellers, were won by their opponents. Henry Ireton, Cromwell's chief subordinate, attacked the whole theory of natural law and "native rights" as an invitation to anarchy or communism; a sincere believer in constitutional government, he believed as sincerely that it must be controlled by men of property. "All the main thing that I speak for," he said (with a fervor that overrode grammar too), "is because I would have an eye to property." Cromwell, a country gentleman, had a more jaundiced eye of the same kind. He branded the Levellers as even more dangerous than the royalists, "differing little from beasts," and laid it down that if England must needs suffer, "it should rather suffer from rich men than from poor men." Under his military Protectorate the country did not suffer from poor men.

No more did it run the risks of republicanism. When in 1657 Cromwell became hereditary Lord Protector—almost a king in name—this only underlined the fact that all along he had ruled more like the absolute sovereign of Hobbes than the Stuarts had managed to. Yet he forced a deeper, more difficult issue than simple tyranny. Always an earnest Puritan, he was no Napoleon hungry for imperial power and fame, still less a ruthless despot. (He took out his ferocity in slaughter of the enemies of God on the battlefield—in particular such enemies as the Catholic Irish.) For all the dispute over the character of Cromwell and his works, we may at least agree that he meant it when he said, "It is not what they want but what is good for them—that is the question." This is indeed the perennial question, forced two thousand years before Cromwell by Plato in his *Republic*, as later again by the Grand Inquisitor. Hence high-minded men of the time could agree that his iron rule was good for them. "We all willingly yield the palm of sovereignty to your incomparable ability and virtue," wrote John Milton, excepting only those ambitious or envious few "who do not know that nothing in the world is more pleasing to God or agreeable to reason than that the supreme power should be vested in the best and wisest." Cromwell himself dismissed the malcontents in the spirit of the Grand Inquisitor: "The people will prefer their real security to forms."

Whatever their preference, the people had to do without the forms of a genuine commonwealth. It is very doubtful whether Cromwell's Protectorate could have survived a free general election, but it is certain that he gave the people no such chance. And the perennial question remains open because at his death it became apparent that his rule had not been really good for them, at least not for the long run. The hereditary Lord Protector left the people only his son Richard, with a godly premonition: "Who knoweth whether he may beget a wise man or a fool?" Richard was neither a wise man nor a strong man. He carried on for some months in the uncertain, unconstitutional role of Lord Protector, amid growing opposition and confusion; even the surviving Levellers intrigued for the return of an honest-to-god king; the Rump Parliament was put together again; and in 1660 the nation turned for "real security" to the dissolute King Charles II. Said the House of Commons: "We submit and oblige ourselves and our posterities to your Majesty for ever."

It set the tone of the obscene aftermath, in which all parties submitted. Sir Henry Vane, greatest of the surviving republicans, was executed. Thinkers vied in extolling the principle of absolute monarchy, Sir Robert Filmer even tracing the sovereignty of the Stuarts to Adam and the Patriarchs. The University of Oxford formally condemned all republican principles, as dutifully banned the works of Milton from its Bodleian Library. Liberty survived most obviously in the notorious license of the Restoration period: an understandable revulsion against the as notorious illiberality of the Puritans—the joyless, humorless zeal expressed in their blue laws and their suppression of the theater—which also emphasized the corruption likely to follow in the wake of revolutionary upheavals, the letdown from the strain of high causes. In *The Character of a Trimmer* Lord Halifax cynically summed up the spirit of the age. While owning a "passion for liberty," the Trimmer noted that the English were not fit for a commonwealth, much preferring the bells and tinsel of monarchy: "there must be milk for babes since the greatest part of mankind are and ever will be included in that lot."

Still, he was a trimmer—not a devoted believer in monarchy. He was contemptuous of Louis XIV, then at the height of his glory, describing him as a vain creature blown up by false worship, "not only an encumbrance, but a common nuisance to mankind." A sincere patriot too, he found it expedient to trim because many other Englishmen had some passion for liberty. If the Commonwealth was dead, so was the principle of absolutism, in both church and state. Like most of the revolutions to come, the Puritan Revolution ended immediately in failure, but its failure was by no means the historic end of the whole drama. As clear in retrospect are the lasting gains, which even the doomed Commonwealth helped to consolidate.

"When civil liberty is entire," wrote James Harrington, the deepest political thinker of the period, "it includes liberty of conscience; when liberty of conscience is entire it includes civil liberty."[7] Though both liberties were far from entire when he wrote (or for that matter are today) he pointed to the fundamental connection that the Puritans had begun to realize under the pressure of events. As an Independent, Cromwell upheld the "natural right" of liberty of conscience. His tolerance was characteristically limited, not extending to Anglicans and Roman Catholics, but he did publicly tolerate all sects—even Jews— except for these dangerous political enemies, and he stepped in to protect individuals from persecution. Above all, he showed some favor to the apparently seditious Quakers, followers of George Fox. Small as this sect was, its rise may be considered the most significant religious development of the period. Quakerism was the ripest form of Protestantism: a religion purely of the spirit or the inner light, in which every man was indeed a priest, as Martin Luther had said and forgotten. It was the most democratic of the sects, the most consistent in upholding the equal rights of men, even of women—Fox was so bold as to say that women too were priests. (Gerrard Winstanley ended in the haven of Quakerism.) And it was prophetic in its open disavowal of original sin, its assertion of the essential goodness instead of the depravity of man.

Accordingly the cause of civil liberty was far from dead either. The arrest of John Lilburne at the outset of the Commonwealth brought on another flood of petitions; and he was acquitted, to an "extraordinary great hum," even though he had published the most violent of his tracts, *The Impeachment of High Treason against Cromwell and Ireton*— a performance unthinkable in the France of Louis XIV. (Lilburne too ended as a Quaker.) Thereafter the rigor of official censorship was

---

[7] Harrington's *Oceana* (1656), though now little read, made a considerable impression on thinkers after him, notably Hume and John Adams. No Puritan himself, he most clearly perceived the social causes of the revolution, and offered the most philosophical, secular argument for a constitutional commonwealth. He would call for more attention here were it not that his ideal was an antique kind of aristocratic republic, not in the line of the future; but at that it anticipated some institutions of popular government, such as compulsory public education.

matched by the resolution of "seditous" writers. The autocratic rule of Cromwell himself, moreover, was qualified by repeated, even pathetic efforts decently to legitimatize his rule, win the consent of the governed. Having done away with the Rump Parliament for the good reason that it was bent on perpetuating its own illegal existence, he continued to summon as well as dissolve Parliaments. He ordered burned a book that identified the right to power with simple possession of it; he refused the crown that was offered him. In keeping with his declared belief in a "Fundamental Law" of the state "somewhat like a Magna Carta," standing and unalterable, he twice tried to give England something it has never had—a written constitution. The English have come to believe that anything so definite, precise, and rigid as a written constitution is contrary to their political genius, but even so Cromwell's efforts were statesmanlike, characteristically earnest, not merely expedient. They help to explain the saying that he founded the English Constitution.

There remains the most obvious, significant fact, that a generation after Cromwell came the "Glorious Revolution." Possibly this might have come about had there been no Puritan Revolution. It is unlikely, however, and still more unlikely that the affair would have been so free from violence. This was indeed a very British revolution, not in the least radical, more sensible than glorious, unlit by flaming idealism, hardly a revolution at all by continental standards. Yet it did unseat a king, bring in a new regime; it could proceed without benefit of new ideas or high idealism because its issues had already been thought out and fought out; and it permanently won the constitutional rights and liberties of Englishmen, the more readily because conservatives could now believe that they were not really won, but only conserved.

4. *The Glorious Revolution*

In the brief honeymoon of the Restoration most Englishmen kept their heads. Oliver Cromwell still served the cause of commonwealth, being exhumed and hanged as the national scapegoat; otherwise King Charles II and his ministers were too wise to call for the blood of the regicides, contenting themselves with the execution of a dozen or so. The Restoration itself had been a constitutional performance, as it was Parliament that summoned the king. He proceeded to confirm the basic concessions that Charles I had been forced to make to the Long Parliament. Royalist nobles and dons might talk wildly of the absolute divine right of monarchs, but Charles II knew better. Although it remained unclear just how much authority Parliament had, he never tried to exercise all the prerogatives that James I had claimed, and by his very skill as a politician he tacitly recognized its authority. The ambassador of Louis XIV reported that this government had a monarchical appearance "but at bottom it is very far from being a monarchy." Charles too had some such idea, for despite his initial popularity he did not trust his subjects, remarking that he would never again go on his travels for anything. Soon disenchanted, his subjects made it plain that the spirit of liberty was very much alive. "Every carman and porter is now a statesman," lamented a noble of the old sack-and-claret school, "and indeed the coffee-houses are good for nothing else. . . . These sober clubs produce nothing but scandalous and censorious discourses." The royal censors again had to contend with seditious books.

Even so, the ensuing conflict with Charles II took place on a considerably lower plane of principle than the struggle against his father. Primarily it was due to religious feeling of an unedifying kind. A Cavalier Parliament soon assured opposition by passing harsh laws against the Puritans, henceforth known as Dissenters, the milder provisions of which excluded them from both the universities and political office. The main focus of opposition, however, was now the feeling against Catholics. Enflamed by the "Popish Plot" concocted by Titus Oates, this was both confused and strengthened by the Catholic sympathies of the king. Charles secretly obtained huge sums of money from Louis XIV on the condition that he make England a Catholic country as soon as feasible, and dissolve or suspend his Parliaments; and at least he did his best to corrupt the House of Commons, by bribery and rigged elections. The gold provided by Louis XIV accordingly helped to found the emerging Tory party, backed by the landowners, the Anglican clergy, and the invincibly conservative universities. Controlling Parliament in the last years of Charles' reign, the Tories distinguished themselves by the extravagance of their devotion to the shameless monarch and the fury of their attack on Dissenters.

By contrast the rival Whig party appeared to considerable advantage. Drawing much of its support from the middle class, including unregenerate Puritans, it professed a devotion to the principles of constitutional government. A Whiggish Parliament put through the Habeas Corpus Act of 1679, one of the cornerstones of the amorphous

English Constitution, providing a formal safeguard against illegal imprisonment. But the Whigs appeared to much less advantage when contrasted with the men who stood out against the early Stuarts—Eliot, Pym, Selden, Milton, Vane, and others. The Puritans were now growing more bourgeois, less militant, reserving more of their fervor for the Sabbath, while many of their gentry turned Anglican to protect their social status. The leaders of the party were mostly only politicians, glad to employ such pawns as the loathsome Titus Oates. (They gave him a pension after his perjury was exposed.) To the high-minded Lord Acton his Whig forebears seemed creatures of expediency when not of vulgar prejudice and self-interest, woefully deficient in both philosophy and passion for liberty.[8]

Hence the conflict did not come to a head until James II, an avowed Catholic, ascended the throne in 1685. Though hailed with giddy enthusiasm by the Tories, he managed to alienate many of them too by abusing his prerogatives to advance the interests of Catholics and attack their enemies, going so far as to imprison Anglican bishops. When a son was born to him, Whigs and Tories were united by their fear of a Catholic dynasty. In 1688 some nobles invited William of Orange, husband of James II's daughter Mary, to come to the rescue of England, and William obliged by landing with an army, favored in crossing the Channel by a "Protestant wind" such as had wrecked the Spanish Armada just a century before. At that, James might well have hung on to his throne had he not taken fright and fled to the court of Louis XIV. Thereupon the "revolution" was won without a battle. Its most glorious protagonist was the foreigner William, who risked a great deal in assuming the role of savior of "the liberties of England and the Protestant religion." The English also owed much to Pope Innocent XI, who out of fear of the arrogant Louis XIV discouraged other Catholics from attacking the Dutch savior. Louis did his bit by providing a threat grave enough to keep the nation united.

Nevertheless, the English now rose to their opportunity with a good sense much more uncommon than heroism. Early in 1689 Parliament drew up the Revolution Settlement, the terms on which it offered the throne to William and Mary. Having thrown a sop to the Tories by

---

[8] The names of England's two great parties were suitably unseemly in origin. Titus Oates was fond of calling anyone who doubted his word a "Tory," the name for the Catholic bandits who preyed on Saxon settlers in Ireland; and his enemies retaliated by calling his supporters "Whigs," meaning the Scotch Covenanters who went in for murdering bishops.

proclaiming that James had "abdicated" the throne, it defined these terms as a reaffirmation of the "true, ancient, and indubitable rights of the people of this realm," and thereby wrote the English Bill of Rights. As for government, it declared that no taxes could be levied, no standing army maintained, and no laws passed or suspended without the consent of Parliament, and that Parliament should be held frequently, election to it and debate within it should be free from any interference. This was all quite conservative, quite legal; so Edmund Burke could rhapsodize over the most "happy" of revolutions, which merely confirmed tradition and introduced no real innovation. Yet it did firmly establish precedent for all time by definitely limiting the power of the monarch, finally spelling out all the basic principles of constitutional government, and swearing the new monarchs to uphold these principles; so Lord Acton could say that the unexalted Whigs of this generation "did more for freedom than any body of men who ever appeared on earth."

In the same year Parliament passed the Toleration Act granting Dissenters freedom of worship—William's answer to the Revocation of the Edict of Nantes by Louis XIV. This now looks like an especially muddled compromise, since out of deference to the Tories it hedged toleration with weird restrictions on civil and political rights that lasted for more than a century; but at least it secured the principle of freedom of worship, and the spirit of toleration soon grew so strong that in practice Catholics too were allowed to worship publicly. A few years later England caught up with Milton's dream of "liberty of unlicensed printing" as censorship was allowed to lapse. Earlier William III had assured an independent judiciary by an executive act appointing judges for life, or on duration of good behavior as determined by Parliament—not the king.

William added to his glory, with the aid of his great general Marlborough, by successfully prosecuting the wars against Louis XIV, who sought to restore James II to the throne. But in so doing he made his major contribution to England by scrupulously adhering to both the letter and the spirit of the Revolution Settlement. He was a strong king, the stronger because he worked with instead of against Parliament. In selecting his ministers, who by accepted theory were still responsible to him alone, he began learning the lesson of the future, that he could accomplish most by choosing ministers able to get the support of Parliament. By such tact he succeeded in giving England the first modern fiscal system, creating the Bank of England and establishing a regularized national debt; he had no trouble financing the wars that bankrupted the government of Louis XIV. Altogether, he helped to assure the real glory of the Revolution: without violence it permanently settled the basic issues that in inglorious ways had brought it on. Thereafter no king ever seriously disputed the essential powers of Parliament or tampered with the laws that protected the basic rights of Englishmen.

The Glorious Revolution was too successful, indeed, as Englishmen waxed so complacent over their Constitution that for a century and a half they resisted all effort at further reform; so presently we must consider the severe limitations of their government by democratic standards. Meanwhile it was more important that the freest of the large nations in Europe enjoyed the stablest government, the largest measure of internal peace. The English could learn to assume the responsibilities of their rights, build up the habits necessary for the maintenance of a free society. The House of Commons, secure in its powers, could atone for the possible stupidity or injustice of its ordinances by cultivating the essentials of political rationality, the simple willingness to listen to the reasons of the other side. In particular the English began developing their distinctive party system. Whigs and Tories would often look as selfish or low-minded as their forebears under the Stuarts, and they were always prone to a narrow factionalism as they put party loyalty first; yet they never succumbed to the obvious dangers of an uncompromising, violent factionalism. As they had managed to reconcile their differences in the Revolution Settlement, so they learned to get along well enough to make further revolutions unnecessary, almost unthinkable. They established the all-important tradition of a loyal opposition.

For such reasons the English system of government was long misunderstood by foreign observers, or for that matter by the English themselves. Thinkers looked for a definite, logical system—something the mother of parliaments did not bother her head about, just as she neglected to write her Constitution; they therefore overlooked the engrained attitudes or habits of thought that most clearly protected the rights of Englishmen. Thus Montesquieu saw the genius of English government in the separation or balance of powers, whereas in fact there was no precise separation, and the House of Commons was well on its way to becoming the supreme power. Under the Hanoverian dynasty of Georges—about the sorriest set of kings in eighteenth-century Europe—the monarch was losing in practice his ill-defined executive powers in theory, so that bad kings were rendered harmless by a tradition that could still make some use of good ones; though as far as law and the Constitution went (or still go) the king might disband the army, sell the navy, trade off some counties to other nations, pardon all criminals, make every Englishman a lord. Likewise there was no prescribed check on Parliament, which overnight might legally repeal the Bill of Rights. And already a new system was emerging, under which the actual ruler of the country would not be Parliament but the Cabinet, headed by a Prime Minister—a system not provided for by the Constitution, not created by an Act of Parliament, not even wanted by Parliament or people. Jealous of the king's ministers, the House of Commons tried to prevent them from sitting in it; while the idea of a prime minister was so abhorrent that Sir Robert Walpole, who early in the eighteenth century was exercising the full powers of one, repudiated the title. More than a century later Walter Bagehot observed that every cabman knew of Buckingham Palace but most had never heard of "Downing Street," the real seat of the government. Quite unconsciously the English evolved this admirable device for assuring strong, undivided executive power, unhampered by the jealousy of legislators, while keeping it responsible to Parliament and the electorate.

Well before this, however, the rest of western Europe had got the main idea. Under parliamentary government, supposedly weak, fractious, and inefficient, England had proved more than a match for the Grand Monarchy of Louis XIV, who commanded about three times as many people. Such republican government had been considered at best a kind of antique luxury that only little countries like Holland and Switzerland could afford. Now a large modern nation was not only managing it but enjoying increasing power and prosperity. English thought acquired a considerable vogue on the continent, especially in France, which in the Age of Louis XIV still knew almost nothing about England. (The earliest French guidebook described it as a land full of demons and parricides; later writers added wolves and fanatics.) And the political thought that was most influential came directly out of the Glorious Revolution. It was above all the thought of John Locke—the philosopher who rationalized the Revolution, and who serves almost perfectly to sum up and round out the whole story to this stage.

As a Puritan, for some years an exile in Holland, Locke was heir to the thought and feeling of the Independents in the earlier Revolution. He also drew on the ideal medieval theory of government as it came down through the "judicious Hooker," including the doctrine of natural law that Bacon and others had authorized as the dictate of "natural reason," and that Coke had more or less identified with the common law of England. He reflected all the major developments of the past two centuries—the humanism of the Renaissance, the discovery of the New World, the rise of the middle class, and especially the rise of science. Hence Locke was quite different from the generation of Puritans before him—less dogmatic and intolerant, if as much less fervent. Temperamentally a man of common sense, philosophically an empiricist, he offered a political theory that was essentially secular, available to men of different faiths, and conducive to more than "Christian liberty."

Although his theory rested on the ancient idea of the social contract, Locke gave this idea a new twist by interpreting it in the light of English experience. He insisted more emphatically that government rested on the consent of the governed, under a contract binding on both parties to it, and he explicitly declared a right of revolution if the rulers violated the terms of the contract. He took a much more optimistic view than Hobbes of "the state of nature," conceiving it as implicitly a civil state, not an anarchic war of all against all, because man is born rational as well as free. "The state of nature has a law of nature to govern it which obliges every one; and reason, which is that law, teaches all mankind who will but consult it that, being all equal and independent, no one ought to harm another in his life, health, liberty, or possessions." Government was necessary only because some men failed to consult this natural law, looking instead to their immediate self-interest, yet it by no means rested on force and fear alone; society was civil because most men could be reasonable enough. Most important, Locke drew from natural law the immensely influential principle of natural rights. Reason taught the self-evident truth that every man is born with indefeasible rights to life, liberty, and property, which it was the main business of government to protect.

Now, it is easy to point out that Locke was often shallow, vague, or muddled, in particular on his not at all self-evident doctrine of natural rights. He himself had refuted the doctrine of innate ideas, he never critically analyzed his premise of natural law, and he never offered or could offer empirical proof of his proposition that all men are born with indefeasible rights. He was as absent-minded in his optimistic assumption that the protection of private rights necessarily promoted the common welfare—an assumption that at most reflected the experience, or the interests, of his class of Englishmen. Hence the "natural man" he pictured was essentially a decent country gentleman, a born Whig; and in arguing for the right of resistance to tyrannical government he tacitly assumed a revolution in which almost no one would be killed—the kind of revolution he was rationalizing. Hardly anticipating more revolutions, much less wishing to stir them up, he remained vague on how or when men should openly resist tyranny, go beyond "the appeal to Heaven." He might have been almost as shocked as Edmund Burke was by the French Revolution, when men took literally his axiom of natural rights.

We shall have to keep returning to the issues raised by this axiom, which became the common sense of the Age of Enlightenment, and in the next century looked more like plain nonsense. But first it recalls us to the primary consideration—the actual revolutionary influence of Locke, in the service of the cause of freedom. The American Declaration of Independence, beginning with an almost verbatim restatement of his political theory, is only the plainest example of it. For Locke did make much good sense. He at least held consistently to the logic of the social contract, that government is properly the servant of the people, rulers are always accountable to the ruled, going so far as to say that absolute monarchy was "inconsistent with civil society." As firmly as he adhered to his moral conviction of the dignity of man, the necessary basis for any logical claims to human rights. He made out a reasonable case for the need of liberty for a potentially rational being, as man must be considered if government by free consent is to mean anything. Even his optimism was reasonable in view of English experience, which indicated that freedom under law, or a bill of private rights, might indeed promote the common good, including the cause of strong government.

In the same view, at the risk of some injustice to his liberal intentions, we may then return to Locke's limitations as a bourgeois philosopher. His objective was constitutional, not popular or democratic government; he was nothing of a Leveller, shying away from the political conclusions that might be drawn from the principle of equality implicit in his doctrine of natural rights. The cue was the axiom he offered the bourgeois, that "the great and chief end . . . of men uniting into commonwealths and putting themselves under government is the preservation of their property." In considering private property a natural right, Locke had his eye on the home and the personal possessions that men naturally do hold precious, and in arguing that men were equally entitled to the fruits of their labor he was still true to the experience of the middle class, who had largely earned their money; yet he ended in a hopeless muddle. While he admitted that most property in his day was in fact conventional, not natural, he neglected to push this idea; he went on maintaining that all property was inviolate. Neither did he look closely into how most property had been acquired, such as the landed estates—the fruits of other men's labor—handed down by inheritance. He showed little concern over the majority who owned no property, went without their natural right, even though he remarked that his theory required that the people should have property, else they would lose the very end for which they had entered into the social contract—"too gross an absurdity for any man to own." It was not too gross for property owners thereafter: to them the absurdity was that men without property should claim a voice in the government. Locke was weak in theory on the rights of minorities, but in effect as weak on the rights of the majority too.

Hence we must finally note that the Glorious Revolution was no more a democratic than a philosophical one. Although it was supported by all classes, and secured some rights for all, it led to no effort to extend the political rights or improve the social condition of the common people. If its principles were not positively betrayed, as the Quakers charged, the reason was that its leaders had made no promises to the common people; unlike the revolutions to come, it raised no banner of Liberty, Equality, Fraternity. It assured only the triumph of parliamentary government, and in Parliament only a small minority of Englishmen were directly represented, the working class not at all. Members of the "Commons" had to be wealthy men, not merely because they received no stipend; in 1710 the House ruled that only men with a considerable landed income (amounting to the equivalent of well over $10,000 a year today) were eligible for membership. Throughout the eighteenth century this meant pure class government, whether Whig or Tory. The loyal opposition offered little or no philosophical, principled opposition to the reigning government. If the ruling class was at best public-spirited, it was nevertheless prone to flagrant abuse of its power and privilege. Beginning with the many small "rotten boroughs" that elected M.P.'s, the whole system made for corruption, which spread through all the major institutions; many a cleric and official collected a salary without performing any duties to speak of, while the universities could sell degrees without bothering to teach or examine the buyer. In this respect the "disguised republic" of England was suitably presided over by its gross Hanoverian kings, the first of whom had abominable taste even in mistresses. Symbolizing the ambivalent myth of majesty, the blend of stately ritual and vulgar theater that helped to unite, inspire, and delude the people, they exposed the obverse of the English policy of compromise: a moderation that was typically due to caution rather than insight, could be a flabby complacence, and generally supported the habit of avoiding the effort at hard, clear thinking.

All in all, Englishmen still had ample reason for their pride as they consolidated the gains of the Glorious Revolution. Through the eighteenth century England remained the freest country in Europe, with the most vigorous press, the most open public debate, the most influential public opinion. A reviewer was only stating the consensus when in 1775 he described the English Constitution as "without doubt the most perfect form of government that ever was devised by human wisdom." Still, it was not quite clear just what was in this most admirable constitution—what liberties it granted and to whom, for what reasons and to what end. Few thinkers were prepared to give a reasoned answer to the reasonable question that would presently be asked by some unfranchised workingmen of Sheffield: "What is the constitution to us if we are nothing to it?" Even as the reviewer wrote, Englishmen in America were starting another revolution for what they called their rights—a revolution that may be viewed as another tribute to this constitution, but was hardly so viewed by the English government. As Americans won their independence and proceeded to write a new constitution of their own, the long process of consolidation in England looked more like a stagnation. Either way, there had been no more creative political thought of consequence after Locke. Having absorbed Locke, France became the main center of ferment.

Chapter Nine | *T H E   A G E   O F*
E N L I G H T E N M E N T

1. *The Ruling Ideas*

Of late the Age of Enlightenment has been going the way of the Renaissance, into the limbo of once celebrated ages. Recent history has been unkind to the optimistic faith it proclaimed. Many writers have been attacking it as the main source of the folly and the evil of our world, describing its faith as at most a "very clever contrivance of human pride." More sympathetic historians have dwelt on the cloudiness and naïveté of this faith, intimating that it was not even clever. Others have remarked that it was unoriginal, much less brilliant than the "Century of Genius," and contributed no really new ideas. Finally some have rebelled against all the popular generalities about the Enlightenment —simplicities belied by thinkers so fundamentally different as Voltaire, Rousseau, Hume, and Kant, not to mention the many lesser men who would have been surprised or scandalized to hear that they lived in an Age of Reason. We now learn that there was no such thing as an "eighteenth-century mind."

As usual, however, such sophistication is also too easy, too simple. It is hardly possible to deny that momentous changes came over western Europe in the eighteenth century, culminating in a great revolution. The "mind" of the century was not discrete and uniform, of course, any more than was the medieval mind; but out of the usual welter of diverse and anomalous tendencies we can readily enough make out certain dominant ones that give the age a distinctive character, a basic continuity if not a clear unity. It was in fact an age of enlightenment by any ordinary rational standards. As unmistakably it effected an emancipation of mind, by not only an actual freedom in thought, a fundamental criticism of traditional belief, but a declared principle of freedom of thought, a militant ideal of rational criticism. It thoroughly earned the abiding hostility of religious and political traditionalists by establishing the basic liberal faith of the modern democracies, ushering in a new age. The student of freedom should realize as always that this was no simple triumph, and today he is obliged to read the works of the Enlightenment in a critical spirit; but his first task remains to understand a revolutionary movement that helped to make such a reading possible, and now imperative.

The ruling ideas of the age were indeed not new. They came directly out of the scientific revolution, as the apostles of the Enlightenment were themselves proud to acknowledge. What was new, however, was the bold, energetic, enthusiastic effort not only to propagate these ideas but to apply them to social as well as intellectual problems. As thinkers the men of the Enlightenment were conscious revolutionaries, very much aware of a "new method of philosophizing" that amounted to a new living faith, the basis for a new social order. If less original than their predecessors, they were in other respects more creative, especially because they exerted a much more apparent influence on society at large.

The obvious lead to their thought remains the conventional one—the key terms that they were wont to capitalize, beginning with Nature and Reason. Although these terms came out of the classical tradition, they now signified a more pronounced shift of interest from supernatural to natural, faith to reason. They stood up on their own, in proud autonomy, no longer overshadowed by such concerns as grace and salvation, at last free from all association with the Devil. They were not mere philosophical abstractions either but honorific terms, freighted with new meanings, or colored by new feeling-tones, owing to the triumph of science. They stood for the pillar of cloud and the pillar of light, beacons on the way to the promised land after long bondage to the past. Alexander Pope wrote the dedicatory verse to the new bible of the Enlightenment:

> Nature and Nature's laws lay hid in night:
> God said, Let Newton be! And all was Light.

Never before had men been so confident that nature was so fully intelligible, and so proper, just an order. There remained metaphysical mysteries, to be sure, but these only proved that metaphysics was foolish and superfluous; the "natural philosophy" of Newton would do for all earthly purposes. Since he had unlocked the secrets of the universe by man's own natural faculties, it followed that human reason was sovereign and self-sufficient. Likewise men might now hope to discover the immutable laws of nature governing man and the social order; from Newton's axiom that "nature is always in harmony with itself" they concluded that it was in harmony with man's purposes too, the source and pattern of both goodness and truth. Science accordingly gave a new authority to the ancient doctrine of natural law, and the modern corollary of natural rights. In the same spirit men sought out the principles of "natural morality" and "natural religion," always equating "natural" with "rational." Hence another ancient Greek idea, restated in Pope's dictum that "the proper study of mankind is man," was given a more radiant meaning, supported by a more benign concept of nature as the guarantor, not the enemy of man's works. Men had the benefit of the optimistic teachings of Christianity, the assumptions of a meaningful universe created by a God of love, which pervaded their feeling when not their thought; while they rejected such seemingly irrational teachings as the idea of a jealous, wrathful God. Above all, they rejected the doctrine of Original Sin. In view of his possession of reason, man was not naturally, incorrigibly depraved. Thinkers differed in sizing up and accounting for the plain fact of evil, and all the grievous evidence of man's irrationality, but they agreed on the essential goodness and perfectibility of human nature.

These optimistic views of Nature, Reason, and Man logically culminated in the crowning faith of the Enlightenment—the novel faith in progress. It was at first not a theory of history, only a general idea that the basic social evils were remediable, and that the future would be better than the past. Exhilarated by their mastery of nature, men felt as they never had before that they might become masters of their fate too. Colin Maclaurin, one of the many disciples of Newton, summed up the new hopes stirred by his triumph: "By proceeding with due care, every age will add to the common stock of knowledge; the mysteries that still lie concealed in Nature may be gradually opened, arts will flourish and increase, mankind will improve, and appear more worthy of their situation in the universe, as they approach more towards a perfect knowledge of Nature." On popular levels this belief came out in the simple, yet extraordinary idea that men could hope to be happier, and that happiness was their due; as Saint-Just would observe, "Happiness is a new idea in Europe." And at length the idea of progress was erected into a formal philosophy of history, notably by Turgot, Condorcet, and Kant. Condorcet epitomized the entire secular faith of the Enlightenment, defining progress in terms of its ruling values, arguing that it was the natural law of history, and concluding that it was inevitable. There was "no limit" to what men might achieve by the power of reason, through science—even "absolute perfection" was almost a certainty.

Condorcet's dreams of the "heavenly city" on earth recall the unmistakably naïve aspects of the Enlightenment. We are obliged to pause over what now seem like elementary fallacies, the more ludicrous in men devoted to reason and science. For these fallacies had much to do with their fervor and their immediate effectiveness, and also with the problems of their heirs—with the reasons why they won the future, and why it has been unkind to them.

To begin with, the Nature they deified was as remote from ordinary experience as their formal or rustic gardens were from jungles and stormy seas. Although they cannot be blamed for failing to anticipate the mysterious, untidy world of quantum physics, any peasant might have told them that nature was neither so perfectly intelligible nor so harmonious an order as dreamed of in their philosophy. As for their doctrine of natural law, the authority they claimed from Newton was got by pure scholastic deduction, and fallacious deduction at that; in any scientific view there was no logical connection whatever between the law of gravitation and the natural rights of man. Worse, their honorific term "natural" was for practical purposes not only vague but dangerously ambiguous. All the custom they deplored as unnatural might as properly be called natural, since it was much older and more nearly universal than the unhistorical standards they set up; while their notions of a natural social order might be arbitrary or artificial. Never clear on just how the children of Nature had managed through the ages to maintain such persistently unnatural behavior, they obscured or evaded the real problem—the ultimate problem of all philosophy and religion—of what is the natural life for man.

Nor did they clarify it by calling it interchangeably the "rational" life. Typically they implied that the Reason they appealed to was cool and clear, dispassionate, wholly objective, so that all men could agree on its dictates—at least if they adhered to "right" reason; but by so qualifying it they only gave themselves away and again evaded the difficult problem, the inability of reasonable men to agree on the right life. In general, they tended to overrate both the theoretical and the practical powers of reason. As they assumed that Newton had revealed the "true system of the world," the "true method of philosophizing," so they often concluded that all rational faiths would finally be reconciled, all real problems finally resolved, in a universally valid philosophy. Meanwhile they assumed that the power of reason was simply a power of light, and that progress in knowledge automatically made for progress in wisdom, virtue, and happiness. Their common idea of man as a rational animal was at once too narrow and too elevated, slighting both the nonrational needs that must condition the life of reason and the irrational drives that always menace it. They had too little of Montaigne's sense of the natural inconstancies and inconsistencies of man, or Pascal's sense of the basic paradoxes of the human condition.

Even short of the extravagances of Condorcet, accordingly, their faith in the progress and perfectibility of man was too simple. While they assumed that progress was natural, at least from the Newtonian era on, in effect they conceived it as a sudden, belated leap into a state that man should always have enjoyed. They had not only little knowledge of the long ages during which man achieved whatever progress he had made, but too little sense of historical development or growth. Chiefly they scorned or resented the past; except for a few ages, such as Periclean Athens, Augustan Rome, and the Italian Renaissance, they saw in it mostly a "code of fraud and woe," a reign of incredible irrationalism. The Middle Ages in particular struck them as so barbarous and benighted that their own enlightenment would seem indeed miraculous, as if God had literally said "Let Newton be!" And the serious trouble with this limited historical sense was no mere failure in respect for the travail of the past: it was a failure to prepare men for the travails of the future, the problems created by their own success. Thinking of progress as a lawful, rational process, by which enlightened men would come naturally into their natural rights, none of the leaders of the Enlightenment anticipated the French Revolution, not to mention its Reign of Terror.

Still, we cannot simply blame them, especially if we lay claim to more historical sense, more respect for the past. We should know that except for the gloomiest prophets, men in the past almost always look shortsighted, and that their foresight may be overlooked because it has become part of our common sense. Enjoying the freedoms that the leaders of the Enlightenment did so much to win, both because and in spite of the simplicities of their ardent faith, men now find it too easy to charge them with all the costs of these freedoms, or to make them the scapegoats for our own failures. They were by no means so foolish as they may seem to critics wise in the ways of revolutions, or weary of them, and blessed or cursed with the further knowledge of the likes of Darwin, Marx, Freud, Spengler, and Pareto. Viewed in their own historical context, their ruling ideas were basically reasonable enough.

However loose their talk about Nature, they were at least looking in a logical direction as they sought grounds for their values. The will of God could no longer do for a Christendom grown sophisticated, hopelessly split over the interpretation of his will. Locke, for example, has been criticized because while identifying natural law with the law of God he failed even to look for it in Scripture, according to him the truly revealed word of God; but had he looked (as indeed he might have) he could not have found it clearly stated there. The works of God offered the only hope of a firm foundation for philosophical knowledge. By "nature," moreover, the men of the Enlightenment often meant human nature, tacitly when not explicitly. It then made more sense to speak of natural laws of justice, corresponding to the needs of a potentially rational animal, or at least to try to ground their norms on the nature of this animal. Similarly with their key term "Reason." It can never be precise, even when written in lower case or given the more modest name of intelligence; but the simple truth remains that they were bound to appeal to it. They saw their society governed by institutions and beliefs that were hallowed by tradition, sanctified by authority, and that nevertheless seemed to them often unjust, barbarous, or absurd; so they had to reject the age-old appeal to custom and authority, the wisdom of the ancestors, and they could do so only in the name of reason, a public standard of truth potentially acceptable to all men regardless of class, nation, or creed.

Granted their tendency to overrate the power of reason, and their own objectivity, their faith in it was generally not so unqualified or extravagant as their fervor implied. In the first place, the leading thinkers of the age were not pure rationalists in the manner of Descartes. They turned away from Descartes, directly attacking the "spirit of system," and took their philosophical cue instead from the empiricism of Locke, which set positive limits to what men could certainly know. Thereupon David Hume demonstrated that even such elemental ideas as matter, mind, and self had no clear basis in experience, and man could no more prove the uniformity of nature than the existence of God—a skepticism too radical for almost all his contemporaries; yet he pointed toward a basic element of skepticism that was essential to the Enlightenment.[1] The final true philosophy that thinkers aspired to still stopped short of the ultimate truth about the cosmos, just as New-

---

[1] Hume concluded his devastating logical analysis on a typically sensible, if possibly illogical note. Expressing dismay over the havoc he had wrought with the claims of reason, he added that "nature herself" dispelled all these clouds of doubt and "cures me of this philosophical melancholy and delirium." The "nature" that did him this charming service was of course simple human nature, not the grand Newtonian synthesis. It recalls that long before Freud, Hume wrote: "Reason is, and ought to be, the slave of the passions, and can never pretend to any other office than to serve and obey them."

ton himself claimed no such truth. "It is a sad lot for our curiosity and our pride," d'Alembert commented, "but it is the lot of humanity." Such skepticism was an immediate reason why thinkers called for freedom of thought—religious absolutism was the major enemy. By the same token, however, they had no doubt that there was such a thing as certain knowledge or truth, and that man could learn a great deal more. The men of the Enlightenment were most attractive in their passion for truth, or in what Kant held was their motto—*Sapere aude,* "Dare to know." In this passion they were liable to dogmatism, as all responsible thinkers are, while to the orthodox they seemed irreverent or irresponsible; and they were also liable to inconsistency, as men of absolute conviction admitting a principle of uncertainty, in effect seeking to combine all the possible values of both faith and doubt. In any case, they conceived reason as a process rather than a pure essence, and science as the unfinished business it actually is.

Their faith in human nature and its perfectibility was likewise qualified. Very few thinkers regarded progress as inevitable, an absolute law of nature or history, or really expected a "heavenly city" on earth. Most had some measure of common sense, even tough-mindedness; no work of the Enlightenment is better known, after all, than *Candide.* They were disposed to some pessimism if only because they saw so much error and evil in the long history of the race, and the forces of superstition, bigotry, and tyranny were still so strong in their own supposedly advanced age. Their optimism came down to the belief that such evils were not simply inevitable; ignorance and superstition could be combated, men could be educated, their condition could be improved. In Kant's words, men were not yet living in an enlightened age, but in an age of enlightenment. Thomas Jefferson summed up a faith that should seem decent and sane if there is any hope at all for man: "Although I do not, with some enthusiasts, believe that the human condition will ever advance to such a state of perfection as that there shall no longer be pain or vice in the world, yet I believe it susceptible of much improvement, and most of all, in matters of government and religion; and that the diffusion of knowledge among the people is to be the instrument by which it is to be effected."

The common ridicule of the apostles of the Enlightenment as enthusiasts drunk on generality and abstraction has obscured both the generosity and the force of their idealism. As their spirit was secular, it may still strike godly men as sinful pride, while sounding quaint in their hymns to "holy Posterity!"—all this fervor on behalf not of God but of unholy men still unborn; yet these proud sinners were spiritual enough to sacrifice their own immediate material interests, crusade without the blessing of special indulgences for their sins. At the same time they were realistic in an ordinary but most important sense. They looked to the immediate source of much apparent evil—unjust laws and irrational institutions. They attacked quite specific practices, such as censorship, religious persecution, judicial torture, and slavery, and they proposed as concrete reforms. They led a humanitarian movement that enlisted both good sense and good will in a belated effort actually to carry out the Christian teaching of the sanctity of the person, or immediately to reduce suffering. It is possible, finally, to make some sense out of even the wildest testaments of their faith. Much of Condorcet's vision may appear reasonable if one substitutes "ought to" or "might" be for what he said "will" or "must" be; but at that he was a fairly remarkable prophet. He foresaw not only a continued advance in the various sciences but a marked increase in population and in length of life, a broad gain in material well-being and leisure, a spread of popular education, a provision for more social security, an extension of political rights to common men, and an awakening of the "backward peoples" of the earth to share in all these goods. Call him ridiculous, Condorcet may then appear sublime: a victim of the French Revolution he had worked for, hiding out in a garret, and in the shadow of death, without hope of heavenly reward, completing his legacy to mankind—a blueprint for the unlimited progress of Posterity.

The issue of progress remains open, given the inability of men to agree on the standards of the good life, and the impossibility of measuring spiritual gains and losses. Still, the Enlightenment opened the issue, made progress a live possibility that cannot be dismissed out of hand. It banked on the indisputable intellectual progress that had been achieved through science. As it attacked some customs that now seem patently irrational or inhuman, so it brought about some changes that are almost universally accepted as for the better, even by its critics. Hence while some of the religious-minded today condemn the idea of progress as heretical, others try to appropriate it, arguing that its ultimate source was not science but the Christian faith. At any rate, there can be no real question that the Enlightenment promoted the cause of freedom, more widely, directly, positively than any age before it. It not only asserted but demonstrated the power of knowledge and reason in self-determination, the choice and realization of human purpose. For the first time in history it carried out a concerted attack on the vested interests that opposed the diffusion of knowledge and the free exercise of reason. Its whole program remains open to criticism, of both its means and its ends; but we need to consider it closely because it was a positive, distinctive program, and on the face of the record a remarkably effective one.

2. The Cultural and Social Program

As France became the main stage for the intellectual and political drama of the Enlightenment, there remained good reason for the air of complacence that pervaded England. It was an air of freedom too, giving some feeling of personal dignity and assurance to the many who had no voice in their government, and allowing ample play to gifted individuals. A lively company of writers offset the torpor of organization men in Parliament, Church, and University. Berkeley and Hume displayed considerably more acuteness than Locke in their critiques of his empiricism, if to little immediate effect. Other English thinkers took a leading part in the much more influential movement of deism, or "natural religion," an effort to reduce Christianity to the simple essentials that all reasonable men might agree on. Literature was distinguished for not only the characteristic lucidity, urbanity, ease, and wit of an age of reason but for the range indicated by such diverse luminaries as Pope, Swift, Addison, Fielding, Gray, Johnson, Sterne, and Blake. In the latter decades England produced the greatest historian of the century, Gibbon, while Adam Smith became the prophet of a new age in his *Wealth of Nations.* By then some agitation for more popular government began to ruffle the assumption that the English Constitution was the last word in political wisdom, or better, began to discover a new virtue in it—an implicit basis for political rights not actually enjoyed by most Englishmen.

Yet this belated discovery also made it plainer that England had not been the leader in the Enlightenment. The great bulk of its philosophy and literature scarcely foreshadowed the revolutionary social and political movements that were gathering force. About the most stirring movement at home was Methodism, another return to pure or primitive Christianity, which in its emphasis on simple faith stirred only the common people, and among other things helped to distract them from efforts at social and political reform. Despite the adventures of individual thinkers, there was generally little intellectual excitement in the air, little energy or fervor for any social cause; "enthusiasm" was a bad word, connoting something of madness. While deism upset the respectable enough to generate some heat, it stimulated little searching thought on either side; skepticism was generally almost as indolent as orthodoxy. Gibbon was surprised by the indignation aroused by his ironical account of early Christianity, and then he became frightened by the French Revolution—the collapse of the old order whose foundations he had placidly worked to undermine. When with Thomas Paine a real religious and political radical entered the scene, it appeared that toleration and freedom of the press had owed largely to indifference, for his publisher was jailed. The major contribution of England to the Enlightenment remained its preliminary one—the work of Newton and Locke.

This was discovered by Voltaire during his three-year stay in England early in the century. Immediately he was impressed by the freedom of the country and the power of its middle class. "See into what horrible decadence the liberty of the press has brought England and Holland," he remarked: they merely "possess the commerce of the entire world." He was more deeply impressed by the prestige of the Royal Society, and in particular of Sir Isaac Newton, whose death at the time was mourned in a manner befitting a national hero. He also came upon the works of Locke, "the only one who has explained human understanding," from whom he learned how much more useful knowledge men might acquire if they were content to study nature instead of trying to divine it as Descartes had. His *Philosophical Letters Concerning the English* acquainted his countrymen with these discoveries, inaugurating the work as a propagandist that was to give him an immense influence—a more direct influence on his age than any writer before him had had. The French authorities responded appropriately: they had the book publicly burned as a "scandalous work, contrary to religion and morals and to the respect due to the established powers."

What Voltaire made of English philosophy is not impressive to rigorous thinkers. Thus he led the way in deriving from Newton authority for the principle of natural law as a moral law absolutely valid, universal, immutable, inviolable; though aware that such a law was not clearly grounded on empirical knowledge, he decided that Newtonian nature—so completely and harmoniously ordered—could not be haphazard or whimsical in the moral world of man, its highest product. He was no more incisive or consistent on the metaphysics of human freedom. At one time he argued for a strict determinism, declaring that, since all nature was governed by absolute law, "one little animal five feet tall" could hardly act to suit himself. At other times he argued that the mere will of this little animal was enough to prove its freedom: "To wish and to act, this is precisely the same thing as to be free"; and he concluded that what freedom really meant was "to know the rights of man"—the natural rights grounded on natural law. At any rate, Voltaire had no serious doubts about such empirical freedom and such rights. Quite logically he concluded that freedom of thought was their essential condition, and he then made this a primary objective of the Enlightenment. The saying attributed to him became legendary: I disagree with every word you say, and will fight to the death for your right to say it. By precept and example, Voltaire did in fact carry on a lifelong battle for freedom of thought. If his own thought would appear not to have been seriously hampered, inasmuch as his published works fill some ninety volumes, he nevertheless had to write outside of France and see the bulk of his work suppressed by church or state. Otherwise the official censorship served to sharpen his wits and his resolve, and to spread his fame; his illegal pamphlets sold thousands of copies, even into hundreds of thousands. No man of his day was more widely admired, feared, and hated, and no man of any day has been a more effective champion of freedom.

As an habitual satirist Voltaire naturally tended to simplify, the more because of his fondness for swift, neat antitheses of actuality and ideal or fiction. By the same token his own ideals were toughened by a live, earthy sense of actuality; in *Candide* he satirized the excesses of the fashionable optimism so devastatingly that simple readers think of it as a pessimistic work. Still, his main point here was that the fashion was not only ridiculous but inhuman, in effect pessimistic; for if this were indeed "the best of all possible worlds," God help man.[2] Actually, man could do much to make it better. As the awful earthquake at Lisbon was followed by an auto-da-fé, so almost all the evils that afflicted

---

[2] It should be noted that Voltaire was unfair to Leibniz, the supposed author of the lunatic optimism he satirized. Philosophically, the best of all *possible* worlds meant that an ideally perfect one was impossible. At that, the refrain was most popular with religious thinkers, and it derived from the ancient idea of the Great Chain of Being rather than the new idea of progress. As Archbishop King of Dublin explained, "God might, indeed, have refrained from creating, and continued alone, self-sufficient and perfect to all eternity; but his infinite Goodness would by no means allow it; this obliged him to produce external things, which things, since they could not possibly be perfect, the Divine Goodness preferred imperfect ones to none at all. Imperfection, then, arose from the infinity of Divine Goodness." Once having got started on the business of creating, God could not deny the blessing of existence to the very lowest orders; complete perfection required every degree of imperfection, the fullest possible world.

Candide were social evils—man's own work, due immediately to class, national, and religious prejudice. If Voltaire had no real hopes of an El Dorado, his Utopian state, he was at least optimistic enough to keep crusading against such prejudice.

His reputation—and the whole work of the Enlightenment—is still clouded by the animus that made Voltaire a scandal in his own day: his main object of attack was the Church. Today his religious satire may often seem obvious and labored, sometimes brutal. He seldom took pains to distinguish between the Church and the gospel of Jesus; his hatred of the "tyranny of priests" verged on a basic hostility to Christianity itself, which grew more pronounced in some of his followers. The Enlightenment accordingly tended to obscure both the historic and the potential services of Christianity to the cause of good will, or its own cause of human dignity. Meanwhile Voltaire's avowed deism— the characteristic religion of the enlightened—was a pretty cool religion. His celebrated remark that if God did not exist he would have to be invented intimated that deity was a mere philosophical or social convenience, and certainly his faith did not kindle in him a warm love of God or man.

Yet those who see only his deficiencies in reverence and charity fail in elementary historical sense. Voltaire's religious satire was not sophomoric at the time, and even when savage had ample excuse in the atrocities still authorized by the Church. His famous motto *Ecrasez l'infame* once rang with a noble indignation, for it was evoked by the judicial torture and murder of the Protestant Jean Calas at Toulouse (which incidentally still celebrated the Massacre of St. Bartholomew as a great feast day); no churchman of his time did as much to make such infamy obsolete. The Church much more insistently obscured the issues of good will by attacking any effort to distinguish between it and the gospel of Jesus. As for deism, its possible inadequacy as a vital inspiration is a proper concern for the devout or for the student of religion, especially because it remains substantially the belief of a great many thoughtful Christians who no longer call themselves deists; but in this history the important point is that it promoted religious freedom, helping to emancipate Christendom from the dogmatism that had long justified persecution. The coolness of Voltaire's religion also meant that like Montaigne he exemplified the values of doubt rather than faith. In his own words, "Doubt is not a very agreeable state, but certainty is a ridiculous one"—ridiculous because it still led the orthodox to claim a monopoly on religious truth.

Somewhat more historical sense is required to do justice to Voltaire's pioneering work in a subject he himself baptized "the philosophy of history." Although he had too little knowledge of other civilizations anyway to be a universal historian, here his temperamental and philosophical limitations united in a kind of systematic abuse of the past. He made little effort to understand, much less to pardon its errors; chiefly he was interested in discrediting it. Among the victims of his own prejudices were the Israelites, whom he sneered at without ever mentioning the loftiness and originality of the great prophets. As for the few societies he could admire, he hailed the Age of Louis XIV as "the most enlightened of all ages." Lessing defined the essential spirit of Voltaire in a laudatory review of his *Essay on Manners*. "What is it to know man in particular? It is to know fools and scoundrels. . . . The case is quite different with the study of man in general. Here he exhibits greatness and his divine origin. Consider what enterprises man accomplishes, how he daily extends the limits of his understanding." Voltaire could be enthusiastic about Man, who in spite of a mostly deplorable history had managed to attain the Enlightenment; only historians are usually supposed to deal with men and societies in particular.

A philosopher of history, however, is properly concerned with the history of Man; and Voltaire was at least attempting a more philosophical study of this than men had before him.[3] "Universal history" had been represented by such parochial works as Bishop Bossuet's *Discourse* on the subject, exhibiting a monumental indifference to all but Christian history. (The bishop gave only a paragraph to Greek philosophy, for example, and ignored India and China.) With Voltaire the classical study of "humanity" took on the new, deeper meaning of "mankind." While he perhaps found it too easy to transcend a Christian point of view, he managed to rise above nationalism too. A declared "citizen of the world" in spirit, not merely by fact of involuntary exile, he was among the first to attack patriotism, war, and the cult of the national hero, usually a great warrior: "I do not like heroes; they make too much noise in the world. I hate those conquerors." For similar reasons he went beyond Montesquieu, who still focused on political history, and inaugurated the study of "the history of the human mind," or of culture: "The progress of mankind can be understood only if one takes into account the growth of religion, art, science, and philosophy." If

---

[3] A significant exception was Giambattista Vico. But his *Principles of a New Science of the Common Nature of Nations* was little known during the eighteenth century, and had no significant influence until the next century.

Voltaire thus celebrated a kind of history in which he and his fellows moved nearer the center of the stage, this was indeed a fundamental kind, as well as the clearest index to the progress of mankind, the soundest basis for the faith of the Enlightenment. By his emphasis on cultural history, and his consequent awareness of "the empire of custom," he anticipated the study of anthropology too.

But immediately he set a rather different example. Faith in the power of reason precluded a full realization of the power of custom or culture. Like Voltaire, thinkers continued to generalize freely about a universal, immutable human nature, befitting Newton's laws; they were more impressed by uniformities than by uniqueness, variety, and flux; and they assumed that custom was a superficial thing, or that their discovery of its empire amounted to a conquest of it (just as thinkers who now announce that all ideas are historically conditioned still assume that this insight is not so conditioned, and that their own judgment—or denial of any right to judgment—is wholly objective). Chiefly they used their slight knowledge of other cultures as another means of exposing the provinciality or bigotry of Christendom, in the fashion set by Montesquieu's *Persian Letters*. The basic program of the Enlightenment remained substantially what Voltaire made it—not so much a dispassionate, scientific study of man as an effort to educate him and improve his society.

Hence its leaders were self-conscious *philosophes*—not formal philosophers or professional scholars. They prided themselves on being men of reason versed in the laws of nature, but otherwise unburdened by technical training, free from pedantry: in effect, up-to-date Renaissance humanists blessed with the knowledge of Newton. As defined by Diderot in his popular article on them in the *Encyclopedia,* the *philosophes* were ideally paragons of wisdom and virtue, civility and social responsibility, by the grace of reason rather than God. In fact they were rare types, if not conspicuously wise or virtuous: less pedantic than most learned men before them and after them, better grounded at once in science and in the humanities, essentially more philosophical, and above all more civic-minded, habitually addressing the general public on matters of public concern. They demonstrated more fully than ever before the possible power of an intelligentsia in the formation of public opinion.

Specifically, they were responsible for the most characteristic, influential single work of the Enlightenment, commonly described as "the great affair of the time"—the *Encyclopedia,* announced in 1750. Unlike an earlier English encyclopedia, this was no mere compendium of knowledge, suited though that would have been to the wide interest in the new knowledge. Diderot, its main editor, frankly avowed that its purpose was "to change the common way of thinking" by diffusing the ideals of the Enlightenment. In other words, it was a work of propaganda, literally subversive, the more so because its radical ideas were typically insinuated under some disguise. (Thus Diderot slipped in a plea for freedom of speech in an article on a piddling Roman divinity.) French authorities kept a suspicious eye on it, while scandalized conservatives charged the Encyclopedists with a conspiracy "to propagate materialism, to destroy Religion, and to inspire a spirit of independence." Though such notoriety harried Diderot during some twenty years of labor, it was good for sales. A growing list of subscribers, who paid the equivalent of a thousand dollars for the complete set, spread the infection through the leading circles of Europe. When the *Encyclopedia* was temporarily suppressed, Frederick the Great and Catherine the Great invited Diderot to finish it in Prussia or Russia.

He confirmed the dreadful charge of "a spirit of independence" by declining the invitation, finishing the last ten volumes almost by himself. Despite his considerable vanity, Diderot did not do himself full justice in his definition of the *philosophe*. He was a philosopher in the modern sense too—a disciplined, acute thinker, and one of the most original minds of the century. Among the first thinkers to take a dynamic view of the universe, he anticipated the theory of evolution, giving a profounder meaning to the popular motto "A new order of things is born"; and he accordingly took a dialectical view of natural knowledge, warning against the assumption of fixities and finalities in philosophy, emphasizing the need of keeping thought open to new possibilities. In his day, however, Diderot was much more influential because of the thought he shared with other men of the Enlightenment, from an initial skepticism as "the first step toward truth" to a high faith in reason and in progress through knowledge.[4] So his hopes for fame rested on his stated aim of enabling "holy Posterity" to become "at the same time more virtuous and more happy."

---

[4] His *Letter on the Blind*, for example, was an acute treatise on epistemology and psychology, exploring the relativity implicit in the nature of sensation and perception, and pointing out that a congenitally blind man would have a different idea of God from the rest of us. While it was admired by contemporaries, most of them saw in it chiefly what the authorities who jailed Diderot saw—another attack on the traditional absolutes, and so another scandal to Religion and Morality. Because of his reputation as an *enfant terrible*, the originality and the remarkable range of his speculation—from physics and physiology to ethics and aesthetics—were not widely appreciated until recent times.

The *Encyclopedia* won immediate acclaim for its articles on science, in particular those by d'Alembert. It carried through the work of Voltaire, popularizing Newtonian physics and the empirical philosophy of Bacon and Locke, again with the object of not merely informing readers but indoctrinating them with the philosophy of science. As formulated by d'Alembert, this involved a distinction not easy to define clearly and maintain firmly: on the one hand, an avoidance of the "spirit of system"; on the other, a welcome of "the true system of the world" revealed by science and an extension of the revolutionary "new method of philosophizing" into all fields of thought. Although the leading Encyclopedists were close enough socially and intellectually to make plausible the charge of a "conspiracy," they scarcely agreed on drawing or maintaining such a line. The spirit of system was especially strong in a school of materialism, represented by Baron d'Holbach's *System of Nature*, which asserted that in a mechanistic universe man too was subject to an absolute determinism. But Holbach thereby made clearer the underlying unity of the Enlightenment. A conspicuously high-minded man, he was impelled to materialism by his felt need of a complete break with the spiritualism or "superstition" of religion; and it turned out that man's behavior was not necessarily determined after all—the real trouble was that he had long been "a mere machine in the hands of tyrants and priests," wicked and wretched because of ignorance. The conclusion was as familiar: man could attain his natural state of virtue and happiness through "Knowledge, Reason, and Liberty."

Diderot himself was largely responsible for another distinction of the *Encyclopedia*, the many lengthy articles on technology. Reflecting the interests of the bourgeois and foreshadowing the Industrial Revolution, these had some philosophical import too. Diderot emphasized the need of being well versed at once in theoretical, experimental, and practical or applied science—the union that the Greeks never achieved, and that has been so fruitful for both science and technology in Western civilization. By contrast, of no less import, he paid little direct attention to theology, or "Divine Science." Wary of the authorities, the Encyclopedists attacked it chiefly under other headings, with cross-references to indicate connections between pagan superstitions and Christian doctrines; otherwise they disposed of its historic pretensions by simply ignoring them. They tended to go further than Locke and Voltaire in excluding revelation and maintaining the complete independence of natural philosophy. While disciples of this philosophy could still believe in the supernatural, some were no longer assuming the naturalness or necessity of such a belief. Diderot himself, who began as a militant deist, moved toward agnosticism and ended in outright atheism—a view deplored by Voltaire as both unphilosophical and impolitic. Likewise in ethics thinkers were moving to purely naturalistic or humanistic grounds, typically retaining the essentials of Christian ethics but rejecting its supernatural sanctions and incentives. It was better to be a good man, said Diderot, than a good Christian.

Hence the standard of freethinkers was now planted well in advance of their highly uncertain rights. Puritan advocates of freedom of conscience had generally assumed that it held only for Christians, not for unbelievers, while Locke had argued for a limited toleration primarily on grounds of practical wisdom, not high principle. Voltaire, much more indignant over persecution, took a more positive stand, and in his *Treatise on Tolerance* argued that it was the very essence of philosophy, which is naturally mild, humane, and reasonable; but one may doubt that he would have fought to the death for the right of atheists to propagate their views. The more radical skepticism or positive disbelief of Diderot, Holbach, and others logically called for complete religious freedom. They upheld the absolute rights of reason, which did not actually require a belief in God. By the end of the century Thomas Paine was attacking mere toleration, as not the opposite but the counterfeit of intolerance. "Both are despotisms. The one assumes itself the right of withholding liberty of conscience, the other of granting it."

Before Paine wrote, Frederick the Great had granted Prussians full religious liberty—still denied to Englishmen as well as Frenchmen. As both pupil and patron of the *philosophes,* Frederick recalls us to their wide influence, and to the broader aspects of the Enlightenment as a whole. Cosmopolitan or universal in its expressed ideals, it became an international movement that affected all the leading powers of Europe, now including Russia. It created something of a stir even in Spain, which by this time astonished travelers as a medieval country centuries behind Europe. In Germany its ideals were absorbed by Lessing, Schiller, and Goethe, helping to inspire the most brilliant period in German literature. In Italy too the stir amounted to a new intellectual renaissance, which brought the land of antiques back into the main stream of Western history. Among the most effective books of the century was Beccaria's *Treatise on Crimes and Punishments,* attacking judicial torture and the common savagery of punishment, starting a movement for legal reform that carried all over Europe.

As the work of an intelligentsia, the Enlightenment likewise cut across class lines. Bourgeois writers indeed took the most prominent part, beginning with Voltaire. Diderot, who played up the practical interests of his class, was a pioneer in bourgeois drama too—a serious, supposedly realistic prose drama, whose protagonists were drawn from the middle class instead of the nobility or royalty who had provided the heroes of Elizabethan and French neoclassical tragedy.[5] A clearer sign of the coming reign of middle-class tastes was the rise of the novel, now on its way to becoming the most popular and characteristic of modern literary forms. Yet these tastes did not set the tone of the Enlightenment. Outside of France, kings everywhere began to pride themselves on being "enlightened," like Frederick the Great, and the fashion spread among the aristocracy. In France the nobility sired some of the most radical thought of the age, notably the works of Condillac, Holbach, and Condorcet. The *philosophes* would have had a much harder time had they not had the support of many persons in high places, from Mme. de Pompadour, mistress of Louis XV (she hated Jesuits), to Malesherbes, official censor during the critical decade when the *Encyclopedia* began appearing. "A man who has read only the books that appeared with the express consent of the government the way the law prescribes," Malesherbes observed, "would be behind his contemporaries almost a century"; and he granted many "tacit permissions" to works he could not give the seal of government approval to.

All this is to say that the times were ripe for the *philosophes*. They profited from not only the popularity of science but the growth of civility, a progress in manners if not in morals, reflected in the currency of a new word—"civilization." This was the great century of the salon in France, and of the art of conversation; Paris, not Versailles, was the mecca of young men with literary ambitions, and fluency and wit might count for more than rank. A growing reading public made it possible for men of letters to be independent and self-supporting. Newspapers and magazines in particular grew rapidly in number and circulation. On all counts much more was heard of "public opinion"—an expression that now appeared in some languages for the first time; the beginning of "the empire of public opinion" may be dated from about the middle of the century. Nevertheless, the *philosophes* did much to create

---

[5] His *Natural Son* strikes us as preposterously high-flown in style and sentiment, and in its blatant aim to edify; it seems true to life only as a revelation of the self-conscious bourgeois, all dressed up in his best moral clothes for the benefit of Posterity. With such similar plays as Lessing's *Miss Sarah Sampson*, it is a sobering example of the relativity of taste that Diderot emphasized in essays on aesthetics, the element of mere fashion that conceivably may cloud the judgment even of our own very sophisticated literary critics.

this empire. Deliberately setting about to educate public opinion, they were as clearly makers as products of "the times," which still produced many more men who regarded "a spirit of independence" as a public outrage. They deserve more credit because they ran the constant risk of jail, even of possible execution—threatened by a Royal Declaration for "any writing tending to attack religion, to rouse opinion, to impair Our authority, and to trouble the order and tranquillity of Our State." Few writers who dared to express an independent spirit enjoyed the security of Voltaire in exile.

Among the harried was the most influential Jean Jacques Rousseau. Priding himself on being "like no one in the whole world," this arch-rebel brings up the further diversities that complicate the Age of Enlightenment, make it both more difficult and more necessary to speak of an "eighteenth-century mind." Excepting Voltaire, no other thinker of the age made so immediate, deep, and lasting an impression; Louis XVI rightly coupled him with Voltaire, remarking "Those two men have destroyed France." Yet Rousseau attacked point-blank the ruling faith of the Enlightenment, anticipating the revulsion of the Romantic movement against it, while he also exemplified its most radical or extravagant tendencies.

Immediately he became famous by his prize-winning essay, the *Discourse on the Moral Effects of the Arts and Sciences*, in which he argued that these arts and sciences—the distinctive values of civilization, and the measure of the progress celebrated by the Enlightenment —were actually the main source of evil. Later Rousseau qualified this argument, or fell into his notorious contradictions, suggesting that science, for instance, was perhaps good for a bad society but bad for a good one, or good only for superior men like himself, bad for common men. At heart, however, he remained a primitivist, and he consistently maintained the claims of the heart, made "sentiment" another key word of the age. The good man for Rousseau was a man of feeling, not of reason. Men had been really good in the primitive or "natural" state of ignorance, long before the rise of science and the "pernicious art" of printing. His own sins, paraded in his *Confessions*, were merely further proof of the sins of the Enlightenment, for he knew—or rather felt—that he was a naturally good man, who had been corrupted by his society. He found peace and joy only when he fled this society, returned to nature. He had known ecstasy when he sold his watch—the symbol of Western civilization, with its bourgeois habits of regularity, its mania for keeping exact time, now its faith in time as the measure or the guarantor of Progress.

Even so, he was very much a child of the Enlightenment. Like all primitivists, Rousseau of course owed his gospel to civilization, as he owed his fame to the "pernicious art" of printing; no primitive could be so lyrical about nature or preach the virtue of "a state of nature." But his gospel was specifically typical of the age in that it was a fervent new gospel, defiant of tradition and authority, and no less fervent for being essentially secular. Though he preached a "religion of the heart" to go with it, summed up in *Emile* as the "Profession of Faith of a Savoyard Vicar," this was a vague deism quite different from the primitive Christianity revived by John Wesley in England. He exhorted men to "follow nature" and be themselves, not to serve God; he traced evil wholly to society, not to original sin. No thinker of the age had a more optimistic view of "nature," or human nature. *Emile* was condemned by ecclesiastical authorities, and Rousseau forced to flee France, primarily because of his heretical insistence on the natural goodness of man. (His native Geneva honored his work by burning it.) Hence, too, no thinker had a more impassioned vision of the perfectibility of man. Differing radically from other leaders of the Enlightenment in his educational program, Rousseau was the most ardent educator among them, convinced that men had a natural right to happiness, and that they could attain it by following their own lights.

In view of his extravagances, it is still necessary to remark that he was no mere fool. The many reputable thinkers he influenced—from Kant and Goethe to Emerson, Thoreau, and Tolstoy—could see that he had his eye on the actual contradictions of civilized society, the actual costs of its values, as well as the deceptions or follies of common sense— "honor without virtue, reason without wisdom, pleasure without happiness." It is even possible to see in Rousseau something of a social scientist, anticipating a new phase of the Enlightenment. He not only took into fuller account than others the sentiments and emotions that in fact govern behavior more than reason does, but made some tentative effort at a scientific analysis. At times he conceived his "natural man" as a logical fiction, a methodological device for penetrating the appearances of any given society and describing the substratum of human nature, or a hypothetical "state of nature" that he could say "perhaps never did exist."

Other thinkers, at any rate, were more consciously groping their way toward the social sciences. Still lacking a solid factual basis, or any clearly formulated scientific method, they were nonetheless attempting studies in a scientific spirit. Among the conspicuous examples were the self-styled Economists or Physiocrats, led by Quesnay, author of a few articles on economics in the *Encyclopedia*. Quesnay was a major influence on Adam Smith, who in *The Wealth of Nations* (1776) made the most comprehensive, systematic effort to treat the subject as a branch of natural philosophy, and by his immediate and immense success became the founder of the modern science of economics. Or "science," some would say, recalling both its uncertain status and the confusions and excesses of the Enlightenment. These students of society were more like pure rationalists than empiricists, given to loose talk about "laws," automatic forces operating uniformly—assumptions no less dangerous because they typically believed that the natural effect of these forces was a rational social order or automatic progress; so liberals have learned to deplore in particular the great influence of Adam Smith on a later age. First, however, they should acknowledge that he was himself liberal in spirit, and that his work was in his own day a major work of enlightenment, potentially of emancipation. He not only preached economic freedom but made men more aware of impersonal economic tendencies, involuntary consequences of their activities. Such understanding made possible more conscious, purposeful, intelligent activity.

Another important influence on Adam Smith, and key figure in the later program of the Enlightenment, was Turgot, economist, statesman, and philosopher of history. In his youthful essay "On the Successive Progress of the Human Mind," he carried through more systematically the idea of progress heralded by Voltaire. He saw this progress as in part the work of reason, culminating in the conscious philosophy of the Enlightenment, but he also saw it as the product of "tumultuous and dangerous passions," the work of ambitious men who had no such end in mind. From this he drew as optimistic a conclusion: "I believe I see an immense army whose every movement is directed by a mighty genius." To Turgot progress was accordingly the design of Providence —an idea that seeped down into the faith of many Christians thereafter, and that was still held by the much more erudite Lord Acton a century later.

By contrast, Condorcet's subsequent outline of the "Progress of the Human Spirit" might be considered more scientific, in that he ignored the undemonstrable genius of Providence and kept history within the realm of purely natural philosophy. His work, however, was more obviously governed by the ruling spirit of the Enlightenment from Voltaire on: primarily it was not a scientific analysis but a program for action, with definite, if utopian objectives. And so even with the crowning work of Kant. There was something of Condorcet—as of Voltaire, Diderot, Rousseau, and Turgot—in the seemingly most sober, dry, abstruse thought of the cloistered German professor. The greatest philosopher to come directly out of the Enlightenment, Kant most clearly and fully exemplifies its basic continuity—the solid core of its faith in reason and rejection of any other authority, beneath the divergent or conflicting tendencies that rose out of the leaven of self-criticism implicit in its faith and its ideal of free thought.

Roused from his "dogmatic slumbers" by Hume's devastating exposure of the limits of reason and empirical knowledge, in particular the inductions on which science rested, Kant responded with his *Critique of Pure Reason*. In this most difficult work he clung to a simple idea. Hume's logic was irrefutable: by direct experience we know only sequences of this *and* that, no necessary connection of this *because of* that, nor can scientists be certain that the future must always resemble the past; yet the plain truth remained that man did know a great deal, and that in science he had discovered the most reliable means to positive knowledge. Kant solved the dilemma by assuming that cause and effect, like time, space, substance, and other basic categories of thought, were necessary modes of understanding imposed by the mind on the sensations coming from something "out there," the unknown and unknowable "thing-in-itself." Granted that his a priori categories are themselves strictly undemonstrable, the important consideration for our present purposes is that Kant provided another buttress for freedom of thought. On the one hand, he denied the certain knowledge of ultimate reality claimed by absolutists, among other things demonstrating that by pure reason one could as convincingly refute as prove the traditional arguments for the existence of God. On the other hand, he confirmed the validity of scientific knowledge, the empirical uses of reason. He added a new dimension of dignity to man as a knower by conceiving the human mind as a dynamic agent, which wrote its own ticket instead of merely recording on a "blank sheet," and attained knowledge by a transaction with nature in which the observer was as indispensable as the observed.

In the *Critique of Practical Reason* Kant dwelt on a plainer source of human dignity, the moral law within man: the categorical sense of *ought*, regardless of selfish desire, that all men have, and that seemed to him as wonderful as the starry heavens above. On these grounds he brought back God and the immortal soul, as the source of this moral sense and the guarantor of the ultimate fulfillment of the will to obey the moral law—a piece of possibly wishful thinking. Empiricists have also complained of the dualism in Kant's lofty categorical imperative, as he absolutely divorced it from all consideration of feeling, sentiment, consequences, or the ordinary requirements of social life—the most apparent source of the moral sense in man. But again our immediate concern is the moral autonomy he conferred on man. He flatly rejected the orthodox Christian scheme of eternal rewards and punishments as a matter of vulgar expediency, insisting that conduct so inspired might be prudent but was not truly moral at all. He erected the fact of the moral sense into his main argument for human freedom, which may seem logically incompatible with both the determinism of scientific law and the concept of an almighty God, but which is nevertheless essential if morality is to be meaningful. And in spelling out the categorical imperative, setting up a rational standard by which a man might determine just what he *ought* to do, Kant asserted the principle of human dignity without any of the qualifications that both theologians and the *philosophes* were wont to add: "So act as to treat humanity, whether in thine own person or in the person of another, as an end withal, never as a means only." If this standard is hardly feasible for social life, which always requires the subordination and to some extent the sacrifice of the person to the common good, it represents a philosophical equivalent of the Sermon on the Mount, the loftiest grounds for claims of the natural rights of man, and especially for the democratic gospel that *all* men are entitled to such rights.

More obviously characteristic of the Enlightenment was Kant's philosophical theory of progress, outlined in his *Idea of a Universal History* (1784). This was an effort of pure reason, based not on an empirical study of history but on a typical premise about Nature: "All tendencies of any creature, to which it is predisposed by nature, are destined in the end to develop themselves perfectly and agreeably to their final purpose." As man's distinctive potentialities derive from his possession of reason, Kant deduced that they would eventually be realized by the establishment of "a universal civil society founded on political justice." His premise, which might seem strange to a naturalist, became more understandable by the end of his argument, when it appeared that behind Nature stood the Providence of Turgot. Otherwise his theory made pretty good empirical sense. He offered it as a hypothesis, claiming no more than probability for it—not the certainty of Condorcet. Sufficiently aware of all the bloody messes in history, he emphasized like Turgot that man had advanced blindly through passion and strife, the "unsocial sociality" that was also natural to him. For so "crooked and perverse" a creature he held out no hope of a heavenly city on earth, anything so utopian as the classless society of Marx. Above all, he was to a notable extent prophetic. As men had learned very slowly, painfully, to live together in great nations, so he argued they would have to learn to avoid great wars between nations, and to live together under some kind of "federal league" or supranational state—comparable to the United Nations that they have in fact established, and that now seems a plain necessity of survival. Before they took this step, Kant predicted, they would go through a "hell of evils." We are obliged to hope that two world wars are enough hell to warrant the rest of his prophecy.

Acknowledging that his theory was not derived from a study of universal history, Kant proposed that scholars might now write such history in order to further the designs of Nature (or Providence), and so carry out the mission of the Enlightenment, which he described as mankind's coming of age. Himself a secluded bachelor, seemingly born to be a professor, he nevertheless had the missionary spirit of the *philosophes*. He ventured to say that the enlightenment of the public was "almost inevitable"—on one condition. "This enlightenment requires nothing but *freedom*—and the most innocent of all that may be called 'freedom': freedom to make public use of one's reason in all matters." Any interference with the cause of enlightenment was a violation of "the sacred rights of man." Living to see these rights drawn up into a constitution during the French Revolution, Kant hailed this upheaval as a phenomenon that could never be forgotten, "because it proves that in human nature there exist an inclination and disposition to the better which no politician ever could have been able to predict by summing up the course of events."

He overlooked, however, a more paradoxical phenomenon. None of the champions of the Enlightenment (including himself), none of the philosophical students of history, had predicted this revolution either. One reason is that none of them really wanted a revolution. None insisted on a popular right to revolution or made popular government the main goal; they rarely used the term "democracy," and then not as an honorific term or a battle-cry. Only some unphilosophical conservatives, frightened by the scandalous "spirit of independence" sown by the *philosophes*, had premonitions of the violent end of the *ancien régime*.

3. Political Thought Before the Revolutions

In the prevailing complacence over their Constitution, English thinkers were naturally least disposed to herald the political revolution in which the eighteenth century culminated. At its liveliest, political thought usually centered on party politics, a choice between the Tory and Whig oligarchies. Some radical ideas that did get into print, with the agitation for parliamentary reform that began in the last decades of the century, had little if any immediate effect and look important only in retrospect, like the lost cause of the Levellers. In their spirit Major John Cartwright attacked the idea that property was the main end of the social compact and the main qualification for a voice in the government; asserting that "all are by nature free, all are by nature equal," he concluded that personality was the foundation of the right to representation. Joseph Priestley, the discoverer of oxygen, took a new tack in arguing for both political and religious freedom, anticipating Bentham's norm of the happiness of the greatest number; he attracted just enough attention to become a victim of the revulsion against the French Revolution, a mob pillaging his house and burning his books. (He sought refuge in America, where he died, but was too radical to be popular there either.) Otherwise the English pretty much adhered to the political thought of Hume, if unthinkingly. Their most brilliant philosopher saw custom, not reason, as primary in social and political life, and believed that conservative prejudices were sounder or safer than the empirically baseless doctrines of natural law and natural rights. In effect he endorsed a seemly obscurantism.

Still, the skepticism of Hume was not really a comfortable philosophy for ordinary conservatives, corroding as it did the religious sanctions of the traditional order. The land of Bacon, Newton, and Locke might be expected to produce some further impetus to new developments. It was in fact starting the Industrial Revolution, the profoundest transformation in man's life since the rise of civilization. And though this would not become apparent until the next century, the political ferment to come also owed something to at least two more thinkers, who were no less typically English for being radically opposed—Sir William Blackstone and Jeremy Bentham.

Blackstone's *Commentaries on the Laws of England* (1765–1769),
immediately recognized as a classic, was a monument to the English
Constitution, and as such was conservative, unoriginal, faithful to its
loftiest ideals and its most glaring inconsistencies. He celebrated at
once the theoretical separation of powers in government, the absolute
sovereignty of Parliament, the higher sovereignty of natural law, the
inalienable rights of the people, the special privileges of gentlemen, the
perfect rationality of the science of law, and the need of keeping this
science properly mysterious, teaching common men to obey laws "without scrutinizing too nicely into the reason for making them." He
warmed up to his subject because "the eternal, immutable laws . . .
which the Creator has enabled human reason to discover" were embodied in the common law of England, and "the rights of all mankind"
were "in a peculiar and emphatical manner" the rights of Englishmen.
The conservative gentlemen who controlled Parliament welcomed
Blackstone's assertion that by the English Constitution "the power of
Parliament is absolute and without control," and that Locke was mistaken in his notion that the people had a right to remove or alter it if
it abused its power. Nevertheless, Americans could and did make of
his *Commentaries* a liberal bible, the basis of their opposition to Parliament. He incidentally granted that "if any alteration were to be
wished" in the essentially perfect English system, it should be toward
"a more complete representation of the people" in Parliament. Most
important, he had piously reaffirmed the principle of natural rights,
which as derivatives of natural law "no human legislature has power
to abridge or destroy." He even declared that "the first and primary
end of human law is to maintain and regulate these absolute rights of
individuals."[6]

Immediately, however, Blackstone's most striking influence was on
Bentham. At one of his lectures Bentham had a sudden, dazzling experience of enlightenment, the revelation that the doctrine of natural
rights was "rhetorical nonsense—nonsense upon stilts." He proceeded
to demolish the *Commentaries*, initiating his crusade against the "tyranny of language," and to work out his purely empirical alternative.
In the flush of his revelation he permitted himself a suggestion of rhetoric, announcing as a "sacred truth" that "the greatest happiness of the

---

[6] In fairness to Blackstone, he was himself sometimes troubled by his apparent inconsistency. On the rights of private property, for example, he recognized that the "sole and
despotic dominion" they bestowed excluded the rights of others, and that they were not
clearly "natural," having been created by human law. He decided that they had better
be regarded as absolute simply for the sake of public order, to avoid too nice a scrutiny.

greatest number is the foundation of morals and legislation." His basic principle of utility was not at all new, having been stated by Hume and popularized by the French philosopher Helvetius, but Bentham became the recognized founder of Utilitarianism because of his methodical application of it to social and political institutions, and his attempt to devise a scientific calculus of pleasure and pain. Though he was long a Tory, bent chiefly on administrative reforms in the interests of efficiency alone, he eventually realized one reason why the rulers of England did not welcome his standard of utility: government was most concerned about the greatest happiness of the upper class. Bentham then called for no mere reform of Parliament but universal suffrage by free, secret ballot. His followers popularized a new word—"radical."

The history of the Utilitarian movement belongs to a later chapter, since its influence did not become considerable until a generation after the revolutions in America and France. At this point we need to remark only Bentham's indirect connections with the revolutionary ferment. A follower of Beccaria (another disciple of Helvetius), he began working immediately for concrete legal reforms, attacking the flagrant corruptions and inequity in the administration of a brutal kind of justice, the legalized savagery of Christendom from which the poor suffered most. Not at all saintly in temper, he exemplified the secular interests that were promoting the humanitarian movement, the active concern over the wretched earthly lot of the many instead of the state of their immortal souls. Despite his scorn of the doctrine of natural rights, Bentham's ruling principle of the greatest happiness of the greatest number implied something like a natural right to the pursuit of happiness. And it was essentially a democratic principle—as conservatives were quicker to perceive.

In France comparably subversive tendencies had swelled the initial popularity of Montesquieu, the first major political thinker of the century, whose *The Spirit of Laws* (1748) soon ran through many editions at home and abroad. It came down to nothing more radical than an argument for limited, constitutional government on the English model. While it popularized the strictly erroneous idea that English government was based on a separation or balance of powers, it reflected the actual preponderance of the aristocracy in England; Montesquieu believed that the nobility, with its tradition of personal honor as well as privilege, could provide the surest check against both the tyranny of the monarch and the possible unruliness of the people. No more a utopian than a revolutionary, he accepted the whole hierarchical, basically feudal order in France. He had less faith in the power of reason than did the *philosophes*, and was less popular with them than he was with later conservatives. But even so he was a major precursor of the Enlightenment.

Montesquieu typified the social, political concerns that dominated French literature in the eighteenth century, and made almost all important writers highly critical of their government. Specifically, his principal concerns were justice and liberty—liberty as the necessary condition of political virtue. He made such a point of the balance of powers because any absolute rule seemed to him corrupt in principle, fatal to political virtue. In this spirit he argued that the common people should have some say in the government, through a representative parliament, and he could therefore describe his model aristocratic state as a republic. His contemporaries were impressed not so much by his idealization of aristocracy as by his criticism of the traditional abuse of power and his hatred of tyranny. They were also properly impressed by his cosmopolitanism and his effort at a fundamental sociological analysis, which led him to conclude that different countries should naturally have different laws to suit their native customs or traditions; but again what stood out was his judgment that England was pre-eminent for political liberty.

The more scandalous works of Voltaire were no more democratic in intent. He expressed little faith in the common people, who in his letters usually figure as the "rabble"; his considered judgment was that "the number of those who can think is excessively small." As a lifelong champion of freedom, he made it plain that the principles of "liberty, equality, and fraternity" are not one and inseparable, in theory or practice. Otherwise he differed most conspicuously from Montesquieu in putting his trust in enlightened monarchy rather than aristocracy. Or more precisely, in enlightened monarchs, such as his friend and patron Frederick the Great. Not primarily a political philosopher, Voltaire worked out no systematic theory of government, but saw immediately that kings might be educated more readily than the masses of people, and freedom—especially freedom from the Church—conferred more promptly from above, by the few who were capable of thinking. A gracious king presided over his ideal state of El Dorado in *Candide*, like the rational, well-behaved God of deism.

The trouble remained, however, that France was not blessed with an enlightened monarch; and the author of *Candide* kept his eye on political realities. Voltaire had no reverence for kingship per se, no conviction of any absolute *right* of monarchs, much less a divine right. He did have a strong conviction of the rights of subjects, based in theory on natural law, but livened by his constant fight for civil liberties. Likewise he had a strong sentiment of natural justice, which kept him critical of the aristocracy—at the time the principal rivals of the king, claiming privileges that were not clearly an enlightened substitute for royal power. In *Candide* Voltaire satirized these hereditary privileges, the distinction conferred on fools or scoundrels by the accident of birth; on the political fighting front he campaigned on behalf of the serfs in backward regions, and he rose to the defense of a critic of feudal rights who had been condemned by the Parlement of Paris, gentlemen who possessed such rights. Altogether, Voltaire never dreamed of working for a popular revolution, even deplored the irreligion of some of the *philosophes* because it might incite the "rabble" by depriving them of their opium; yet he was for good reason a popular idol, wildly acclaimed on his home-coming to Paris in his old age—a tumultuous celebration that was perhaps the clearest portent of the French Revolution. The common people of Paris could see why Voltaire was anathema to the supporters of the *ancien régime*.

And so with the diverse or inconsistent political thought of the *philosophes* as a whole. Some emphasized more than Voltaire the principle of natural rights, with its implication of equality. In an *Encyclopedia* article on the subject Diderot used the term "inalienable" rights, and elsewhere he set sharp limits to all political authority: "No man has received from nature the right of commanding others." On the other hand, Diderot also sounded a bourgeois note that might muffle the principle of political equality: "It is property that makes the citizen," gives him a right to a voice in the government. None of the *philosophes* prepared a program or drew up a constitution for a full-fledged democracy. Holbach, in his *Social System* the most radical and utopian of them, specifically ruled out violent, revolutionary means. Yet all of them contributed to the democratic revolution, in ways apparent to alarmed conservatives.

Most obviously they undermined the traditional authority of the Church and the monarchy. If their attacks on authority need not have led toward popular government, in a society still aristocratic through and through, this was still a natural outcome. They popularized not only a spirit of independence or potential revolt but a principle of reasoned dissent, which weakened any claims to privilege or power based merely on custom, as the claims of a hereditary aristocracy substantially were. Their assertion of natural rights was linked with a broader principle of human dignity, the grounds for claims to equal rights. In rejecting the doctrine of Original Sin they emphasized instead the inherent or potential goodness of man, which implied that he was fit for freedom. They declared that his natural goal was self-realization on earth, no doubt having in mind chiefly gifted men like themselves, but again encouraging the assumption that common men were entitled to the pursuit of happiness. With the idea of progress they spread a *will* to progress, the belief that something should and could be done about apparent evils and inequities. All in all, they propagated a spirit that we may now see as "liberal" (a term not yet in their political lexicon), but that in their day was more strictly "radical" (a term also unknown to them), because rooted in a fundamental incompatibility between their principles and the principles of the *ancien régime*, and that under the momentum of circumstances might become revolutionary.

They accordingly help to explain why there was no immediate sensation when this latent revolutionary spirit finally became explicit in Rousseau's *Social Contract* (1762), far and away the most influential political treatise of the century. This at first caused so little stir that it was not even condemned in France. (Geneva alone honored its son once more by banning and burning the book.) With the outbreak of the French Revolution, however, men evidently began to realize what the authorities had overlooked. In the next decade more than thirty editions of the *Social Contract* were printed in France, while it appeared in a dozen or so editions in other Western languages—starting on the career that would carry it into Hungarian, Greek, Polish, Czech, Russian, and Turkish as well, usually at a time of revolutionary ferment. For Rousseau was literally radical in both a philosophical and a political sense: going to the very roots of the problem of political authority, the legitimacy of coercive government; ignoring or rejecting the most familiar arguments derived from the will of God, tradition, or expediency; and setting forth principles absolutely irreconcilable with the claims alike of the French monarchy and the aristocracy.

The *Social Contract* is also shot through with contradictions, beginning with its famous first sentence: "Man is born free, and is everywhere in chains." It was almost bound to be inconsistent as Rousseau tried to make over his "natural man" into an ideal citizen, but it was the more so because of his uncompromising spirit, his refusal to put up with any nuisance jeopardizing "the reign of virtue" in his ideal republic. We have at once to distinguish two Rousseaus, inasmuch as both emerged in the Revolution and both have been alive and kicking to this day: one an ultralibertarian, the *bête-noire* of conservatives; the other as extreme an authoritarian, the *bête-noire* of liberals.

Behind both was his central concept of the "general will"—the will of the people for the common good. In adopting the familiar idea of the social contract, Rousseau emphasized more than any thinker before him its logical implication that sovereignty derived from the people, the state existed only to serve them; he insisted on the absolute, inalienable, indivisible sovereignty of the people. Likewise he more sharply distinguished the state from the government, the set of officials that at any given moment constituted it, and that represented merely a commission. Whereas Hobbes had argued that rulers were not bound by the contract, Rousseau asserted that they were not even a party to it. He proclaimed the revolutionary doctrine "that the depositories of the executive power are not the masters of the people, but its officers; that the people may establish or remove them as it pleases; that for these officers there is no question of contracting, but only of obeying; that in undertaking the functions which the State imposes on them, they only fulfill their duty as citizens, with no right of any kind to dispute the terms." All this applied to kings too; he scoffed at the hereditary rights that enabled imbeciles or monsters to wear the crown. Though the people might establish monarchy, they retained the right to change at will whatever form of government they chose, to "limit, modify, or recover" the powers they had delegated. And though Rousseau did not argue that democracy was the best form of government, considering it feasible only for small states, he did spell out the democratic implications of popular sovereignty. All citizens should enjoy the same rights, "every vote must count." The first important political thinker to be *of* the people, and an outsider all his life, Rousseau was temperamentally disposed to take a kindlier view of common men than Voltaire did, but his logic also led him to declare, "The voice of the people is, in fact, the voice of God."

Up to this point, his premises were similar to John Locke's. Rousseau went on, however, to a radically different interpretation of the social contract. According to Locke, men in "the state of nature" surrendered a measure of their God-given freedom in order to secure their basic rights, especially their property; the state was in effect a necessary evil. According to Rousseau, men made no real sacrifice; they surrendered only their "natural independence," which was not real freedom, and in return got not only security but civil liberty, including property *rights* instead of mere possession. It was the state that created rights, gave men equality. For all serious purposes, in other words, man was not born free and in forming the state did not put on chains. It was indeed strictly meaningless for Rousseau to speak of a social contract at all, since men came to know of conscious rights and liberties only after they had agreed to this imaginary contract, and he insisted that the government was no party to it.

Despite this inconsistency, he was accordingly closer than Locke to the basic facts of social life, and the historic origins of the state. Locke has been endlessly criticized for the bourgeois atomic individualism implicit in his concept of political society as merely a contract instead of an organic growth. Rousseau, as often condemned for his cult of the ego, here remained faithful to the classical tradition that conceived man as by nature a social animal, and the state as indispensable to his self-realization. In this regard the modern democracies have more nearly followed his way of thinking. By Locke's way—long the favorite American way—government was at best a policeman, every gain in its power was at the expense of individual liberty, and so the less government the better. In Rousseau's view government had a more positive role in promoting the common welfare, and might go on to provide more real freedom for the people, as in time it did most obviously by establishing free public education. Granted that its power always limits individual liberty (policemen are a serious embarrassment to thugs), it might nevertheless secure still more effective freedom for the many by taking on more powers—restricting the liberty of some individuals, say, to work children twelve hours a day in their factories. To a greater or less extent, all the modern democracies have become "welfare states."

Yet all history demonstrates that there is much truth too in Locke's view of government, and always good reason to fear its power. In Rousseau's own day man was indeed in chains almost everywhere. His earlier *Discourse on the Origin of Inequality* had pictured the state as the author and guarantor of flagrant inequality and injustice, and he was now proposing a different theory because men did not actually enjoy the rights that ideally the state created. Even so he conferred on it all the power that Hobbes had given Leviathan: "The social compact gives the body politic absolute power over all its members." He proceeded to specify drastic restrictions on individual liberties, which the modern democracies have eschewed but the totalitarian countries have imposed on principle—a principle essentially his own. We are brought to the basic ambiguity of Rousseau's thought, specifically to the authoritarian in him, whose "reign of virtue" helped to authorize the Reign of Terror in the French Revolution.

The key remains his concept of the general will. At times Rousseau described this as simply a social fact, amounting to tribalism—the common sentiments that actually hold a people together and make it a people. More often he described it as a norm of public virtue and justice: being a will to the common welfare, underlying all the particular selfish interests of individuals, it was perforce always right. It became a kind of Platonic Idea—an Enlightened Sovereign transcending all mere appearances. Rousseau then worried over the problem of how to make out and spell out this nebulous general will, which was no mere sum, could not be got at by any mere counting or subtracting of particular wills, and in practice always needed to be enlightened, as the people did not know the good they willed. But in his passion for pure legitimacy he insisted anyway on the absolute sovereignty of the general will, and therefore of the state that perforce represented it. All members of the body politic "really" share in this will, the sovereign "neither has nor can have any interest contrary to theirs"; so any misguided individual who refuses to obey it "shall be compelled to do so by the whole body," and this coercion will still be no real infringement of his liberty —it "means nothing less than that he will be forced to be free." So far from being anything like tyranny, it assures "the reign of virtue" too: "virtue is nothing more than this conformity of the particular wills with the general will." Rousseau went on to denounce such institutions as parliaments, holding that long debates only proclaimed "the ascendancy of particular interests and the decline of the State." On the same grounds he banned political parties and private associations: "there should be no partial society within the State." He even set up a "civil religion" for purely political purposes, with compulsory belief in the dogmas decreed by the State; unbelievers were to be banished or executed, not as godless but as "antisocial" persons. In short, this archindividualist did his best to rule out individual decisions, this archrebel made conformity the sovereign virtue.

In thus laying down the principles of totalitarianism, Rousseau exposed the limitations and the dangers of the ardent rationalism of the Enlightenment. The "natural" social order to which the *philosophes* aspired was a uniformly rational order. Though devoted to ideals of freedom, they did not habitually stress either the fact of individual differences or the value of diversity of opinion. Reason as they saw it made for uniformity, which might encourage a demand for conformity to their own rational ideals; and since they tended to identify reason with virtue they were liable to impatience with frail, fallible humanity. The plebeian Rousseau remained a harsh critic of the *philosophes*, but his ardor for public virtue carried him further from the real life of ordinary men, closer to the possible tyranny of abstract idealism. And en route he found a guide in Plato's *Republic*. He had earlier glorified Sparta as a model of simple, unspoiled virtue, contrasting it with corrupt, cultivated Athens. Plato's disillusionment with Athenian democracy, which allowed men to live as they pleased, supported Rousseau's inclination to such paradoxes as forcing men to be free—free in ways not of their own sweet pleasure.

Like the author of *The Republic*, however, he did not actually compose his *Social Contract* in an enthusiastic or optimistic spirit. He believed that the best possible constitution could not indefinitely prevail against the invariable tendency of government to obstruct the general will, but in particular he was oppressed by a keen sense of the political realities of his day. In his letters he wrote despairingly of the prospects of getting citizens enlightened enough to discern the general will, patriotic enough to act upon it; about the only country he thought capable of freedom was Corsica (which would presently give birth to Napoleon). He had no real hope or even serious thought of a French Republic. And so he brings up some excuse for the sweeping generalities to which both he and the *philosophes* were addicted. De Tocqueville, among the eminent critics of their excesses, himself remarked this excuse, pointing out that they saw around them "so many absurd and unjust privileges . . . so many ridiculous, ramshackle institutions," and that they could hardly press for sensible, gradual reform in "the total absence of any political freedom." As for Rousseau's general will, it is very hard at best to distinguish this actual, essential will for the common good, which may be misrepresented by the particular will of a majority at any given moment—the democratic way of getting at it; but it was especially hard in the France of his day, when "the people" had no means of expressing their will. No more could a thinker appeal to the rights of Frenchmen, corresponding to the rights of Englishmen, for there scarcely was such a thing—there were only the privileges of "estates," supplemented by a jumble of particular privileges of towns, guilds, universities, and other medieval orders. However vague the idea of "the rights of man," it made more sense.

Before writing the *Social Contract*, Rousseau had contributed to the *Encyclopedia* an article on "Political Economy" in which he outlined the contract on which he said his society was actually based: "You need me, for I am rich and you are poor. Let us therefore make a contract with one another. I will do you the honor to permit you to serve me under the condition that you give me what little you still have left for the trouble I shall take in commanding you." This account, typical of the radicalism of Rousseau's feeling, was perhaps no more unrealistic than the accounts of the *ancien régime* drawn up by its defenders, or by some lovers of medieval hierarchy today. In any case, it summed up the way a great many inarticulate Frenchmen felt; and it explains why, without plan or plot, they made a revolution that he scarcely anticipated either.

Chapter Ten | *T H E   A G E   O F*
R E V O L U T I O N

1. Stage, Cast, and Plot

Although the French Revolution has been played down by professional revolutionists in our time, it still looks like the great turning point in modern history. Revolutions have been going on ever since. Waves of them spread over western Europe in the last century; they were followed by upheavals in the Ottoman Empire, China, and czarist Russia; and lately they have become a commonplace all over the world. Now a permanent possibility, they remain the nightmare of conservatives everywhere. To be sure, the French Revolution was not the sire of all these revolutions. It was preceded by an American revolution, which made a considerable noise on the continent (though many Americans have forgotten that this noise included a ringing declaration of the right to revolution) ; and since Marx the specialists in these affairs insist that the kind they make is fundamentally different. Nevertheless, the French set the most influential example for the Old World. Out of their revolution came the ideals, or the slogans, of most of the later ones. It gave the word its common meaning of a popular rebellion, in the avowed cause of freedom or justice—an idea taken over by the Communists too. For the Glorious Revolution that a century earlier had made England a major influence on the continent had by no means made revolution the political mode, since it was essentially a classless as well as bloodless affair, without manifestoes. To many Englishmen, notably Edmund Burke, it made the French Revolution simply shocking, virtually incomprehensible.

Burke led the immediate revulsion, even before the advent of Napoleon, that still makes a sober comprehension of it difficult. Many Frenchmen were of course much more shocked, and never got over it; among its lasting consequences was the deep cleavage between Left and Right —names derived from French politics—which has prevented France from ever achieving so stable a democracy as England, and has impelled

French historians to continue fighting the Revolution to this day.[1]
Subsequent revolutions, which everywhere intensified such partisan-
ship, have made it no easier to size up fairly. Hence we now have a wide
choice in or between extremes. The French Revolution was historically
inevitable, or wholly unnecessary; it was a spontaneous outburst of
righteous indignation, or an eruption of mad violence; it was the work
of the bourgeois, the rabble, or the devil; it emphatically vindicated,
betrayed, or discredited the faith of the Enlightenment; it proved the
practical force of utopianism, or its utter futility; it signaled the triumph of democracy, or the beginnings of totalitarianism; or in the very
long or lofty view of some universal historians it made little difference
to speak of—it only marked another recurrent phase in the endless cycle,
another transparent delusion of the Earthly City. Yet in view of all
this to-do, certain conclusions remain fairly evident. The French Revolution did usher in an age of revolution—something quite new in history by any ordinary standards, and quite real and important to men
who have to live in it. Like the age it heralded, it was a deeply confused,
contradictory affair, not at all pure or simple for better or worse. Out
of it nevertheless came more rights for ordinary men, positive gains by
democratic standards—standards that after it became ever more generally and widely accepted. Even so, most men outside the Communist
world would agree that revolution is not an ideal, civilized mode of
progress, and that it never assures progress.

And so with the immediate question, why it broke out at this late
stage in Western history, and remained the political fashion. The Revolution was not clearly inevitable. Without question it was not planned
by the men who started it; they foresaw neither its early course nor its
outcome. If they were agents of some iron law of revolution, its irresistible logic still collides with immovable historians. Most clearly this
was a unique event. Nothing like it had occurred in earlier civilizations, including the Greco-Roman; history testified rather to the natural conservatism of the race, the "law" of inertia, the unlikelihood of
any such national effort to overhaul the entire state. The invariable
incongruities—between words and deeds, beliefs and actualities, expectations and outcomes—were more pronounced because the Revolution
was so novel an affair, so exciting to idealists and shocking to traditionalists. At the same time, it remains quite intelligible. It was no mere

---

[1] An eminently balanced, judicious, but sympathetic account of it, Georges Lefebvre's *The
Coming of the French Revolution*, was suppressed by the Vichy government during World
War II.

accident and was due to no simple perversity either; we can make out specific social and economic causes for its outbreak, as specific effects of ideal aspirations on its course. Both the material and the spiritual factors, especially the latter, were abetted by peculiar Western traditions; for if we looked only to poverty and misery—the obvious causes—we should expect to find perpetual revolution in the history of civilization. All this becomes still clearer, if also more complicated, in the light of contemporary uprisings all over Europe, which have been largely forgotten because of the pre-eminence of the French Revolution. And though later revolutions were all different, generally more deliberate and sometimes plotted, we can discern a significant continuity up to the Russian Revolution that has proved so crucial in recent history.

For the sake of a calm perspective, accordingly, we might pause to review the distinctive developments in European history that prepared for this decisive epoch. To begin with, there were the many popular uprisings—much more numerous than in any other civilization—from the Middle Ages on. (Even in sober England Sorokin has counted 162 "internal disturbances" violent enough to get into the record—an average of about one every eight years since Anglo-Saxon times.) They remind us of a tradition of violence and war, feudal in origin, later intensified by ethnic and religious hatreds; rebellious peasants might be fired by ugly prejudice rather than passion for liberty or justice. They also drew, however, on Christian idealism. All along some simple men like John Ball kept taking seriously the ideals of equality and fraternity. Indignation at social injustice had flared out repeatedly, seldom in high places, as seldom to any lasting effect, but keeping alive a tradition that reformers could appeal to. In the eighteenth century, when Christianity was on the defensive as never before since the Roman Empire, it perhaps contributed most to humanitarianism, for it still colored the thought and especially the moral feeling of secular reformers (like Condorcet), whose followers mostly still thought of themselves as good Christians. It helps to explain why the *philosophes* showed more enthusiasm over the doctrine of natural law than its Greek and Roman authors had, and why they made so much more of the corollary of natural rights. When during the Revolution the Jacobins introduced purely secular versions of Christian rituals, such as love feasts and altars to Reason, they were no doubt caricaturing the religion of Christ, but they were also paying tribute to its living ethical inspiration. In no Hindu, Buddhist, or Confucian society of the time could the slogan of Liberty, Equality, and Fraternity have stirred such fervor.

Similarly one reason why "Liberty" got into the trinity is that the medieval commonplaces about the sovereignty of the people had survived the rise of absolute monarchs and the disappearance of national parliaments. In seventeenth-century France some jurists still recalled Machiavelli's praise of the French Constitution, which ostensibly bound the king by the laws of the land. At the end of the century Cardinal Fénelon offset Bishop Bossuet's emphasis on the absolute authority of the king by insisting rather on his obligations. "He has all power over the people," Fénelon conceded in *Telemachus*, "but the laws have all power over him"; kings who recognized no law but their own will "have no longer a People, they have only slaves." In the eighteenth century local parliaments more openly opposed the royal will, generally in a selfish or reactionary spirit, with an eye to aristocratic privileges rather than popular rights; but they were nonetheless helping to maintain the tradition of constitutional government, a measure of political liberty.

This recalls, too, the vitality of the classical tradition. The writers of the Enlightenment typically shared Diderot's youthful enthusiasm for the classics, on which they had been brought up. Though they were still given to a romantic idealization of antiquity, now beginning to feature more radiant Greeks to go with Roman patriots and tyrannicides, and to inspire a revival of classical forms in public architecture, this revival was no mere anachronism. Thinkers were giving closer attention to the political thought and the civic ideals of the ancients. Whereas in England the idea of freedom, associated directly with the historic rights of Englishmen, was buttressed by the individualism of Locke and his class, in France it was associated more closely with the Greek ideal of rationality, the needs of a rational animal. The French Revolution had more philosophy behind it, and though unpremeditated, could soon issue in a philosophical Declaration of the Rights of Man.

Most conspicuously, however, the Enlightenment marked the critical difference between Europe and antiquity: the more active faith in the power of reason and knowledge, now fired by the novel idea of progress. It was promoted by another revolutionary development, made possible by the printing press that the ancients lacked—not only the growth but the spread of knowledge. In 1670 William Berkeley, governor of Virginia, had thanked God that there were "no free schools, nor printing"; and he added, "I hope we shall not have any these hundred years; for learning hath brought disobedience and heresy and sects into the world, and printing hath divulged them and libels against the best government." He was quite right in his fears, though not his hopes: learning and printing were indeed proving fatal to the cause of religious and political orthodoxy. In the Enlightenment Voltaire was only the conspicuous example of the influence wielded by a horde of pamphleteers, mostly now forgotten; France was eventually flooded with tracts as England had been during the Puritan Revolution. Literacy was still confined to a minority, enjoyed by relatively few workers and fewer peasants, but it had become extensive enough to provide a substantial public for the breeders of "disobedience and heresy." The rapid growth of newspapers evidenced the growing interest in public affairs, or in the divulgence of "libels against the best government"—i.e., a growing concern over apparent misgovernment. Even peasants mentioned "the rights of man" when they drew up the *cahiers* of their grievances on the eve of the French Revolution.

So we are brought back again to the key role of the bourgeois. Although by and large they were no more bent on revolution than they had been in the Middle Ages, it was primarily through them that education was spreading, to the continually expressed alarm of men high in state and church. From their ranks came the great majority of the writers and the readers who were creating public opinion, and through pamphlets, newspapers, reading clubs, and private societies (such as the Freemasons) were popularizing ideas about freedom of all kinds, religious, intellectual, political, economic. Their activity on behalf of the Enlightenment befitted a class that from the beginning had shown much more energy, enterprise, and independence of spirit than had the businessmen of Rome, Islam, or any great Eastern society. Long since a recognized Estate, they were now ready to take the stage and play the historic role assigned them in Marxist theory, as their forebears had neglected to do in earlier civilizations. To all but devout Marxists it looks like a confused role; they were scarcely a united class, their motives were generally mixed; but there is no question whatever that they took a leading part in both the French and American revolutions.

They also had considerable to do with most of the other revolutionary movements that in the closing decades of the eighteenth century erupted over Europe—in Ireland, Holland, Belgium, Italy, Switzerland, Germany, Poland, Hungary. These were diverse in cause and outcome; not all were radical, violent, or momentous enough clearly to warrant the name of revolution, still less to illustrate any simple thesis about it. They had enough in common, however, to warrant our speaking of an age of revolution. Generally they reflected the wide-spread ferment of the Enlightenment. (As one example, the works of Locke, Voltaire, Diderot, Rousseau, and others were translated into Polish.) Most were movements toward more popular government, emphasizing that the French Revolution was neither accidental nor perverse; in the Low Countries they made current the word "democrat" before it became a red-letter word in France. As popular movements they were mostly unsuccessful, concluding immediately in victory for the monarchy or the aristocracy; but thereby too they afford a perspective on the much more significant French Revolution.

Ironically, though understandably, the age of revolution followed upon the fashion of benevolent or "enlightened despotism" represented by such eminent monarchs as Frederick the Great of Prussia, Joseph II of Austria, and Catherine II of Russia, and approved by Voltaire. This may be viewed as a culmination of the best tradition of early monarchy, which had brought order out of feudal and religious disorder, as kings now concentrated on the task of modernizing their government, introducing more efficiency and more rationality, in keeping with an age of Enlightenment. It became so much the royal fashion to patronize philosophers, and to rule in their rational, liberal spirit, that even Spain conformed to it under Charles III. The chief exception was France, the land of the philosophers. Here Louis XVI made some efforts at reform, trying out the likes of Turgot as minister, but he was neither enlightened nor strong enough to play the part; so with better luck France might conceivably have escaped its revolution. Yet benevolent despotism proved to be only a transitory fashion. The reasons why it was not for Europe the road to advance are plain enough in the contrasting careers of Frederick the Great and the Hapsburg Joseph of Austria.

Frederick was by common consent the greatest king of his day, dazzling contemporaries by his brilliance at once as a soldier, a diplomat, and a philosopher-king. A self-conscious Machiavellian in his foreign policy, who felt obliged to act on principles he deplored in his philosophical reflections, he was at least consistently loyal to his declared role as "first servant of the state." Throughout his long reign (1740–1786) he made no effort to dazzle by maintaining a Versailles or setting up as a "Sun King," but devoted his exceptional talents wholly to building up his state. In spite of limited natural resources he succeeded in making Prussia a major power. This he managed by a strictly disciplined bureaucracy, based on merit rather than patronage or favoritism; the Prussian bureaucracy was a striking creative achievement, which by standards of efficiency enabled Frederick to give his people the best government in Europe. To contemporaries his rule also seemed the most enlightened because of his religious tolerance, his advancement of public education, and his concern with justice. The celebrated Prussian General Code that was drawn up at his orders, and hailed as the greatest legal achievement of the Enlightenment, included provisions about "the rights of man," grounded on the "natural liberty" of all to seek their own welfare so long as they respected the rights of others.

Actually, however, this was no landmark. The "rights of man" took hundreds of pages to spell out because the Code declared that they "arise from his birth and his estate"; it rigorously systematized all the traditional class distinctions in an aristocratic society, binding most peasants to serfdom. For Frederick the Great had not attempted any basic reorganization of Prussian society, much less reform on behalf of the common people. Rather he had strengthened the privileges of the nobility or Junker class (including such families as the Bismarcks), favoring them as he staffed his army and his bureaucracy. He rightly called himself the servant of "the state"—not the people. He proposed no new ends in keeping with new aspirations, introducing only more efficient means of achieving the traditional ends, primarily the aggrandizement of the Prussian state. He won his military fame in wars of aggression, playing the "hero" deplored by his friend Voltaire, never seriously distracted by his interests in philosophy or the supranational ideals of the age; thus he joined Russia in the cold-blooded First Partition of Poland, which began the extinction of an ancient state. Prussia as he left it was indeed a remarkable creation because a deliberate creation of a national state, without benefit of a rich cultural tradition; as the military virtues of the Junkers were harnessed by the discipline for which the nation was to become known, he rightly boasted that it was the Sparta of north Europe; but like Sparta it was built to no end more ideal than national power. And in raising some question about how enlightened Frederick's despotism was, it accentuates the fact of despotism: apart from religion, his autocratic rule entailed a rigorous regulation of both public and private life. If it may have been good for the Prussians of his time, it could not satisfy peoples who were being stirred by the ideals of the Enlightenment—as the Prussian state itself made plainer by collapsing ignominiously in the Napoleonic Wars.

Joseph II, on the other hand, was so completely devoted to these ideals that he has gone down in history as "the revolutionary emperor." Frederick the Great had helped to prepare for him during the reign of his pious mother, Maria Theresa, by aggressions that exposed the weakness of the sprawling, backward Hapsburg kingdom; though not addicted to philosophy, she became an earnest reformer. After serving as co-ruler for some years, Joseph tried to go much further and faster during his independent reign (1780–1790). He directly attacked the bulwarks of the traditional order—the Catholic Church and the nobility. Among many other things, he suppressed most of the monasteries, forbade pilgrimages, made marriage a civil contract, abolished such legal "crimes" as magic and apostasy, granted full toleration to Protestants, and renovated the curriculum of the universities. His social reforms included the abolition of serfdom and other ancient privileges of the aristocracy; he sought to make noblemen equal before the law, even to make them pay their full share of taxes.[2] In general, Joseph attempted to reorder the whole society, emancipate and enlighten all its members, and so actually institute the rational ideals that with Frederick the Great came down to a hobby or closet pastime. As a philosopher-king he was much more thoroughgoing.

Only he was as much less effective in his day: the great bulk of his reforms died with him. Their immediate effect was to stir up violent opposition all over the Hapsburg dominions, especially Belgium; here Joseph brought on a full-fledged revolution. For he had tried to put through his reforms simply by royal decree, not by constitutional means. However selfless and public-spirited, he could appear as despotic as Frederick, the more so as he depended on a secret police to spy out his enemies. However selfish the opposition, it could therefore stand on grounds of high principle. Although he found some support among the bourgeoisie and the intelligentsia, he was generally hated as an enemy of "liberty"—i.e., the medieval liberties that mostly amounted to special privileges of the few, but still constituted the principal legal check on the absolute power of the monarch.

One may say simply that Joseph II was bound to fail because he was too radical, as his more prudent mother could have told him. Still, Frederick the Great and above all Peter the Great had not inched along as they set about modernizing their countries, with much more success, and Communists in recent times have managed well enough to cast some doubt on the invariable wisdom of gradualism. It may be

---

[2] The ghost of Machiavelli might have rejoiced over his younger brother Leopold, who ruled the grand duchy of Tuscany for twenty-five years in a similar spirit. Following the lead of Beccaria, Leopold abolished torture and the death penalty, and made criminal procedures uniform for all classes.

more illuminating to consider the specific reasons for Joseph's failure, with an eye to the French Revolution that was under way by his death.

Now, he had good excuse for his highhanded methods. While most of his decrees were clearly in the public interest by democratic standards, he still lacked not only wide public support but any ready means of organizing effective support. Outside of Belgium, the middle class in his dominions was small and politically inexperienced. The great majority of his subjects were illiterate peasants, who naturally welcomed his efforts to remedy their grievances, but as naturally had little understanding of national government or due process; articulate leaders of peasant insurrections in Hungary could only declare their complete loyalty to their absolute monarch, as against their lords. Nobody called for universal suffrage, which would have been hopelessly impractical. The problems faced by Joseph II explain why the *philosophes* generally put their faith in reform from above, or government for rather than by the people, and why Rousseau believed that democracy was feasible only in a small city-state. There was no such thing as a "general will" in the heterogeneous Hapsburg kingdom.

There were, however, some organized political bodies; and these were almost uniformly hostile to the program of the revolutionary emperor because they expressed the will of the privileged few. Hungary and Bohemia retained their traditional diets, parliaments virtually monopolized by the greater landowners. Belgium had a large assortment of guilds, assemblies, town corporations, and provincial estates that made it the freest land in his realm, but that represented chiefly the vested interests of local aristocracies. And though the Hapsburg realm was on the whole more backward than western Europe, it was in this respect typical. Even apart from the nobility in every country, the principle of aristocracy not only permeated Europe but was gaining political strength. As the upper class now had a high culture— interests generally spurned by the feudal barons of the Middle Ages— the eighteenth century was more than any other the age of aristocracy.

The nobility itself was on the ascendant, regaining the political power it had lost during the growth of absolute monarchy. In England it controlled Parliament, the real ruler of the country; in Sweden it dominated the Diet that ruled without royal interference during the so-called Age of Freedom (1719–1772) ; in Prussia it won the royal favor without struggle, anticipating the coming alliance with kings that now seems quite natural but had not been the general rule; and in Russia Catherine the Great recognized the spirit of the times by issuing a

Charter of Nobility that guaranteed "independence and liberty to the
Russian nobility for all time by inheritance in future generations."
(For more feminine reasons she also gave away about a million serfs to
her favorites, or her lovers.) If the nobility suffered somewhat from the
growing ambitions of the bourgeois, it compensated by a more conscious
pride in birth and rank, exalted feelings that had not yet been given the
vulgar name of "class consciousness." While the wealthier bourgeois
tried to buy their way into its ranks, it was paid a seemlier compliment
by other established orders, in town and guild as in church and university. These middle orders were everywhere aping it by settling down
as closed orders, dominated when not legally ruled by a hereditary elite.
The tendency was especially marked in the "free" cities of Holland,
Belgium, Switzerland, and Germany, though here it might seem igno-
ble because another name for a merchant aristocracy is "plutocracy."
The nobles who ruled the nominal republic of Venice tacitly recognized this sordid aspect of the universal tendency by disdaining the
commerce on which their ancestors had grown wealthy.

Even so, this ordered society of the eighteenth century had the perennial appeal of the aristocratic principle, or of hierarchy. Some historians
still dwell on its ideal aspect as a series of orders, perhaps rather untidy
but on the whole harmonious, in which every man had his place, was
associated with other men of the same occupation and interest, knew
both his rights and his duties, and so could enjoy the freedom of psychological security. Granted that not every man was in the right place,
still the few at the top might be bred to the responsibilities of command,
the many might be free from the frustrations and anxieties bound to
attend any struggle based on the always uncertain standards of merit.
At that, it was not a caste society, but made some provision for "natural" aristocracy; men of exceptional energy and ability could rise to
the top, especially in England and France. With the help of such new
blood the aristocracy cultivated a gracious, civilized way of life, perhaps best symbolized by the music of Mozart, which nourished the arts
and sciences. In any case, its authority seemed natural to most men, not
inherently a form of tyranny. Many complained of particular abuses
or hated particular noblemen; few protested against the principle of
aristocratic rule or the existence of a noble class. The enlightened generally agreed with Montesquieu that it was essential to political freedom, as a safeguard against royal absolutism.

Yet only the most sentimental apologists for the *ancien régime* can
argue that the nobility as a class, and all the other hierarchical orders,

were much concerned about any freedom other than their own rights or privileges. By its nature the regime was set against ideals of freedom, for its essence was status, not contract; the orders were not free associations, freely chosen. A basically nonrational system, it was most clearly "natural" as a rationalization of medieval custom; de Tocqueville—himself an aristocrat—observed that behind its many absurd or pernicious regulations one could always find some financial expedient that had crystallized into an institution. The most privileged nobility was most vulnerable to criticism since it was based on an enforced, not a natural inequality of men, and many of its members were obviously not superior in personal merit or intelligence. It contributed a good deal to the systematic mismanagement of affairs, the more because a dignified place had to be found for all its younger sons in government or army, church or university. As for culture, the nobility was generally more decorative than creative; it contributed most conspicuously to the growing tyranny of mere fashion, in literature as in dress and furniture. Other words for its gracious style of life are "classy" and "rococo."

Neither was the society as a whole a clearly harmonious order, for by its nature the regime also made for narrowness and partiality in outlook, blindness to considerations of the general will. "The nation," Turgot reported confidentially to Louis XVI, "is an aggregate of different and incompatible social groups whose members have so few links between them that everyone thinks solely of his own interests; no trace of any feelings for the public weal is anywhere to be found." And again the nobles were apt to be the most irresponsible, despite their tradition of *noblesse oblige*. In their pride they were often more lawless and ungovernable than the "rabble" they despised or feared, while they were never so proud as to disdain sinecures or royal handouts. The badge of nobility that they most stubbornly, fiercely clung to was exemption from most common taxation—the privilege of not paying their share in the upkeep of the society that maintained them so handsomely. Thereby they contributed more than their share to the chronic difficulties of royal government in the eighteenth century.

This apparent inequity, which was increasingly resented, leads us to the heart of the drama in the age of revolution. It meant more hardship for the many poor who had to pay the taxes, and who in general had fared badly in the material progress of the century, remaining at the often untender mercies of noble landowners and town oligarchs. Hence the hierarchical order that ideally produced the freedom of psychological security actually produced much bitterness, alienating the

ruled, then making the rulers more fearful. As the upper classes—
noble and oligarchic—got embroiled in conflicts with both kings and
popular movements, they revealed that there was less enlightened aristocracy than enlightened despotism.[3] Thus in Poland a revolution
ended in the setting up of a Constitution (1791) that was moderate
enough to delight Edmund Burke, extending some rights to burghers
and especially the lesser nobility while leaving the serfs pretty much
as they were, yet the greater landowners would have none of it; they
promptly made war on the new regime and succeeded in crushing it,
with the help of Catherine the Great—whereupon followed the Second
Partition of Poland. In western Europe the Belgians forced the issue
more sharply by their successful rebellion against Joseph II. When a
democratic party proposed equal representation for all citizens in the
liberated country, an abbot of Tongerloo summed up and gave away
the case for the aristocratic orders: "The abbots as a group represent the
secular and regular clergy, and indeed they represent the whole rural
country as well, being the largest landowners; and, finally, usage has
always been this way and should remain so, since it is constitutional
and the Constitution cannot be changed." The democrats lost out, and
the regular clergy then followed usage by leading a reign of terror
against them—another privilege that had long been exercised by the
nobility in putting down rebellious peasants, but that appalled Edmund Burke when it was usurped by revolutionary leaders in France.

France had lagged somewhat in the resurgence of aristocracy. Finally,
however, the French nobility took the lead in starting what became the
French Revolution. For every fault of theirs, this turned out to be a
democratic revolution, quite different from all the others on the continent, which permanently ended the *ancien régime* in France. But a
further reason for this outcome was the revolutionary example of
America. The "New World" had long been enflaming the imagination
of Europe, stimulating such advanced thinkers as Montaigne, More,
and Bacon, providing the natural setting for Utopias, New Atlantises,
and El Dorados—anticipating the saying that the invention of America
was more important than its discovery. Now the Americans had demonstrated that a free society was no mere philosopher's dream, proclaimed
to the Old World the real hope of a new order. Upon winning their

---

[3] A premonitory instance was Maria Theresa's effort to abolish judicial torture. She ended
it in her hereditary domain of Austria but was unable to do so in Beccaria's native duchy
of Milan; its Senate declared that torture was essential to sound government. Joseph II
finally abolished it in Milan by first doing away with the Senate.

independence they had given substance to Rousseau's concept of the general will by drawing up a Constitution that began "We the People of the United States," and proceeded to lay down articles designed to "promote the general welfare, and secure the blessings of liberty to ourselves and our posterity." Without this example the French might very well have made their revolution anyway, especially because they saw in America what they already believed or what they wanted to see; but the fact remains that the curtain on the great revolutionary drama went up in America.

2. *Revolution in the New World*

Although Americans have long been united in a conviction of the necessity, propriety, and beneficence of the American Revolution, there has been a growing disposition to regard it as not really a revolution at all—only a war of independence, in defense of traditional rights. This disposition obviously reflects the conservative mood of a nation grown fearful of revolutionists (not to mention the attitudes of such bemused or benighted groups as that oddly named the Daughters of the American Revolution). It points, however, to some significantly unconventional aspects of the affair. Up to a point this was in fact a conservative affair, inspired by no idea of revolutionizing either the social or the political structure. It was led by the upper class; the signers of the Declaration of Independence were exceptionally solid, respectable men, almost all of high social standing. The rebellion did not go the way made familiar by later revolutions, into a Jacobin reign of terror or the dictatorship of a Napoleon. Foreigners might add that it was not a very fierce or heroic struggle, and that it was won largely by default of the English, with the substantial aid of the French monarchy. A rather small minority of Americans behaved like crusaders for freedom, firing "shots heard round the world."

Nevertheless, their war of independence was strictly illegal—a violent rebellion against constituted authority. It was therefore opposed by American Loyalists, who initially made up at least a third of the population (and had much the same attitudes as the D.A.R.). The Loyalists were subjected to enough terror so that many thousands fled the country; one reason why Americans came to agree on the complete propriety of their rebellion is that they eliminated the opposition more thoroughly than the Jacobins did, in time remembering only that there had been some "traitors" in their midst. Their Declaration of Independence was plainly a revolutionary manifesto, asserting the right to revolution. Thereafter there were enough radicals among them to push the un-formed nation closer to democracy than most of its leaders wanted. Their Constitution set up a new kind of government, not so demo-cratic in intent as most Americans now fondly believe, but more demo-cratic than any other of its day. They soon became proud in the belief that theirs was a new land, quite different from the musty motherland —a pride expressed in the motto *Novus Ordo Seclorum* that is still inscribed on their most cherished national document, the dollar bill. Even as they tried vainly to keep out of European affairs, all "foreign entanglements," some began conceiving their manifest ideal destiny, to assure that government of, by, and for the people should not perish from the earth.

In any case, the doings in America looked like a revolution to con-temporaries. Indisputably they had a revolutionary influence in Europe, as the shots were indeed heard round the world. They would be signifi-cant enough merely as a successful war of independence, launching the career of a nation due to become a world power; but at this stage they were more significant as a major episode in a larger revolutionary movement.

From the day of its discovery the New World was never isolated, of course, immediately influencing history in Europe and always being influenced by it, remaining essentially European in culture. The diverse native peoples naturally made some difference, but not primarily by their own will. Thus in Central and South America, where the Span-iards ran into civilizations rich in silver and gold, it was the metal that made the big difference. Otherwise these American civilizations may be dismissed very briefly here, for despite their intrinsic interest they added little of consequence to the world's treasury of culture, and nothing whatever to the tradition of freedom. While from impulses most likely come from Asia they had gone on to develop a distinctive high cul-ture of their own, they had settled down into the basic pattern of the sacred monarchy that prevailed in all the early Asiatic civilizations. A priestly aristocracy, in time headed by kings, ruled over masses of peas-ants or serfs, and apparently tended to a brutal tyranny. The Aztecs, the latest comers in Mexico before the Spaniards, seem the bloodiest because of their custom of human sacrifice to the gods, who on high occasions demanded thousands of victims; but the common fate of violent destruc-

tion that overtook the royal or religious centers in Central America—
violent beyond the ordinary destructiveness of barbarians—suggests the
fury of people long oppressed. Although the Spaniards might still have
learned something from the civilizations they destroyed (beyond the
cultivation of some crops), they were bent chiefly on exploiting their
subjects, and they destroyed the more wantonly because Indian art
was unchristian.[4] On the whole, the good fortune met by the Spaniards
brought out the worst in them.

In North America colonists encountered only primitive Indians,
from whom they could learn nothing but some New World agriculture
and woodlore. At first mostly friendly, the Indians helped to inspire
the popular idea of the "noble savage," heralding the primitivism that
Rousseau made fashionable. (The colonists might have been more impressed by the Iroquois confederacy, which achieved a remarkable
measure of representative democracy in the maintenance of internal
peace and mutual aid.) They became chiefly a nuisance when not a
menace, however, as the colonies began to expand. Too independent to
be enslaved like the peasants in Latin America, they had to be pushed
back, and they then acquired a worse reputation than they deserved;
their "savagery," intensified by an understandable hatred of the white
men, was exaggerated because the colonists had to justify their own
tactics of chicanery and brute force. The self-righteous Protestant English made little effort to convert the Indians, sending out no such missionaries as the French to the north of them and the Spaniards to the
south.

Yet this ugly story points to other basic differences of potentially
more ideal consequences. The Spanish *conquistadores* came as adven-
turers and gold seekers, and though their feat of winning an empire
was more astounding in that they managed it largely on their own, with

---

[4] In fairness to these societies, which in a history of freedom call for no more than a footnote, I should at least emphasize that they had some highly impressive feats to their credit.
The Incas in Peru managed to become great builders and administrators even though they
had not acquired the art of writing—the only recognized civilization to lack this art. Among
the brilliant achievements of the early Mayans was a calendar more accurate than that
of the Spanish conquerors. The conquerors themselves were awed by the monumental
architecture of their victims.

As for the rest of early American art, I should confess to some difficulty in appreciating
it because its subject or apparent intent is so often repulsive; I find its "archaic" phases
generally more attractive than its "classical" ones. (One early culture in Mexico stands
out for a singularly lively, humanistic art.) At any rate, these societies are further witness
that neither art nor religion is *ipso facto* a clear mode of freedom. As in many other
societies, art was dedicated primarily to the service of unspiritual gods, or immediately
of despotic priests and kings.

little aid from the Spanish crown, as freebooters they were not men to organize an empire. Within a generation the royal government stepped in, to assure a more regular flow of precious metal. In administering the "Indies," it sent over governors and granted business monopolies to royal favorites; there was no question of self-rule or liberty for the colonists. The Spanish Church was no more a pure boon to the colonists than to the Indians. It promptly began accumulating land and collecting a large share of the imperial revenues, eventually owning about half the property. While some of its missionaries recorded their indignation over the callous treatment of the Indians, it was mostly content to build hundreds of churches and monasteries, keep the faith pure by installing the Inquisition, and bring the spiritual comforts of mystery and miracle to the exploited, while leaving them in poverty and ignorance. Together, Church and Crown maintained the colonial empire for almost three hundred years, and as effectively prevented the growth of freedom until the English colonies infected Spanish America with their revolutionary example.

The first Englishmen to settle in America likewise came seeking gold, and so had a wretched time of it in Virginia until they discovered the possibilities of tobacco. In Massachusetts, however, the Puritans settled for quite different reasons; seeking a haven from persecution in the Old World, they were the first to give the new one its ideal meaning in the history of freedom—a land where men might live by their own lights, be their own masters. In both colonies, and all later ones, the emigrants settled down to the normal pursuits of agriculture and commerce, not living as conquerors; one reason why they neglected to send out missionaries to the Indians was that they were busy making their own living, fashioning a new life for themselves. And in varying degrees they were governing themselves, under charters suited to English tradition. Virginia's charter included the famous clause that all English colonists and their offspring "shall have and enjoy all liberties, franchises, and immunities . . . as if they had been abiding and born, within this our realm of England." The Pilgrims in Massachusetts had drawn up their more famous Mayflower Compact, in which all agreed to abide by the will of the majority—one reason why the historical myth of the social contract might not seem like a mere fiction to American thinkers. Other colonial charters, as in Pennsylvania and Georgia, expressed the hope of an ideal commonwealth.

Needless to add, all the colonies fell far short of this ideal. By the end of the seventeenth century England was supervising their affairs more systematically, through royal governors, and internally they were

A *condottiere*—
Gattamelata by Donatello (p. 128)
Alinari-Art Reference Bureau

Pope Leo X by Raphael—
at right Cardinal Giulio de' Medici,
the future Clement VII (p. 125)
Alinari-Art Reference Bureau

An auto-da-fé—
anonymous engraving (p. 173)

Witches—
woodcut after Hans Baldung Grien (p. 154)

Founder of the House of Fugger (p. 187)
Courtesy of the Lilly Library

The Sun King:
Louis XIV, by Rigau
(pp. 210 ff.)
*Alinari-Art
Reference Bureau*

The Court of Louis XIV: Versailles (pp. 211 ff.), *French Government Tourist Office*

Hall of Mirrors, Versailles, *French Government Tourist Office*

City plan of Amsterdam (p. 229). *Netherlands Information Service*

Domestic life
in the Dutch Republic:
The Mother,
by Pieter de Hooch
(pp. 229 ff.)
*Marburg-Art
Reference Bureau*

The "High Mightinesses" of the Dutch Republic:
The Syndics, by Rembrandt (p. 226), *Bruckmann-Art Reference Bureau*

FRANCISCI
DE VERULAMIO,
Summi Angliæ
CANCELLARII.

Multi pertransibunt & augebitur scientia

LONDINI
Apud [Joannem] Billium,
Typographum
Regium.

Voyage to the "New Intellectual World"—
frontispiece of Bacon's *Novum Organum* (pp. 186, 242)

Isaac Newton (pp. 267 ff.)

Mining Operations,
from Agricola's *De Re Metallica* (p. 239)

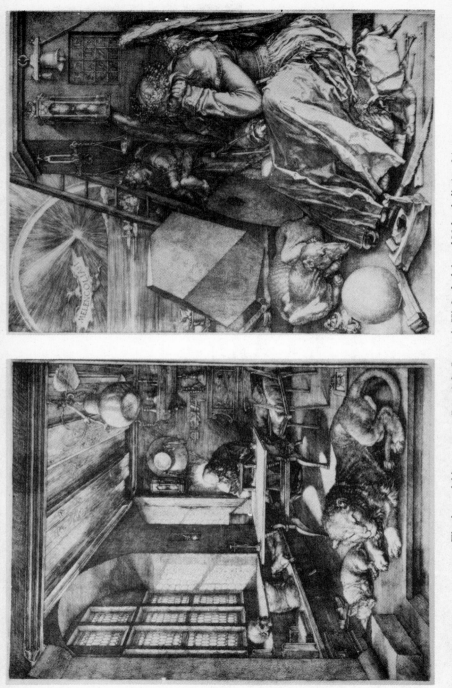

The shape of things to come: Dürer's St. Jerome in His Study, left, and Melancholia (p. 263)
The Metropolitan Museum of Art

The type of the Grand Inquisitor:
Cardinal Guevara, head of the Spanish Inquisition, by El Greco
(p. 173), *The Metropolitan Museum of Art*

Henry VIII by Holbein (pp. 281 ff.)
Alinari-Art Reference Bureau

Philip II of Spain, by Titian (pp. 288-289)
Anderson-Art Reference Bureau

THE
"MIGHTY
OPPOSITES"

Queen Elizabeth of England (pp. 287 ff.)
National Portrait Gallery from Art Reference Bureau

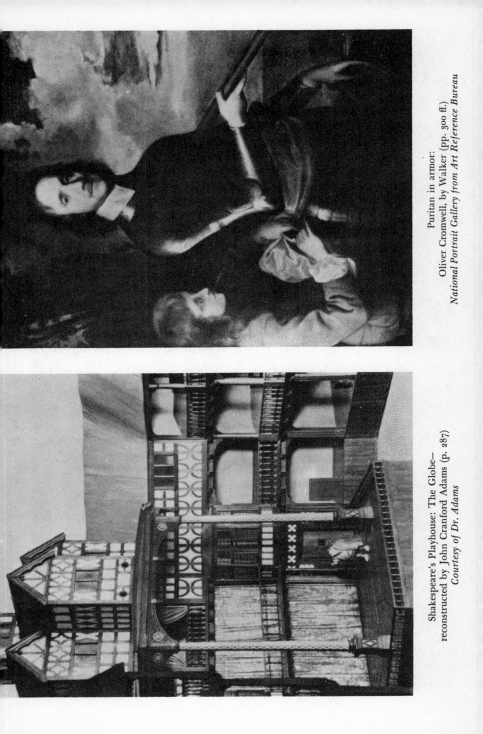

Puritan in armor:
Oliver Cromwell, by Walker (pp. 300 ff.)
National Portrait Gallery from Art Reference Bureau

Shakespeare's Playhouse: The Globe—
reconstructed by John Cranford Adams (p. 287)
Courtesy of Dr. Adams

The Declaration of Independence, by John Trumbull (p. 361)
Yale University Art Gallery

The Oath of the Tennis Court, by David (p. 387)
Fogg Art Museum from Art Reference Bureau

The costs of Napoleon's dream: Execution of the Citizens of Madrid, by Goya (p. 394)

dominated by aristocratic or oligarchic interests. But at least they were not subject to purely arbitrary or despotic rule. They enjoyed considerable self-government through popularly elected assemblies, which in most of the colonies managed to hold their own against the meddlesome tendencies of the governors. While the vote was usually restricted to property owners, there were so many of these—in New England a distinct majority of adult males—that the colonial assemblies were more nearly democratic than any such bodies in Europe. The idea of government by consent of the governed was no revolutionary ideal in America, but was pretty much taken for granted.

Similarly the colonists came to enjoy an exceptionally large measure of religious freedom. The early Puritans in New England wanted such freedom only for themselves, of course, and their leaders were no more disposed to democracy—"the meanest and worst of all forms of government," according to Governor Winthrop; Massachusetts under the Saints was much like Calvin's Geneva. In as due course, however, the theocratic dictators stirred the independent, rebellious tendencies of other Puritans. Roger Williams, one of the first rebels, was the most advanced too, preaching no mere toleration but full freedom of conscience. At Providence he founded a settlement where all men could enjoy full political rights regardless of their religious beliefs, thereby establishing the first government in history devoted to religious freedom; and these terms were incorporated in the charter later granted to Rhode Island. Meanwhile Lord Baltimore had been granted the territory of Maryland as a haven for Catholics, whom he protected against inroads of Protestant settlers by persuading the local assembly to pass a Toleration Act. Later the Quaker William Penn carried out in Pennsylvania his "Holy Experiment" in republicanism and religious freedom, with immediate success. Elsewhere the Anglican Church was generally favored, but not so firmly established as a state church as it was in England. Everywhere toleration was forced on the many intolerant Americans because they belonged to so many different sects. Religion was accordingly not a vital issue in the American Revolution, nor clearly a vital inspiration. "It will never be pretended," John Adams wrote later, "that the men who set up the American governments had interviews with the gods, or were in any degree under the inspiration of Heaven." In fact it was so pretended, or at least "divine Providence" was dutifully called in to bless the Declaration of Independence; but Providence could oblige more readily because most Americans had stopped quarreling over its designs or its political demands.

As an old man, John Adams also anticipated the popular saying that

Americans were free men long before they became technically independent. The war with Britain was "no part of the revolution," he wrote, only a result of it: "The revolution was in the minds and hearts of the people . . . before a drop of blood was shed at Lexington." Despite its popularity this idea was substantially true, and as significant of the New World; but on all counts it therefore calls first for some serious qualifications.

A great many Americans did not come to the new land as free men, but arrived as indentured servants. To pay their passage they sold themselves into servitude for some years, on terms that permitted their masters to resell the indenture and in other respects treat them as slaves; and there were still several hundred thousand of these at the time of the Revolution, or about a tenth of the population. Much more ominous was the early introduction of outright chattel slavery—the last word in unfreedom. Negroes were found most useful on Southern plantations, but New Englanders too were pleased to specialize in the always lucrative slave traffic. (In Boston Peter Faneuil built his famous hall out of his profits in this traffic.) Although Congress prohibited further importation during the Revolution, smugglers had little trouble, stirred as little feeling of public outrage. Congress had also deleted a condemnation of slavery in Jefferson's draft of the Declaration of Independence, addressed to a "candid world," which proclaimed that all men are created equal. Later the constitutions of Southern states specified, candidly or carefully, that only "all freemen" are equal. What Jefferson denounced as a "cruel war against human nature itself" brought out some national aptitude for self-righteousness or possible hypocrisy before it brought on the fiercest war of the nineteenth century, which among other things demonstrated that Southerners had become slaves of their anachronistic system.

With its plantation economy, the South was likewise most conspicuous for the colonial aristocracy that belied the alleged native passion for equality. Thus a thousand or so families completely dominated the society and controlled the local government of South Carolina. In the North political power was largely in the hands of a commercial aristocracy, in which rich Quaker merchants figured as prominently as the erstwhile Saints of New England. Everywhere the leaders of society held it as axiomatic that only men of property were entitled to full political rights. The many businessmen and land speculators among them were also leading the way to the reign of the almighty dollar, or what Americans would characteristically call the "acquisitive instinct":

a frank materialism that pointed up the notorious rawness of early American life. The few colonial cities of any size—Boston, New York, Philadelphia, Charleston—were small islands of civility in a vast rude sea; most "free" Americans lived in huts or cabins on half-cleared farms and enjoyed a pretty meager culture, if they enjoyed it at all. A generation after they won the Revolution that was only a postscript to the revolution they had made long before, the *Edinburgh Review* published its celebrated taunt: "In the four quarters of the globe, who reads an American book? Or goes to an American play? Or looks at an American picture or statue?"

Still, this taunt was something of a tribute to the new nation. In winning their independence, Americans had won enough attention in all quarters of Europe to embarrass their former masters, worry traditionalists everywhere; they had at least written political documents that were widely read. They had a plain excuse, moreover, for the rawness of their life, since so many of them perforce lived on frontiers, and the nation concentrated on the immense physical job of clearing the land. The materialism for which they would become known round the world was inseparably connected with the ideals that also made America a world symbol. "Opportunity" became a national byword because the New World was in fact a land of opportunity for common men, as some million had testified by leaving their homeland; and the first thing they wanted, naturally, was to make a better living. They had the simple dream that would sustain the many more millions to come, the hope that their children would enjoy a better opportunity than they themselves had. Apart from all those who had sought a haven from religious or political oppression, Americans became freer men in spirit because they had much more chance to fulfill such dreams than ordinary men had in Europe.

Granted the servitude of many, the simple truth remains that the poor in general were always better off in America. As laborers in colonial cities, for instance, they earned wages about four times the wages paid in London. If most of them remained poor, very few were paupers, a great many were independent farmers or artisans. Always some kept acting out the favorite national legend, the story of the poor boy who made good; Benjamin Franklin himself wrote as well as exemplified the story. Most took for granted that in America one could always "make something of oneself," "better oneself." Individualism was no mere theory, but to a considerable extent a simple fact of American life.

Granted, too, the power and privilege of the colonial aristocracy, this was still quite different from the aristocracy that reigned in Europe. Mostly it was an industrious class, only in South Carolina conspicuously a leisure class. It was not a legal caste, with titles and hereditary privileges, nor was it entrenched in such traditional orders and estates as ran all through European society. (Genealogy did not become the fashion until the nineteenth century, if only because few Americans could trace their ancestry to noble families, and there had to be a Revolution before there could be Daughters.) An aristocracy that worked for its living and included many self-made men tended to be less disdainful of ordinary workers, and in any case it was accorded no such deference as the nobility in Europe; de Crèvecoeur observed that the ordinary man in America forgot "that mechanism of subordination, that servility of disposition which poverty had taught him." There was considerably more democratic feeling of equality, in a much more fluid, mobile society. It appeared in the continual local revolts against the gentry or oligarchy. It took more sociable form in the popular sentiment that every man ought to be given a fair chance, and in concrete efforts to equalize opportunity. Massachusetts had set an unprecedented example in 1647 by making primary schooling not only free but compulsory; other New England settlements soon followed suit. At about the same time Massachusetts adopted by far the most humane law code of the seventeenth century, when savage punishment was the common rule for even the petty crimes of the poor.

Such innovations were also signs of a broader disposition to experiment, more openness to change than in the Old World. The too familiar commonplaces about the pioneers and life on the frontier, and today the sluggish response to exhortations to open "new frontiers," are likely to obscure the living truth of early American life, the extent to which men actually thought, felt, and behaved like pioneers in a new world. Hard as life was on the frontier, it not only demanded energy and enterprise but promised to reward them. With the expansion of the country came more feeling of expansiveness, more sense of "wide-open spaces." The idea of progress was in America no mere historical theory but a vital optimism, rooted in the fact of material progress and the obvious potentialities for further progress. De Crèvecoeur summed up the new mentality:

> An European, when he first arrives, seems limited in his intentions, as well as in his views; but he very suddenly alters his scale; two hundred miles formerly appeared a very great distance, it is now

but a trifle; he no sooner breathes our air than he forms schemes, and embarks in designs he never would have thought of in his own country. There the plenitude of society confines many useful ideas, and often extinguishes the most laudable schemes which here ripen into maturity. Thus Europeans become Americans.

By the same token Americans were less disposed to reverence for authority, tradition, the past. That a custom or institution was old was not automatic proof that it was sound; appeals to the wisdom of the ancestors carried less weight for men who had left the land of their ancestors, often in discontent. In ordinary Americans this disposition might come down to a simple ignorance of the past, or a brash contempt of it. It plainly accentuated the crudeness of American life, as de Crèvecoeur noted; it was allied with the national traits of restlessness and rootlessness, the frontier tendencies to lawlessness or anarchic individualism; and in few Americans was it a seriously reasoned attitude, worthy of being dignified as a philosophy. Yet it helped to give America its especial significance for thoughtful Europeans in an age grown critical of venerable institutions and beliefs. Thomas Paine struck the new note in his insistence that first and last the living should be accommodated, not the dead: "Every age and generation must be free to act for itself in *all cases* as the ages and generations which preceded it. The vanity and presumption of governing beyond the grave is the most ridiculous and insolent of all tyrannies."

All this helps to explain the suddenness of the official American Revolution—and let us add at once, its inglorious aspects, the reasons why it was not born of the simple love of freedom featured in all American textbooks until recent times. Ten years before it broke out there was hardly a thought of open rebellion, still less a general desire for independence from England, in colonies that were markedly prosperous. The immediate causes of agitation were obviously economic, and were played up by a small minority of colonists. When the war was started by some "embattled farmers" in Lexington and Concord, Americans proclaimed their perfect union but in fact they were still far from united in any agreement on what they wanted, and why; apart from the many convinced Loyalists, as many more were half-hearted because they felt free enough or well enough off. Their most famous Declaration of Independence (which incidentally was not signed on July 4) was agreed upon primarily as a means of securing aid from France. The British helped out immeasurably by hiring Hessian mercenaries, who did most to keep alive resentment of the mother country. Even so the war settled down into a pretty dreary, muddled affair, among the least heroic struggles in the history of freedom, as neither side showed much stomach for it. George Washington exerted the most heroic effort simply to hold together a dwindling army, a feat he barely managed. The states were too suspicious of one another to entrust strong power to their Continental Congress, most Americans too independent, fractious, or self-seeking to heed its pleas for men and money. Very possibly they might not have won the war except for French aid.

Involuntarily, the French had also helped to bring on the Revolution by the Seven Years' War with England. This struggle for the mastery of North America, which ended their empire on the continent, emboldened the English colonists by freeing them from fears of dangerous enemies on their borders.[5] At the same time, the war had almost doubled the national debt of England; so the royal government decided that the prosperous colonists should pay a larger share of its upkeep, which included the costs of protecting them. The Stamp Act of 1765 touched off the uproar in the colonies. Though shortly repealed, it was followed by more or less blundering efforts to impose taxes or import duties, coupled with other restrictions on colonial trade, which led to more violent indignation, such impromptu defiance as the Boston Tea Party, and by 1774 the concerted defiance of the First Continental Congress.

Now, the many grievances detailed as "facts" in the Declaration of Independence, dressed up with such epithets as "absolute tyranny" and "cruelty and perfidy scarcely paralleled in the most barbarous ages," were grossly exaggerated. The tyranny had produced nothing more atrocious than the "Boston Massacre," in which a few Americans were shot during the confusion of a riot. The colonists bore a much lighter tax burden than did the English themselves, or any other people in western Europe. If they had good English precedent for their slogan

---

[5] The story of the French in America is another that need not be detailed here. Their colonization had been managed chiefly by the government rather than private initiative, and Louis XIV, intent on his imperial ambitions in Europe, failed to back up the vision of such bold missionaries and explorers as Marquette and La Salle. The Frenchmen who settled in Canada to exploit its fisheries and furs had little evident zeal to make a new life for themselves, especially because Protestants were not allowed to join them; at the time of the Seven Years' War, New France had only a very small fraction of the population of English America. Its survival in the French-speaking inhabitants of Canada was at this stage of negligible consequence in the history of the Western world.

"No taxation without representation," the great majority of English-men were not represented in Parliament either; and at that there is little question that the colonists would have remained dissatisfied had they been granted some members, since Parliament would have pro-ceeded to tax them anyway. In the Declaration of Independence they never even mentioned Parliament, or "the rights of British subjects" that they had been clamoring about for ten years. They singled out the king as the villain, making him responsible for all the intolerably oppressive measures, though these had been quite constitutional pro-ceedings. If George III was asserting himself more than the witless Georges before him, he was hardly the absolute tyrant they made out.

Nevertheless, the colonists did have some genuine grievances. For more than a century they had been treated as stepchildren, not as equals in the national commonwealth. Both their trade and their in-dustry had been kept under restrictions, immediately for the benefit not of the commonwealth—as Adam Smith pointed out—but of British merchants; these merchants annually made millions off them. Thus the tax on tea was hated the more because it was a pure gift to the East India Company. As the controversy went on, the royal governors grew more dictatorial, threatening the rights of the colonial assemblies. And the very prosperity of the expanding colonies made all such interfer-ence seem more intolerable. "There is something absurd," exclaimed Paine, "in supposing a Continent to be perpetually governed by an island." In England William Pitt anticipated such common sense, warning Parliament that England might better retreat while it was still able to do so: "you cannot conquer the Americans." Pitt also answered the conservative argument that like all Englishmen Americans were "virtually represented" in Parliament, describing such nominal repre-sentation as the "most contemptible" idea that had ever been dreamed up.

That Englishmen would continue to put up with such inequities well into the nineteenth century only emphasized the change that had come over their fellows in the New World. Americans, including both John and Sam Adams, had dutifully paid tribute to the English Constitution, describing it as admirably calculated "to preserve the blessing of liberty"; but their economic grievances made them aware that in fact it was preserving chiefly the interests of oligarchy. Parliament kept resisting all reforms, fearful of the "leveling principle," which as one member warned made "the people imagine they themselves shall be judges over us." Americans were given to imagining precisely this, and they soon made foremost the issue of their political rights.[6] The more radical, like Sam Adams, took to democratic slogans, developing a skill at revolutionary propaganda that Americans may now fail to appreciate. Tom Paine had an immense popular success with his tract *Common Sense,* in which he attacked not only George III but monarchy itself, and made the first appeal for an American Republic. And by this time even the conservative leaders of the colonists were being impelled to take up strictly radical positions. Since their legal case against Parliament remained weak, and most Britishers did not enjoy the rights they claimed, they shifted their grounds: these provincials began asserting universal principles, philosophical rather than merely traditional or customary. In the Declaration of Independence they made no mention of "the rights of British subjects" because they were claiming rights simply as men—rights proper for all men—as the British had not done in their Glorious Revolution.

The doctrine of natural law and natural right here affirmed may therefore look like mere rationalizing. Certainly it was a kind of afterthought, not the direct "cause" of the Revolution. As certainly its principle of equality was more radical in implication than most of the signers of the Declaration really meant; they were by no means so devoted to popular government as their inescapable appeal to the sovereignty of "the people" might suggest. But neither were they merely dressing up or disguising their class interests, any more than the Revolution itself was clearly due to inexorable economic necessity. Their interests as aristocratic landowners or bourgeois merchants would as naturally have inclined them to be Loyalists, as a great many of their fellows in fact were. (A historical materialist finds it hard to explain, for instance, why Virginia was so much more revolutionary than New York.) Once committed, at any rate, the American leaders made it plainer that fundamental principles were at stake, first of all the principle that government derived its just power only from the consent of the governed. Call their Declaration of Independence a rationaliza-

---

[6] The economic interpretation of history has inspired such typical verdicts as Louis Hacker's, that "the struggle was *not* over high-sounding political and constitutional concepts . . . *but* over colonial manufacturing, wild lands and furs, sugar, wine, tea and currency." (Italics mine.) I am as usual substituting "both-and." Here it seems to me especially clear that low-sounding economic interests were the immediate cause of the conflict, but that the political concepts became as vital a factor and for the long run were much more significant. Rebellious colonists had largely forgotten sugar, wine, tea, etc. by the time they were declaiming "Give me liberty, or give me death!"

tion, by the same token it brought the American cause into the main stream of European thought.

The content of its Preamble was of course not at all original. Jefferson explicitly disclaimed any originality, emphasizing that every idea in it was "hackneyed"; as he later wrote, his object was simply "to place before mankind the common sense of the subject." This sense came directly out of English political thought, in particular Blackstone and Locke. Jefferson had not only read Locke, like most educated Americans, but reread him, learned him almost by heart. Likewise the Preamble echoed the thought of the Enlightenment, which was as well known to Americans. The rather casual reference to "Nature's God" recalls that the leaders of the Revolution were mostly deists—not ardent Puritans—who were inclined to be more worshipful of Nature than of God, and of Newtonian than of scriptural revelation. Hence these highly debatable principles could be proclaimed in all simplicity and sincerity as "self-evident" truths. Hence, too, they were liable to the charge of "glittering and sounding generalities" that conservative Americans later echoed; and admirers of Jefferson may grant that the happy phrases or noises came too easily, without the excuse of intense feeling. Yet the Preamble remains a simple, plain, on the whole typically dignified statement of principles that to men of the Enlightenment seemed truly self-evident. Without question it was these ideal principles that gave the American Revolution its enduring historical significance for the Old World, and made it in European eyes strictly a revolution, not merely a war for independence.

If they failed to inspire many Americans in the often sorry struggle that followed, they were at least repeated in the constitutions that the various states adopted during the war, and that were widely studied in Europe. Pennsylvania's constitution was notably democratic, as more embattled farmers wrested power from Quaker patricians tending to be loyalist. Elsewhere not many more Americans were directly enfranchised, but the common people asserted themselves enough to support the common charge of Loyalists that the Revolution was all their doing, too much democracy was the root of the trouble. Their leaders justified Condorcet's observation of the great advantage Americans had in not having a nobility and as privileged a clergy, estates tied to a venerable tradition of flagrant inequity and misrule; they were mostly responsible or prudent enough to remain loyal to the declared principles of the Revolution. Abroad the new nation had an ideal ambassador in Benjamin Franklin, at once a plain man of the people, thoroughly American, and a civilized man of the world, the ideal type of the *philosophe*. At home George Washington, the hero of the war, refused the crown offered by his army, the chance to become a Cromwell or a Napoleon. In general, there was relatively little tyranny or terror except in the treatment of Loyalists. The American Revolution did not "devour its children" as the French one would.

The major test came when the victorious states proceeded to draw up a federal Constitution that made them a nation, the United States. This too was something essentially new in Western history, as "the people" proved their nominal sovereignty by deliberately creating their form of government. The Constitution itself was as novel in providing for federation with a strong central government, which Holland and Switzerland had lacked, and in setting up an elaborate system of checks and balances, such as Montesquieu and others mistakenly saw in England. The aged Franklin, a member of the Convention that wrote it, accordingly viewed it with some misgiving, uncertain whether it signified that the sun was rising or setting on the new land. Although he finally rejoiced in the conviction that it was a rising sun, "the people" were mostly far from enthusiastic over their new Constitution. They had reasons that still make it a controversial subject.

To a great many men the Constitution looked more like a conservative reaction against the Revolution than a democratic fulfillment of it. Condorcet deplored its "aristocratic spirit," Jefferson saw it as an "oligarchic" effort to suppress democracy, others anticipated Charles Beard's economic interpretation of it as the work of men of property seeking chiefly to protect their interests. The Founding Fathers themselves made no bones about the supreme importance of property, as both the means and the end of good government; they worried a great deal over the possible tyranny of the majority, much less over the much more common tyranny of minorities. Farmers and artisans were not represented in the Convention that drew up the Constitution, in secrecy. The American people knew almost nothing about its deliberations until fifty years later, but they could guess that the celebrated system of checks and balances was designed primarily as a check on the common people, who directly elected only the lower house of Congress and at that were not granted universal suffrage. The Fathers quite ignored the principle of equality asserted in the Declaration of Independence, and in effect forgot too their previous indignation over the idea of taxation without representation; many agreed with Elbridge Gerry that democracy was "the worst of all political evils." They argued against a Bill of Rights as dangerous or at best superfluous, later accept-

ing it only as a grudging concession to the democrats, in order to over-
come popular opposition to their handiwork. Even so it took a hard
fight to get the Constitution ratified, for in some states—notably such
key ones as Massachusetts, Virginia, and New York—there was at first
a positive majority against it. In the processes of ratification many of
the people had no direct representation, and many others who were
entitled to vote were too apathetic to do so; about 5 per cent of the
adult males actually voted on the Constitution that most Americans
now revere as the great symbol of their democracy. Political theorists
may add satirical comments on the mess of compromises that constitutes
the American system of government.

Yet these compromises point to the most significant facts: that concessions were made to small states and little men, a Bill of Rights was
added, and the Constitution was submitted for ratification to representative bodies in which the people did have some say. Saddled with less
crusted tradition than the aristocracy of Europe, the American ruling
class proved less stubbornly conservative, or more enlightened in self-
interest. The task of the Constitutional Convention was properly a
conservative one in so far as the plainest need at the time was not
revolution but stability and order, and a great deal of mature, responsible thought went into its proceedings, which James Madison among
others thought might "decide forever the fate of Republican government." *The Federalist* in particular was an amazingly reasonable,
measured discourse for a campaign document, or work of propaganda.
It remains a classic of political theory—in the judgment of Jefferson
himself perhaps "the best commentary on the principles of government
which has ever been written"—because in defending the Constitution
it went much deeper than any ordinary rationalization of property
interests. The system of checks and balances was also inspired by a
thoroughly realistic analysis of the dangers of power, no less when
exercised by the superior few. Madison summed up the whole problem
in *Federalist No. 10,* granting that faction inevitably arises from the
unequal distribution of property, and that there was no hope of completely subordinating moneyed interests to the public good, but adding
that neither the faction nor the inequality could be eliminated without
destroying liberty; so he maintained that the nation could only seek
to control their effects, minimize the mischief. Similarly the Founding
Fathers had more than selfish reasons for their distrust of simple, direct
rule by the majority; for the Bill of Rights itself put the basic rights of
Americans beyond the will or whim of any transient majority.

At least the United States was unquestionably the most democratic nation of the time. In spite of property qualifications for voting, a large majority were authorized voters in some states, a large proportion in all states, while the Constitution specified no such qualifications for holding office, as no religious qualifications either. And the event proved Franklin right: it was a rising sun. Under this new form of government the nation not only prospered but grew more democratic.[7] The Revolution had not really ended after all—it had only begun. Add that the Constitution became a national myth, we may then append the extravagant conclusion of Lord Acton: initially a "monstrous fraud" by liberal standards, it nevertheless produced "a community more powerful, more prosperous, more intelligent, and more free than any other which the world has seen." Today it remains the oldest of written constitutions.

In this view the immediate aftermath was suitably ironic. Obsessed by their fear of "faction," the Founding Fathers devoutly hoped to escape the evil of political parties (an attitude shared by the leaders of most of the new nations in the non-Western world today) ; but parties began forming in the controversies over the Constitution itself, and before long the nation was on its way to the two-party system that is now its boast. The Federalists took command under the presidency of Washington, a conservative who dutifully aspired to be above partisan politics but gave increasing support to Alexander Hamilton, the ablest and most ardent partisan for strong central government controlled by the upper class. Although Hamilton generally concealed his contempt for that "great beast" the people, he did most to foster the growth of a rival Republican party by his resolute efforts to strengthen the propertied and commercial interests of the country. The Federalists grew more frightened of democracy as the French Revolution ran its course, and under the presidency of John Adams they forced through the notorious Alien and Sedition Acts, proceeding to victimize chiefly Republican newspaper editors. The "Federalist reign of terror" became a major issue in the ensuing presidential campaign, which Thomas Jefferson called "the Revolution of 1800." When a Republican Congress was elected with him, the lame-duck Congress packed the judiciary with Federalists, setting an example in the uses of the Constitution for

---

[7] An incidental example of its success was the first modern census, carried out by the United States in 1790. Colbert had begun collecting and analyzing statistics for Louis XIV and the practice spread in the eighteenth century, but it remained unpopular; subjects resisted it on the assumption that it would benefit only their government, at their expense. The American census demonstrated a rare measure of popular trust in government.

hamstringing the popular will—a trick that American politicians would develop a genius for.

Jefferson, the foremost champion of democracy, also remains vulnerable to ironic contemplation. He had opposed the strong central government pushed by the Federalists, attacking it in favor of states' rights, which would become the bulwark of slavery, and in this century would be revived by a very different Republican party for its conservative purposes; but as President he advanced the powers of the executive, consulting neither Congress nor the states when he purchased the Louisiana Territory from Napoleon. The Napoleonic Wars led him to modify as well his opposition to Alexander Hamilton's policy of protecting and developing the nation's manufactures. He still wanted America to remain predominantly agricultural and rural, however, believing that big industry and big cities were alike a menace to democracy; so Hamilton more clearly foresaw the future, given the Industrial Revolution already under way—the conditions under which democracy would willy-nilly have to make out as best it could. Jefferson's possible sentimentality about the virtues of rural life, easy for a wealthy plantation owner, recalls his possibly complacent facility as a spokesman of the democratic faith.

Still, he remained loyal to this faith, under a severe enough test. As leader of the democratic party he had been subject to violent abuse, reflecting both the deep anxieties of a revolutionary period and the deep divisions of a nation not yet bred to a faith in a party system, democratic processes, and popular suffrage. As President he nevertheless went out of his way to emphasize the "sacred principle" of the rights of minorities, even to the expression of opinions that would today be damned as un-American. "If there be any among us who would wish to dissolve this Union or to change its republican form," he said in his first inaugural, "let them stand undisturbed as monuments of the safety with which error of opinion may be tolerated where reason is left free to combat it." One of the few thinkers of the Enlightenment to emphasize the positive value of diversity of opinion, he was among the still fewer to declare and stick to a trust in the common people. Hence he was likewise one of the first to proclaim the ideal mission of America as "the world's best hope." He called upon Americans to bury their private differences and their selfish interests because "the last hope of human liberty in this world rests on us," and their failure would "seal the heresy that man is incapable of self-government." In ordinary Americans this idea was already engendering simple conceit, the habit of telling the world that theirs was the greatest nation on earth—a piece of news that the rest of the world might hope they would keep to themselves more often. In Jefferson's own feeling there was little national conceit, no idea that Americans were God's chosen people—he was only emphasizing the universalism of the democratic gospel. He meant it when he said, "We are acting for all mankind."

More to the point, many Europeans agreed with him. Early in the American Revolution Turgot had declared, "This people is the hope of the human race." If without this hope Europeans might have gone on to make the same history they did, it was clearly a stimulus, and the major meaning of America for the rest of the world. In England it intensified the agitation for parliamentary reform, which culminated in the Westminster Convention of 1780; this drafted a report demanding full democracy, anticipating all the major articles of the famous People's Charter a half century later. While nothing came of it at the time, England contributed to the popular cause by its own unpopularity on the continent. Resentful of its wealth and power, royal governments were generally pleased by the difficulties it was having in America, and therefore permitted the publication of a deal of subversive thought in the guise of pro-American sentiment; thus the revolutionary state constitutions were widely published and cited. In far-off Poland, where a popular uprising was led by Kosciusko, a fighter in the American Revolution, an editor exclaimed over the new era that had begun in Europe, unlike anything since the Crusades: "As men then fought for the Holy Land, it is now for Holy Liberty that they fight." Such excitement was least apparent in Spain, where censors kept on their job; but within a generation it lost its colonies in America as these rebelled in the name of the ideals proclaimed in the Declaration of Independence.

Most plain and immediate was the impact on France. An early symptom was the extraordinary enthusiasm in Paris when Benjamin Franklin, the popular representative of the New World, embraced the aged Voltaire, the great fighter for freedom in the old one. The cause and perhaps the deepest effect were summed up by the enraptured Condorcet. It was not enough, he wrote, that the sacred, long-forgotten rights of man were written in the books of philosophers: it was necessary that ordinary, ignorant men "should read them in the example of a great people"—and "America has given us this example." In drawing up their state constitutions the Americans were actually forming a "social contract," incorporating the ideals of the Enlightenment. They were showing that evil was due primarily to bad institutions, man was naturally good. They were substantiating Condorcet's belief that the human race was making a new start, and one that was bound to be better.

3. *The French Revolution*

As everybody knows, the French Revolution was fought under the banner of Liberty, Equality, Fraternity, it declared the universal Rights of Man, it proclaimed a new era of universal peace and justice; and it culminated in a Reign of Terror, dictatorship, and imperialistic wars involving all Europe, heralding the World Wars to come. So we had better begin, a little wearily, by rehearsing the obvious ironies of a drama considerably more ambiguous than the American Revolution. Unforeseen by not only the philosophers and the great monarchs of the day but the men who precipitated it, the Revolution emerged as a popular revolution on the famous day of July 14, 1789, when a Paris crowd impulsively stormed the Bastille. Then followed a peasant revolution, directly inspired by no passion for liberty but by the "Great Fear," mass hysteria over rumors of an aristocratic conspiracy; the peasants believed that they were carrying out the will of their "good king." By the end of 1789, which had produced the Declaration of the Rights of Man and Citizen, there was still no thought of overthrowing the monarchy, no idea that the Revolution was only beginning. When two years later the new republican Constitution finally went into effect, Robespierre said: "The Revolution is over." The ensuing Reign of Terror was presided over by Robespierre, who also said that he would rather see France ruled by a king than by a dictator. Upon the end of the Terror the Republic soon ended too, and France got its dictator. Napoleon put a stop to the revolutionary nonsense at home, only using its slogans to pose as a liberator when he marched out to fulfill his own grandiose, bloody dream of empire.

At every point we have to keep an eye on such incongruities, which were by no means incidental or accidental. Yet we now have to be wary too of the sophisticated reaction against the popular simplicities, the tendency to dwell chiefly on all that was unconscious, involuntary, irrational, unideal, or a matter for irony. If the Revolution was unforeseen by men in high places, it was nevertheless prepared for by not only

Western tradition but recent crises that lesser men were alert to. "One opinion pervaded the whole company," reported Arthur Young, a contemporary English traveler in France, "that they are on the eve of some great revolution in the government: that everything points to it"; and among the signs he noted was "a great ferment amongst all ranks of men, who are eager for some change, without knowing what to look to, or hope for." If what followed was neither a premeditated revolution nor a spontaneous uprising of a liberty-loving nation, it did enlist a great deal of deliberate thought and effort, arouse a great deal of spontaneous fervor. Young noted too the "incredible" business going on in the pamphlet shops of Paris, "nineteen-twentieths" of it in favor of liberty. Once the movement was under way, men were extraordinarily quick to respond to the opportunity, and decide "what to look to, or hope for"; within a few months the National Assembly was drafting the revolutionary Declaration of Rights. If by this time the movement was already split, it was also more clearly a national movement, involving "all ranks of men," in whom Turgot some years before had found no concern whatever for the public weal. It broadened out into a conscious effort to make over the entire society—an effort that naturally made confusion and contradiction more pronounced, and no doubt failure more certain, but that emphasized how radically different this was from other contemporary upheavals. The highly critical de Tocqueville later judged that in all his study of history he had never run across a revolution in which "so many men displayed a patriotism so intense, such unselfishness, such real greatness of mind"; and let us add that no great revolution can ever be made without a great deal of idealism, and some impossible hopes of lasting peace and justice. On all counts we need to consider the French Revolution more closely than the relatively simple American one.

Unquestionably it grew out of a revolutionary state of affairs, if of a paradoxical kind that the *philosophes* understandably overlooked. This was not a state of intolerable misery or grinding oppression. France had prospered in the eighteenth century, a rapid growth in population matching the growth in building, industry, and foreign trade, keeping it the greatest nation in western Europe; Necker, minister of finance for Louis XVI, estimated that it owned nearly half the cash of Europe. Although its wealth was of course far from evenly shared, on the whole the common people were better off than in most other countries, and in any case they did not start the Revolution: this was the doing of the prosperous. Peoples who have been ground down can tolerate almost anything and ordinarily do not make revolutions—they merely riot or lash out in frenzy; until recent times, major revolutions have been a kind of luxury that only relatively prosperous societies could afford. Frenchmen had plenty to complain about in their condition, but what made this a revolutionary condition was a higher standard in what was "tolerable," a growing disposition not to endure what men had put up with over the centuries. It was the critical attitudes sown by the *philosophes.* Thoughtful Frenchman had already answered the question Edmund Burke would ask. Instead of inventing novelties to correct abuses, he wrote, why not return to your old traditions, the "ancient common law of Europe"? What they objected to was no mere abuses but precisely those traditions or that common law.

The immediate target for the aggrieved was naturally, though somewhat mistakenly, the government of Louis XVI. He himself was a weak king, not at all brainy, who in his stubborn or frustrate moods might sound off in the tradition established by Louis XIV and restated emphatically by Louis XV: "In my person only does the sovereign power rest. . . . From me alone do my courts derive their existence and their authority. . . . To me alone belongs legislative power without dependence or division. . . . Public order in its entirety emanates from me." In fact a vast deal of government emanated from the king, spreading into the management of all other institutions, reaching down into every hamlet, intruding on the private lives of families. The motive behind all this bureaucratic regulation was no aspiration to totalitarianism but a compound of earnestness, suspicion, incompetence, fussiness, and blind adherence to custom, or lack of motive. One result was the popular tendency to blame everything on the ubiquitous government when things went badly, as they generally did. A perpetual grievance was the preposterously confused, inefficient, inequitable system of taxation, the costlier because the collection of indirect taxes was farmed out to private enterprise; as France prospered, its government got ever more heavily in debt, until more than half its expenditures went into servicing the debt. But its fundamental weakness lay in a sickly, impotent kind of absolutism, perfectly symbolized by Louis XVI, that made it seem both more unenlightened and more despotic than it actually was, and deprived it of the support of both conservatives and progressives.

On the one hand, the royal government was liberal and incompetent enough to stimulate a growing spirit of independence in its subjects, who were openly critical of it. On the other hand, it was not liberal on principle or by statute; its critics enjoyed an uncertain, hence possibly unwholesome kind of freedom. It made no provision for constitutional means of reform, as none for a representative national parliament or a responsible opposition. All men could see its glaring faults, including the extravagance of the royal court (not to mention the indiscretions of Marie Antoinette, who was never so dear to her people as she became to Edmund Burke). Most failed to appreciate its serious efforts at reform. While a series of royal ministers—Turgot, Necker, Calonne—kept trying to modernize it, in particular to reform the tax system, thoughtful Frenchmen kept suspicious of them as agents of absolutism, and generally paid less heed to the reasons why their efforts had little success. They were constantly impeded by the antique orders that now charm lovers of hierarchy, and in matters of taxation they were thwarted by the opposition of the nobility. The nobility was indeed serving as a bulwark against absolutism; but it brings up the confusions and anomalies that long obscured the basic issues of the Revolution.

Although this was not a homogeneous class, ranging from an exclusive old nobility of "the sword" to many needy gentry, it was set apart by the possession of feudal privileges, such as exemption from the basic income tax known as the *taille*. Now it was growing more assertive, with the help of royal partiality. Whereas Louis XIV had drawn his high ministers from the "vile bourgeoisie," Louis XVI chose almost none but nobles, while his army too was exalted by an ordinance requiring all officer candidates to have at least four generations of noble blood. (A royal genealogist was added to the bureaucracy to provide the necessary certificates of purity.) Outside the royal government aristocrats were flexing their political muscles in the local parlements, or law courts, which had survived the disappearance of the national Estates-General, and which they dominated from seats owned as personal property. Abolished by Louis XV when they claimed the right to pass on his edicts, the parlements were restored by the grace of Louis XVI. But in spite—or because—of such gains the nobility felt discontented. Some, who had become liberal under the influence of the Enlightenment, wanted truly constitutional government in the public interest. Most simply wanted a fuller restoration of their ancient power, a more direct, assured role in government. And these traditionalists did most to prepare the way for the Revolution.

They agitated directly through the parlements, which presently began asserting that together they constituted a kind of Parlement of all France, represented the nation. The most influential parlement of Paris gave away their selfish interests plainly enough when Louis XVI made the reformer Turgot his chief minister. In denouncing Turgot's moderate proposal to maintain the royal highways by a small tax on all landowners, instead of the compulsory labor of nearby peasants, it declared that the first principle of civil government was to uphold both the rights of property and "rights attached to the person and born of prerogatives of birth and estate"; and it went on to prove that the idea of "an equality of duties" was a most dangerous threat to not only the nation but the very principle of civil society, "the law of the Universe," the order ordained by God. Nevertheless, the parlements won the support of public opinion, especially of the enlightened. They were not only showing courage but asserting more revolutionary principles than they intended. Thus they stoutly maintained that no law or tax edict was valid without the consent of the nation, meaning their own consent, but implying the ultimate sovereignty of the people. In defending this claim, which Louis XIV would have considered treasonous and blasphemous, they imported the vocabulary of natural law, popularizing such concepts as "citizen" and "natural and imprescriptible rights." When Louis XV suppressed them he only proved that the French monarchy was a "despotism"—another term they used freely. They had amply stocked the revolutionary arsenal by the time, on the eve of the Revolution, the rest of the nation finally woke up to what de Tocqueville called their demagoguery.

One important exception to the awakening was the clergy, nominally the First Estate. The Church too was a privileged landowner, possessing about a tenth of the kingdom. While legally entitled to collect the tithe, a tax on all products of the soil, the clergy remained exempt from direct taxation; in return for state support it contributed to the king only a "free donation," fixed by itself. In 1789 all the bishops without exception were nobles, and most were as hostile as other nobles to tax reform at the expense of their privileges. Lord Acton accordingly lamented that the last time the Church played a decisive part in Western history found it still resisting the cause of liberty and popular rights. Actually, its part was somewhat confused, and not clearly decisive. Ordinary Frenchmen resented only its privilege of the tithe, the proceeds of which went largely to the higher clergy instead of the local parish and the poor. Parish priests, who were almost all commoners, tended to share this feeling; they lent support to the popular cause in the critical early days of the Revolution. Their superiors hardly justified their high rank and privilege by any high order of spiritual leadership, any clear demonstration of either moral or intellectual superiority, but for the same reason they were largely ineffectual.

By contrast considerably more idealism was displayed by the bour-geois, leaders of the lowly Third Estate, which comprised about 95 per cent of the population. Their ideals were impure, it is true, blended with class and property interests that upon their triumph would become more conspicuous. Wealthy merchants and bankers, who had always wanted nothing better than to be like the aristocrats, were very insistent on the forms of their own gentility—a rank consciousness that was as marked in the lesser members of the middle class, making them all look very bourgeois. But even their vulgar aspirations were at this point a boon to the popular cause. They were united in an increasing resent-ment of the nobility who looked down on them, echoing the question that the Figaro of Beaumarchais asked of his great lord: "What have you done to deserve all these blessings? You took the trouble to be born, and nothing more." Naturally they resented as well their exclusion from direct political power, the more because the nobility were now insisting that high office should be restricted to men of high birth. And many, too, were earnest devotees of the Enlightenment. Only the most rabid medievalists or Marxists deny that there was much genuine ideal-ism in the men who wrote the Rights of Man into the new French Constitution.

The skilled workers and independent craftsmen toward the bottom of the middle class shaded off into journeymen and wageworkers, who in Paris made up a substantial proletariat. Although it was chiefly these lower ranks who stormed the Bastille, Marxists agree that they were not yet a class-conscious proletariat, aware of their independent historic destiny as a "fourth estate." There has been much controversy, however, about the much more numerous French peasantry. Michelet, the ardent democrat, presented most graphically what is still perhaps the conven-tional view, picturing an utterly wretched, oppressed class. Enemies of the Revolution then set out to prove that on the contrary the peasants were free men, mostly quite well off; their accounts of rural life under the *ancien régime* verged on the idyllic.[8] Later Marxist historians lent

---

[8] Among the more temperate versions is the popular history of Pierre Gaxotte, who argued that there was "a great affectation of distress" in order to fool tax collectors, but behind "this cloak of rags" was hidden a life that was "tranquil, often easy, and sometimes ample." On the other hand, the ultraconservative Taine dug up a wealth of evidence that sub-stantiated Michelet's account of the misery and degradation of the peasants; Taine's point was that their bestiality helped to explain the mad violence of the Revolution, which he saw as primarily the work of the *canaille* and a lesson to all democrats. In looking forward to the day when adequate data would enable historians to be wholly objective, Lord Acton wrote that they would then all present the same French Revolution. The point of this footnote is that that day has not yet arrived.

the conservatives a hand, if not in a fraternal spirit: they discounted the misery of the peasants because they were bent on proving that the Revolution was the work of the bourgeois. But the great mass of social and economic data that they helped to accumulate makes it easier to reach the commonplace conclusion that the truth lies between these extremes.

Almost all French peasants were indeed legally free men. Serfdom, still the rule in central and eastern Europe, had disappeared almost everywhere in France so long ago that men had forgotten just when. So many peasants owned their own land, moreover, that Arthur Young was startled; he had had "no idea that such a state of affairs existed anywhere"—as in fact it did not in England. An unenterprising nobility had spared the French peasant the jolt of the enclosure movement, and thus helped to mold the type that has persisted to this day— independent, technologically backward, devoted to property, set in his narrow ways. He might seem more oppressed than he was because he had enough spirit to complain, put up some resistance to the authorities. Nevertheless, he had obvious reason for complaint. He still owed feudal dues and services to the seigneurs; he alone was subject to the royal *corvée,* compulsory unpaid labor in maintaining roads and assisting troop movements; almost alone he drew lots for compulsory service in the militia, which was so wretchedly housed and fed that (an economist explained) "it would be sheer cruelty to conscript men not belonging to the lowest class"; and almost alone he paid the *taille,* while also paying much more than his share of other taxes that the wealthy could largely manage to evade. If he owned his land, it was usually so small a plot that he had a hard time making his small ends meet, and could do so only by hiring out as a laborer. He shared as little in the cultural progress of the age, remaining illiterate, mostly ignored when not despised by his betters; nor was he helped much when Rousseau made it a fashion to celebrate his simple virtues and innocent pleasures. Rather, his troubles worsened toward the end of the century.

The rising prosperity of France came to a halt about 1770. Thereafter a series of crises, due to economic depression or drought, left many men jobless and hungry. Just before the Revolution an exceptionally bad harvest doubled or tripled the price of bread and pauperized millions; a primary cause of the momentous upheaval was simply the price of bread. Such acts of God, which grievously complicated the financial problems of the hapless Louis XVI, recall the reasons for doubting that the French Revolution was strictly inevitable. The loans that kept the government going became ever harder to float as the debt soared into the billions. Yet this desperate financial crisis also recalls us to the human agencies in the revolutionary conditions, and specifically to the basic failings of the *ancien régime*.

A new minister, Calonne, saw that short of declaring bankruptcy there was no way out but to make the privileged classes bear a fuller share of the tax load: there was more than enough wealth in the grand monarchy if everybody paid in. Though the reforms he proposed were still modest, not even touching the exemption of the nobility from the *taille*, the parlements would have none of such infraction of the divine rights of birth and estate. Aristocrats waxed more indignant when he appealed to the country and complained of the abuses of privilege—lending official authority to so subversive an idea. At this juncture Louis XVI moved to the fore with the characteristic unstately irresolution that made him a key figure in the Revolution, if in a role not precisely as a historical determinist would cast it: a stronger king might have made considerable difference. First he bowed to the furor, dismissing Calonne; then, after a new minister tried vainly to put through milder reforms, he lost patience with the parlements and by royal edicts took away their political powers; and when this outrage against the "defenders of liberty" touched off a universal uproar, Louis caved in again. He agreed to meet the conditions the defiant Parlement of Paris had set for its approval of further loans: he would summon a national Estates-General to consider ways and means of dealing with the national emergency. So the curtain rose on the drama summed up by Chateaubriand: "The patricians began the Revolution; the plebeians finished it."

Louis proceeded to contribute somewhat more than his bit by decreeing that all delegates to the Estates-General should be elected by their own estates. For the aristocracy these elections were a simple enough matter, but for the Third Estate they were wildly exciting. Amounting to a national election—the first such opportunity the people had ever had—they even approached universal suffrage, as the seemingly harmless peasants were encouraged to participate. The people were stirred up the more because their assemblies were asked to draw up *cahiers* enumerating their grievances. That the bourgeois completely dominated the complicated processes of election, very few if any peasants or workers being chosen as delegates, was neither surprising nor lamentable for popular purposes. The bourgeois virtually monopolized the experience, learning, and professional skills required for political leadership; and their delegation not only was much abler than either the noble or the clerical delegation but turned out to be more radically independent than a plebeian body would likely have been. For the aristocratic "defenders of liberty" at last succeeded in giving away their hand.

The Estates-General that convened at Versailles, in May of 1789, had been irreconcilably split beforehand. Necker, the latest reform minister of the king, had suggested that the Third Estate ought to have double representation in order to give it an equal voice with the two upper orders. The Parlement of Paris had promptly ruled that each order should be equally represented as in medieval times, thus assuring a majority for the aristocracy; whereupon it instantly lost its popularity in another national uproar. Had the aristocracy made some concession comparable to the House of Commons in England, the Revolution might well have been averted. As it was, the aroused bourgeois refused any longer to accept a subordinate role. The Abbé Sieyès forced the issue in his enormously popular tract on the Third Estate: "What is the Third Estate? Everything. What has it been until now? Nothing. What does it ask? To be something." Denied equality, it set about becoming everything. Its delegation refused to co-operate with the other estates, presently renamed itself the "National Assembly," and prepared to draft a constitution for the nation. As it had the support of some liberal nobles (such as Condorcet, Mirabeau, and La Fayette) and won increasing support from the parish priests, it hoped to get the king's approval; but when Louis XVI vacillated as usual it took the famed Oath of the Tennis Court, almost to a man swearing never to break up or go home until it had completed and securely established a constitution. At length the king gave in ("Oh, well, the devil with it— let them stay"), ordering his recalcitrant nobility to sit in the National Assembly.

So far the bourgeois were winning a popular revolution without the use of force. It was Louis who brought on a stormier phase by moving in troops, with the apparent intention of sending home the National Assembly. All Paris had been following the news from Versailles with intense interest, then with growing alarm over what the king and the aristocracy were up to; and when word came that he had dismissed Necker, the people rose. After taking the Bastille by assault they set up a new municipal government, put La Fayette in command of a citizen militia. The common people accordingly inaugurated the deplorable method of violence. There is no question, however, that immediately the storming of the Bastille acquired the ideal significance that has made July 14 a red-letter day in the history of freedom. The news from Paris set off wild enthusiasm throughout France, towns everywhere installing new governments that took orders only from the National Assembly. It thrilled dreamers all over Europe—dreamers like the father of the Danish writer Steffens, who hurried home to tell his family that a new era had begun in which poverty would vanish, all men would face life on equal terms.

As spontaneous, if less edifying, was the peasant revolution that followed. This was essentially an independent affair, neither instigated nor led by the bourgeois. Enflamed by wildfire rumors of an aristocratic conspiracy to crush them by means of the "brigands"—paupers who were begging or robbing their way around France—the peasants took up arms and settled their grievances on their own, wrecking manor houses, burning the records of their obligations to the seigneurs. So far from following any lead from the National Assembly, they were an embarrassment to it; lacking troops to take charge, it could only accept the *fait accompli* despite the menace to the rights of property. The consequence, at any rate, was again epoch-making, for the National Assembly passed a series of resolutions that went far beyond the hitherto expressed intentions of its leaders. In a single night, August 4, 1789, it practically ended the feudal regime, following up by doing away with the tithe too.

In the same famous month of August it approved the Declaration of the Rights of Man and Citizen as a preamble to a new constitution. Today this may seem a tame as well as vague bourgeois manifesto, since it hedged on such fundamentals as religious toleration and universal suffrage while declaring property "an inviolable and sacred right." Yet the Declaration was a truly revolutionary document for its day, and a credit to the bourgeois leaders who pushed it through against considerable opposition from their own ranks. Its first article, "Men are born and remain free and equal in rights," was to contemporaries not at all vague, but a positive, explicit condemnation of the *ancien régime*. The seven articles devoted to the "imprescriptible rights" of liberty likewise referred plainly enough to specific abuses. The elementary principle, for instance, that no man should be arrested or detained except by law, all should be presumed innocent until judged guilty, was contrary to both ecclesiastical tradition and common royal practice. And immediately the Declaration was printed in hundreds of thousands of copies, publicly posted throughout France. Its immense potential influence as

a manifesto of democratic principles was soon indicated by its translation into a dozen languages, and by the fact that in most countries it
could not be so posted.

The business of drawing up the Constitution itself was considerably
more prolonged, complicated by the refusal of Louis XVI to give his
sanction to the August decrees, and by growing dissension within the
National Assembly over the question whether his sanction was necessary. The common people of Paris again settled the immediate problem
of the king's passive resistance by rising up in the "October Days": an
impromptu army of them marched on Versailles, frightened Louis into
submission, and brought him back to Paris, where he might be preserved from evil counsel. The Constitution that was finally adopted,
after two more years of debate, was still a compromise by democratic
standards, setting up a limited monarchy with limited suffrage, but it
went well beyond the English Constitution by doing away with all the
ancient orders and estates, and giving the vote to more than half the
adult males. So it was now, in 1791, that Robespierre pronounced the
Revolution to be over.

What ensued was its bloodiest, most familiar, and most controversial
phase. Within a year the royal palace in Paris was stormed and the
monarchy overthrown, this time by a well-planned uprising. Then came
the September Massacres, which took at least a thousand lives. Another
year and the Terror was on, under a Committee of Public Safety headed
by Robespierre: a systematic persecution organized, its apologists say,
to prevent indiscriminate massacre; or as Robespierre put it at the
time, "the despotism of liberty against tyranny." In any case, it was a
pure enough despotism, denying all the basic freedoms, violating the
rights of the person to an extent that the government of Louis XVI
never had. The victims of the "holy guillotine" numbered up to 20,000
and perhaps as many others died without trial or formal execution,
while some hundreds of thousands were jailed. (Revolutionary statistics
are sadly inexact.) Besides the royal family and many nobles, the victims included many moderate men of good will who had worked for
the Revolution. And all this took place in the name of democracy, an
ideal now popularized by the Jacobins and incorporated in a new
Constitution that provided for universal suffrage. Recent history has
made the terror and the tyranny seem much more ominous as the beginning of totalitarianism.

Hard as it is to view these portentous events calmly, and impossible
to pretend to complete detachment and impartiality, some important

considerations seem reasonably certain. The Jacobins had this much excuse, that by 1792 some kind of action was clearly necessary to preserve the gains of the Revolution. European monarchs, slow to realize that the goings on in France were not a local, transient disturbance, had at length come to the support of Louis XVI; Prussian and Austrian armies were invading France. In this national emergency, the leaders of the Revolution could hardly be expected to deal leniently with their many enemies at home. They had better excuse for guillotining Louis XVI than the Puritans in England had had for beheading King Charles; never having welcomed the new regime, the king was plainly disposed to conspiracy against it, or what now amounted to treason. More plainly the nobility were finally vindicating the popular fears of them all along, conspiring with the foreign enemies of France to crush the people's government.

At the same time, the Terror was not primarily the work of the "rabble." The common people had indeed shown themselves ready enough to employ violent means (as did the Americans, for that matter), and most of them may have approved the reign of violence, if only because their betters had not bothered to educate them or share with them the amenities of civil society. But beginning with the overturn of the monarchy, all key decisions were made and carried through by an ever smaller, more tightly organized minority, the Jacobins. None were submitted to the people for ratification, nor was the new democratic Constitution ever put into effect; the democratic slogans merely concealed the absence of democratic procedures. The common people had had but a slight recent experience in such procedures, after all. Hence the logic of the Committee of Public Safety. "The transition of an oppressed nation to democracy," ran one of its decrees, "is like the effort by which nature rose from nothingness to existence. You must entirely refashion a people whom you wish to make free, destroy its prejudices, alter its habits, limit its necessities, root up its vices, purify its desires." On the one hand, this meant an idealistic or silly effort to refashion all social conventions, from a new calendar with its mellifluous months (*thermidor, fructidor, brumaire,* etc.) to a new religion with cults of Reason, the Fatherland, the Supreme Being. On the other hand, it meant the Terror—destroying all public enemies, rooting out all signs of faintheartedness over the brave new world. On both counts it introduced immediately the now familiar story of revolution, repeated in Russia, of the moderate party losing control and the extremists taking over. More significantly, it introduced the kind of democratic absolutism, or tyranny in the name of liberty, equality, and fraternity, that has remained a permanent element in Western tradition.

If some of the Jacobins were corrupt and more were corrupted by power, there is no mistaking their initial idealism, above all the uncompromising idealism of Robespierre. Starting out as "Societies of Friends of the Constitution," little if any more extreme than other friends, they developed by complete dedication to the cause the superior organization and iron party discipline that enabled them to win control. (And let us remember that the more numerous moderates were a diverse group, far from united on either means or ends, by no means so uniformly sensible or high-minded as we might like to think.) In the process the Jacobins learned the arts of propagandizing, browbeating the opposition, staging "spontaneous" riots—they beautifully mastered the strategy of crisis, or the art of revolution as later practiced by the Communists: a feat the more remarkable because they had no precedent to guide them and the "laws" of revolution had not yet been written. Still, they did have some historical authority for their policy. The most apparent reason why Jacobinism has remained embedded in our tradition, despite the obvious failure of their very brief regime, is that it was already deeply rooted.

Christendom had always been prone to an uncompromising war on error or evil. The notorious example was the Inquisition, or the extermination of heretics by the medieval Church. Heretics themselves often made as plain the potential tyranny of salvationist creeds. The recurrent millennarian or messianic movements down through the Reformation anticipated both the ends and the means of the Jacobins, in their vision of an egalitarian heaven on earth and their frequent addiction to holy bloodthirstiness. Calvin's Geneva also intimated the possible terrors of rule by the righteous, as did some of the Puritan saints in the English Revolution. Robespierre himself was a puritanical type. While the Jacobins grew hostile to official Christianity, he accentuated the religious quality of their idealism by declaring war on the atheism of the Encyclopedists. He insisted on the need of faith in a Supreme Being who might not look like the Christian God, but was as hard on unbelievers.

Short of the terror, the totalitarian policies of the Jacobins came out of a long tradition, from Plato through Louis XIV to the fashion of "enlightened despotism"; and directly they stemmed from the rationalistic excesses of the Enlightenment. Preoccupied with the uniformities rather than the diversities of human nature and culture, the *philosophes* were the more inclined to minimize the problem of accommodating the wayward dispositions of men, and the varied interests of individuals, because they typically assumed that evil was due only to irrational institutions. The chief exception to their optimism, an often low opinion of common men, only confirmed their belief that reform had to be imposed from above. Few showed much concern with free institutions beyond a free press; most went on talking like individualists but neglecting the political conditions of individual freedom. The Physiocrats set a striking example as they coupled their doctrine of *laissez faire* in economics with the most explicit absolutism in politics, banking on untrammeled state power to achieve the efficiency they set their hearts on; as Quesnay wrote, "Any system of opposing forces within a government is highly objectionable." But in particular the Jacobins looked to the now most popular Rousseau—to the authoritarian in Rousseau, who had said that men must be forced to be free, in obedience to the infallible general will. Inevitably they drew the conclusion stated by Robespierre: "Our will is the general will." Austere, puritanical, incorruptible, Robespierre would never permit the license of freedom to impede the reign of the "Republic of Virtue." As Rousseau had written, "To permit vice, when one has the right and the power to suppress it, is to be oneself vicious."

Behind all such logic lay the fundamental difference between the French and the Anglo-American political tradition. After prolonged debate, the authors of the French Constitution had rejected the American principle of a balance of power. Too suspicious of the king to provide for a strong executive, too fearful of the nobility to establish a Senate or House of Lords, they had concentrated all power in a single body, the National Assembly. When the Jacobins succeeded in controlling this, there was no legal check on their power except the declared rights of man and citizen, and no strong tradition to support these rights; they could and did abuse their power as the sovereign English Parliament would never dare to. Debaters before them had denounced the English party system as merely a means of delaying action or blocking reform. So they put in a better light the muddle of the Anglo-American way. Although its spokesmen—especially in America—were sufficiently fond of glittering generalities, they remained basically empirical, pragmatic; they were always likely to disappoint both idealists and rationalists by seemingly flabby compromise, in effect trusting less to virtue or logic than to the method of "bumps and grinds"; but thereby they established the tradition of liberal democracy. They remained truer to the declared moral ends of democracy, upholding the abstract rights of man by more respect for the rights of fallible individuals to pursue happiness in their different ways.

Immediately, the Jacobins proved much more fallible. A terrible failure by democratic standards, their regime was no less a failure by ordinary practical standards, lasting only a year or so. When Robespierre himself went to the "holy guillotine" in July, 1794 (or Thermidor, year II), largely through the machinations of Jacobin speculators and profiteers, his party had nothing better to offer a demoralized populace. The Directory that took over the government put an end to the bloody circuses, but failed to give the people enough bread either; depending increasingly on the army for support, it called in Napoleon Bonaparte to put down a royalist uprising in Paris, and thus helped to realize the danger feared by Robespierre. As the Jacobins had made over the Revolution by a series of *coups d'état,* Napoleon ended it by a final *coup* in 1799, on the 18th Brumaire of their calendar, overthrowing the Directory and setting up a military dictatorship. He concluded his proclamation that he was a man "above party" with a bit of balderdash worthy of a modern dictator: "Conservative, protective, and liberal ideas have resumed their sway."

In view of Napoleon's genius and the tremendous power of his personality, historians are still debating his motives and intentions, the springs of his personality; but there is little question about his immediate achievements. He gave France what perhaps it chiefly needed at the time—order and stability, with a more efficient government than it had ever had under either its grand monarchs or the Jacobin National Assembly. In the process he not only kept up some democratic appearances but consolidated some of the gains of the Revolution, most notably by the enduring Napoleonic Code. Even his admirers, however, have seldom pretended that he was fired by revolutionary zeal, or any passion for liberty, equality, and fraternity. Though he employed only a judicious measure of terror, he suppressed all organized opposition, kept the press under censorship. To strengthen his position he signed a Concordat with the pope that officially restored the Roman Church to its privileged status as the national church. ("For my part," he confessed, "I see in religion not the mystery of transubstantiation, but the mystery of social order.") In getting himself elected emperor by a plebiscite, he may have sought primarily to legitimatize his sovereignty, but he also revealed some dynastic ambitions, trying to seat his family on European thrones. In any case, he eased the way for the return of the Bourbons to the throne of France.

As for Napoleon's military career, in which his genius was most apparent, there is no need of detailing it here, nor of going into the vexed question of how sincere his patriotism was. (Pieter Geyl has filled a volume with contradictory estimates by French historians.) The exploits that brought on the greatest wars in Western history to that time, putting some three million men in arms, left the map of Europe unchanged; here the important point is that they were surely not inspired by the cause of mankind, any ideal beyond nationalism, the *gloire* of France. As surely Napoleon's motives included personal ambition, to an extent that may look like megalomania. ("Three more years," he told the Bavarian general Wrede in 1811, "and I am master of the universe.") At most he was a great "hero," a type that Hegel would celebrate but that Voltaire had deplored; his exploits amounted to a betrayal of the ideals of the Enlightenment.[9] The outcome, of course, was disaster for both France and Napoleon. In a history of freedom Waterloo is just another battle, of little immediate importance except for the outside chance that victory might have enabled Napoleon to rule another little empire, which might have lasted a little while.

Inevitably we recall the dreams of Condorcet, one of the "moderates" who fell victim to the Terror. "Everything tells us that we have come to one of the great revolutions of the human race," he wrote in his hideout, and he concluded that for guidance in this new start for the race there was no real need of consulting history. "The actual state of human enlightenment guarantees to us that this revolution will be a happy one."

Its end was on the whole happy enough for the bourgeois—the class who according to Sieyès had been everything and nothing, and wanted only to be something. They at least succeeded in achieving their less exalted aims, or purely class interests. Excepting Rousseau, the thinkers of the Enlightenment had not been radical on the subject of property or the economy in general; those most interested in economics, the Physiocrats, proposed nothing more revolutionary than *laissez faire*. Likewise the radicalism of the Jacobins had involved no disrespect of

---

[9] His fame, incidentally, was enhanced by some precocious genius as a publicity man. Napoleon was the first to use the military bulletin for propaganda purposes, writing or editing most of his many bulletins, which helped to build up the legend of his military infallibility. In the midst of the appalling disaster of the Russian campaign that cost France half a million lives, one bulletin reported that "the health of His Majesty was never better."

the rights of property, save only that of "enemies" of the state. Under the thoroughly bourgeois Directory Sieyès himself helped to organize the *coup d'état* that put Napoleon in power, in order to assure the rule of the "notables," and Napoleon reciprocated by treating the bourgeois as a main prop of the state, in his Code safeguarding above all the rights of property. Under the Bourbons they weathered a violent reaction of die-hard aristocrats, and in 1830 took charge of the government; so from now on they were really "something."

The poorer classes, especially the city workers, fared worse in the last years of the Revolution. As an army officer Napoleon helped to put down the one potential uprising on their behalf, a ludicrous conspiracy of a small party led by "Gracchus" Babeuf. Its *Manifesto of the Equals* proposed a kind of socialistic state, trumpeted by a prophetic announcement: "The French Revolution is but the forerunner of another revolution, far more grand, far more solemn, which will be the last." After the execution of Babeuf an ardent disciple, Philippe Buonarroti, devoted his life to spreading the gospel of egalitarian communism, though in a spirit reminiscent of the Jacobins: he attributed "the loss of democracy and of liberty" in the French Revolution to "the diversity of views . . . the want of virtue, of unity," in particular the failure to "invest a man of Robespierre's stamp with a dictatorship." Workers at least felt that common men had been betrayed, and never forgot the Bastille; so revolution remained the mode—tried again in 1830, 1848, 1870. The cleavage between Right and Left was deepened by spiritual descendants of the old aristocracy and clergy, who never forgave the Revolution. In a sense France never recovered from it.

More portentous for Europe was an unforeseen by-product. In his early tirades against the Revolution, Edmund Burke predicted that for a long time to come once mighty France "need no longer be reckoned with as a military power"; but it soon built up the mightiest force since antiquity, which made all Europe reckon with it. The people's armies that defended revolutionary France fought with much more zeal than the professional royal armies, for they were patriots, defending "their" country; presently they were carrying the flag of France into other countries, ostensibly to liberate their peoples; and Napoleon continued using the revolutionary slogans to justify his wars of conquest, at first with enthusiastic popular support. The later cult of Napoleon as a national hero accentuated a paradox as disagreeable as understandable. Popular government, proclaimed by the National Assembly as a universal ideal and a means to universal peace, was intensifying nationalism and war. Thus the French people had submitted to nationwide conscription, a compulsory service that Frederick the Great had said no monarch would dare impose on his people, and that Americans would also submit to in their Civil War. Another sign of the new times was Napoleon's internment of enemy aliens, a measure that other European nations then denounced as barbarous, and that has since become routine. With the rise of democracy, war was on its way to becoming all-out, "total" war.

Yet the primary fact in a history of freedom is that democracy *was* on the rise. A primary reason was the French Revolution, which had by no means ended in simple failure. Most obviously, it had done away with the feudal regime for good; titles remained and with them some honorific social privileges, enough to keep aristocrats feeling superior, but also bitter at the permanent loss of their former privileges. Napoleon had assured this much by his celebrated Code, which affirmed the principles of civil equality and civil liberty. While re-establishing the Catholic Church he established religious liberty too; Protestants and Jews were assured equal status with Catholics. The Bourbon monarchy restored under Louis XVIII was a constitutional monarchy, and it retained the popular reforms in spite of a "White Terror" staged by furious royalists. The reputedly lucid, logical French were set on the confused, erratic course that so far has produced a dozen constitutions and five republics, an alternation of liberal and reactionary governments unable to win the consent of many of the governed; but no government ever dared to repeal the August decrees of the National Assembly, or flatly to renounce the principle of equal rights. While there remained marked inequalities in actual power and effective rights, enough apparent social injustice to keep common men permanently aggrieved, there remained enough freedom to enable them to keep struggling. The dominant bourgeois class always included influential men loyal to the principles their forebears had stated in the Declaration of the Rights of Man and Citizen.

Abroad, the French Revolution soon exposed the basic weaknesses of the *ancien régime*. At first quite blind to its danger, monarchs were slow in adjusting their mutual suspicions and jealousies, the habits bred by the wars they were accustomed to making on their own. As a contemporary observed, "They do not want, nor are they able, to understand that this is a *revolutionary* war which must be waged in a revolutionary way with weapons adapted to the genius and the means of their enemy." Hence Napoleon was able to pick them off one by one, inflicting humiliating defeats on each in turn, in this impartial way serving as "the son of the Revolution" that he proclaimed himself; he made their regimes look as obsolete as the Holy Roman Empire he put a decent end to. Thus the Prussian state fashioned by Frederick the Great, which collapsed ingloriously after the disastrous battle of Jena, responded by putting through a series of radical reforms, beginning with the abolition of serfdom. And Napoleon continued to serve the popular cause, if still less voluntarily, as he began to look like only another conqueror and oppressor. Other peoples acquired the patriotic fervor of the French, England emerged as the champion of the liberties of Europe. Immediately the patriotism strengthened the monarchs who finally united to defeat Napoleon, and thereupon inaugurated the reactionary era presided over by Metternich; but it also stirred up much more political activity, including agitation for more liberty at home. In England an extreme Tory reaction after Waterloo succeeded only briefly in suppressing the agitation for reform, the ferment that had been stirred by such revolutionary works as Tom Paine's *Rights of Man* and William Godwin's *Political Justice*. On the continent it soon became apparent that Metternich's regime had not extinguished the enthusiasm stirred by the fall of the Bastille.

It may be hard to realize now what de Tocqueville remarked, how unprecedented and astonishing the French Revolution initially was as a "political revolution that sought proselytes all the world over." It was in this sense more religious than the Puritan Revolution in England: a universal gospel of Liberty, Equality, Fraternity, which could inspire no less idealism and heroism because it was expressed in secular terms, or what now seem abstract terms. Call them rhetorical nonsense, crude slogans, myths, this is only to emphasize their actual popular appeal. So by 1830 men were beginning to make more revolutions—revolutions that immediately almost always failed, but that nevertheless marked the advance of the popular cause. A simple measure of the historic change is that in 1789 absolute monarchy was almost universal in Europe, outside of England, and a century later representative, constitutional government was nearly as universal, outside of Russia. Another measure was a note of the youthful Wordsworth in 1794: "I am of that odious class of man called democrats"; a century later "democracy" was a good word and its enemies were on the defensive. Condorcet was right, after all, in believing that the French Revolution heralded a new era for man. He had added an important proviso to his guarantee of a happy revolution—"that we be able to make use of all our strength";

and in his wretched garret, in the shadow of the guillotine, he exemplified what proved to be the irresistible force of the new hopes for history, the new confidence that men had the strength to make it to suit themselves.

All in all, the French Revolution was far more successful than all the other contemporary revolutions in Europe, including those attempted by "moderates." If in humanity we may rightly deplore the method of revolution, on the record we cannot easily maintain that it is bound to defeat its ideal purposes, and that the men who stormed the Bastille were simply misguided or deluded. It seems fairly certain that peaceable, sweetly reasonable means would not have ended the *ancien régime*, whose defenders were never averse to violent means; but in any case the success of the revolutionists—in France as in America— has made it possible for most of us in the democracies to be moderates, and more comfortably to deplore their methods. Likewise we need to qualify the blanket condemnations made easy by our painful experience with revolutionists in recent times. Although the French Revolution was no doubt a precursor of the Russian one, to some extent a model for it as a basic course in the studies of Marx and Lenin, the Communists rightly maintain that their revolution was quite different. The Jacobins were children of the Revolution, late-comers who for a year or so won control of it, then went down, and were pretty thoroughly discredited long before Marx discovered that they were only bourgeois. The Russian Jacobins, well schooled beforehand, won their revolution, proceeded to create the Soviet, and forty years later are still in control. Now we may add that lately they have grown critical of Stalin's Reign of Terror, and their epigoni are displaying some inclination to a bourgeois kind of materialism; so possibly they too may be discredited by the "verdict of history"—the only verdict they officially recognize. Meanwhile they recall the rest of us to the elementary conditions of historical judgment, which has always to deal with mixed fruits.

THE WAVE OF
THE FUTURE

"If a great change is to be made in human affairs," wrote Edmund Burke, "the minds of men will be fitted to it; the general opinions and feelings will draw that way. Every fear, every hope will forward it; and then they who persist in opposing this mighty current in human affairs will appear rather to resist the decrees of Providence itself, than the mere designs of men. They will not be resolute and firm, but perverse and obstinate." Burke wrote this long before it was clear that the wave of the future in Europe was carrying toward popular government, the revolutionary ideas he had for years so vehemently opposed. He has been much praised for his honorable admission of possible perversity in his stubborn conservatism, which today would be labeled "reactionary." He indeed pointed here to a kind of wisdom that is more imperative in our own much more revolutionary age. Those who are not historical determinists have especial need of pondering the mighty currents in human affairs, which involve strictly irresistible, irreversible forces, such as modern technology—forces that drastically limit our choices in possible futures, set the conditions under which we have to work out our designs. Like Thomas Jefferson, we might prefer a simple agricultural society; but short of the collapse of our civilization there is no chance whatever of dismantling our industrial machinery and going back to such a society.

Still, there is much more to be said on behalf of the "reactionary" Burke. By common consent he was the philosophical father of political conservatism, the first to offer a self-conscious, coherent, comprehensive defense of this oldest and commonest of attitudes. He made out perhaps the strongest case for the value and the necessity of the perennial conservative principle, which remains among the given conditions that all political thinkers must take into account. While he has become the

god of the "new conservatives" in America, liberals too must acknowledge that he was by no means simply obstinate or perverse in opposing
the revolutionary doctrines of his day, in particular the invitations to
popular tyranny or Jacobinism. And we must add some reservation
even about his honorable admission, now that the mighty current is
no longer clearly carrying toward democracy. It may be that the future
belongs to Communism, as Marxists insist; but if so, many of us would
persist in opposing it, be "reactionary" as a matter of integrity. Neither
wisdom nor virtue obliges one to vote the straight ticket of the future—
else principles would mean nothing and brute force always have its way.

Burke was hardly a farseeing prophet, aside from his limited understanding of the French Revolution. The mighty current was much more
complex than he ever perceived: no mere wave rolling straight to
democracy but a swirling tide, with many eddies rising from deep
confusions and contradictions, and always a powerful undertow. Yet he
remains among the significant thinkers of the age of revolution, aside
from his considerable immediate influence. Aroused by the upheaval
in France, he was fundamentally more concerned with the possible con-
tagion in England, or in general with the threat to traditional society
itself. He was acute enough to discern the basic, abiding issues beneath
the immediate conservative reaction. By both his insights and his over-
sights he may afford us a clearer, calmer, fuller parting view of this
age, the prelude to our own revolutionary age, and the direct source
of the principles to which most of us in the democracies are still
committed.

As a conservative perforce supporting tradition, Burke followed
Hume in basing government on convention or custom, ultimately a
principle of utility, rather than natural law or "imaginary rights."
"Nothing universal," he declared, "can be rationally affirmed on any
moral, or any political subject." What he meant in this somewhat
loose statement was that no philosopher could prescribe the right kind
of government for all mankind; good government was always a matter
of "political convenience," adjusted to the needs of a particular people
under particular circumstances. Otherwise he affirmed sufficiently universal principles, as the necessary bedrock of a conservative philosophy.
He attacked the appeal to reason because in practice it meant allowing
men "to live and trade each on his own private stock of reason." It was
never right "to turn our duties into doubts"; it was always necessary
to respect tradition, which embodied the accumulated wisdom of the
ancestors. "The individual is foolish . . . but the species is wise." Unlike

Locke, Burke emphasized above all the fact and the supreme value of community. In his most famous passage he gave most eloquent expression to the classical organic concept of society and the state:

> Society is indeed a contract. Subordinate contracts for objects of mere occasional interest may be dissolved at pleasure—but the state ought not to be considered as nothing better than a partnership agreement in a trade of pepper and coffee, calico or tobacco, or some other such low concern, to be taken up for a little temporary interest, and to be dissolved by the fancy of the parties. It is to be looked on with other reverence; because it is not a partnership in things subservient only to the gross animal existence of a temporary and perishable nature. It is a partnership in all science; a partnership in all art; a partnership in every virtue, and in all perfection. As the ends of such a partnership cannot be obtained in many generations, it becomes a partnership not only between those who are living, but between those who are living, those who are dead, and those who are to be born. Each contract of each particular state is but a clause in the great primeval contract of eternal society, linking the lower with the higher natures, connecting the visible and invisible world, according to a fixed compact sanctioned by the inviolable oath which holds all physical and all moral natures, each in their appointed place.

Behind this primeval contract lay the will of God. Essential to its maintenance was "the spirit of religion" on which European civilization had depended for ages.

Burke accordingly asked pointed questions of the radicals who were undermining the traditional sanctions. What did they mean by "the will of the people" on which they said government must rest? In practice this turned out to be the will of a majority, which was not at all sacred and might well be no more sensible. What alone made "a people" was a common respect for their tradition and their law, for the obligations imposed by the partnership between the living, the dead, and the unborn—duties that were strictly as involuntary as were the benefits conferred on all. Tell the people that their will or whim was sovereign, tell them (as Paine and Jefferson would) that every generation should be perfectly free to act for itself, you let in the Jacobins. Or your gift to posterity might be a Bonaparte: years before Napoleon came to power Burke foresaw that a popular general was likely to become master of the supposed republic. He had other prophetic things to say about the shameless irresponsibility to be expected in popular government, and the possible tyranny of multitudes.

Similarly he turned the tables on the apostles of Reason and Nature. Government must indeed be founded on human nature, but they were "so taken up with their theories about the rights of man that they have totally forgotten his nature"—and first of all his plain need of a restraint upon his passions. By liberal standards Burke took a more reasonable view of man than Hobbes had, not considering him so innately selfish and lawless as to require an ironclad contract of absolute submission; he defended "the real rights of men," as to the fruits of their industry, or in general all the historic rights of Englishmen; and he assumed that the species was wise enough to achieve a measure of progress, as exemplified by the glorious English Constitution. At the same time, man was obviously given to self-seeking and was not primarily a rational animal either; so Burke held that the good in him could be brought out only by a constant discipline of his passions, an insistence upon his duties rather than his rights. As for his "natural" right to liberty, who rejoiced when a criminal or a lunatic regained it? So far from being necessarily a good thing, liberty was a positive evil when men talked chiefly of being free to live as they pleased instead of how it ought to please them to live. Liberals, one might add, are now least disposed to rejoice over the way most free Americans are pleased to live.

Their complaints over the common uses of freedom lend more weight to Burke's further charge, that the democrats or "levelers" also perverted "the natural order of things" by their "monstrous fiction" of equality. The "true moral equality of mankind" consisted in a recognition of the inevitable inequality, a respect for the necessary order of civil life, in which those destined for a humble state obeyed their natural superiors. Tailors, carpenters, and the like ought not to be oppressed by the state, but neither should they be allowed to oppress the state by their rule. The wisdom of the ages was a virtually complete agreement that common men were incapable of judging either the public interest or their own best interests. One had to recognize their limitations out of regard as well for their own happiness—their real rights. Burke did not go so far as to insist, like the Grand Inquisitor, that freedom was an intolerable burden for the masses of men; but he did argue that democratic aspirations could only aggravate the real inequality of men, embitter the lives of the lowly, while imperiling the civil order that alone could give them a decent security and honest self-respect.

As a philosophical conservative Burke naturally looked to history, the study of which Condorcet thought was no longer really necessary. Here he was ahead of his time, anticipating a major preoccupation of the nineteenth century. He had a truer insight than any of the *philosophes* into the organic processes of history—all that had grown rather than been made deliberately by men, because of which a genuine community is much more than a mere contract. By the same token he made some provision for continued growth. Himself at first a Whig, he took up some still-unpopular causes, such as religious toleration and the grievances of the American colonists. He insisted only that reform be gradual, corresponding to the decent kind of evolutionary rather than revolutionary change that he saw in English history. From history he drew a lesson that liberals can never afford to ignore—the supreme importance of facing up to *"difficulty."* We may all agree with his charge that the popular leaders of the French Revolution were too intent on evading difficulty, too fond of "tricking short-cuts."

Although the Americans whom Burke defended soon left him behind, moving toward the popular government he dreaded, his stand may now look more dignified by contrast with a radically different kind of conservatism, just beginning to emerge in his day, that was destined to ride high on the wave of the future. This evaded difficulty by emphasizing above all the economic rights of individuals, not their social duties. When it came to dominate government in America, it paid nominal obeisance to Christian convention, but it was scarcely animated by "the spirit of religion," and it had little if any reverence for tradition, the past, or the state itself. It was supported by as little philosophy, beyond a crude version of Adam Smith's thesis that the unrestricted pursuit of self-interest would automatically promote the public good, coupled with a convenient forgetfulness of Smith's belief that merchants and manufacturers "neither are, nor ought to be, the rulers of mankind." Its business spokesmen tended rather to a growing distrust of intellectuals—the more unfortunate for their society because as hardheaded men they were mostly quite incapable of doing any hard thinking on their own about social and political problems. Their insistently practical spirit took on an ever more naïve air; for these political conservatives were economic revolutionaries, busily promoting an industrial revolution—profoundly transforming their whole society, and thereby outmoding their own doctrines, making their slogan thinking more hopelessly unrealistic.

Yet thereby, too, they put Burke in a less favorable light. Granted the value of the conservative principle, it is still inadequate for a world of revolutionary, ever more rapid change. The best wisdom of the ancestors might not do for radically different conditions that they never anticipated or could anticipate, just as the sage counsel of George Washington about avoiding foreign entanglements served only the cause of the benighted when the youthful nation had grown into a world power. Burke hammered down a motto he said could not be repeated too often, *"To innovate is not to reform";* but men would keep on revolutionizing the whole economy anyway, and government everywhere was obliged to risk some innovation. Likewise he may have been right that it was the misfortune, not the glory, of his age that "everything is to be discussed"; but it was no longer possible to avoid the misfortune so long as thought remained at all free. Thomas Paine spoke more to the point in his insistence that when precedents fail us we must return to first principles, and *think* as never before.

Immediately, Burke illustrated the besetting danger of the conservative principle by a growing inflexibility, reflecting a kind of "trained incapacity" for understanding and adapting himself to his revolutionary age. Even before the French Revolution turned him into a Tory he began betraying his own principle of wise government, "to know the best time and manner of yielding what it is impossible to keep." He opposed any effort at parliamentary reform, denouncing the most modest proposals as efforts to disgrace Parliament, destroy the English Constitution. As time went on, he reversed himself by voting against religious toleration, then against the abolition of the slave trade. He branded any suggestion of democratic principles as a defiance of the divine will, bound to bring on "the dissolution of civil society." Such extravagance, unbecoming his later reputation as a model of conservative sobriety, was due in part to the emotional instability and violence of temper that made him distrusted by his contemporaries, but it was more significant as a symptom of his hysteria over the French Revolution—the blend of complacence and dread to which conservatives would remain prone in a revolutionary world. Much of Burke's rhetoric would be called demagoguery if it were employed by a democratic orator, while his celebrated picture of the *ancien régime* in France—all chivalry, gallantry, fidelity, dignity, honor, in which service of the adorable Marie Antoinette expressed only an "exalted freedom"—was as ludicrous as any that Condorcet painted of the heavenly society of the future.

Only in this sense was Burke a man of vision. His most radiant vision was of past achievement, such as the establishment of the sovereignty of Parliament in England. It lit up not the arduous effort that had gone into this achievement, the defiance of custom or convention, the rebellion against constituted authority, the heroism of some individuals—it lit only the misty notion of the "great primeval contract," a wisdom restricted to "the species." Otherwise it exposed a symptomatic deficiency in Burke's own wisdom. He made a great point of eschewing the abstract principles of the *philosophes,* sticking to experience, appealing to utility or practical convenience, stressing the real needs of particular peoples under particular circumstances; but he was most vulnerable precisely to the charge of vagueness and want of realism at the critical points in his argument, or in his own terms, an evasion of the serious *difficulties* it involved.

Thus with his reverence for tradition—the essential principle of conservatism. The plain difficulty with any given tradition is that it is a mixed affair, inviting rational criticism because it embalms not only the tested wisdom of the ancestors but some deal of obsolescent custom and belief, prejudice and inequity; and it would seem as plain that any old tradition will not do for men grown at all thoughtful. One reason, again, why Burke could not understand the French Revolution is that he never clearly perceived that French tradition did not incorporate the rights he thought proper for Englishmen. His wisdom was of still less avail to most other European peoples, notably Russia—a nation now emerging as a world power. Russian tradition, barely ruffled by the unholy thought of the Enlightenment, enshrined a form of government that he himself deplored; and just what would he have had the Russian people do about the despotism and the serfdom to which they had been condemned by their ancestors? For that matter, even English tradition might have given Burke more pause, in view of the stirrings in his age. Once he had casually noted, for example, the "strange and ridiculous" condition "that those who labor most enjoy the fewest things and those who labor not at all have the greatest number of enjoyments' ; but he did not propose to do anything about this condition. Venerable though it was, the many poor toilers were at least capable of judging that it was not in their best interests, and seemed unjust. They might have wondered when Burke insisted that government was founded on "political convenience." The convenience of the rulers? Or the ruled?

According to him, they were "destined" to their lowly status; but he remained as vague on the difficult issues raised by his cardinal principle of aristocracy. To be sure, he wanted a "natural" aristocracy, rule by men of "virtue and wisdom"; he disclaimed any "vulgar admiration" for the titled class. Nevertheless, the aristocracy that actually prevailed in England and everywhere else on the continent was hereditary, it was bent on maintaining a forced inequality, and it was given to shameless abuses of its unearned privileges.[1] While he consistently emphasized the "absolute necessity" of an aristocracy in government, he never indicated how a natural one might be constituted and maintained. His lordly neglect of this problem has remained typical of aristocratic critics of democracy down to this day. Thus Burke's disciples now cite with approval the wisdom of Irving Babbitt, allegedly another disciplined, realistic thinker: "One should in the interests of democracy itself seek to substitute the doctrine of the right man for the doctrine of the rights of man." Liberals might be pardoned for hanging on to the doctrine of rights so long as the Burkes and the Babbitts fail to specify just who should pick out the right man, by what public standards, and just how society should go about putting and keeping him in the right place.

On the indispensable "spirit of religion" Burke became most specific in his horror of "infidels": he would have "the laws rise in all their terrors" against these "outlaws . . . of the human race." Otherwise he ignored the plain fact that the spirit of religion could support almost any kind of state, and throughout the ages had supported mostly despotic ones. He disregarded as well some plain texts in the Christian Gospels that rebuked his aristocratic sentiments. And another possible reason for his oversight was a somewhat inconsistent sympathy with the rising business interests. While Burke lamented that an age of "sophists, economists, and calculators" had succeeded the age of chivalry ("and the glory of Europe is extinguished for ever"), he encouraged these impious conservatives of the future by giving a religious gloss to the views of Adam Smith: "The laws of commerce are the laws of nature, and therefore the laws of God." This typically sonorous dictum, in which he managed to confuse the different meanings of the word "law" more thoroughly than the *philosophes* had in their doctrine of natural law, reminds us that conservatives too have some natural fondness for "glittering generalities." So with his favorite: "the great law of change"

---

[1] It helps to explain, incidentally, why Burke himself could be rather shameless in financial matters. While a member of Parliament he accepted payments by the colony of New York, as well as thousands of pounds from an English peer, and he sought government favors for his family, including a cousin who at the time was involved in fraudulent deals at the public expense. In Burke this was not simple graft or corruption: he was merely reflecting the low standards of political morality in the aristocratic regime he stood for.

—"the most powerful law of Nature"—which decrees that "change shall proceed by insensible decrees," and which men somehow manage to break, as did Luther and Calvin, Henry VIII, and the leaders of the Puritan Revolution.

Burke may fairly be called a romantic. Most clearly, if unconsciously, he heralded the future as a forerunner of the Romantic movement. Like Rousseau a champion of sentiment rather than reason, he anticipated it as well by his reverence for the past, his celebration of national tradition, his appeal to religion. His thought may accordingly be viewed as a wholesome corrective to the narrow rationalism and limited historical sense of the Enlightenment. Yet he was as liable as Rousseau to the obvious excesses of the new movement, beginning with simple sentimentality. He neglected to pay the intellectual and moral import duties on the feeling he indulged over a highly romanticized past, in which he saw little worse than the "pleasing illusions" of the *ancien régime*, overlooking the millions of poor devils who took little pleasure in them. In particular he foreshadowed the mystiques that would supplant the cult of Reason, and that involved potentially more dangerous illusions.

The worship of the nation-state was not, after all, a peculiarly democratic heresy. Burke himself raised an altar to it in his celebration of the "great primeval contract of eternal society," which perpetuated the venerable confusion of the state with society. From his pronouncement that "society is indeed a contract" he glided in a sentence to his famous description of the state as a partnership in all science and art, every virtue and all perfection; and since he believed that God himself had " willed the state," he added elsewhere that "in a Christian commonwealth the church and the state are one and the same thing." Citizens of the democracies might be prone to Burke's worshipful attitude out of patriotism, but from the beginning they had taken pains to protect themselves against the state by bills of rights; they were more apt to realize that all perfection is not in fact owed to the state, which is neither primeval nor eternal, and which looks less sacred in its necessary guise as a government, a set of mortals like as not wanting in science, art, and virtue. (In America patriots were likely to feel that the worst rascal was the President—the head of state.) Immediately, Burke's sentiment found more favor among the German Romantics. Some dressed it up with a metaphysics suggesting the abstractness he attacked, but possibly more becoming than the pragmatism he affected; most wedded it to a more fervent nationalism—a sentiment more ominous because they no longer associated it with notions of liberty and universal rights as it had been in France and America. Hegel completed the apotheosis of the nation-state, describing it as "the march of God through the world." Though he did not foresee either that the march would lead to totalitarianism, he provided its political ethic by grandly resolving Burke's worries over "imaginary rights" and the dangers of allowing men to trade on their "private stock of reason." "Positive freedom," he declared, could be achieved only by "utter obedience" to the State, "complete abnegation of one's own opinions and reasonings."

Likewise Burke's conception of history anticipated the kind of historicism that enabled conservatives to give a Hegelian blessing to the *status quo,* affirm that what had come to be was not only necessary but right. By his logic, the mere existence of a social or political system testified that it was better than any imaginary one philosophers might conceive. His true insight into the process of organic growth was clouded by the dubious implication that the process was providential or virtually automatic, the wisdom of the species somehow prevailing over the foolish wills of the individuals who make up the species. Hence to Burke (as later to Hegel) the root folly of the revolutionaries was their belief that they could *make* a new constitution to suit themselves, whereas even to make one over ever so slightly was a perilous business. In attacking the very modest proposals to reform Parliament, he explicitly argued that it was too delicate, complex an institution to be tampered with by mere mortals. We may therefore understand why, despite his initial sympathy with the Americans, he never discussed or publicly mentioned the constitutions they drew up. They were flagrantly violating "the great law of change."

And they were getting away with their impudence, really making their own history. In the light of Burke's thought—reputedly the best wisdom that the perennial conservative has to offer—we might now reconsider why the "mighty current in human affairs" moved away from him. He may help us to realize how literally revolutionary the popular cause was, and how remarkably bold an adventure, inasmuch as the wisdom of the ages and the weight of the historic record were indeed on his side. At the same time, he may serve to deepen our respect for the liberal faith of men like Thomas Jefferson, through a clearer awareness that this was neither so facile nor so naïve as critics of the Enlightenment have made it appear. Believers in the democratic cause may better appreciate the value of the conservative principle now that they have much to conserve, against the forces of tyranny; but I should say that they still need most to pay heed to the inherent dangers of this principle, and to the bolder temper of Jefferson.

"We have admired our ancestors less," wrote Chastellux on behalf of the Enlightenment, "but we have loved our contemporaries better, and have expected more of our descendants." First of all, Jefferson represented a more generous, humane credo than Burke's, involving a much livelier concern for the rights of the living. Instead of a "true moral equality" that effectively condemned most men to a menial status with little enjoyment, he maintained the moral ideal of equal rights to life, liberty, and the pursuit of happiness, and of a state that should serve equally the interests of all. To him the Christian spirit illumined "the palpable truth that the mass of mankind has not been born with saddles on their backs, nor a favored few booted and spurred, ready to ride them legitimately, by the grace of God." And with a greater charity he held out a more positive faith and hope. Complacent though Burke was over the English Constitution, he displayed less faith than fear as he demanded of his countrymen only that they sit tight and guard against any "innovation"—insisting that all was for the best as it was, and all was in dire peril. Jefferson set his descendants a more invigorating challenge by his insistence on both the need and the possibility of much improvement.

His casual remarks about how "a little rebellion, now and then, is a good thing," and for liberty's sake "God forbid we should ever be twenty years" without one, perhaps came a little too easily, revealing his kind of complacence. Yet they pointed to an uncommon kind of wisdom, suited to a revolutionary age that he made every effort to keep abreast of. Having sworn "eternal hostility against every form of tyranny over the mind of man," Jefferson perceived that the most common, everlasting form was the tyranny of the past. Openness to innovation and experiment—one of his favorite words—was required by the growth in knowledge he expected, by the "moral emancipation" he hoped for, and above all by the very nature of American democracy, which as a new, untried form of government was itself an experiment. Convinced that his generation had deserved well of its country, he nevertheless warned against a "sanctimonious reverence" for its work, beginning with the Constitution: "No society can make a perpetual constitution, or even a perpetual law." Hence he even assumed that posterity not only would but should scrap some of his own cherished opinions. When "Jeffersonian democrats" made a fetish of such opinions as the impor-

tance of states' rights, they betrayed his spirit. His wisdom was a rare
blend of firmness in principle and flexibility in policy, alike necessary
for the maintenance of a free society.

More clearly and fully than any other thinker of the age Jefferson
recognized the logical implications of a faith in freedom, and faced up
to the risks or the *difficulties* of a democratic state. If he had too placid
a conviction that truth could stand by itself and would always prevail
over error in a free market, he knew from his own political experience
that freedom of speech and press was bound to be abused, and at any
rate he gave the necessary answer. The diversity of opinion that resulted
from allowing men to trade on their "private stock of reason" was no
mere social evil but a positive good, the necessary condition of intellectual progress; and better such abuses of freedom than the no less inevitable abuses of coercion or suppression, which over the centuries had
failed anyway to produce uniformity, succeeding only in making "fools
or hypocrites" of men. Similarly he accepted the stresses and strains of
democratic processes, which neither Burke nor the Jacobins could
abide. He assumed all the intellectual and moral obligations of his
commitment to popular government, no less resolutely after the reign
of violence and terror in France. Attributing this to the poverty and
ignorance of a long-oppressed people, denied their birthright of natural dignity, he held that men would not run wild if they were brought
up in freedom. His lifelong concern with the extension and improvement of education sprang from the faith on which democracy must
finally rest: that on the whole, in the long run, ordinary men had
enough potential good sense and good will to be capable of self-
government.

Tradition made it easy for Burke to reject this novel faith—indeed,
somewhat too easy. Jefferson was at bottom not only more idealistic
but more realistic, keeping a sharper eye on political actualities and
alternatives. He of course knew that men were not equal in ability or
merit, he believed in natural aristocracy, he wanted government by the
best; but the practical question was, how better to achieve it than by
democratic processes, backed by education, that gave freer play to natural ability? He emphasized education so much because he agreed with
Burke that government had to be fitted to the capacities of a people.
(For this reason he was skeptical of the prospects of the Spanish American colonists, foreseeing not only their revolutions but the military
dictatorships that would commonly follow.) It was Burke who was doc-
trinaire here, insisting on the "absolute necessity" of aristocracy in

government, while his alternative came down in practice to rule by a patently artificial aristocracy, on its historic record in Europe hardly distinguished for virtue or wisdom.[2] In America the only real alternative was rule by men of property, the colonial aristocracy to which Jefferson himself belonged; and he remarked that in his observation men's wisdom, virtue, and honesty did not increase with their riches. His judgment would be borne out by the coming plutocracy.

That democracy would have to make its way in an industrial, urban society not to his liking gives more point to the "verdict of history," the tribunal to which Burke ultimately appealed. For an empiricist this is surely a mixed, tentative verdict: the obvious shortcomings, the abiding problems, and the uncertain prospects of popular government are matter enough for another volume. But as surely it has at least worked out far better than Burke ever thought possible.

As the democratic principle kept spreading, conservatives kept repeating the stock arguments of its critics from Plato on: democracy meant mob rule, its natural outcome was civil war, anarchy, tyranny. "It has never happened in the world, and it never will," declaimed Fisher Ames in America, "that a democracy has been kept out of the control of the fiercest and most turbulent spirits in the society." In Europe the alarm of Burke was echoed in more dreadful prophecies as ordinary people were made equal by being lumped together in a monstrous abstraction, "the masses"—by definition blind, barbarous, lawless. "The world, gentlemen," Donoso Cortés told an assembly of the gentlemen, "marches with rapid steps toward the establishment of the greatest and darkest despotism in human memory." Today aristocratic thinkers are resurrecting these prophecies as proof of their ageless wisdom: "the masses" have brought on totalitarianism, established the worst despotisms in history. So it becomes necessary to state some obvious truths. The established democracies have not been controlled by fierce, turbulent spirits, but over the past century have generally maintained the

---

[2] Jefferson's low opinion of this class was echoed by the conservative John Adams, who observed that the *aristoi* were "the most difficult animals to manage in the whole theory and practice of government." The American counterpart of Burke, Adams took as pessimistic a view of ordinary human nature, was more fearful than hopeful in his political thought, and worried over assuring "the rights of the rich"; but he was too realistic to be so devoted to tradition. Aware of the corruption in the British aristocracy and Parliament, he saw more clearly that power tends to corrupt, was more concerned about limiting it, and therefore supported the democratic principle of a legislature in which the people too would have some power. Nor were his fears so obsessive as to make him despair of American democracy after his defeat by Jefferson in the bitter presidential campaign of 1800. Their mellow correspondence in their old age might remind us that "Jeffersonian democracy" was not the creation of one man.

stablest government. They have never been ruled by despots either. Despotism was established rather in Russia, Germany, Italy, Spain— countries long dominated by a monarchical, aristocratic tradition, commonly supported by an established church. It has so far met its strongest resistance from countries with the strongest democratic tradition.

Among the evident reasons for their relative success has been the democratic sentiment of equality. So far from producing anarchy, this tended to generate the pressures to conformity that early alarmed de Tocqueville (a much more subtle, acute critic of democracy than Burke). As he recognized, however, it also generated a spirit of independence and promoted more equity. Men were no longer disposed to put up with such "strange and ridiculous" conditions as Burke had casually noted —neither the ancient inequities nor the new evils that grew up with industrialism. Popular elections, which he abhorred as a "mighty evil," likewise encouraged a constant criticism of the government, impeding the growth of tyranny. Especially in America the greater writers and thinkers were rarely so complacent as he was about the English system of government, but typically remained critical of their whole society by democratic standards, impatient of both its political and social shortcomings. And behind the general belief that something could and should be done, quite deliberately, about all such matters lay the faith in progress stemming from the Enlightenment. Touching the thought of Burke himself, this came through the revulsion against the Enlightenment and the French Revolution, and presently flourished on the material progress being made through technology and science. It became most conspicuous in America, where it was most uncritical and naïve too; but this only calls attention to how much difference it made in everyday thought and feeling.

It accordingly brings us back to the fundamental issue of "human nature." Implicit in all political theory, this became most explicit and controlling in the secular thought of the Enlightenment, in which Nature and Nature's God served only to endorse the rights of man conceived as a rational, perfectible animal. While Burke called on God for his conservative purposes, and reverted to the traditional emphasis on the frailty of human nature, he also anticipated the deeper confusions to come with the study of history and the sciences of man. On the subject of rights and liberties he talked like a relativist: he asserted that nothing universal could be rationally affirmed about them, insisted on the primacy of convention or custom, grounded his values on historical or cultural tradition. On the subject of duties and the requirements of social order he talked like an absolutist: now he implied that human nature was immutable, men everywhere had the same invariable passions and needs, and common men in particular were uniformly inferior, obliged to accept the lowly status natural to them. Burke's appeal to history thus enabled him to have it both ways —always a convenience for political philosophers as well as ruling classes. Yet by this appeal he also gave away more than he realized. He spoke as a conservative English gentleman, proud of English tradition and the apparent difference it had made in the English character; he pointed to the basic fact of cultural diversity, with its implication of the power of custom or "second nature"; he pointed to a similar diversity by his stress upon the natural inequalities of men, which might have made him more aware of the vast range in kinds and degrees of interest, ability, and virtue in common men; and he admitted just enough change, through the wisdom of the species or the English ancestors, to imply some possibility of improvement in men. In other words, "human nature" was not actually so uniform, immutable, and incorrigible as conservative tradition had it.

So liberals too may have it both ways. Obliged to recognize the underlying uniformities—in structure, need, desire, fate—that alone make it possible to speak of *man*, they have in fact emphasized these uniformities by declaring the cause of Humanity, the principle of equality, the rights of all men to life, liberty, and the pursuit of happiness. At the same time, they may emphasize the facts of cultural diversity and historic change, the apparent plasticity of human nature —the basis of their hopes of improving the human condition. They have been largely responsible for spreading an idea that is now commonly taken for granted, even by conservatives: the idea that man has a natural passion for freedom, his whole history has been a struggle for freedom. (Dwight Eisenhower, for instance, concluded an address on the State of the Nation with the prophecy that "humanity shall one day achieve the unity of freedom to which all men have aspired from the dawn of time.") Actually, once more, this idea is belied by most of his history, which more clearly supports the thesis of the Grand Inquisitor. Still, it truly reflects the history of Western civilization, especially in recent centuries. It points to a significant change in the basic mentality of ordinary men, or to some extent their "nature." Today it reflects the extraordinary stir all over the world, as "backward" peoples are beginning to realize possibilities and demand opportunities that through the ages they scarcely dreamed of. With this stir the revolutionary doctrine of the Rights of Man that terrified Edmund Burke has swept the world as has no other idea, or no religion. If it is still widely violated in practice, it is now universally accepted in theory as the bill of "human rights" affirmed by the United Nations.

Like all the issues of freedom, this remains wide open. But at least it gives some reason to hope that the Grand Inquisitor may be wrong, and to believe that once men have known freedom, or known of it, they become "naturally" disposed to cherish it and will not knowingly surrender it.

BIBLIOGRAPHY

The following bibliography is a selective one designed solely for the general reader. It is comprehensive only in the rough sense of including representative works on all the major topics covered in this volume.

GENERAL

Acton, Lord: *Essays on Freedom and Power,* New York (Meridian Books), 1955.

Ausubel, Herman (ed.): *The Making of Modern Europe,* Book One: *The Middle Ages to Waterloo,* New York, 1951.

Brinton, Crane: *A History of Western Morals,* New York, 1959.

Bronowski, J., and Mazlish, Bruce: *The Western Intellectual Tradition,* New York, 1960.

Burckhardt, Jacob: *Judgments on History and Historians,* Boston, 1958.

Bury, J. B.: *A History of Freedom of Thought,* New York, 1913.

Cassirer, Ernst: *The Myth of the State,* New Haven, 1946.

Friedell, Egon: *A Cultural History of the Modern Age,* Vols. 1 and 2, New York, 1933.

Hauser, Arnold: *The Social History of Art,* Vol. 2, New York (Vintage Books), 1957.

Jouvenel, Bertrand de: *Power, the Natural History of Its Growth,* London, 1945.

———: *Sovereignty,* Cambridge, 1957.

Mayer, J. P., and others: *Political Thought: The European Tradition,* New York, 1939.

Mumford, Lewis: *The City in History,* New York, 1961.

———: *Technics and Civilization,* New York, 1934.

Niebuhr, Reinhold: *The Nature and Destiny of Man,* 2 vols., New York, 1941-43.

Randall, J. H., Jr.: *The Making of the Modern Mind* (revised), New York, 1940.

Rougemont, Denis de: *Man's Western Quest,* New York, 1957.

Ruggiero, Guido de: *The History of European Liberalism,* London, 1927.

Sabine, George H.: *A History of Political Theory*, New York, 1955.
Schlatter, Richard: *Private Property*, London, 1951.
Schumpeter, Joseph A.: *History of Economic Analysis*, New York, 1954.
Singer, Charles, and others: *A History of Technology*, Vols. 2 and 3, Oxford, 1956-57.
Ward, Barbara: *Faith and Freedom*, New York, 1954.
Watkins, Frederick: *The Political Tradition of the West*, Cambridge, 1948.

PROLOGUE: THE RISE AND FALL OF ISLAM

Arnold, Thomas, and Guillaume, Alfred: *The Legacy of Islam*, Oxford, 1931.
Becker, C. H.: *Christianity and Islam*, London, 1909.
Brockelmann, Carl: *History of the Islamic Peoples*, New York, 1947.
Gibb, H. A. R.: *Mohammedanism, An Historical Survey*, London, 1949.
Guillaume, Alfred: *The Traditions of Islam*, Oxford, 1924.
Ibn Khaldun: *The Muqaddimah*, trans. Franz Rosenthal, 3 vols., New York, 1958.
Lewis, Bernard: *The Arabs in History*, New York (Harper Torchbooks), 1960.
Lybyer, A. H.: *The Government of the Ottoman Empire in the Time of Suleiman the Magnificent*, Cambridge, 1913.
Schroeder, Eric: *Muhammad's People*, Portland, 1955.

PART I: THE ORIGINS OF WESTERN CIVILIZATION

Adams, Henry: *Mont-Saint Michel and Chartres*, New York, 1905.
Bibby, Geoffrey: *The Testimony of the Spade*, New York, 1956.
Bryce, James: *The Holy Roman Empire*, London, 1904.
Burns, C. Delisle: *The First Europe: A Study of the Establishment of Medieval Christendom, A.D. 400-800*, London, 1947.
Carlyle, A. J.: *Political Liberty, A History of the Conception in the Middle Ages and Modern Times*, Oxford, 1941.
Cheyney, E. P.: *The Dawn of a New Era (1250-1450)*, New York, 1936.
Childe, V. Gordon: *The Prehistory European Society*, London, 1958.
Cohn, Norman: *The Pursuit of the Millennium*, New York (Harper Torchbooks), 1961.
Coulton, G. G.: *Medieval Panorama*, New York, 1938.
Dawson, Christopher: *The Making of Europe, 400-1000 A.D.*, London, 1934.
————: *Religion and the Rise of Western Culture*, London, 1950.
Fremantle, Anne: *The Age of Belief*, New York (Mentor Books), 1955.
Huizinga, J.: *The Waning of the Middle Ages*, London, 1924.
Ker, W. P.: *The Dark Ages*, New York (Mentor Books), 1958.
Lloyd, Roger: *The Golden Middle Age*, London, 1938.

Maritain, Jacques: *True Humanism*, New York, 1938.
McGiffert, A. C.: *A History of Christian Thought*, Vol. 2: *The West from Tertullian to Erasmus*, New York, 1932.
Origo, Iris: *The Merchant of Prato*, New York, 1957.
Pirenne, Henri: *Economic and Social History of Medieval Europe*, New York (Harvest Books), 1937.
————: *Medieval Cities*, Princeton, 1925.
Rashdall, Hastings: *Universities of Europe in the Middle Ages*, Oxford, 1895.
Stephenson, Carl: *Mediæval Feudalism*, Ithaca, 1942.
Taylor, Henry Osborn: *The Medieval Mind*, London, 1911.

PART II: THE GROWTH OF A REVOLUTIONARY WORLD

Baron, Hans: *The Crisis of the Early Italian Renaissance*, Princeton, 1955.
Burckhardt, Jacob: *Civilization of the Renaissance in Italy*, London, 1929.
Butterfield, Herbert: *The Origins of Modern Science*, New York, 1951.
Ferguson, Wallace: *The Renaissance in Historical Thought*, Boston, 1948.
Friedrich, Carl J., and Blitzer, Charles: *The Age of Power*, Ithaca, 1957.
Hall, A. H.: *The Scientific Revolution*, Boston (Beacon Books), 1956.
Haller, William: *The Rise of Puritanism*, New York, 1938.
Harbison, E. Harris: *The Age of Reformation*, Ithaca, 1955.
Klarwill, Victor von (ed.): *The Fugger News-Letters*, 2 vols., New York, 1924-26.
Lewis, W. H.: *The Splendid Century*, Garden City (Anchor Books), 1957.
Martin, Alfred von: *Sociology of the Renaissance*, London, 1944.
Meinecke, Friedrich: *Machiavellism*, London, 1957.
Norton, Lucy (ed.): *Saint-Simon at Versailles*, New York, 1958.
Nowell, Charles E.: *The Great Discoveries and the First Colonial Empires*, Ithaca, 1954.
Olschki, Leonardo: *The Genius of Italy*, New York, 1949.
Parry, J. H.: *The Establishment of the European Hegemony: 1415-1715*, New York (Harper Torchbooks), 1961.
Roeder, Ralph: *The Man of the Renaissance*, New York, 1933.
Santillana, Giorgio de: *The Age of Adventure: The Renaissance Philosophers*, New York (Mentor Books), 1956.
Schevill, Ferdinand: *History of Florence*, New York, 1961.
Smith, Preserved: *The Age of Reformation*, New York, 1920.
————: *A History of Modern Culture*, Vol. 1: *The Great Renewal*, New York, 1930.
Tawney, R. H.: *Religion and the Rise of Capitalism*, New York (Pelican Books), 1947.
Taylor, Henry Osborn: *Thought and Expression in the Sixteenth Century*, New York, 1920.

Tilley, Arthur: *The Decline of the Age of Louis XIV*, Cambridge, 1929.

Whitehead, A. N.: *Science and the Modern World*, New York, 1925.

Willey, Basil: *The Seventeenth Century Background*, London, 1934.

Wolf, A.: *A History of Science, Technology and Philosophy in the Sixteenth and Seventeenth Centuries*, 2 vols., New York (Harper Torchbooks), 1959.

PART III: THE RISE OF DEMOCRACY

Becker, Carl: *The Declaration of Independence*, New York (Vintage Books), 1958.

————: *The Heavenly City of the Eighteenth Century Philosophers*, New Haven, 1932.

Beloff, Max: *The Age of Absolutism 1660-1815*, London, 1954.

Brinton, Crane: *The Anatomy of Revolution*, New York (Vintage Books), 1957.

Bury, J. B.: *The Idea of Progress*, London, 1921.

Cassirer, Ernst: *The Philosophy of the Enlightenment*, Princeton, 1951.

Gay, Peter: *Voltaire's Politics*, Princeton, 1959.

Gershoy, Leo: *From Despotism to Revolution 1763-1789*, New York, 1944.

Geyl, Pieter: *Napoleon For and Against*, London, 1949.

Gooch, G. P.: *English Democratic Ideas in the 17th Century*, New York (Harper Torchbooks), 1957.

Lefebvre, Georges: *The Coming of the French Revolution*, New York (Vintage Books), 1957.

Maitland, F. W.: *The Constitutional History of England*, Cambridge, 1955.

Mattingly, Garrett: *The Defeat of the Spanish Armada*, London, 1959.

McCutcheon, Roger P. (ed.): *The Present-Day Relevance of Eighteenth-Century Thought* (Symposium held by the American Council of Learned Societies), Washington, 1956.

McIlwain, C. H.: *Constitutionalism Ancient and Modern*, Ithaca, 1940.

Palmer, Robert R.: *The Age of the Democratic Revolutions*, Princeton, 1959.

Perry, Ralph Barton: *Puritanism and Democracy*, New York, 1944.

Rowse, A. L.: *The Expansion of Elizabethan England*, London, 1955.

Sampson, R. V.: *Progress in the Age of Reason*, London, 1956.

Stephen, Leslie: *History of English Thought in the Eighteenth Century*, 2 vols., New York, 1949.

Talmon, J. L.: *The Origins of Totalitarian Democracy*, New York, 1960.

Tocqueville, Alexis de: *The Old Régime and the French Revolution*, Garden City (Anchor Books), 1955.

Trevelyan, G. M.: *History of England*, New York, 1928.

Wilson, Arthur M.: *Diderot: The Testing Years*, New York, 1957.

Woodhouse, A. S. P.: *Puritanism and Liberty*, Chicago, 1951.

INDEX

ABOUT THE AUTHOR

Herbert J. Muller is Distinguished Service Professor at Indiana University, where, since 1956, he has been Professor of English and Government. He has also taught at Cornell, Purdue, and the University of Istanbul. He has traveled extensively, particularly to the sites of ancient cities. Mr. Muller has written for numerous periodicals and is the author of a number of books, best known of which are *The Uses of the Past, The Loom of History, The Issues of Freedom,* and *Freedom in the Ancient World.*

HARPER COLOPHON BOOKS